Mastering
Communication

KT-447-081

to be returned on or before the last date

Accession 27

grave Master Series

ccounting
counting Skills
dvanced English Language
dvanced Pure Mathematics
Arabic
Basic Management
Biology
British Politics
Business Communication
Business Environment
C Programming
C++ Programming
Chemistry
COBOL Programming
Communication
Computing
Counselling Skills
Counselling Theory
Customer Relations
Database Design
Delphi Programming
Desktop Publishing
e-Business
Economic and Social History
Economics
Electrical Engineering
Electronics
Employee Development
English Grammar
English Language
English Literature
Fashion Buying and Merchandising
 Management
Fashion Marketing
Fashion Styling
Financial Management
Geography
Global Information Systems

Globalization of Business
Human Resource Management
Information Technology
International Trade
Internet
Java
Language of Literature
Management Skills
Marketing Management
Mathematics
Microsoft Office
Microsoft Windows, Novell
 NetWare and UNIX
Modern British History
Modern European History
Modern United States History
Modern World History
Networks
Novels of Jane Austen
Organisational Behaviour
Pascal and Delphi Programming
Philosophy
Physics
Poetry
Practical Criticism
Psychology
Public Relations
Shakespeare
Social Welfare
Sociology
Spanish
Statistics
Strategic Management
Systems Analysis and Design
Team Leadership
Theology
Twentieth-Century Russian History
Visual Basic
World Religions

www.palgravemasterseries.com

Palgrave Master Series

Series Standing Order ISBN 0–333–69343–4

(outside North America only)

You can receive future titles in this series as they are published by placing a standing order. Please contact your bookseller or, in case of difficulty, write to us at the address below with your name and address, the title of the series and the ISBN quoted above.

Customer Services Department, Macmillan Distribution Ltd
Houndmills, Basingstoke, Hampshire RG21 6XS, England

Mastering
Communication

Fourth Edition

Nicky Stanton

First published 1982 by Pan Books as *The Business of Communicating* in the Breakthrough series.

Second edition published 1990 by Macmillan Press Ltd as *Communication* in the Professional Masters series.

Third fully revised and updated edition published in 1996 by Macmillan Press Ltd in the Masters series.

Fourth edition 2004
Published by
PALGRAVE MACMILLAN
Houndmills, Basingstoke, Hampshire RG21 6XS and
175 Fifth Avenue, New York, N.Y.10010
Companies and representatives throughout the world

PALGRAVE MACMILLAN is the global academic imprint of the Palgrave Macmillan division of St. Martin's Press, LLC and of Palgrave Macmillan Ltd. Macmillan® is a registered trademark in the United States, United Kingdom and other countries. Palgrave is a registered trademark in the European Union and other countries.

ISBN 13–978–14039–1709–6
ISBN 10–14039–1709–4

This book is printed on paper suitable for recycling and made from fully managed and sustained forest sources. Logging, pulping and manufacturing processes are expected to conform to the environmental regulations of the country of origin.

A catalogue record for this book is available from the British Library.

Library of Congress Cataloging-in-Publication Data
Stanton, Nicky, 1944–
    Mastering communication / Nicky Stanton. – 4th ed.
      p. cm. – (Palgrave master series)
    Includes bibliographical references and index.
    ISBN 1–4039–1709–4 (pbk.)
      1. Communication. I. Title. II. Series.

P90.S787 2003
302.2–dc22   2003053651

10 9 8 7 6 5
13 12 11 10 09 08 07

Printed and bound by Creative Print & Design (Wales), Ebbw Vale

Contents

Preface to the fourth edition

When I first wrote *What Do You Mean, Communication?* and *The Business of Communicating* in 1982, I had no idea that they would remain popular for so long. The two books have since been combined into one, but it has not really been necessary to make any radical changes along the way. Similarly, in this, the fourth edition, now established as simply *Mastering Communication*, I and those who have helped me by using and reviewing the book have needed to make only minor changes.

Perhaps we should not be surprised. After all, the subject of the book is the way in which human beings communicate with one another in words and actions, and essentially this will always – at least in the foreseeable future – remain much the same: to think carefully about what we want to say and how we want to say it and then, perhaps more difficult, to translate these thoughts into words and actions so that we are understood in the way we intend.

True, over the centuries, the means of communication have changed dramatically from the quill pen to the telephone and typewriter through to a world in which almost everyone, in the developed world at least, has access to PCs and mobile phones. True, our relationships with others have perhaps become more friendly and informal and, because of education and the expansion of the media world, our messages have become more sophisticated and yet sometimes more informal. But our task remains the same: to find the most appropriate words and actions to convey our thoughts and meaning.

As with previous editions, the main changes in this edition have therefore been concerned with updating dates, recommended books and sources of advice; names of journals and institutions that have changed; words that have had to alter in response to social changes and pressures; and the effect of office and personal technology. Gone are 'salesman' and 'chairmen' replaced by 'sales people' and 'chairs'! Gone are stencils and carbon copies, typewriters and eradicating fluid, replaced by word processors and extremely high quality printers at a price almost every office, however small, can afford. Gone are blackboards and the problems of managing 16 mm film projectors, replaced by video machines and computer controlled projection. Gone is the ability to blame the typist or the printer for our mistakes; most of us at work now key in our own data and messages and can no longer escape responsibility for the accuracy and quality of the final message.

However, in a world in which electronic communication appears to be able to carry out miracles of transmission, in which with the press of a few keys we can chat on screen within seconds to almost anyone in the world, perhaps we now appreciate personal communication even more. How good it is to hear a voice on the phone that sounds like a real, live, breathing human being instead of a computer voice or someone simply reading a script. How pleasant it is to receive a handwritten letter from a friend, or a business letter that seems to have been written by a real person with a name, in a style that seems to convey that they really mean what they are saying, rather than a series of selected standard paragraphs that sound like the outpourings of an emotionless computer. How rewarding it is to have a face-to-face meeting in which we can see people's eyes sparkle with enthusiasm, detect from a subtle smile that they are actually being humorous and ironic, recognise that someone has been hurt by thoughtless remarks and put it right there and then, rather than spending all our time addressing a telephone answering machine or a computer screen.

In this world, it is all too easy to be lulled into believing that the machinery will do the thinking for us. It is perhaps, therefore, even more important than ever to stop and think:

Is this the best way to communicate?

Is this the effect I meant to achieve?

IS THAT WHAT I REALLY WANT TO SAY?

NICKY STANTON

◤ Introduction

Why? The purpose of this book is to help anyone who is interested in improving their communication skills and their knowledge of the way in which communication functions in business, by providing a self-contained book which will both stand on its own without the aid of a teacher, and complement a taught course.

Who? It is intended to help:

- students on NVQ/SVQ, BTEC/GNVQ Intermediate and Advanced, Higher level courses, A-level and AS-level students and students on other professional courses to improve their skills in communicating by learning and practising techniques on their own; this is also an Open University set book;
- teachers in colleges and universities, whether communication specialists or not, who are concerned with improving their students' communication skills, but who find there is never enough time in the timetable to give students sufficient chance to get the practice which is so essential if their knowledge and skills are really to develop satisfactorily; and
- anyone interested in communication and keen to become a more effective communicator but who is unable to take advantage of a course at a college, university or at work.

What? The book covers the main communication tasks with which you are likely to be confronted – telephoning, interviewing, meetings, giving talks and oral presentations, writing letters, reports (long and short), questionnaires, e-mails and so on. In addition you will find chapters on non-verbal communication, listening and reading, and the use of visual aids – boards, projectors, videos and the like, and on visual communication – graphs, charts and so on.

The final part deals with the basic elements of English grammar and usage and is intended either to help you brush up your knowledge of English or to act merely as a quick reference section together with some useful reference lists in the appendices at the back of the book.

How? In order to help you check your progress as you work through the book, you will frequently come across questions and exercises.

Self-checks are usually short questions or exercises to test your understanding of what you have just read, or to find out what you know already, before reading on. Try not to read on to the discussion of these questions until you have at least attempted an answer for yourself. Try not to cheat – it will only hinder your progress – but if you are really stuck, then read on or check back over the last few pages.

Exercises are similar to self-checks but come at the end of a chapter or section to test your understanding of the whole chapter. Again, if you have difficulty answering these, go back over the previous section or chapter. You can find suggested answers to these exercises at the back of the book.

Assignments are longer exercises, usually at the end of chapters to help you apply your knowledge and practise the skills and techniques you have learned. However, sometimes these activities occur in the middle of a chapter and ask you to carry out some observations or do some research over a longer period of time. Make a note of them when you get to them to remind you what to do or what to look out for during the next few days or weeks.

In writing this book my aim has been to adopt a tone and style of writing which both reflects acceptable current practice and makes the reader's task as easy as possible. I have therefore not always adhered strictly to some of the older 'rules' of writing, which the purist would regard as essential to good writing style. As I have explained in Chapters 19 and 20, on English and grammar, the English language has gradually changed over the centuries, and these changes are still taking place. I believe my task is to indicate to the reader what is acceptable to good, modern business writers now, in the twenty-first century.

However, in 'breaking' one rule, I have perhaps been particularly controversial. Normally in formal business writing nowadays we would still probably try not to use contractions ('don't' for 'do not', 'can't' for 'cannot') unless we know the reader well and were permitted by the circumstances to write in a more casual style. I have chosen to use contractions and a generally informal, although I believe correct, style of writing in order to lighten the tone of the book and give the reader, particularly the self-study reader, the feeling that I am talking rather than writing, and that we are working together.

In order to avoid accusations of sexism and yet to avoid the rather clumsy 'he/she' form I have often used the plural form 'they' or 'their' even when referring back to a singular noun, for example, 'anyone who wishes to improve their communications skills'. This may offend the purists, but it is now a broadly acceptable way of avoiding the 'his/her' problem.

When? The chapters in this book inevitably develop from one another. However, each chapter is designed to be complete and self-contained, enabling you to pick up the book and make use of those odd hours between other demands on your time.

Where? Armed only with this book and a pen and paper, you should be able to work through the various chapters at home, at college, in a library, on buses, trains and even planes. However, in some of the chapters that deal with speaking skills you may find a small tape-recorder useful, in which case you may prefer to work in privacy.

So – good luck, and above all, enjoy yourself! Learning should be fun and the way in which human beings communicate is always fascinating even when we fall short of perfection, which we all too often do.

NICKY STANTON

Acknowledgements

No idea can really be said to be original – for every 'new idea' is a development of the countless ideas which have gone before. Any book is therefore merely an expression of the knowledge, experience and skill acquired during the author's lifetime of contact with other people. To all those people who have in any way been influential in my own development and learning and who have therefore contributed, often without my knowing, to the ideas expressed in this book, I owe my gratitude.

However, my special thanks are due to my colleagues at the University of the West of England, Swindon College and Rede Group, and to all my students, in colleges, universities and in industry and commerce, with whom over the years I have learned about the process of communication.

For their patient and tireless, practical and moral support I thank especially my husband, Mike, and my two children, Matt and Abi, and the help and support of my parents, Jo and Gordon.

NICKY STANTON

The author and publishers wish to thank the following for permission to use copyright material:

British Standards Institution for extracts from BS 5261: Part 2: 1976 (1990).

Guinness Publishing Ltd for Figures 18.12 and 18.18 from *The Guinness UK Data Book*. Copyright © Guinness Publishing Limited 1992.

Crown copyright material is reproduced with the permission of the Controller of HMSO and the Queen's Printer for Scotland.

The National Audit Office for an extract from 'Evaluating the Applications to Run the Lottery', 1994–5.

Longman, for the example of an algorithm from D.M. Wheatley and A.W. Unwin, *The Algorithm Writer's Guide* (1972) in Chapter 18.

Flamingo Modern Classics for an extract from Robert Tressell, *The Ragged Trousered Philanthropists*, 1991.

Every effort has been made to trace all the copyright-holders, but if any have been inadvertently overlooked the publishers will be pleased to make the necessary arrangement at the first opportunity.

◾ **1** ▮ The process of communication

The Process of Communication

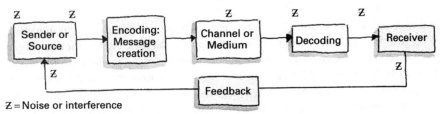

Z = Noise or interference

Human communication is fraught with problems and difficulties. How often do we say or hear statements like 'I didn't really mean that' or 'You still don't see what I mean', or 'You don't seem to have grasped the point'? Whatever we try to communicate, something often seems to get in the way and we are not understood in the way we intended. But even when we are understood we often fail to get people to think or behave in the way we would wish, since when we communicate we really have four main objectives.

Self-Check

Can you suggest **four** general objectives which are true of all efforts to communicate?

1.1 The objectives of communication

Whether we are writing or speaking, trying to persuade, inform, entertain, explain, convince or educate or any other objective behind the particular communication task we are engaged in, we always have four general objectives.

Check-Points: The Objectives of Communication

- to be received (heard or read)
- to be understood
- to be accepted
- to get action (change of behaviour or attitude)

When we fail to achieve any one of these, we have failed to communicate. This can often lead to frustration and resentment expressed in phrases like 'Don't you understand plain English?'

But what is 'plain English'? English after all is only a code which we use to express the thoughts in our head, and a code can only be understood if both parties give the same meaning to the symbols that are used. Words are only symbols that represent things and ideas, and we attach slightly different meanings to the words that we hear and use. The meanings that we give to words result from the way we each interpret the world around us, and for each of us that world is seen and understood differently.

1.2 The meaning of words

It is therefore our individuality that is the main barrier to effective communication. While it is true that we all went through the process of learning our mother tongue and we learned to give roughly the same meaning to words as those around us, we must nevertheless recognise that the only connection between a word and the thing it represents is whatever association a particular group or people has chosen to make.

What does the word 'dap' mean to you? Depending on what part of the country you come from, it may mean nothing, or it may mean what others may call a 'plimsoll', 'tennis shoe', 'pump' or 'trainer'. The thing itself may be roughly the same but what you call it will depend on what community you lived in, when you learned the word, agreed, rather arbitrarily, to call it.

With concrete words – words which describe things we can touch, feel, hear, see or smell – we may have fewer difficulties in explaining what we mean because if all else fails we can point to the things. Provided that the other person has experienced that thing before, they will recognise it and therefore understand us. But what about abstract words – words that describe sensations, feelings, emotions, ideas? How can you be sure that someone else gives the same meaning as you to words like 'danger', 'love', 'hate', 'beautiful' and so on? The meanings attached to these words will be the result of each person's past experience. For example, if you spend much of your life climbing mountains or driving racing cars the word 'dangerous' will have a very different meaning from that given to the words by, say, the parent of a toddler, or a high-powered business tycoon.

1.3 Non-verbal communication

Of course we don't only use words to communicate. Every time we communicate we are sending out messages by means of all sorts of other things. In fact, even when we are not actually writing or speaking we are still communicating something, even if unintentionally.

Self-Check

Make a list of the other ways we communicate when we speak or write – the **non-verbal** means of communication. You will find more about these in Chapter 4.

Obviously we may use pictures to communicate our message, either to replace words or more importantly to reinforce our verbal message. But, consciously or unconsciously, when we speak we will also communicate by other means.

Check-Points: Non-verbal Communication

- facial expression – a smile, a frown
- gestures – movement of hands and body to help to explain or emphasise our verbal message
- body posture – how we stand or sit
- orientation – whether we face the other person or turn away
- eye contact – whether we look at the other person or not, and the length of time that we look at the other person
- body contact – a pat on the back, an arm round the shoulder
- proximity – the distance we stand or sit from the person
- head-nods – to indicate agreement or disagreement or to encourage the other to go on speaking
- appearance – physical grooming and choice of clothes
- non-verbal aspects of speech – variations of pitch, stress and timing; voice quality and tone of voice (these are sometimes called 'para-language')
- non-verbal aspects of writing – handwriting, lay-out, organisation, neatness and visual appearance generally

---

All these non-verbal elements of communication are sometimes called 'meta-communication', from the Greek word 'meta' meaning 'beyond' or 'in addition to'. 'Metacommunication' is therefore something 'in addition to the communication' and we must always be aware of its existence.

It is essential to remember that the metacommunication which accompanies any message is very powerful. The receiver will use these clues to help them to interpret what you mean, but more importantly they will often take the meaning from the metacommunication rather than from the words themselves, particularly when what you are saying conflicts with what you are *doing*. If, for example, you are angry but trying to hide your anger you must be aware of your body posture, the way you use your eyes, gestures and facial expressions, and the tone of your voice, which may well give you away. Similarly, in writing, the 'tone of your voice' may show.

1.4 The context or situation

Just as the words (the verbal message) and the non-verbal message may be interpreted differently by different people, so the same person may attribute different meanings to the same words at different times and in different contexts. After all, we don't communicate in a vacuum; the art of communication always takes place within a situation or context. The situation will have a history and particular characteristics which will make it different from any other situation. Certainly in order to communicate at all, we learn to recognise similarities in situations so that we can learn from our experiences. This is obviously essential or we would never know what to do or what to expect.

But, just as this looking for similarities in situations can be helpful, it can also be harmful for there is always a danger that we will *assume* a situation is familiar and therefore *assume* we know what to say and do. For example, supposing you have only met a person once, and on that occasion they behaved in an arrogant and dictatorial manner. Is it not likely that when you meet them again you will expect them to behave in the same way? However, while you are assuming that the situation is the same and that therefore their behaviour will be the same, you may have neglected to recognise that the two situations are different and that therefore they may well behave very differently in each. The danger lies in your expectations: for, if you expect them to be arrogant and dictatorial, you may react to them in an aggressive way and it may be precisely that aggression which causes them to feel insecure and under attack, resulting in their adopting an arrogant and dictatorial stance in order to stand up to you. You leave them, content that your impressions were right – they are arrogant and dictatorial and therefore unpleasant. But, in a different situation they may behave and therefore speak differently, and if you had behaved differently towards them they might not have been arrogant and dictatorial to you this time. Remember! Behaviour breeds behaviour.

1.5   Barriers to communication

Now let's look at some factors which can cause problems for communication and which we must be aware of if we are to overcome them or communicate in such a way as to minimise their effect.

Differences in perception

The way we view the world is largely determined by our past experiences, so people of different ages, nationalities, cultures, education, occupation, sex, status, personality and so on will each have different perceptions and will each perceive situations differently. Differences in perception are often at the root of many of the other barriers to communication.

Jumping to conclusions

We often see what we expect to see, and therefore hear what we expect to hear, rather than what is actually there. This may lead us, as the saying goes, 'to put two and two together and make five'.

Stereotyping

Because we have to learn from our experiences, we run the risk of treating different people as if they were the same: 'You've met one copper/student/foreigner/car salesman, you've met them all!' we often hear, or words to that effect.

Lack of knowledge

It is difficult to communicate effectively with someone who has a very different background from yours, or whose knowledge of the particular subject of discussion is considerably less than yours. Of course, it is possible, but it requires skill on the part of the communicator to be aware of the discrepancy between the levels of knowledge and communicate accordingly.

Lack of interest

One of the greatest barriers to overcome is the receiver's lack of interest in your message. You should always be alert to this as a possibility, since it is so easy to assume that everyone is as concerned about our interests as we are. Where the lack of interest is obvious and understandable you must work particularly hard to angle your message to appeal to the interests and needs of the receiver.

Difficulties with self-expression

If, as the communicator, you have difficulty finding the words to convey your ideas this will clearly be a barrier and you must work at improving your vocabulary. But lack of confidence, which can also cause difficulties in expression, can be boosted by careful preparation and planning.

Emotions

The emotions of either receiver or communicator can also prove to be a barrier – any strongly felt emotion is liable to prevent almost anything but the emotion being communicated. The moral, of course, is to try to avoid communicating when a strong emotion is liable to make you incoherent or when it will totally distort what you mean to say. However, any audience knows that a speaker with no emotion and enthusiasm in their voice is likely to be a dull speaker – so emotion can be a good thing.

Personality

In the example above about someone who appeared to be arrogant and dictatorial we saw that it is not just the differences in people's personalities that can cause problems: often our resulting behaviour can then affect the behaviour of the other person. This kind of 'clash of personalities' is one of the most common causes of communication failure. We may not be able to change the personality of others, but at least we should be prepared to consider our own personality to see if a change in our behaviour may result in more satisfactory relationships – however unpalatable this sort of self-analysis may be.

These are only a few of the many factors which can cause communication to be less than effective or even fail completely. But it is quite a good place at which to end this discussion of potential barriers because it leaves us with the recognition that it is up to us, either as the receiver or the communicator, to make conditions as satisfactory as possible so that communication – a far from perfect process – stands a chance of being effective.

So far, we have looked very briefly at some of the more important factors which affect our success in communicating. Now let's move on to examine ways in which we might make sure that we communicate as effectively as possible. The first golden rule is to *think ahead*. If we can predict some of the likely problems *before* we communicate, we may be able to avoid them.

1.6   Why? Who? Where? When? What? How?

Whatever communication task you are undertaking, asking these six simple questions *before* you start will give your communication a better chance of success *and* make the task easier. Check-points follow each question.

Why? (Purpose)

- Why am I communicating?
- What is my real reason for writing or speaking?
- What am I hoping to achieve? Change of attitude? Change of opinion?
- What do I want the receiver(s) to do as a result of my communication?
- What is my purpose? To inform? To persuade? To influence? To educate? To sympathise? To entertain? To advise? To explain? To provoke? To stimulate thought?

Who? (Receiver)

- Who exactly is my audience (listener or reader)?
- What sort of people are they? Personality? Education? Age? Status?
- How are they likely to react to the content of my message?
- What do they know already about the subject of my message? A lot? Not much? Nothing? Less/more than I do?

Where and When? (Place and context)

- Where will they be when they receive my message? In their office close to other relevant material? Or isolated from the problem so that I may need to remind them of the facts?
- At what point in the total matter does my message come? Am I replying to something they have raised? Or will my message represent the first they have heard about this topic/problem/issue?
- What is my relationship with the receiver? Is the subject of my message the cause of controversy between us? Is the atmosphere strained or cordial?

Answers to these questions will help you to find answers to the next set of questions more easily than if you jump straight in with 'What do I want to say?'

What? (Subject)

- What exactly do I want to say?
- What do I need to say?
- What do they need to know?
- What information can I omit?
- What information must I include in order to be:

  – Clear?   – Constructive?
  – Concise?   – Correct?
  – Courteous?   – Complete?

(the six Cs of effective communication)

How? (Tone and style)

- How am I going to communicate my message? With words? Or pictures? Or both? Which words? Which pictures?
- Which medium of communication will be most appreciated? Written or spoken? A letter or a personal chat or interview? A report or an oral presentation? An e-mail or a phone call?
- How will I organise the points I want to make? Shall I use deductive sequence (start with my main points and then go on to the explanation/examples/illustrations)? Or inductive sequence (start with the explanation/examples/illustrations and build up to the main point at the end)?
- How am I going to achieve the right effect? What tone must I use to achieve my purpose? Which words must I use/avoid in order to create the right tone?

In some cases the answers to these questions will come quickly. In fact, they may seem obvious. But beware – it is very easy to jump to conclusions, to see the problem from your point of view and forget that your listeners or readers may see things differently. It is always worthwhile going through these questions before you communicate anything difficult or of some length and it is useful to bear them in mind even when you are communicating spontaneously. They act as a gentle discipline to stop you 'opening your mouth without thinking'-particularly easy when e-mailing.

But with more difficult problems or sensitive issues, it is often worthwhile pondering over these questions even for several days and sometimes weeks before you write or speak.

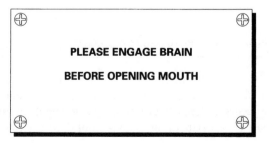

PLEASE ENGAGE BRAIN

BEFORE OPENING MOUTH

1.7   Planning the message

Only when you have given some thought to these six essential questions are you ready to plan your message.

Stage 1   write down your purpose

It is always a good idea to write down (preferably in one or two sentences) exactly what you are trying to achieve by your message. You will then have it always before you to help you to organise your material and avoid straying from the point.

Stage 2   assemble the information

Using notes on paper, index cards or notes on your PC, especially if it is to be a fairly long message like a report or oral presentation of some kind, jot down all the ideas or points which you think you need to make.

At this stage you need to select only the essential, relevant information and reject the irrelevant, however much you may feel tempted to include it. Ask yourself questions like 'Is this really relevant to my message?' 'Does my audience (listener or reader) really need to have this information if they are to understand my message?' 'Will this help me to achieve my purpose?'

Stage 3   group the information

Now consider your list and look for links between the bits of information. Rewrite your notes in clear groups. It helps to give each group a heading. The groups will probably become the paragraphs or sections in your finished message and the headings will either remain as headings (if headings are appropriate) or contain the gist of each group and will therefore help you to compose the main sentence of the paragraph, often called the 'topic-sentence'. Remember that all paragraphs should have only one main idea. All the other ideas in the paragraph will be supporting material – examples, elaboration, illustrations and so on, of the main idea (see Figure 13.1, diagram of a paragraph, on p. 185).

Stage 4   put the information into logical sequence

Your next task is to put the groups of information (still only in note-form) into some sort of sensible order which your reader can follow.

Self-Check

What are the most commonly used methods of ordering material?

- *Chronological order* – this is sometimes called historical order and is perhaps the most common method, which merely presents the material in the order in which it occurred or occurs in time. On occasions, presenting the material chronologically is the most appropriate order to adopt, but don't use this method without some critical thought. Since most of the things we need to write about in business have a time sequence, there is always a temptation to use this method even when it is not the most appropriate. Always try to look for some other logical link between the sections of your material.

- *Spatial (or place) order* – effective for describing machinery, buildings, furniture, geographical location. Facts are presented on a geographical basis – from place to place: from north to south, top to bottom, left to right, high to low, in and out, up and down or near to far.
- *Order of importance* – descending order of importance (or deductive order): starting with the most important point to gain the reader's attention; or ascending order of importance (or inductive order): starting with the least important point. Inductive order is not usually advisable in business writing except in persuasive writing where it can be very effective.
- *Ascending order of complexity* – simpler ideas first followed by increasingly difficult or complex material.
- *Descending order of familiarity* – moving 'from the known to the unknown'.
- *Cause and effect* – put simply, cause and effect means '*because of this, then that*'. In other words, 'because this happened, that happened'.
- *Topical* – sometimes of course there appears to be no real link between the chunks of material and no obvious pattern of development. In this case, all you can do is deal with each chunk on a topic-by-topic basis.

Stage 5 produce a skeleton outline

By working through the previous four stages you will have produced in effect a plan or skeleton outline of your finished message, but if this outline is not clearly on your screen or a piece of paper and your message is fairly long, it is essential to produce this plan which you can then use to work from. It will make the job of writing or presenting your final message much easier and the receiver's job of understanding you also much easier.

Stage 6 write the first draft

Now you are ready to start writing. Write the first draft to yourself. Don't worry at this stage about the style and the words – that can come later. Many people find that actually starting to write, particularly anything of any length and complexity, is the most difficult barrier to get through. However, if you take this advice and you have done the necessary preparation and planning, including some thoughts on what you are going to put in the introduction, the main body of the message, and the conclusion, you will probably find that the words themselves come much more easily.

Stage 7 edit the rough draft and write the final draft

Once you have written the first rough draft you must put yourself in the shoes of your receiver. Read your draft through their eyes, checking for ambiguities, errors, awkward expressions, lack of signpost words ('first', 'second', 'finally', 'on the other hand', 'consequently', etc.) which are essential to guide your reader along the route of your argument, and, above all, aiming for a concise, easily understood style.

Check-Points: Editing Check-list

- Vary the length of the sentences but keep them on the shorter side: 18–22 words should be the average.
- Paragraphs should have only one main idea.
- Use words that the reader will understand.
- Avoid unbusinesslike colloquialisms (e.g. 'to cut a long story short').
- Omit unnecessary words ('serious' in 'serious crisis').
- Use the shorter rather than the longer word or phrase, if appropriate: 'start' rather than 'commence'.
- Avoid hackneyed expressions (clichés – 'please find enclosed', 'If I can be of further assistance, please do not hesitate to contact me).
- Avoid needless repetition of words and phrases – find alternatives wherever possible.
- Use sincere words – don't overstate or exaggerate.
- Use positive words rather than negative words if possible.
- Use the active rather than the passive voice (for an explanation of this and other aspects of grammar and style refer to Chapters 19 and 20).

Summary – how to communicate

This introduction to communication is intended to provide you with a basic understanding of the communication process and the principles you should bear in mind particularly when writing. The remaining chapters deal in more detail with the particular characteristics of different communication tasks.

Assignment: Briefly describe a communication incident and list the barriers to communication which prevented the right message getting through.

Exercise 1.1 (Answers will be found at the end of the book): List and explain the main potential barriers to communication between two people who officially speak the same language.

☑ **2 Speaking effectively**

The art of speaking

'Jan, can you spare a minute?'
'Hi Dave. What's the matter?'
'Well, while you were away, the others decided to go ahead with their request for a crèche. I'm supposed to see the boss about it tomorrow.'
'Oh?'
'Well, I've thought about it and I think we'd stand a better chance if you come too. You're a better talker than I am.'
'Well, thanks but I'm really not sure…'
'Oh! Don't worry, I'll give you all the details. We decided that…'

Supposing someone did ask you to do this. How would you react? Would you go along and just trust to luck that the right words would occur to you when you needed them? Or would you plan your approach? If the boss didn't give in easily to your request, would you become aggressive? Or would you keep calm? If Dave wasn't presenting a very good case, would you butt in impatiently and take over?

How do you estimate your ability at effective speaking? Not just the formal occasion but in face-to-face discussions and interviews, at meetings and on the phone?

Perhaps because we learn to speak before we write, or perhaps because speaking is so much a part of our everyday life, we are liable to take speaking for granted and as Chapter 1 implies, 'open our mouth before engaging our brain'. But it is not just the 'big occasion' which requires care and attention.

In Chapter 1 we looked at the problems in the communication process. The same principles apply in the countless speaking situations which present themselves at work. They may involve you in simply answering a phone call; on the other hand, they may involve participation in group discussion, giving information, instructing someone new in the procedures of your department, presenting an idea at a meeting, or making oral reports to your manager or head of department. They may also involve you in giving short talks at work or as part of your social activities. Later on, they may involve interviewing and acting as chair. In Chapters 1–11 we shall look in more detail at each of these situations. In each of them you will be drawing on the range and flexibility of your communication skills as you try to express what you have to say in clear, precise and forceful spoken English.

Let's look first in this chapter at the basic skills of speaking which apply in any situation:

(a) personal qualities and
(b) vocal qualities – enunciation and pronunciation.

2.1 Basic speaking skills

Assignment: First of all, think of someone whose speaking ability you admire.

- What are the qualities and characteristics which contribute to their success when speaking? Make a list.
- Have they any qualities which distract or irritate you? List these.

Now think of someone you regard as a poor speaker. Add to your list ways in which you think they could improve their skill at speaking.

Keep this list – it represents what you think constitutes good and poor oral communication and it should form the basis for all your efforts to increase your own skills as a speaker.

Personal qualities

Clarity

To be a good speaker you need first and foremost to be able to express your ideas clearly. Your language should be simple and your material organised so that it can be easily followed. You should avoid trying to impress by using long, complicated words. Of course, you may have to use specialised vocabulary or jargon in some situations but you should take care to explain any terms that may be unfamiliar to your audience.

As well as clear thinking, speaking clearly also means uttering the words distinctly so that they are easily recognisable.

Accuracy

You should also make sure that the words you use say exactly what you mean. You therefore need a reasonably wide vocabulary so that you can choose words with precise meanings to suit your purpose.

The facts you use should be correct, so you should take care to research your subject thoroughly and ensure that any authorities you quote are reliable. You should also avoid making statements which go beyond the facts and which might therefore be challenged. Statements which begin 'Everybody thinks...' or 'Nobody in their right mind would accept ...' are always dangerous and open to challenge, especially since they are likely to create a hostile reaction.

Empathy

Always try to be courteous and friendly. However angry you feel, try to control your emotions and at least remain calm. Perhaps the best way to be courteous and polite is to put yourself in the other person's place. Try to make yourself feel what the other person is feeling. Putting yourself in the other person's place in this sense helps you to establish *empathy* for that person. This doesn't mean that you have to agree with them or their ideas, but it does help you to be understanding and be patient. Facial expression and tone of voice are obviously important here, especially in group discussions and interviews.

Sincerity

This really means being natural. There is always a danger when talking to strangers or people of higher status of becoming stiff and awkward, and trying to put on an act. This usually stems from lack of confidence. Of course, when you talk to your boss you may not talk in exactly the same manner as you would when you talk to a friend or colleague, but you should strive to be yourself as much as you can in all situations.

Assignment: Consider how you normally speak when talking to friends or members of your family. Then think about how you speak when talking to your boss or someone very senior to you.

- Does your voice sound much the same in both instances? If so, then you probably speak in a natural way most of the time. (Of course, your choice of words and phrases may, and probably should, be rather different.)
- Do you freeze up when talking to certain people?
- Does your voice become higher or lower?
- Does your rate of speech speed up or slow down?
- Do your movements and posture become stiff and awkward?
- Does your accent change?

Relaxation

The best way of getting rid of these unnatural speech characteristics is to relax. When our muscles are tense, we have difficulty expressing ourselves naturally. Awkward movements are also the result of tension.

Try taking a deep breath. This may help you to relax. If you freeze up with tension, you probably begin holding your breath without realising it. If you can remind yourself to breathe in a natural manner, or even more deeply than usual, your muscles will be more relaxed, and you will be too.

Eye contact

In Chapter 4 which looks at the importance of body language, we will see that *direction of gaze* and *length of gaze* are important factors in synchronising speech and signifying desire to be friendly, but it is worth reminding ourselves here how crucial eye contact is whenever people are speaking to one another.

Assignment: Have you ever been in conversation with someone who seems unwilling to look you in the eye and intent on looking almost everywhere but at you? How does this make you feel? Write down your feelings and/or discuss them with others in a group.

A speaker who never looks at his or her listeners may be conveying messages like 'I am not very interested in you', 'I don't like you', 'I am not very sure of myself', 'I am not sure about what I am saying' or even 'Don't believe what I am saying'.

So when you are speaking give your listeners their fair share of eye contact. Don't keep your eyes on the desk, or in your lap or out of the window, and when you are talking to a large group move your eyes around the room, treating your audience as individuals. They will prefer a slightly hesitant speaker who shows interest in them by looking at them, to a highly fluent speaker who reads with head down over their notes.

Appearance

How you look can affect how well others understand you. Your appearance reflects how you see yourself – 'self-image'. Since your listeners cannot help but notice your appearance they will receive metacommunications from the way you dress and your general grooming. In most speaking situations (apart from phone conversations and the radio) people see the speaker and form judgements about them even before they speak.

Attractive dress and good grooming are obviously important in formal situations: the public meeting, the job interview and so on. But being 'dressed up' or 'dressed formally' is not always practicable or even appropriate and in some jobs it would be absurd. Supposing you are in the middle of a dirty job and you are called to the manager's office or asked to explain something to a visitor, what then? Well, your personal appearance should commend you. Even oil-stained overalls can convey the impression that they are well cared for and that you consider personal cleanliness and tidiness are important even when you have a dirty job. There are therefore two important things to consider

- personal cleanliness and tidiness
- dress and appearance appropriate to the situation.

Even as a new employee, you should realise that the way you look affects the impression you make. Take your cues from the others around you and dress accordingly. This doesn't mean losing your individuality completely but it does mean being flexible and ready to adapt your appearance to suit particular circumstances. So, if you go for extremes in fashion when you are not at work, tone things down for work.

Posture

Good posture is also important. Someone who props up the wall or slouches in their chair as they speak conveys a message to their listeners which may surprise them. Their attitude is showing. They are either tired or bored or careless, or all three! And the listeners are not likely to be impressed.

Another important reason for examining your posture – how you sit and stand when you are talking – is that posture is related to voice quality.

If you slouch over, hang your head or let your shoulders droop, the quality of your voice will not be good, because your breathing is affected. You cannot draw as much breath into your lungs, nor do you have complete control over how you let out the air.

Furthermore, if you slouch or bend your head down, your throat muscles, jaw and vocal chords do not operate as freely as they should, with the muffled, poorly pronounced results we have seen.

Poor posture also affects your voice psychologically as well as physically. The sense of not caring about yourself or about anything – communicated by poor posture – creeps into your voice as well. If you have a hangdog look, your voice will probably have a hangdog sound. It will be listless and spiritless. A whining quality which most people find unpleasant may very well colour the tone of your voice.

By improving your posture when talking, you can do much towards instilling in your voice and your whole manner four characteristics of good voice quality.

Check-Points: Characteristics of Good Voice Quality

- alertness
- pleasantness
- distinctness
- expressiveness

Vocal qualities

Don't think that you can't change the way you speak. You can and do control your voice all the time. Listen to the way you use your voice in different situations, raising and lowering the volume, adjusting the tone to suit particular circumstances and so on. You can improve your voice if you want to, but you have to work at it. The first step is to be aware of the factors which affect the sound of your voice.

The mechanics of speech – speech involves many mechanical skills. It requires a complicated manipulation of the diaphragm, the lungs and muscles of the chest as well as vocal chords, mouth, tongue and lips.

The vocal chords are rather like rubber bands stretched across the interior of a kind of box called the larynx behind what we call the Adam's apple. As the air in your lungs is forced up through the larynx and past the vocal chords, sound is produced. The sounds are affected first by the vocal chords, and then successively by the position of the jaw, the interior of the mouth, the tongue, teeth and lips. Of course, you are not aware of all this when you speak, unless excessive speaking, tiredness or emotion draws your attention to your voice.

To ensure that the sounds you produce are clear, your throat muscles must be relaxed, your jaw must not be taut or rigid and your lips must be flexible and capable of assuming a variety of positions. If you have ever had an anaesthetic injection at the dentist you will know what it does to your ability to move your lips properly to pronounce the words.

Pitch – a person whose voice has a high pitch may sound thin or squeaky or shrill. A person with low pitch will sound deep or throaty. When your vocal chords are stretched tight, the sound will be higher as the air is forced past them causing them to vibrate (like plucking a tight elastic band).

When people are frightened or tense, their vocal chords stretch tight and their voices tend to squeak. One way to relax your throat muscles is to practise this simple exercise:

Practice

Take a deep breath then, as you breathe out, say several short syllables, for example:
'She gave us all a short talk on art.'
Try it. Notice how the tightness disappears as you exhale. It is in fact, physically impossible to breathe out and keep the muscles tight at the same time. This is why deep breathing can help you relax.

Volume – volume is more easily controlled than pitch, but practice is still required to get the right volume. Proper breathing is essential to volume control and good speaking. Practise taking deep breaths and letting out the air with just enough force to generate the right volume. Learn how to *project* your voice so that you can be heard at great distances without yelling or sounding strained.

If you can control your voice and speak clearly without appearing to strain or shout or run out of breath, you will impress your listeners by the quality of your voice alone. They are very likely to assume that you also know what you are talking about and will find it worth their while to listen to you.

The right volume depends on the situation. You should therefore note:

– where you are speaking (in a small room or a large lecture room; in a room where sound carries well; in a room where sound echoes; indoors or out in the open), as the location will affect how well your words can be heard;
– the size of the group to whom you are speaking;
– background noise, for example the noise of air conditioning.

Diction and accent – diction is the way in which you say or pronounce words, and is acquired. To some extent it is affected by your accent. Someone from the north will have different diction from someone who comes from London or the South. Diction depends on 'articulation' and 'enunciation', which are terms used to describe how you pronounce words:

– articulation refers to the way people pronounce consonants
– enunciation refers to the way people pronounce vowels.

If people articulate and enunciate well, that is clearly, they will have good diction. Good diction is generally considered to be the result of being well educated and well informed.

However, it is important not to confuse diction with accent. Whatever your accent, you should pronounce your words clearly. Listen to television and radio announcers to hear the difference between accent and diction. There was a time when 'BBC English' was held up as 'the way to speak'. Nowadays, every possible regional accent is represented and is quite acceptable because the speakers pronounce their words clearly; so like your accent, your diction will tell your listeners something about you.

If you mispronounce words, for example, 'labratry' instead of 'laboratory', 'nucular' instead of 'nuclear' or drop your 'h's' or 't's', as in 'Ave you go' the le'er?', or slur your words, you won't impress your listeners. In some situations this may not matter. In others, such as a job interview, it could mean the difference between getting something you want or need and not getting it.

Assignment: Record your voice and think about the way you speak – the physical process you use to produce the sounds.

Now write a short critique of your speaking style. Include good and bad points.

Vocal tension – blurred, indistinct speech can be caused by a tight, rigid jaw or tight lips. If your throat is tight, it is almost certain that your jaw will be tight. The jaw should be relaxed and ready to open and close freely as required. If it doesn't do this, the sounds come through a half-closed mouth and consequently are unclear. It is also impossible to get expression into a voice produced under these conditions and the result is a voice which lacks vitality and sounds monotonous.

Practice: Testing your Jaw Movement

Test your jaw movement for yourself. Tighten (i.e. half-close) your jaw and say, 'A cleverly devised scheme'. Notice that your teeth and lips hardly moved.

Now relax your jaw and let your teeth and lips move freely while you say the phrase again. You should be able to detect the difference quite easily. If not, try it again with a tape-recorder. Repeat the exercise and see if you can detect the difference.

Practice: Jaw Relaxation

Grit your teeth and tighten your jaw. Hold this position for a few seconds.

Then let your lower jaw sag. (It may help to let your mouth drop open as you do this – best done in private perhaps!) Note that while your lower jaw is sagging you can put your tongue between your teeth. This tells you that your jaw is relaxed.

Often when we are lying down and think we are relaxed, our jaw is tight as a result of inner tension. Practising this exercise when trying to get off to sleep can be very effective.

Tight lips, or lips which do not move very much during speech also affect the sounds which are made. Billy Connolly, a Glaswegian, when asked if he made an effort to change his accent when he came south of the border said 'No! I just open my mouth more. Glaswegians have mouths like letter-boxes. They don't open their mouths much when they speak.'

This emphasises the difference between accent and diction. If you have a strong regional accent don't try to change it, but do make sure you open your mouth and use your lips flexibly to pronounce your words clearly.

Practice

Try this experiment. Set your lips in a straight line (like a letter-box!) and try to say the words 'bit', 'team', 'fill', 'kite', 'see' and 'chap' without changing the position of your lips. Now try 'hip', 'load', 'murmur', 'no', 'rain', 'yet' and 'weigh'.

Notice how the pronunciation was affected. This is because the lips should take a different position in order to produce the first letters in each of these words.

Now try saying the words again naturally.

The good speaker would have ranged through all the lip positions. A small range of movements automatically means that some consonants and vowels become difficult to distinguish and this results in poor communication. Even listeners with good hearing rely more than they think on 'lip-reading'. If the speaker's lips do not move very much, the words can be more difficult, if not impossible to understand.

Practice

If you are aware that you don't move your lips very much when you speak, practise this exercise.

Say 'soon', 'seen', 'sand', 'sawn', 'sow', 'side', 'such' – concentrating on putting your lips in clearly different positions.

At first you will find it helpful to exaggerate each movement, but don't exaggerate your lip movement when you are talking to other people. However, when you are speaking in a very large room to a very large audience, it may be helpful to make your lip movements slightly more pronounced than normal, to cope with the distance your sounds must carry.

Speed

The speed at which you talk will also affect the message you are sending. Speaking very quickly conveys a sense of urgency to the listener. This may be useful at times, but speaking rapidly all the time, pouring out your words in a great rush, may cause your listeners to switch off because they have learned that the implied emergency does not really exist. Speaking too quickly may also make it difficult for you to be understood, and you probably won't pronounce each word clearly and carefully.

Most people who speak in public actually speak at a slower rate than they do in normal conversation. But, of course, this depends on their normal speed, and they cannot afford to speak so slowly that the minds of their listeners wander, or their listeners become bored or lose track of what they are saying.

The good speaker varies their pace according to the relative importance of what they are saying; thus unimportant words and phrases are spoken quickly while important words or phrases will be spoken more slowly.

The use of the pause

If you spoke with long pauses between each word or series of words, you would very quickly lose your audience. However, the pause, carefully used, can be a very effective device for getting your message across.

A good speaker will pause briefly at the appropriate places to give their listeners the opportunity to take in what they have said. They will also occasionally pause before or after a word to give it emphasis, or before making a particularly important point.

Tone

The inflection, or 'up-and-down' movement of your voice – tone also affects the way in which your message is received. Variations in tone are often associated with pitch and speed in giving interest and emphasis to your speech.

However, quite apart from the words you are saying, tone can betray your attitudes and emotions. Your attitude to your listener or listeners and to your message or subject is often indicated by the tone of voice you use.

Your tone can convey whether you are happy or angry or sad. You can sound humble and frightened, or commanding and patronising. You can even make the same word mean several different things by the tone you give it:

'I've finished all those letters.'
'Good.'
'They're being typed now and should go out this afternoon.'

The word 'good' could mean 'I understand' or 'Well done – you've worked amazingly fast' or 'It's about time too!' depending on the tone of voice used.

It is easy to give the wrong impression by carelessly using the wrong tone and, of course, it is easy to convey what you really think even when you don't want to.

Just as tone is important in informal speaking, so it is an essential part of a talk given in a formal situation. If you are speaking on a subject which is of no interest to you, it is easy for the listeners to detect this in the tone of your voice. Of course, if you are enthusiastic about it and pleased to be speaking on a particular subject, it is good to let the audience recognise this. But negative, adverse feelings should be disguised. If the subject really *is* a bore, then concentrate on doing a good job in spite of it, and you will find the tone of your voice will work with you and not against you.

In other words, it is important to guard against letting your tone betray your attitude and feelings unless you want it to do so.

2.2 Qualities to aim for when speaking

- *Alertness* gives your listener the impression that you are aware of and interested in what is happening around you and what you are saying. They are more likely to feel it is worthwhile to listen to you.
- *Pleasantness* is partly being polite, but also striving to give a friendly tone to your voice by smiling and looking pleasant.
- *Distinctness* is speaking clearly so that your listener can hear and understand your words without straining. This includes pronunciation, of course. It requires you to breathe properly, to move your lips, tongue and jaw freely and easily. It also requires you to talk directly to the listener.
- *Expressiveness* is putting feeling into your voice. To be expressive, you must avoid the low droning monotone which will turn off your listener. It is easier to be expressive when you maintain good posture, and are interested in your subject and concerned about your listener.

Summary – good speaking

Effective speaking is therefore the result of several things over which you do have control. First, Personal Qualities – clarity, accuracy, empathy, sincerity, relaxation, eye contact, appearance and posture which have a lot to do with what you say and how you behave; and second, Vocal Qualities – the mechanics of speech, pitch, volume, diction and accent, vocal tension, speed, the use of the pause and tone, all of which affect the way you use your *voice*.

Assignment: Choose a passage from a book or magazine article and read it aloud (tape-recording if possible) four times: first concentrating on sounding **alert**, then concentrating on sounding **pleasant** (smiling helps!), then concentrating on sounding **distinct**, and finally, aiming for **expression**.

Now play back the four versions of the passage. Can you hear any difference between them? Did you succeed in emphasising each of the four qualities?

Finally, read and record the passage again, aiming for **all four** qualities this time.

Further reading

Bradbury, Andrew, *Successful Presentation Skills*, Kogan Page, 2000

▮ ▾ 3 Listening

Speaker and Listener

We have all met them:

- *the person who looks at you with glazed eyes, so intent on working out what they're going to say next that they hear nothing you say and cut you off in mid-sentence to say something that bears very little relationship to what you have just been saying;*
- *the manager who says: 'Never hesitate to come and see me if you've got any problems,' and when you do make an appointment to see them they spend all the time talking about their own problems;*
- *the student who complains about every lecture, switches off after about the first five minutes, barely stays awake and says everything is boring and a waste of time;*
- *the person next to you at the conference who, as the last speaker sits down, says: 'Well that was pretty awful. The man didn't know what he was talking about and anyway I can't stand people who wear their handkerchief in their top pocket!'*

Perhaps you are one of those people!
So, how good at listening are you, and why is listening important anyway?

3.1   Listening – the neglected skill

We have already seen that in an attempt to meet the increasing demands of people to be kept informed, and in an attempt to improve morale and productivity, there has been a fever of activity in many organisations aimed at increasing the quality and quantity of written communications. Yet we have also seen that merely subjecting people to more and more information does not necessarily improve the communication climate in organisations.

Much of this activity stems from two beliefs. First, to judge from the contents of most training courses aimed at improving communication skills, the answer lies in improving people's ability to *transmit* information more effectively – to write more clearly and concisely and to speak with more confidence and sensitivity to their audience; and yet those who study the way in which human beings communicate have discovered that it is our ability to *receive* information which is just as much in need of improvement.

Check-Points: How Well Do We Listen?

- Listening tests have shown that the average person can remember only 50 per cent of what they have heard immediately afterwards, and only about 25 per cent two months afterwards.
- Worse still, one study has shown that only 10 per cent of the original message remains after three days!

The second belief – very commonly though perhaps unconsciously held – that has led to this concentration on producing more and more written and printed information, is the belief that the higher up the ladder of success we go and the more we find ourselves in positions of responsibility, the more our activities shift from listening and receiving messages to giving out and telling others what to do and even how to do it. In fact, this is exactly the opposite of the observable fact.

Check-Points: How Much Do We Listen?

- One study which looked at how white-collar workers spent their day, by logging them at intervals of fifteen minutes over a two-month period, discovered that seven out of every ten minutes awake were spent in some form of communication activity. It broke down like this:

9%	writing	
30%	speaking	= 39% transmitting
16%	reading	
45%	listening!	= 61% receiving

- If this statistic is correct, and there have been many other studies which support it, the average white-collar worker spends 45 per cent of all communicating time listening and about 31.5 per cent of *all time awake* listening.

It is listening, then, which in most organisations carries a large part of the communication burden.

If we compare the rather alarming findings about the quality of our listening with this tendency to rely more and more on oral methods for transmitting information both in our social lives and at work, we can see that, far from being an unimportant and automatic skill, it is perhaps the most important area in communication, and desperately in need of some attention.

Were you taught to listen?

'I do wish you'd listen!' 'Do you ever listen to anything I say?' or just simply 'Listen!' probably sum up, for most of us, all the help and instruction we were ever given in this very important skill.

At school, you were probably taught to write, from the first day to the last; you were taught to read and speak, at least up to a basic level of ability. Whether you received any more instruction on reading and speaking once you could 'do it' probably depended on the particular school you went to, but most of us were left to our own devices, perhaps refining our skills a little, more by luck than judgement.

As for listening, it seems to be assumed that as long as we don't have a physical hearing deficiency, we are automatically capable of listening from the day we are born, and do not therefore need to be taught. Yet a few minutes' thought will probably enable you to recall many instances when people you talk to, and you too (if you're honest), seem to go through the motions of listening but, in reality, are either thinking of other things or, more particularly, thinking of what they are going to say next.

Listening, therefore, seems to be sadly neglected, and is sometimes written off as a merely passive skill, about which we can do very little. But it is crucial to good communication, for as we have seen it is really the receiver – the listener – who communicates, rather than the speaker.

Unless somebody listens to the message and understands it, there is no communication, only noise.

3.2   Reasons for improving listening

Effective listening produces many salutary results:

- *Encouragement to others* – when others note that you listen to them in a non-threatening manner, they in turn lose some or all of their defensiveness and will usually try to understand you better by listening more effectively to you; thus your effective listening often results in making others good listeners.
- *Possession of all the information* – to solve problems and make decisions more effectively, it is necessary to obtain as much relevant information as possible. Good listening helps you to get as much information as the speaker possesses. Your careful listening will usually motivate them to continue talking and to cite as many facts as they can. When you have as much information as possible, you are in a position to make accurate decisions.
- *Improved relationships* – effective listening usually improves relationships between people. It gives the speaker the opportunity to get facts, ideas and hostile feelings off their chest. You will understand them better as you listen; they appreciate your interest in them; and friendship may therefore deepen.
- *Resolution of problems* – disagreements and problems can best be solved when individuals listen carefully to each other. This does not mean that they must each agree with the other's point of view; they must merely show that they understand the other person's point of view. Everyone wants understanding, and there is no better way of expressing this quality than through sensitive listening.

    Listening may also help the other person to see their own problems more clearly. Usually when any of us can talk through a problem, we can more easily work out possible solutions.
- *Better understanding of people* – listening carefully to another person will give you clues on how they think, what they feel is important and why they are saying

what they are saying. By understanding them better, you will be able to work better with them, even if you do not particularly like them. Knowing that Jan is an extrovert, that John is an introvert, or that Mike needs frequent praise, leads to better understanding and thus harmony.

The good listener gains four things.

Check-Points: Benefits of Listening

- information
- understanding
- listening in return
- cooperation.

We all need to listen

Finally, then, listening is vital for students whose success depends on how well they retain ideas, and for managers who must know what is taking place in many areas if they are to make intelligent decisions and ensure the morale of staff. Sales staff must listen to their customers. Parents must listen to their children. And there are several professional areas where effective listening is the main stock-in-trade: psychiatry, educational and marriage guidance, personnel interviewing. In medical training, too, increasing emphasis is being placed on the skills of listening, since patients are the main source of information on which their doctors base much of their diagnosis.

This is not to say that we should all become full-time listeners, or that those who tend to be very quiet, diffident people can afford to pat themselves on the back, for as one writer commented:

A man who listens because he has nothing to say can hardly be a source of inspiration. The only listening that counts is that of the talker who alternately absorbs and expresses ideas.

How, then, can we train ourselves to really listen to what we hear? Or, perhaps, you think you already do!

3.3   Are you a good listener?

Assignment: If you are interested in finding out how well you listen as a matter of habit, answer the following questions. This 'test' is easy to 'beat', and if you are happy to cheat, go ahead, but don't be fooled by your answers. However, if you are honest with yourself, you have a chance of estimating your listening ability. Just answer 'yes' or 'no'.

1 Do you place yourself in the room so that you are certain you can hear clearly?
2 Do you listen for underlying feelings as well as facts?

3 Do you take no notice of a speaker's appearance and watch out only for the ideas they are presenting?
4 Do you 'pay attention': do you look at the speaker as well as listen to what they have to say?
5 Do you allow for your own prejudices and feelings as you evaluate what the speaker has to say?
6 Do you keep your mind on the topic continuously and follow the train of thought being presented?
7 Do you try consciously to work out the logic and rationality of what is being said?
8 Do you restrain yourself (you do not interrupt or 'stop listening') when you hear something you believe to be wrong?
9 In discussion, are you willing to let the other speaker have the last word?
10 Do you try to be sure that you are considering the other person's point of view before you comment, answer or disagree?

- If you answered all the questions with a definite 'yes', then you were not being honest with yourself. You may like to believe that you do all those things, always, or you may intend to do them, but – be honest! – listening as well as that is hard work and none of us can keep it up all the time.
- If your score was around 5 then you were probably being honest and are pre- pared to admit that even the 5 to which you answered 'yes' cannot be maintained without frequent lapses when you forget to try. However, you obviously make some attempt to remember that, despite what your real opinions are, everyone is entitled to a reasonably fair hearing. Which ones did you answer 'no'? What does that signify about you as a person? Do you find it difficult to concentrate? Can you only listen effectively when you like someone or agree with their views? Do you tend to switch off if you don't like their appearance, or at least tend to let their appearance affect your assessment of their ideas?
- If you scored under 5 then you are either being disarmingly honest or falsely modest, but you are in danger of being the sort of person you don't like – self-centred, only interested in your own ideas, narrow-minded and unwilling to accept that other people's views may be just as valid as your own, unprepared to recognise your own prejudices and … well, just not very keen on making much effort to listen to other people.

Assignment: Now, go back to those 'listeners' at the beginning of the chapter and use your imagination about how they might have answered the questions or, rather, since they may not be too honest, answer the questions on their behalf.

As you work to improve your listening performance, the preceding ten questions should be your guides, for they include the most significant listening problems which occur in personal and organisational communication.

However, here are some more practical suggestions which, if seriously practised in organisations, might double or treble communication effectiveness, and help you to become a more effective part of any organisation.

3.4   Ten aids to good listening

Perhaps the simplest way of ensuring good listening is to concentrate. 'Easier said than done', you might say; 'but *how* does one concentrate?' The guidelines suggested here include ways of improving concentration.

Be prepared to listen – listening is not a passive skill but one that requires active hard work. Communication is a two-way process and so we must share the responsibility for effectiveness with the speaker: try to think more about what the speaker is trying to say than about what you want to say.

Being prepared also means getting into the right mental attitude – ready to maintain attention, increase awareness and elicit comprehension – and having the right background knowledge to understand what is being communicated. This means doing some homework for the meeting, the interview or the lecture, so that you start off with a common frame of reference.

Be interested – 'If they can't make it interesting, they can't expect me to listen!' is a comment frequently heard after lectures or speeches. Remember – the listener is equally responsible. Look for ways in which the message might be relevant to you, your job, your interests. Any message, any time, could be relevant. Ask questions like: what is being said that I can use? How can I use this information to give a better service, improve morale, be more efficient, learn something about myself or other people?

And look interested – after all no one wants to speak to a 'blank wall'. Put yourself in the speaker's shoes and imagine how you would feel.

Keep an open mind – being open-minded means being aware of your own prejudices or you may 'tune out' those messages that don't fit your bias. Don't feel threatened, insulted or resistant to messages that contradict your beliefs, attitudes, ideas and values.

Being open-minded also means trying to ignore a speaker's appearance and manner of presentation. Just because you don't like the look of them, don't be put off their ideas. If you know your own prejudices, you are more likely to control them and take them into account.

Never jump too quickly to conclusions about the speaker's personality, their main message and your own response. You may be wrong and if you make up your mind too soon, you may block out any chance of hearing the truth. In other words, delay judgement.

Listen for the main ideas – poor listeners are inclined to listen for the facts only. Learn to discriminate between fact and principle, idea and example, evidence and argument.

The ability to extract the main ideas depends on your ability to recognise the conventional methods of structuring a message, transitional language and the speaker's use of repetition. The main points can come at the beginning, middle or end of a message, so you must always be alert. If the speaker gives a preview or a summary, listen especially carefully.

Listen critically – you should be critical, in an unbiased way, of the assumptions and arguments the speaker is using, and weigh up carefully the value of the evidence and the basis of the logic behind the main message.

Resist distractions – concentrating is only another way of saying 'resist distractions'. Attention is fluctuating and selective. Your own experience will tell you that it is very easy to 'switch off'. Of course the speaker has a very real responsibility to attract attention and to keep it. But the best orator in the world can fail if the listener is not prepared to make an effort.

The natural attention curve for most people is quite high, drops off as the message continues and increases again at the end. You should try to combat this tendency by making a special effort in the middle of the message and trying to keep it constant.

Don't be distracted by the speaker's dress, appearance, vocabulary, style of presentation, use of visual, oral and written aids. Above all, don't let other people in the audience distract you. They may not be good listeners; prove you are.

Take notes – if the message is essential to you, you will need to make an outline of the speaker's main ideas and particular examples which you might otherwise forget. But, remember that note-taking can be a distraction, so be flexible. It might be better to listen attentively and then make notes after the speaker has finished.

Help the speaker – we have already noted that it helps the speaker if we try to look interested, but in conversation there are other ways in which we can encourage the speaker. These 'listener responses' are very brief comments or actions that the listener makes to the speaker, which convey the idea that you are interested and attentive and wish him to continue. They are made quietly and briefly so as not to interfere with the speaker's train of thought – usually when the speaker pauses. There are five types of listener response.

Self-Check

Can you think of typical 'listener responses' which convey your interest in the speaker? Picture the last conversation you had. What did you do while you were listening?

Check-Points: Listener Responses
- nodding the head slightly and waiting
- looking at the speaker attentively
- remarking 'I see', 'Uh-huh', 'Really?' etc.
- repeating back the last few words the speaker said (but be careful – if this becomes a habit, it can be irritating)
- reflecting back to the speaker your understanding of what has just been said ('You feel that …')

How many did you get? The value of listener responses is that they provide feedback to the speaker and tell them that you are still with them and want them to continue.

Reflect back – the last of the listener responses mentioned. It is such an invaluable tool for the good listener that it is worth a special mention.

Check-Points: Reflecting Phrases

If you don't understand what has been said or you want the speaker to elaborate on a point, try to introduce the thought with a reflecting phrase, such as:

- 'you said'
- 'you mentioned'
- 'you suggested before'
- 'you described'

After repeating the idea, follow with a question beginning with

- 'who'
- 'what'
- 'where'
- 'when'
- 'why'
- 'how'.

Reflecting phrases are designed to give you a second chance of receiving something you missed the first time round.

Reflecting back the speaker's own ideas in this way has the added advantage of showing the speaker that you are really listening to what they are saying. In addition it allows you to check that you have really understood what the speaker meant to say. Most of us are so intent on how we are reacting to the speaker's words that we don't really listen to them. One psychologist was so aware of this problem that he developed a game to delay argument and encourage people to really listen to one another. He suggested that before people can make a point in a discussion, they should first be able to summarise the last person's contribution to that person's satisfaction. Try playing this game and see for yourself how very difficult it is not to prepare mental arguments while the other person is talking, with the result that you miss most of what is really being said.

Hold back – Perhaps the hardest thing about being a good listener is trying not to interrupt. Even when there is a pause, it doesn't always mean that the speaker has finished, so be patient.

Listening is a process of self-denial
(A.C. Mumford)

Exercise 3.1

1 What percentage of communicating time does the average white-collar worker spend listening?
2 What proportion of the original message is remembered after three days, according to one study?
3 List and explain the five ways by which we can show we are listening.
4 How can a listener resist distractions?
5 Now look back at the four 'listeners' at the beginning of the chapter. Which of the aids to good listening would be particularly helpful for each one?

Summary – good listening

- *Results of effective listening*
    1 Encouragement to others
    2 Possession of all the information
    3 Improved relationships
    4 Resolution of problems
    5 Better understanding of people

- *Aids to good listening*
    1 Be prepared to listen
    2 Be interested
    3 Keep an open mind
    4 Listen for the main ideas
    5 Listen carefully
    6 Resist distractions
    7 Take notes
    8 Help the speaker
    9 Reflect back
    10 Hold back

Assignment: For your next face-to-face listening situation, write down the ten aids to good listening on a card and intentionally practise each and every one. Try the same exercise on a televised party political broadcast, preferably that of a party you would not normally support.

Assignment: Try the listening game. Have a discussion with a friend but institute the rule:

Each person can speak only after they have first restated the ideas and feelings of the previous speaker accurately and to that person's satisfaction.

At the end of 20 minutes, discuss the difficulties of this method and the advantages in terms of effective listening.

4 Human interaction and non-verbal communication

Everything we do is a form of communication

Ian Baker had just had a flaming row with his wife and walked out of the house with the sound of his wife's angry words echoing in his ears. While he sat impatiently in traffic jam after traffic jam, he went over in his mind what he would really like to have said to his wife (and to his mother-in-law, for that matter!)

What had caused the row? What had he said and done that had made things worse? What had she said and done that had annoyed him?

He arrived at work late, frustrated and angry. As he pushed open the swing doors he was met by the cheery smile and bright 'good morning' of Jayne Pembroke, one of his most loyal and hard-working employees. He pushed past her, as if he hadn't even seen her.

Ian Baker had never cut her dead before! What had she done? She began to wonder...

It is impossible *not* to communicate – that is, the absence of words does not mean that there is an absence of communication.

We have seen that even when we are not making any conscious effort we are constantly receiving messages from the world outside us; in the same way, we are always communicating something to other people, whether we mean to or not. Everything we do is a form of communication, even when we are not saying a word. And how we feel about the world, other people and ourselves will influence – consciously or unconsciously – how we communicate.

4.1 Metacommunication and paralanguage

Non-verbal communication is anything other than words that communicate a message. The way we stand, walk, shrug our shoulders; the clothes we wear, the car we drive, or the office we occupy all communicate ideas to others.

You may say of someone: 'She *said* she thought it was a good idea, but I got the feeling that she wasn't very happy with it.' How did you get this feeling, this message? It may have come from a particular expression on her face, which seemed to imply that despite what she said, she did not like the idea. It may have been something in her tone of voice which did not sound very enthusiastic: something which, in effect, did not fit with what she was saying.

All these things which we take into account in interpreting what someone is saying, over and above the actual words, are referred to as 'metacommunication'. 'Meta' is from the Greek and means 'beyond' or 'in addition to'; hence, metacommunication is something 'in addition to communication'.

In the example just given, if you got the impression that the speaker was unhappy with the idea because of the expression on her face, or because something in the movement of her body told you she was not enthusiastic, she communicated this by means of metacommunication.

However, if you got the impression from the inflection of her voice, then she communicated this by means of what we call 'paralanguage'. Frequently, paralanguage conveys the opposite of the words themselves. When this happens, we usually pick up the meaning of paralanguage rather than the meaning of the language being used.

It's not what he says, but the way he says it.

For example, a sarcastic parent may comment on something very *un*helpful that a child has done by saying, 'Thank you very much', in such a tone of voice, and with a particular emphasis on the 'you' perhaps, that leaves the child in no doubt at all that the parent is *not* thanking them at all, just the opposite!

Of course, we often communicate in a completely non-verbal way by means of gestures, facial expressions and other body movements. A shrug of the shoulders (indicating, 'Don't ask me, I don't know'), or a hand-clap (expressing appreciation), or someone storming out of the room and slamming the door (indicating anger) communicates every bit as effectively as words might have done.

Although you cannot help but be affected by this non-verbal communication, it is often interpreted subconsciously. Similarly, you may be unconscious of the ways in which you may be inadvertently communicating.

*Non-verbal channels are the ones of which we seem to be **least** aware in ourselves, but **most** aware in others.*

Since non-verbal communication is such an important part of the process of communication, you should know what is involved, so that you can become more consciously aware of non-verbal messages and make them work for you, rather than against you.

In this chapter we shall look at the language of

- silence
- time
- body language and
- the underlying psychology that underpins human interaction.

4.2 The language of silence

Have you ever been 'cut dead' by someone? How did you feel? The speech or lecture is finished and the person in the chair asks for questions – how do you feel about the silence?

'Silence is golden', so the saying goes, but is it? Ian Baker in the opening extract above was silent, but he communicated very 'loudly', and Jayne Pembroke did not find the silence very golden. A long period of silence may be golden for some people in certain circumstances, but in Western society most people find that it can be embarrassing and sometimes even threatening.

When someone asks us a question and we fail to answer, we communicate something. When a speaker reaches the end of their talk, invites questions and there is total silence, the audience is also communicating. It may be difficult for the speaker to interpret the silence correctly – boredom? disagreement? total rejection? total satisfaction? Without any clearer feedback, the silence is ambiguous and the speaker is left to guess the meaning – perhaps wrongly.

We are social creatures and our society is made up of responses to each other. We need reassurance from those around us: not just that we exist, but that those around us are friendly and not hostile. One of the cruellest social punishments is to 'send someone to Coventry'; one of the cruellest official punishments, and the most damaging, if it lasts for a long time, is solitary confinement. So although holding one's tongue can sometimes be wise, it can also be an act of rejection; silence builds walls – and walls are barriers to communication.

On the other hand, by using silence carefully at strategic times – by being prepared to listen, in other words – we may encourage someone to carry on talking or reveal certain feelings and attitudes which they might not otherwise have done. Silence can be an effective technique in encouraging feedback, or real two-way communication.

Silence is a powerful tool of communication, but it must be used skilfully.

Assignment: When you next watch television or overhear a conversation in a bus or train, be aware of silence. How and why are people using it, and what effect is it having?

4.3 The language of time

Assignment

1 Think about your attitude to time. Does punctuality matter to you? Always or only on some occasions? If so, which ones?
2 Can you recall an incident lately when you noticed that someone else's attitude to time was different from yours? What effect did it have on you?
3 Can you recall turning up for a meeting at work, or with a friend, early? late? You may have had good reasons but how might the other person have interpreted it?

It is easy to assume we all experience time in much the same way. After all an hour is an hour, isn't it? And yet time is experienced differently by different nationalities, societies and cultures.

In Western European/Christian culture, time has been divided into years which consist of 365 days ($365^1/_4$ to be exact), whereas the Muslim year is 10 or 11 days shorter. Christian years are numbered from the year of the birth of Jesus Christ, whereas the Muslims start in AD 622, the year in which Mohammed fled from Mecca to Medina. So in the Christian year 1979 the Muslims started their fourteenth century.

Even within a particular culture, different communities will divide time into different periods. The business community will concentrate on the commercial week from Monday to Friday, while the shop-owners' week will be Monday to Saturday; the retail trade will see their year divided into the periods of Christmas, the January sales, the summer sales and perhaps the summer months if they are in a tourist area, whereas a farming community may well not be so conscious of weeks and weekends and will track the course of time according to farming activities and the seasons – the ploughing season, the sowing season and the haymaking season.

Check-Point

What is perhaps more important because it is not always so obvious is that individuals have different time-scales too. In the context of their own position and circumstances, people will value time differently. The time of a nation's president will differ from that of a retired couple whose 'time is their own'.

Assignment

- Would you describe yourself as a person for whom time is very important?
- Are you a fast-moving, energetic person? Or a slow, cautious person?
- Do you expect other people to be like you?
- Does it irritate you when they are not?
- For example, do you get irritated by people who are always rushing about at work? Or by people who seem to do everything at an infuriating snail's pace?
- Have you ever thought that your attitude to time may annoy other people?

The different values we attach to time are reflected in the words we use. The busy executive may impatiently describe a 30-minute chat with someone they did not want to see as having 'wasted hours'. Most children will know only too well how ambiguous the phrase 'just a minute' can be when uttered by a harassed parent. It could mean literally 'one minute'; it could mean 'when I've finished this'; it could (and frequently does) mean 'never', unless the child keeps pestering. One person may say they will do a job 'as soon as possible' and mean that they will do it immediately after finishing a couple of more important or urgent jobs; someone else may say the same thing but mean that they will not get round to it until you have reminded them two or three times.

Perhaps even more significant in its effect on communication is the way we use time. If you arrange to meet someone at 10.00 a.m. and turn up at 10.30 a.m. you would be communicating something – about your attitude to the meeting, or to the other person, or about your attitude to yourself and the importance of time to you. If you turn up early to a lecture it may say something about your interest and enthusiasm. You would be using time to communicate your eagerness.

Again there are cultural differences in the use of time, which the business executive would do well to be aware of. In Western society, business people tend to move pretty much by the clock, with clocks and watches, diaries and calendars almost governing our lives – a 2 o'clock appointment usually means 2 o'clock or within 5 or 10 minutes of it. But in some other cultures, a 2 o'clock appointment may mean 3 o'clock; and if you arrive to transact business at the appointed 2 o'clock, you may actually offend the other person.

Similarly, if you are invited to a meal in the West it is usually considered impolite to leave immediately it is over, whereas in Saudi Arabia, for example, the socialising and chatter usually take place before the meal, and guests commonly leave as soon as the meal is finished. At a business meeting in Britain, it is customary to exchange a few short pleasantries and then get down to business quickly, but in Saudi Arabia, because the Saudis set more value than we do on the exchange of small favours in their everyday affairs, no business is discussed at all until coffee or tea has been served and time has been spent on elaborate personal exchanges. Undue haste to get down to business is taken to be a sign of bad manners and possibly even lack of business expertise. However, at the end of the meeting your host, no matter how busy they are, will press you to stay; but you should still leave politely.

Check-Point

Before you travel and/or do business abroad you should check carefully on local customs, cultures and communication and remember that people do things differently just as people within your own culture have different values, attitudes and customs.

4.4 Body language or kinesics

Assignment

- Do you think a person's appearance matters?
- What factors make up 'appearance'?

A favourite sport of many people is 'people watching'. Indeed Desmond Morris has called his very popular book, *Peoplewatching*. While waiting on a railway platform or even in a doctor's waiting room, have you ever watched the crowd and tried to imagine the occupation, the problems and the thoughts of various people? Have you ever tried to work out what sort of person someone is from the way they are dressed? Have you watched two people talking out of earshot and tried to guess from their gestures, facial expressions and manner of walking and standing what they might be talking about and how they feel about one another?

Whether we are aware of it or not, each of us spends a lot of time decoding body language, or as it is also known, 'kinesics'. These body movements should be considered in relation to the message itself; however, the non-verbal communications often come through louder than the words that are actually being spoken and are frequently the means by which we reveal the emotional side of our communications.

In recent years, more and more interest has been taken in body language and researchers have tried to establish the exact nature of the relationships between this kind of non-verbal communication and the effect it has on the receiver. Although this research is still in its infancy, there are already several books which cover the subject of body language in far more detail than is possible in this book. However, no book on communication would be complete without at least an introduction to the subject, since it is essential that anyone trying to improve their communication techniques should be sensitive to the human relations aspects in the communication process – and these human elements are often vividly revealed in body language.

Assignment

- How do you know that someone agrees with you, when you are speaking to them?
- Can you tell whether someone has understood you, from the way they look?
- List **five** examples of body language and what message they each convey.

The non-verbal messages of a speaker tend to reveal the degree of presence of sincerity, conviction, honesty, ability and knowledge; they reveal, too, a lot about the speaker and their attitude and feelings about the message they are transmitting. Body language of the receiver also reveals a lot about them and their feelings. But, more important, it frequently tells the speaker the extent to which their audience is accepting or not accepting the message. In other words, body language provides instant feedback to the speaker and tells them how they are doing. If this feedback is available but the speaker is insensitive to it, not aware of its significance or unable to interpret or read the language, a valuable contribution to their communication effectiveness is being wasted.

Check-Point

It follows that to be a good reader of body language you need to sharpen your powers of observation and your ability to decode the messages; you need to be more aware of the presence of these messages and their possible meanings; to be constantly alert to the effect of your body language on other people and constantly alert to the feedback available so that you can immediately use your other communication techniques if the feedback tells you it is necessary.

Space

Before we look at the way we move the various parts of our body, we should first examine our attitude to the space in which that movement takes place. Just as silence and time speak, so does space. Not only does space affect the way we communicate, but we also *use* space to communicate.

First each of us has spaces that we feel are our own. The 'Three Bears' complaint that 'someone's been sitting in my chair' may seem petty, but reflects a very real sense of possession of space and invasion of privacy. Many families have a particular chair which is 'Dad's chair' and woe betide anyone who dares to sit in it.

Similarly it would be unthinkable for a subordinate to walk into a boss's office and sit down in the boss's chair, unless specifically invited to do so; and 'Old Tom' may become quite upset if an unsuspecting stranger should inadvertently sit on 'his' stool at the bar.

Assignment

- Do you have a particular space which you feel is your own?
- If you are a student, do you always tend to sit in the same place in the lecture room? What do you do to this space to show it is yours?
- Do other people seem to have this attitude to 'their space'?
- What effect does it have on other people's behaviour?

Space and status

In business offices, space is usually directly related to status, in that the higher up the organisational ladder people go, the more square feet of floor space they have in their offices. Some large companies even have rules which lay down the amount of room, and possibly even the size of desk top, to which a particular level manager is entitled. At lower levels in the organisation, too, acquisition of private space is reflected in the fact that it is better to be given an office on your own, even though it may have a smaller floor area, than one which you have to share with others.

Even in open-plan offices, which are more common nowadays, there may be subtle ways in which status or responsibility reveals itself.

There are cultural differences in the way we use space to say something about status, particularly in formal situations like offices. Europeans, for instance, are more likely to put their desks in the centre of the room, as authority is seen to flow outwards from the centre. Proximity to the centre is one way of saying, 'That person is important'. Americans, on the other hand, tend to distribute their working space around the edges of a room, leaving the centre open for traffic and casual conversation.

Territory

Our apparent need to stake a claim on a particular area of space seems to stem from the instinctive need of animals to guard their territory. Whether it is inherited or not, observations of our fellow-men indicate that there is little doubt that most of us have a sense of territory, which prompts us to erect fences around our garden and protect our home against the uninvited stranger. Even in public spaces – in a classroom, in the underground or in a lecture hall – as long as there is freedom to choose, most people will tend to sit as far as possible from strangers.

Next time you go to the seaside, watch the way a beach fills up. First thing in the morning, when there are few groups on the beach, each new arrival will find its own territory, virtually equidistant from its nearest neighbours. The territory will then be staked out by means of towels, windbreaks and so on. As the beach fills up, each new arrival fills in the available spaces, until by the peak period you may find yourself practically sitting on the towel of a complete stranger; but had you sat that close to a total stranger first thing in the morning when the other person was the only one on the beach, your behaviour would have been regarded as extraordinary and the stranger would have made it very obvious that you had invaded their territory.

Assignment

- How do people at work stake their claim on a particular territory?
- How do you stake your claim?
- How do you indicate to the rest of the world that this is your patch, whether it is your office space or your work station or your room at home?
- How do you feel when people invade your territory?

Personal space

Possibly in an attempt to carry our territory around with us we behave as if we are surrounded by a 'space bubble' or sense of personal space; that is, a distance at which we are prepared to interact with others. We are prepared to vary this distance according to how well we know someone and the activity or type of communication taking place. For example, while you may be quite happy for a close friend or relative to carry on a fairly intimate conversation at very close quarters, you are likely to become very uneasy if a total stranger speaking on a very formal matter were to stand only one foot away from you.

These 'space bubbles' or distances seem to fall into four types (each of which has a close phase and a far phase):

Intimate distance

Close phase (actual contact or touching): this is reserved for making love, for very close friendships and for children clinging to a parent or to each other, but it would also include wrestling or fighting. In our culture it is acceptable between women, and between men and women on intimate terms, but it can be embarrassing between men, or between men and women not on intimate terms. However, in Arab culture it is perfectly normal to see men walking in the street with their arms round one another.

Far phase (up to $\frac{1}{2}$ metre): still close enough to clasp hands but not acceptable for people not on intimate terms, unless circumstances, like a crowded lift or underground train force it. In this case, other behaviour – drawing away, tensing muscles, avoiding eye contact – sends the message: 'I am sorry to intrude on your private space. I don't mean anything intimate by it.' If the rules of acceptable behaviour are broken, then trouble can ensue.

Personal distance

Close phase ($^1/_2$–$^3/_4$ metre): this distance is reserved for more than just a casual friend or fleeting encounter. Contact is possible but more difficult. Where people stand in relation to each other signals their relationship, or how they feel towards each other, or both. A wife can stay inside the circle of her husband's close personal zone with impunity. For another woman to do so is an entirely different story.

Far phase ($^3/_4$–$1^1/_4$ metres): the limit of physical domination. It provides a degree of personal privacy to any encounter but close enough for personal discussion. Two people who meet in the street may stop to chat at that distance, but at a party they tend to close in to the close phase of personal distance. This distance can communicate various messages, from 'I'm keeping you at arm's length', to 'I have singled you out to be a little closer than the other guests'. Moving too far in when you have a far distant relationship could be interpreted as 'I'm available'.

Social distance

Close phase ($1^1/_4$–2 metres): used for impersonal business and casual conversations – the businessman or woman meeting a new client, a prospective employee or perhaps an unknown colleague; the householder talking to tradespeople at the door or in a shop. This distance can be manipulated to indicate domination, superiority or power without having to speak any words.

Far phase (2–4 metres): used for more formal social and business relationships. The chief executive may actually have a large enough desk to ensure that this kind of distance is maintained, but if they come out from behind the desk and reduce the distance, they are signalling a willingness to be more personal, less superior. This distance allows greater freedom of behaviour: you can keep working at this distance without being rude, or you can stop working and talk. Similarly people on very intimate terms may assume this for social distance to relax. A husband and wife, for example, can talk to each other if they want to or simply read instead of talking.

Public distance

Close phase (4–8 metres): suitable for informal gatherings such as a manager talking to a meeting of staff or a lecturer talking to a room full of students.

Far phase (8 or more): usually reserved for politicians and public figures, since it provides the necessary security and emphasises domination particularly where a platform must be provided to ensure that all can see and hear.

You may feel that these rather exact distances are a little far-fetched or arbitrary. They are only an attempt to standardise what observation seems to indicate and are based on the way in which people do tend to interact, rather than on strict measurement.

If someone moves closer than is appropriate for the activity and relationship, we may become tense or even hostile, and this will affect the nature of the communication that is possible.

However, here again there are cultural differences. Most North Americans and British prefer a certain distance for normal conversation. They feel more comfortable if that space between themselves and the other person is maintained. This can often cause problems for American or British business people visiting Latin countries, for example, where a smaller distance is preferred, or Japan where crowding together is often welcomed and not seen as an invasion of personal space.

When there is an invasion of territory or personal space, the person who feels invaded will often retreat to maintain the distance. But when they can retreat no further they may, if they are aware of what is going on, start to advance in turn in order to threaten the invader, so forcing them to retreat. While this return invasion might work in North America or Britain, it would probably fail in Latin countries where the new proximity would be welcomed.

Check-Point

Since space and its use make such a contribution to your total communication effort, you should know how to encode and decode these 'space messages' in order to avoid unconsciously offending others or being offended.

Touch

Touching is obviously closely related to the idea of personal space. Although it was probably among the earliest form of communication and is still used by small children when they are unable to communicate verbally, we tend to be very cautious in our use of touch as a means of communication. In times of trouble or sorrow it can be one of the most effective methods of communicating sympathy or protection, but generally North America and Britain would not be described as tactile societies, and touch is usually reserved for the intimate distance mentioned above, and for communication between close friends or relatives. While it is acceptable for women to touch in public, it is still less appropriate for men to do so. Quite small boys soon learn to shake off physical signs of affection from even their mothers and fathers in embarrassment.

Assignment

If touching can be so effective in times of trouble and to show affection, do you think communication could be improved if we were less inhibited in our use of touch? Give some examples to support your argument.

Orientation and posture

We can influence communication and signal our attitudes not just by our proximity to others but by the position and posture we adopt. Experiments have shown that people who want to cooperate will tend to sit or stand side by side whereas if they feel in opposition they will tend to position themselves head-on or opposite the other person. Watch the behaviour of people at meetings and you will often see that people tend to argue far more with people across the table than with those alongside them. A wise chair may, in fact, contrive to seat potential opponents along the same side of the table if they particularly want to avoid conflict at a meeting. Similarly, a good interviewer will recognise that seating a candidate directly opposite and with a desk between them will not be conducive to the kind of easy cooperative conversation which they want to create. For this reason you may frequently find that you are shown to an easy chair near a low table and the interviewer will sit at roughly a ninety-degree angle in relation to you in a chair the same height, as this kind of arrangement has been shown to encourage easy, non-threatening discussion.

In the same way bodily posture can communicate, often involuntarily social status or the desire to be dominant or submissive. Hunched shoulders and a lowered head may signal shyness and inferiority; standing erect, with head tilted back and hands on hips, may indicate superiority and self-satisfaction.

People all have different styles of walking, standing, sitting and so on, which may reflect past and present roles – as in the case of a police officer – or they may reflect a person's self-image, self-confidence or emotional state.

Assignment

Look at the drawings of body postures in Figure 4.1. Which of the following adjectives describes which posture?

angry	dominating	resigned	surprised
aloof	doubtful	sad	suspicious
ashamed	impatient	self-conscious	undecided
casual	modest	self-satisfied	uninterested
describing	questioning	shy	

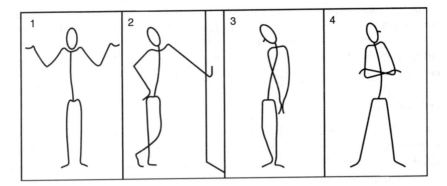

Figure 4.1 **Body postures.**

Psychologists have found in experiments that these four postures tend to be associated with certain emotions and activities in the following way:

Posture 1	*Posture 2*	*Posture 3*	*Posture 4*
uninterested	self-satisfied	shy	surprised
describing	impatient	self-conscious	dominating
resigned	describing	ashamed	suspicious
doubtful	casual	modest	undecided
questioning	angry	sad	aloof

How well did you read these examples of body language? How often do you communicate your mood or your emotions to other people by means of your posture?

> **Check-Point**
>
> Change of body posture can also, of course, signal the beginning or end of an encounter or the desire to speak. The good communicator will be on the lookout for these signals.

Head nods

In most Western countries we shake our heads up and down to indicate agreement or to encourage another person in what they are saying or doing. In fact, as we have seen, a good listener would do well to remember this as a means of encouragement. It is also one of the non-verbal signals we use to control or synchronise speech when we are conversing with other people, so that we speak in turn. However, whereas in Britain a nod gives the other person permission to go on, a rapid succession of head nods indicates that the nodder wants to speak himself. In India shaking the head up and down means 'no' or disagreement.

Facial expressions

Of all body movements, facial expressions are the ones we are most able to control. Although a person's face may provide a continuous commentary on their reaction to what you are saying – surprise, disbelief, agreement, disappointment, anger and so on – and you can learn much about a person's true feelings from studying their facial expressions, they should be read in relation both to the words being uttered and to other body movements which are more reliable as communicators of real feelings because they are so much more difficult to control.

Eye movements

In contrast to other body signals, movements of the eyes have an effect quite out of proportion to the physical effort exerted; some eye movements are quite uncontrollable but nevertheless send out very strong messages which we receive almost without being aware of them.

The movements of the eyes perform a number of important functions in social interaction.

To indicate interest – when two people are engaged in conversation they look each other in the eye intermittently. Usually each looks for between 25 and 75 per cent of the time. The glances vary in length but we tend to look twice as much while listening as while talking. The amount of look is related to the amount and kind of interest: if we are interested in someone or what they are saying we will look at them, whereas we will tend to direct our gaze away if we are uninterested. Long periods of looking indicate a desire for intimacy, so in our culture there tend to be unwritten rules about the length of time we may look at a person in certain circumstances. In a crowded lift or train we may glance but not stare. For an unwary male to stare at a woman longer than is proper in a public place is to court all sorts of unpleasant consequences. However, there are obviously moments when longer periods of looking are expected, even desired. When people are interacting but are far apart, they will tend to look more, as if to compensate for the distance.

To gain feedback – people look primarily to obtain information: people look while listening to get visual messages to supplement the words to help them understand what they are hearing. They look while they are talking to get feedback on the person's reactions. If a speaker looks while talking, then not only will the other person feel that the speaker is really interested in them rather than just the subject of conversation, but they will also feel that the speaker is more confident, more believable. These impressions seem to be justified since people look more when they like the person they are talking to and when they are telling the truth.

To synchronise speech – eye movements, like head nods and grunts, are also used to synchronise speech. The speaker will tend to look away from the other person just as they start talking. This seems to be because they want to avoid distraction from too much incoming information, just at the moment they are planning and organising what they are going to say. Similarly they may look away when they are speaking hesitantly, but when they are speaking faster and more fluently they will look at the other person; and more important, at the end of what they are saying they will give their listener a prolonged gaze. This is because they need to see how the other person is reacting; although, unconsciously perhaps, they also signal to the other person that they have finished what they want to say. At pauses in the middle of long speeches, they will look for permission to carry on; the other person will usually nod or grunt if agreeable to this.

To show attraction – for many people one of the most fascinating discoveries that have been made about eye movements is that the pupils of the eye dilate or grow bigger when we look at something which arouses or excites us. Although the pupils normally dilate in darkness and in response to certain drugs, experiments have shown that women's pupils dilate especially when they are shown pictures of babies, and men's in response to pictures of naked women. This rather special movement of the eyes which is beyond our control, also communicates the other way. Not only does pupil dilation reveal arousal and interest, but it also tends to make a person look more attractive, so it is likely that the attraction can become mutual without either person being precisely sure why they are attracted.

The eyes do not communicate in isolation. There is an endless number of messages which can be sent when one thinks of eyes combined with different movements and positions of eyelids and eyebrows and other parts of the body. As with all forms of non-verbal communication, messages sent by the eyes should be decoded in terms of the words accompanying them.

Gestures

Other movements of parts of the body – hands, arms, even legs and feet – grouped under the heading of gestures are perhaps the most commonly thought of method of non-verbal communication. We probably all know someone who 'talks with their hands'. Some people punctuate their communication with such extravagant gestures that it is almost dangerous to stand too close when they are talking.

The kinds of meaning conveyed by gestures are certainly too numerous to mention here, but generally speaking gestures serve the following purposes.

Communicating information – a hand raised in greeting, the 'V' sign of Winston Churchill, a clenched fist, the pointed finger are all examples of the ways in which non-verbal communication can be used either to supplement the meaning of words or, in some cases, even replace speech altogether, where normal speech is either difficult or impossible. Examples of hand movements and gestures becoming highly developed and systemised into a language which can replace speech completely are the sign languages used in television broadcasting studios, by ground crews on airfields, by those who are deaf/without speech and by some Australian aboriginals.

Although the meaning of gestures will often vary between cultures, there appear to be certain basic gestures that have the same meaning in many cultures.

Communicating emotion – as with gestures used to communicate information, there appear to be a few specific gestures like hands raised to the mouth in surprise or fist-shaking which have been found to accompany particular emotions in widely varied cultures. This suggests that such expression may be innate and universal.

General emotional arousal tends to produce diffuse, apparently pointless, bodily movements: a nervous lecturer may appear to be constantly on the move. On the other hand, more specific emotions tend to produce particular gestures – hand-clapping (appreciation), fist-clenching (aggression), face-touching (anxiety) and so on.

Supporting speech – while a person is speaking they move their hands, body and head continuously. These movements are closely coordinated with speech and form a part of the total communication.

Head and body movements are often used to give emphasis and meaning to words, to point to people and objects and to give illustrations of shapes and sizes or movements; but they are also closely related to the pattern of speech, so that gestures often reflect the structure, that is, large movements correspond to large verbal units like the paragraph, and smaller, finer movements which may be barely visible are related to sentences, phrases or even individual words.

An obvious example might be a speaker raising his arm in a wide gesture with three fingers raised as he says: 'There are three main reasons…' Then as he deals with each reason in turn he raises one finger, then two and finally three to reflect non-verbally that he has got to the third reason.

These kinds of gesture are often the equivalent in speech of the signposts used in writing which we look at in Chapter 13 on better reading.

Gestures also contribute to the synchronisation of speech between two or more people. A raised hand may indicate that the listener wants to interrupt the speaker to say something himself or to ask for clarification. A gesture extending an upturned palm may indicate an invitation to the other person to speak.

Expressing self-image – you may convey the image you have of yourself by body movements and gestures. If you have an extrovert personality, you may subconsciously communicate this to the world by means of wide, energetic gestures; whereas, if you are rather a shy, retiring personality your gestures may be less frequent, smaller and restricted to the area close to your body.

Assignment

- Next time you are in conversation, try clasping your hands together so that you can't move them.
- Does it feel awkward, as if your hands are fighting to get away?
- Do you find it difficult to talk naturally?

Some speakers who may nervously grasp the edges of the lectern, or plunge their hands deep into their pockets, reveal that they are restricting their natural gestures, as their hands still try to move either in rather a tied-down way on the lectern, or causing the sides of their jackets to flap rather like bird wings!

Expressing relationships – those who study the way in which body language can reflect attitudes and emotions, have discovered that we often tend to adopt or 'mirror' the gestures and body movements of other people with whom we are talking. These shared postures and movements often reflect mutual interest or shared points of view. For example, if two people are chatting and are either attracted to one another or are in agreement, when one crosses their legs, the other person is very likely to do the same. This kind of mirroring of gestures and postures is usually completely subconscious and goes unnoticed by the participants, but it can be fascinating to watch this behaviour as an onlooker from a distance. Desmond Morris in *Peoplewatching* includes some convincing photographs of 'postural echo'.

4.5 The underlying psychology: NLP, EI and TA

Neuro-Linguistic Programming (NLP)

In fact, in the 1970s, Richard Bandler and John Grinder, working in linguistics, psychology and psychotherapy, began to help people to develop *conscious* techniques and strategies to change their behaviour quite dramatically and so communicate with and influence others more effectively. Put simply, the underlying belief was 'Hey – if that guy can do it, why can't we?' and Bandler and Grinder began examining the behaviour of people and analysing it into its component parts so that the behaviour could be modelled and others could copy and so perform effectively too. Bandler and Grinder's work gave rise to further development by others – Steve Andreas and Connie Rae, Joseph O' Connor and John Seymour, and more recently Sue Knight – and the approach, which came to be known as Neuro-Linguistic Programming (NLP), has become recognised by many as one of the most revolutionary approaches to personal development, interpersonal skills and communication. It is particularly pertinent to this chapter since NLP concentrates especially on face-to-face communication and provides techniques for building rapport by picking up on and *consciously* 'mirroring' voice, speech and body-language signals of others, and learning how others perceive the world so you can present ideas in ways they will accept.

However, the techniques that have been developed also claim to help you to accelerate the ability to learn, improve the quality of the way you relate to people with whom you live and work, develop flexibility so that you have more choice over your behaviour and therefore more influence, improve your ability to gain the cooperation of those around you, and manage your thoughts and feelings so that you can become the master of your emotions.

Emotional Intelligence (EI)

The best oral communicators don't just use well-chosen words, in well-structured sentences within a well thought-through structure: these are essential pre-requisites, but are not enough in themselves. For instance, the clearest speech, dully presented, has little effect – may not even be listenable to.

Emotional Intelligence (EI) has come to be a generic name for the set of abilities (or competency framework) that covers handling ourselves and relating to others: broadly, people skills, as distinct from cognitive and technical skills. Its formal definition is 'the capacity for recognising our own feelings and those of others, for motivating ourselves and for managing emotions effectively in ourselves and in others … a learned capability that contributes to effective performance …' The EI competencies fall into four categories:

Self-Awareness
Social Awareness
Self-Management
Relationship Management (or Social Skills)

This set of definitions was popularised by Daniel Goleman in his books, *Emotional Intelligence, Working with Emotional Intelligence* and *The New Leaders* (with Richard Boyatzis and Annie McKee). His work drew on earlier research by John Mayer and Peter Salovey, who used a somewhat different definition originally. Goleman's research was based on studies of children, and an analysis of the McBer (now HayGroup) company's database of competencies of people in a wide range of jobs – particularly focusing on people who are successful at what they do. It has recently been revalidated and redesigned (2002).

One of the key EI competencies for communication is emotional self-control; another is empathy. Others are self-confidence, transparency, organisational awareness, service orientation and influence. In simple terms, if you are going to be a good oral communicator, you need to be able to listen, controlling out your personal expectations and preferences; be self-assured; speak in accordance with your values (people can spot insincerity); understand and allow for the climate and culture within which you are speaking; match the needs of your customers (audience); engage your audience, and anticipate the effect of your actions and words.

Transactional Analysis (TA)

Transactional Analysis focuses on people's external behaviour and, secondarily, on the internal psychological processes which underly their behaviour and communications. It is a relatively easy model for the layman to understand; this is perhaps confirmed by its having stood the test of time: four decades. Eric Berne designed Transactional Analysis (TA) as a way of understanding interactions between people. It has been used more and more by trainers and their students to understand what is actually going on when people interact with one another and to modify behaviour which is causing conflict and unhappiness when communicating with others.

Parent/Adult/Child ego states

Berne made complex interpersonal transactions understandable when he recognised that all people, whatever their actual age or state, interact from one of three 'ego-states' – Parent, Adult or Child – and that these interactions can occur at overt and covert levels. Each one of the ego states is in effect a system of communication with its own language and function:

- The Parent is a language of values.
- The Adult is a language of logic and rationality.
- The Child is a language of emotions.

Berne maintained that, if we are to function effectively in the world, we depend on the availability of all three, intact and undamaged ego states. But, in business situations, we need to be in the Adult state as much as possible – although others may not be. Through training it is possible to recognise what ego states people are transacting (or communicating) from, and to follow the transactional sequences that people engage in as they interact with each other. We can then improve our own communication skills, and even those of others.

Games, strokes and scripts

Berne, perhaps most famous for his book *Games People Play*, originally published in 1968, also described the 'games' or rituals people use to score points or get control, or become victims or to receive the positive or negative 'strokes' they feel they need, often subconsciously. These, although fascinating, are beyond the scope of this book.

TA as a communication skill

While the efficient, yet insightful, method that TA teaches makes it ideally suited for helping people to cope with their place in the world, it is also a relatively quickly learned technique for understanding and improving our own communication.

We can all improve our communication skills by learning to identify our ego states and evaluate and improve ways in which our ego states function so as to stay in Adult as far possible.

We can develop our skills in analysing transactional patterns so that we are able to understand, predict and help improve dysfunctional, unproductive, uncooperative interactions between people at home and at work.

Assignment: Next time you are in a group conversation, look at the posture and gestures of those in the group and see if there is a link between shared gestures and posture and shared opinions and attitudes.

Not all body language is easily read, but we ignore it at our peril.

Concentrating only on what we say and what we hear, rather than how it is communicated, can lead to bad feelings, misunderstandings and missed opportunities for really effective communication.

4.6 Conflict between verbal and non-verbal communication

Finally, then, everything you do is a communication; actions speak louder than words. Quite often a verbal message is sent with a non-verbal one; you may be greeted at a friend's door by a welcoming 'Hi! Come in! Cup of coffee?' But the non-verbal communication, consisting of frequent but surreptitious glances at the clock, may indicate that you are not so welcome after all. Then there is the employee who tries to sound relaxed and comfortable when talking to the boss, but the toe tapping on the floor or the fidgeting hands tell another story.

Whenever the meaning of the non-verbal message conflicts with the meaning of the verbal message, we are more likely to believe the non-verbal message.

If we are alert, we will detect the anxious person who really exists behind the good-humoured, back-slapping 'hail-fellow-well-met' facade; we will recognise the rocky relationship of a married couple, despite their protestations of undying love; we will discern the worried, unhappy employee fighting to get out from behind the apparently carefree mask … *if* we are alert!

Summary – the importance of paralanguage in human interaction

Paralanguage and human interaction is a fascinating area of study. Many people are devoting their lives to a study of this subject, and much remains to be learned about it. By becoming a better observer, by sharpening your powers of perception and by knowing as much as possible about yourself and those you are communicating with, you should be able to translate more accurately the non-verbal and verbal messages, as well as understand what you are really communicating to others and how they 'read' you.

Assignment: Have a discussion with a friend about how you each use body language, time and silence to communicate.

How do you each feel about the non-verbal communication of the other? Is it helpful?

Does your friend tell you that sometimes your non-verbal signals communicate things you don't want to? Make a mental note of things you might like to adjust gradually in your behaviour so that it doesn't give the wrong signals.

Exercise 4.1

1 What is 'metacommunication'?
2 How can silence serve as an effective method of encouraging communication?
3 If you arrive half an hour late for an interview, without apologising, how might the interviewer interpret your late arrival?
4 What is the term given to the science or study of body language?
5 Human beings seem to have a sense of 'personal space' which is divided into four types of distance each appropriate for different kinds of interaction and relationships. What are the names of the four types of distance?
6 Other things being equal, what is the impression you are likely to convey if you look at someone while you are talking?
7 When two or more people are conversing they must take it in turns to speak, and usually achieve a fairly smooth pattern of synchronising. Which non-verbal signals in particular are used in controlling the synchronisation of speech?
8 If the verbal message and the non-verbal message conflict, which are we likely to believe?

Further reading

Argyle, Michael, *The Psychology of Interpersonal Behaviour*, Harmondsworth: Penguin Books, 1995

Bandler, R and Grinder, J, *Frogs into Princes, Neuro Linguistic Programming*, Utah, Real People Press, 1979

Berne, Eric, *Games People Play: The Psychology of Human Relationships*, Penguin Books, 1968

Bradbury, Andrew, *Develop Your NLP Skills*, Kogan Page, 2000

Goleman, Daniel, *Emotional Intelligence Why It Can Matter More Than IQ*, Bloomsbury, 1995

Goleman, Daniel, Boyatzis, Richard, McKee, Annie, *The New Leaders*, Time Warner Books UK, 2002 (originally published in US by Harvard Business School Press, 2002)

Goleman, Daniel, *Working with Emotional Intelligence*, Bloomsbury, 1998

Harris, Thomas, A, *I'm OK, You're OK*, Arrow, 1995

Harris, Amy and Harris, Thomas, A, *Staying OK*, Arrow, 1995

Knight, Sue, *Introducing NLP*, Chartered Institute of Personnel and Development, 1999

Knight, Sue, *NLP at Work*, Nicholas Brealey Publishing, 2002

Morris, Desmond, *Peoplewatching*, Vintage, 2000

O'Connor, Joseph and Seymour, John, *Introducing NLP Neuro-Linguistic Programming*, Aquarian/Thorson, 1993

Pease, Allan, *Body Language: How to read others' thoughts by their gestures*, Sheldon Press, 1997

Tannen, Deborah, *You Just Don't Understand*, Virago, 1991

Tannen, Deborah, *That's Not What I Meant*, Virago, 1992

◪ 5 Talking on the telephone

Crossed wires

'Hello.'
'Hello.'
'I'm ringing up to report a pothole in the road outside my house. It's been getting bigger and bigger and it's time something was done about it before someone has an accident. Can you get someone to see to it?'
'Yes. Where exactly is the pothole?'
'Right outside my house.'
'Yes, but ... where is that?'
'Oh, I see ... yes, you want my address – it's 29 Maud Rise ... Have you got that?'
'Yes. Thanks for letting us know.'
The girl wrote '25 Moor Drive' on a piece of paper and immediately went along to the Highways Section to report the pothole.

Assignment: What do you think might have been the likely outcome of this telephone conversation? Imagine the possible sequence of events. Make a list and then alongside, list what should have been done to avoid these consequences.

Nowadays, even with e-mail and the Internet, the telephone is still probably the most common means of communication in business, and used efficiently it has two advantages.

Check-Point: Advantages of the Telephone

- it is fast
- it allows people to converse even when they are unable to meet
- it is a great leveller: status, physical appearance and surroundings don't show
- it is a great focuser: it removes the social and emotional distractions of a face-to-face encounter

---

5.1 Telephone problems

The telephone, for all its convenience and speed, also has the power to convey rapidly a poor impression of the efficiency of individuals and organisations and create considerable confusion and irritation.

Self-Check

List the ways in which inefficient use of the telephone has irritated you.

Assignment: Ring up five organisations and make notes of how you are dealt with.
What impression did you get of each organisation?

Cost

Certainly telephone calls seem cheaper than sending a letter. Many organisations calculate that the average cost of sending a letter, taking into account the staff time involved and overheads as well as postage, is about £25, which would buy quite a lot of telephone time even at current rates and, of course, accounts for the rapid rise in the use of e-mails and fax machines. But telephone calls do not necessarily save time – and in business time is money. We have all suffered from the irritating waste of time caused by bad telephone manners:

- having to listen all through a menu of six destinations before we can press a button to make a choice
- trying to get a line
- the person required not being available and having to listen to their message before we can give one
- being left hanging on (albeit to the sound of Mozart or Dave Brubeck!) by an operator who appears to have gone to lunch
- being passed from department to department (or even diverted from phone to phone without our knowledge!) in an effort to find someone who can answer the query
- wrong or engaged numbers
- a caller who seems to have all the time in the world to chat when we are busy.

Any one of these time-wasters can take longer than it takes to write or dictate a letter.

First impressions count

But the telephone can exact other costs. Frequently, the first contact a caller has with an organisation is with the person who answers their first call. That person, either through a lack of courtesy, lack of knowledge about the organisation, or how to use the telephone itself can, however innocently, create an initial bad impression of the organisation which it is difficult to correct.

The faceless voice

Perhaps the principal cause of much of this apparent inefficiency is that although the standard telephone allows oral communication, most do not yet transmit visual communication. We have seen in Chapter 4 how important non-verbal messages can be in complementing the verbal message. Facial expressions, gestures and posture not only help to convey the real meaning of words, but are often the principal means of feedback in face-to-face conversation, allowing misunderstandings to be instantly corrected. Without this visual communication and consequent feedback these problems are typical of those which occur during telephone calls:

- words are missed
- words are misheard
- the message is misunderstood because the visual cues and feedback are missing
- the conversation somehow just doesn't seem so immediate.

Not only does this lack of visual communication cause messages to be *received* incorrectly, but it can also cause messages to be *transmitted* incorrectly by putting callers at what they feel to be a psychological disadvantage. Many people have developed a positive dislike of the telephone because they cannot see the person to whom they are talking, with the result that they lack the confidence to make and answer calls clearly and efficiently. The proliferation of voicemail and answering machines has, for many people, made this fear even worse.

Given the importance of the telephone in modern business operations and the prevalence of bad telephone habits (of which we are all guilty at times), it is surprising that very few books on business communication offer more than a paragraph or two on the subject of telephone technique. For this reason, this chapter is aimed at correcting the balance somewhat by

- providing guidance on making and answering calls efficiently and therefore
- cutting the cost of telephoning.

Picking up verbal clues

The telephone is not merely a second-rate communications channel. For most purposes, a telephone conversation is as effective as a face-to-face meeting. Indeed, given the saving in travel time and costs and the facility of audio- and videoconferencing (see Chapter 9 on Running and Taking Part in Meetings) it is set to replace most meetings.

Check-Point: Being a Verbal Detective

- Trust your intuition when picking up clues about the other person's personality, feelings and mood.
- Stay relaxed and allow ideas about the speaker to drift into your mind; unforced impressions can prove to be remarkably accurate.
- Look out for hesitations, self-mocking comments and other clues about the speaker's state of mind.

- Check your hunches by replaying your impressions to the caller, use 'reflecting back' phrases (remember Chapter 3 on Listening) like 'What you seem to be feeling is ...'
- Use 'anticipatory feedback' to guide your conversation: imagine the other person's response to a statement you are about to make and then modify what you actually say to achieve the intended result.

5.2 Basic telephone rules

Be brief

But not at the expense of making yourself clearly understood and not to the extent of being abrupt and discourteous. Lack of telephone confidence often causes people to talk for longer than they would in face-to-face conversations.

Be courteous

This is especially important when telephoning to avoid creating a bad impression which is so difficult to correct. Your tone of voice is crucial in conveying a courteous, cheerful impression as are the words you use. Remember too, that even if you are not yet using a video phone, your facial expression affects the tone of your voice. Smile!

Check-Point

A smile can be heard – in the tone of voice, which will sound pleasant and interested. If you scowl or frown, your tone will be unfriendly and uninterested.

Be resourceful

Don't be clueless. Always think of ways in which you can be most helpful. If you are taking a message for someone else, use your local knowledge to suggest helpful ways of getting the caller and the recipient of the message in touch with one another so that the caller can judge in an informed way what they want to do. If the caller has been put through to your department but no one in your department knows anything about the matter, think quickly. Who else in the organisation might know something and be able to help? If you are really unable to help, sound sincerely concerned, not uninterested.

Speak clearly

Enunciate and articulate your words particularly clearly to counteract both the poorer acoustic quality of a telephone line and the absence of lip movements to help the listener. When giving names and numbers, if there is any possible ambiguity use the phonetic code used by all emergency services and some call centres to clarify messages.

A for Alpha	J for Juliet	S for Sierra
B for Bravo	K for Kilo	T for Tango
C for Charlie	L for Lima	U for Uniform
D for Delta	M for Mike	V for Victor
E for Echo	N for November	W for Whisky
F for Foxtrot	O for Oscar	X for X-ray
G for Golf	P for Papa	Y for Yankee
H for Hotel	Q for Quebec	Z for Zulu
I for India	R for Romeo	

Remember that 5 and 9 sound very similar. Take a tip from the police who say 'fife' and 'nina' to distinguish between them.

Speak more slowly

When you are talking on the telephone it is a good idea to slow your speech down. When your voice is being mechanically transmitted, the words seem to move together faster. That is the reason television announcers often speak at a slower rate than is normal in everyday conversation. Remember too that someone may be trying to take notes as you talk. This is particularly important when speaking to an answering machine. Don't rattle off your phone number at a rate of knots – remember the poor person on the other end trying to write it down.

Building a positive telephone personality

How do *you* come across on the phone? What sort of personality do you convey down the line?

Check-Point: Building a Positive Telephone Personality

- Don't worry what you look like when you're on the phone; use as much (or as little) body language as you wish.
- Focus your concentration on what you're saying and what's being said to you.
- Mirror positive feelings in your facial expressions; if you smile while you speak, you'll put a smile in your voice.
- Try to relax; stretch to loosen your muscles and breathe evenly – tension can feed straight into your voice and create a negative image.
- Don't use specialised language (company or professional jargon): what's jargon to you may be a foreign language to the other person.
- Avoid clichés ('with all due respect', 'between you and me', 'to cut a long story short', etc.) that say one thing and clearly mean something else.
- Remember, when you tell a lie your voice rises involuntarily; on the phone this is easily detected.
- Punctuate your conversation with 'you', 'your' and occasionally the person's name.
- Replace some of your body language (head-nods, quizzical expressions) with verbal equivalents: 'Yes', 'Of course', 'I'm not sure I understood that last point. Could you...'

5.3 Switchboard operators

Although telephone operator training was at one time standard practice in business, some organisations seem to put their least able employee on the switchboard.

> **Assignment:** We have all suffered at the hands of switchboard operators who behave as if taking a call is an inconvenient interruption.
>
> If you were selecting a receptionist or switchboard operator, which **six** personal qualities would you look for?

The operator is typically regarded by callers as the representative of the whole organisation. They should be very carefully selected and trained, and should possess six essential qualities.

Check-Point: Qualities of the Switchboard Operator

- verbal intelligibility
- speed
- courtesy
- accuracy
- discretion
- resourcefulness.

These qualities are just as essential in anyone who is allowed near a business telephone.

Help the operator

The good switchboard operator is indeed an organisation's ambassador: they welcome your callers, introduce you, apologise for your absence or try to get you on another line, often take messages – and are frequently blamed for your shortcomings. Seven ways in which you can help the operator.

Check-Point: Making your Telephone System Work

- understanding how the telephone system used in your organisation works
- giving the number you want (including the STD code)
- not disappearing immediately you have asked them to ring a number for you
- answering the phone after the first ring (when they call you back)
- acting upon messages without delay
- telling them in advance when you are likely to be absent
- providing your potential callers with your direct line number so that they don't have to go through the operator.

5.4 Making a call

Before

1 Answer the six questions of effective communication (see pp. 6-7).
2 Make notes of what you want to achieve, the main points/queries you must include and any dates, facts and so on, you may need to refer to.
3 Have ready any files, correspondence and so on which you may need in the course of the conversation; don't keep your receiver waiting while you ferret around for the relevant papers or turn your computer on and find the right screen.
4 Have ready a plain piece of paper for your own notes.
5 Know the name of the person to whom you need to speak; sometimes this may be impossible but, at least, keep a personal telephone directory of names and numbers you ring regularly.
6 Remember there are certain times when calls are cheaper – can your call wait?
7 Dial the number carefully (or tell the operator clearly); wrong numbers are the most common cause of frustration and time-wasting, but are usually the fault of the caller.

During

1 Give a greeting ('Good morning', etc.); state your name (and organisation) and the name of the person to whom you want to speak.
2 Wait patiently to be put through; you may be put through to a secretary or the department telephone, in which case you will have to go through Step 1 again.
3 If you are cut off, replace the telephone receiver, wait a few seconds and ring again.
4 Keep it short: most calls can achieve their purpose in 20 seconds – 20 seconds … time to run 200 yards! Time for a jet to fly 4 miles!
5 State your subject/query clearly – enough to put the recipient in the picture.
6 Refer periodically to your notes.
7 Pause occasionally to get feedback that your message is understood.
8 Spell names and addresses; repeat any numbers.
9 Take notes, especially the name and number of the person to whom you are speaking.
10 Summarise main points of a long conversation at the end and always conclude by confirming any action required or date to be met.
11 If you have to leave a message for someone else, help the person who answered the phone to take the right message; don't just ramble on making them get the gist of it; tell them which are the main points to write down.
12 Be polite: thank the receiver for their help, even if you haven't got the information you wanted – fostering goodwill is not just part of being courteous, but will help future relations.
13 Telephone etiquette officially requires that if you are the caller you decide when the call ends but, since not everyone knows this, use your judgement.

After

Immediately, before you forget:

1 Fill in your notes so that they will be comprehensible at a later date.
2 Date the note and file it.
3 Put any relevant dates for future action or follow-up in your diary.
4 Pass on the results of your call to anyone concerned with the matter.

Check-Point: Controlling the Flow of Conversation

- Be sure you understand exactly what you want the call to achieve.
- Take the initiative; this gives you the right to take the lead and choose when to end the call.
- Begin every call with a verbal 'handshake' by saying who you are and why you are calling.
- Mirror the conversational style and vocabulary of the other person to generate rapport.
- Keep your line of argument simple: state your case and persist until the message gets through.
- Keep the conversation flowing by asking plenty of questions, but also be generous with information of your own.
- Search for areas of agreement rather than points of difference.
- Use silence for emphasis and to prompt the other person to respond.
- Offer alternatives when seeking agreement.

5.5 Gathering information by telephone

In gathering information for the preparation of a report, or merely as part of your day-to-day job, you may need to contact original or primary sources of information, or someone else who has access to secondary information you need. Telephone calls are widely used by business and industrial firms who may need certain information very quickly, and, made correctly, these calls can be very effective.

Before

1 Work out exactly what information you need.
2 Frame a series of increasingly specific questions which will give you what you want to know, for example,
   'Do you have the unemployment figures for the Bristol area over the last six months?'
   'Does this include a breakdown by age groups and sex?'
   'Can you tell me the unemployment figures for girls aged 16–25 for each month since June?'
   … and so on, to the level of detail that you need.
3 Decide which firm, individual, office, government agency, organisation or business might possibly have at hand the information you need.

During

1 When you get through, be polite but specific.
 Don't say: 'I wonder if you happen to have anyone there who knows something about unemployment...' and so on. Instead say: 'I need some information concerning the unemployment figures for the Bristol area over the last six months. Can you help me?' (Remember politeness and courtesy can be conveyed in your tone of voice.)
 Then, depending on the response, go on to ask a more specific question.
 If they can't help say:
 'Could you please give me the name of someone who can?'
2 Don't be discouraged if the first place you try can't help you; try another place – you will eventually get what you want if you keep trying (providing that it is not your telephone technique which is putting them off!).
3 Make sure you are talking to the right person; ask to speak to the 'personnel manager' or 'the person in charge of buying' or whatever is appropriate.
4 Write down the information immediately – don't rely on your memory; read it back to the person you are questioning.
5 Remember to say 'thank you'.

5.6   Answering the telephone

In some organisations the job of answering the telephone is given to the most junior employee. This is unwise as far as the organisation or department is concerned, and unfair on the junior, who through lack of confidence and lack of experience in the organisation usually creates a poor impression.

However, more senior employees may be just as guilty: through laziness, apathy or thoughtlessness they can create an equally poor impression.

Check-Point

Anyone who answers a telephone anywhere must be courteous, helpful and efficient.

Before

1 Know how the telephone system in your organisation works, especially how to transfer a call. (Being cut off is probably one of the most frustrating experiences – (it wastes time and creates a bad impression.)
2 Never answer a telephone without a pencil and paper.
3 Keep near your own telephone:
 • a pencil and message pad
 • an internal telephone directory
 • an appointment diary (if appropriate).
4 Stop talking to anyone else and reduce any other noise *before* picking up the telephone receiver.

During

1 Think about the needs of the receiver and give them (as fast as possible) everything they need to know, for example,
   - announce your name and department or section (in a cheerful voice!)
   - if the call has come through the operator, the receiver will already have been given the name of your organisation
   - if the call is directly from outside, announce the name of your organisation first, and then your name and department (if relevant).

   A common fault is to start speaking a second or two before picking up the receiver or, more commonly on the switchboard, before pressing the button on the console. I have heard *half* the name of more organisations than I care to remember, for example,

   '... oyce plc. Good morning.' '... dons Ltd. Good morning.'

   Many organisations have a standard practice for greeting a caller – know your house rules, for example,

   'Simmonds, Personnel Director, speaking', 'Mrs Boff's secretary speaking', 'Good morning. The Dispatch Department, Matthew speaking.'

   Don't rush this greeting. Because you have to say it so often it is tempting to rattle it off, with the result that at best it sounds completely insincere and monotonous or at worst it is incomprehensible to an outsider and therefore pointless. Many people are amused or even irritated by the common greeting: 'Whitaker plc. Tracy speaking. How may I help you?' Make it sound as sincere and spontaneous as possible.

2 Be prepared to answer the query, or take a message for someone who can, or transfer the call.

3 If you are acting as secretary you may be expected to filter calls for your boss; know whether:
   - they may wish to be 'unavailable'
   - they want some people put straight through to them – if so, know who they are
   - they want you to deal with certain routine calls yourself – if so, know which types of call you should deal with.

   You will therefore have to ask for the name of the caller and politely ask the purpose of the call. But use tact. Don't be over-protective or you might cause resentment in the caller and your boss.

4 Listen carefully to what the caller has to say and take notes; they will form the basis either of your action or of a message if you have to pass one on. Check that you have the right facts in the message – don't assume the eventual recipient of the message will know what it's all about.

5 Don't hesitate to ask the speaker to slow down or to spell names and addresses if they are unclear, and always read them back.

6 Compensate for the lack of visual communication: the nods of normal conversation must be conscientiously replaced by verbal equivalents, for example,

   'Yes, I see ...', 'Fine, I'll let him know ...',
   'I'm not sure I agree with that ...', 'Really?'

But avoid using over-familiar or slang expressions like 'You're not serious!', 'Yeah', 'Good God!' – and if the message is for someone else, avoid speaking *for* them, committing them or imagining negative attitudes on their behalf, unless you are authorised to do so; for instance: 'Oh he'll be over the moon about *that!*' (said either sincerely or in a sarcastic tone of voice).

7 Don't be distracted by anything going on around you, or someone else trying to attract your attention and *never* try to hold two conversations at once.

8 Be just as keen as your caller should be to save time and money.

9 Avoid asking the caller to 'hold the line' while you go on a paper chase; offer to call back.

10 If you are cut off, put the telephone down and wait for the caller to call you back.

11 Before the call ends, repeat back the main points of the conversation and always read back any names, addresses, numbers, dates and times, to give the caller a chance to correct any errors or omissions.

12 Agree what happens next, especially if you are taking a message for someone else, for example,
   'I'll tell her that you'll ring again on Thursday morning', or 'I'll ask him to ring you back as soon as possible.'

13 Telephone etiquette requires that since the caller is paying, they should be the one to decide when the call ends; however, since not everyone seems aware of this, be prepared to use your judgement.

Dealing with difficult calls

THINGS TO REMEMBER

Always volunteer to help rather than wait to be asked.

Always personalise the conversation by introducing yourself and getting the caller's name.

Always let the caller let off steam without interruption until their anger is spent.

Always show you are taking a serious interest by playing back the details of the complaint in your own words.

Always encourage callers to voice all their complaints before starting to deal with any of them.

Always offer sympathy to the caller ('I can understand how annoying that must have been') but without overdoing it.

Always finish by summarising what you've offered to do – and agree it with the caller.

THINGS TO AVOID

Don't attempt to reason with someone while they're still angry.

Don't suggest or agree to a solution (or take the blame) until all the facts have emerged.

Don't offer excuses or look for sympathy; don't dump the blame on some third party ('the supplier let us down') or on unusual circumstances ('everyone had the flu') – those are your problems, not the customer's.

Don't take the complaint personally; be as objective as you can and avoid getting angry yourself.

Don't assume the complainer is unique (suggest that they are the only person to have had a problem) – research shows that for every person who rings to complain, there are six who don't.

Don't agree to do something you are not in a position to deliver; if

Always call the customer if there's a further problem; don't risk angering the customer twice.

necessary, offer to call the customer back after you have taken advice.

After

1 Fill in your notes so that they will be comprehensible to you later and particularly to the recipient if you have taken a message.
2 Act on the notes immediately, telling anyone else who is concerned; write any letters or e-mails now, if possible, while the matter is clear in your mind.
3 If you have a message for someone else, put the date and time of the call on the message and deliver it immediately or place it in a prominent position on the person's desk if they are out; remind them when they return.
4 Update any documents necessary; write dates in your diary.

Check-Point: Being a Good Telephone Listener

- Don't listen on 'auto pilot' or while doing something else; make a conscious effort to pour all your energy into listening.
- Eliminate as many external distractions as possible; ignore what's going on around you.
- Erase internal distractions as well; stray thoughts about other matters should be curbed as soon as they occur.
- Take notes to keep your 'eye on the ball'; jot down your own reactions as well as points of hard information.
- Demonstrate to the speaker that you're paying attention by making regular 'continuity' noises; don't let them have to say: 'Are you still there?'
- Keep a hold on your emotions; getting emotional interferes with your ability to listen clearly.
- Read Chapter 3 on listening.

5.7 Voicemail

Many organisations now have voice messaging (Voicemail) systems. These allow each member of staff who is on the system to access a personal 'mailbox' in which others may leave messages, and to leave messages in colleagues' mailboxes. Some systems automatically re-route unanswered calls to a voice mailbox.

Check-Point: Advantages of Voicemail

- **cost reduction** – message-taking by secretaries or colleagues is avoided
- **personalisation** – the caller feels confident that they have left a message because they have recorded it personally after having heard the recorded voice response of the person they are trying to contact

- **circulars** – most systems allow a message to be sent to many people at once
- **accessibility** – you can access the system from any telephone, anywhere
- **ease of use** – leaving an oral message is, for many people, easier than typing an e-mail
- **avoidance of 'telephone tag'** – each calling one another back only to find that the other person is not there.

Check-Point: Disadvantages of Voicemail

- Most, preferably all, of the staff of an organisation need to be on the system.
- The system only works if everyone accesses their mailbox frequently.
- Abuse of the system, for example, by leaving long messages (there is usually a maximum of 3 minutes or so, but listening to a series of 3-minute messages twice daily can be wearing).
- Some people keep their voicemail on all the time, so that it seems almost impossible to talk to the actual person.

Check-Point: Tips for Effective Voicemail Use

- Only use voicemail for short messages.
- Never use two or more 3-minute 'slots'; if the message is that long, write a memo (preferably using e-mail): reading a memo takes a fraction of the time of listening to a message.
- Always access the system three times daily.
- Leave a special message if you are away for a period and unable to access the system.

5.8   Mobile phone manners

No chapter on telephoning nowadays would be complete without some reference to the mobile phone but, since in parts of the developed world almost everyone has a mobile phone and copes with the ever-increasing range of facilities and services with very little difficulty, I shall limit my remarks to suggesting ways in which we can all make the best use of the mobile without inconveniencing others (or indeed endangering life and limb!).

- Never use a mobile while driving a car – there is considerable evidence that even with a hands-free system the distraction, both physical and mental, caused by operating the phone causes accidents.
- Always switch your mobile off when in a cinema, theatre or social gathering.
- Always switch your mobile off when in a hospital, surgery or in a plane. People do not seem to realise that the mobile interferes with essential equipment and electronic systems, and again there is increasing evidence that several plane crashes have been caused by interference to flight control systems.

- Consider those around you. As Lady Celestria Noel, author of *Debrett's Guide to The Season*, commented, 'At its most basic level, all rudeness is selfishness. With mobile phones this most commonly takes the form of thinking that you are moving around in an impenetrable bubble.'
- If you must keep the mobile on in a public place or on a bus or train, turn the ring tone down or preferably switch it to vibrate rather than ring.
- Similarly, don't text with your keypad tone set on loud, or pass time by going through your entire ring tone collection.
- Don't shout. Why is it that people seem to assume that their words are not being transmitted with the aid of a microphone? And even at normal volume, be aware that people can overhear you. Use discretion when discussing personal or sensitive business facts or conversations on public transport or in a public place. Otherwise, at best you could appear very foolish and at worst you may be betraying secret company information.
- Don't pay too much attention to your mobile, especially on a date or in the company of others. Accepting calls or spending the entire time with your eyes firmly fixed on your mobile as you read or send yet another text message is extremely rude.
- And finally, take care when using your mobile in the street to remember to look where you are going! And if you are using a hands-free system in the street be aware that passers-by when catching sight of you apparently talking to yourself may draw their own conclusions!

Assignment

1 Find out now how your organisation's telephone system works, including these points:
   - Does a call come straight through to you, or through an operator?
   - Does your organisation expect you to answer a telephone call in a particular way? If so, how?
   - How do you transfer an internal call? An external call?
   - How do you get an outside line? Ask the operator? Or dial a particular number?
   - How can you divert your calls to another phone?
2 Find out when telephone calls are charged at the cheap rate, and what the different rates are.

Assignment: Decide on a particular piece of information you need; work out which firms or organisations might be able to help you and make the necessary telephone calls to get the information.

If you are not successful, analyse your telephone method and work out why. Try again – for some new information.

Assignment: Discuss with your colleagues which of the mobile phone habits mentioned above particularly annoy each of you, and re-write the list of do's and don'ts in order of importance.

Exercise 5.1

1 Telephone messages

What problems might arise for the recipient of the messages in Figure 5.1?

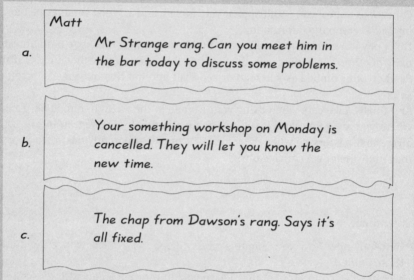

Matt

a. Mr Strange rang. Can you meet him in the bar today to discuss some problems.

b. Your something workshop on Monday is cancelled. They will let you know the new time.

c. The chap from Dawson's rang. Says it's all fixed.

Figure 5.1 **Telephone messages**

2 Most organisations have their own telephone message pads or obtain them from stationery suppliers. Design a telephone message pad for your organisation (or your home).
3 Reduce the length of this telephone conversation making it more efficient on both sides. Invent any extra details which seem necessary.

The number is ringing.
'Paul Jeffries. Can I help you?'
'Er … Are you Mr Sloan's assistant? Is he about?'
'Well, he's in the building, but I'm afraid he's not available at the moment. Can I get him to ring you back? Could you give me your name and number?'
'Yes – tell him it's Trent of Partridge's. My number is Manchester 675071 but I won't be in after 4 o'clock this afternoon.'
'Can I tell him what it is about?'

'Well – I've arranged to meet him in London tonight and I said I'd let him know when I'd be arriving at the airport. He thought he might be able to meet me at the airport.'

'Well, I'll get him to ring you back before 4.00.'

'When do you expect him back?'

'Well, he said he'd be back by 3.00 p.m. but you know what these meetings are like. They usually natter on even when the business is done.'

'Oh – but supposing he hasn't rung me before I leave for the airport? I shan't know whether he's meeting me or not.'

(Silence)

'Are you still there?'

'Yes. I was just thinking … Well, I can't see what else I can do. He never likes to be disturbed in these meetings.'

'So you'll try to get him to ring me then?'

'Yes, I'll do what I can. Thank you. Goodbye, Mr Trent.'

'I've just thought of …' (sound of receiver being put down).

Summary – good telephoning

Remember! When you speak on the telephone the efficient reputation of both you and your organisation is in your hands.

Further reading

Maitland, Iain, *Make That Call!*, Kogan Page, 2000

▼ 6 Interviewing

Room 101

For many people, 'interviewing' means job-hunting. Indeed for many of us the job or selection interview is probably the most important interview we ever take part in. However, employment is only one of many reasons for participating in an interview. Every business day millions of interviews occur for purposes of giving and receiving instructions, selling ideas or products, appraising performance, handling complaints and grievances or solving problems. Add to that list the number of interviews that occur between doctors and their patients, lawyers and their clients, teachers and their students, police and the public, journalists and the public and so on, and it is easy to see that interviewing and being interviewed are something we are all involved in everyday – talking and listening to people, at home, at work and at leisure.

This chapter will therefore be concerned not just with the more formal kinds of interview, but with general principles which apply to all interviews, even fairly informal interviews which are all too easy to take for granted.

6.1 Interviewing weaknesses

Perhaps it is because we are all involved in this activity so often that we tend to take all but the most formal occasions for granted. We become complacent and, as with so many other communication activities, interviews can often be ineffective and a waste of time.

Assignment: Think back over the interviews that you have taken part in during the past week. Perhaps your boss called you into his office to discuss something, or asked to see you at a specific time; perhaps you made an appointment to see him; perhaps you visited the doctor; or had occasion to speak to a tutor at college on a one-to-one basis. In some of the interviews you may have been the 'interviewer' – the one who asked for the interview – in others you may have been the 'interviewee' in that the other person may have been in control. In either case, think about these interviews critically and jot down a list of things which you feel were wrong with them, things which prevented the interview being as effective as it might have been.

Check-Points: Ineffective Interviews

You list will probably include some of the following:

- took longer than necessary
- rambled off the point into a discussion of irrelevancies
- one or other party talked too much, not letting the other get a word in edgeways
- left you feeling dissatisfied in that the interview didn't achieve what you had expected or hoped
- left you wondering what the purpose of the interview really was
- developed into an argument or even a slanging match
- did more harm than good.

Assignment: Now focus on one of those interviews and ask the following questions. **Write down** the answer to the first question, if you know the answer:

1 Why did the interview take place?
2 Was the purpose of the interview clear? To both of us?
3 Was it with the right person?
4 Was it held at the right time and in the right place?
5 What did I expect or hope to achieve by it?
6 Did I achieve what I had hoped or expected?
7 Did I listen sufficiently? Did I talk more than I should have done?
8 Did I consider the other person's point of view fairly?
9 Did they consider mine fairly?
10 How long did the interview take? How long should it have taken?
11 Was the time well spent?

Now write down ways in which you could improve the process if you could go through the same interview again.

In general terms, interviewing consists of talking and listening and forming conclusions. Talking and listening to other people are the basis of good communications at work and in our personal relationships; but it is not just a question of encouraging people to talk to one another more, but a question of improving the quality of the talking and listening that takes place.

6.2 What is an interview?

For the purpose of this chapter we shall define an interview as being

Definition

Any planned and controlled conversation between two (or more) people which has a purpose for at least one of the participants, and during which both speak and listen from time to time.

Chance meetings in corridors, lifts or canteens often result in conversations, but we shall not consider these interviews as such, since the definition we are using contains the crucial idea of *purpose*, as well as the aspect of planning and controlling the conversation.   In remembering the reasons why some interviews you have taken part in were unsatisfactory, you may well have deduced that many interviews tended to become merely meandering chats precisely because no one seemed to be too clear exactly what the interview was intended to achieve.

Check-Points: The Effective Interview

To be effective, an interview must have:

- purpose
- planning
- controlled interaction.

Whether you are likely to be mainly the interviewer or the interviewee will depend, of course, on your circumstances, but you can learn a great deal about the art of 'being interviewed' by learning how to 'interview'. From understanding the objectives of an interviewer and being aware of the methods used to achieve those objectives, you can gain insight into how best to perform as the interviewee, and to cope with or help the less-than-good interviewer, of whom there are many.

6.3 The purposes of the interview

The purpose of an interview may be very specific – selecting someone for a job; hearing about someone's complaint; reprimanding or disciplining someone for a misdemeanour; or determining how someone is progressing – and there are many more. But all interviews will be concerned with:

- obtaining information
- passing on information
- clarifying information.

In other words, *exchanging information.*

It is the *reason* why this information is exchanged which forms the purpose of a particular interview, and researchers normally conceive of four basic purposes of interviews.

> **Check-Points: The Purposes of Interviews**
>
> 1 dissemination of information (teacher – student interviews, news journalism interviews)
> 2 seeking belief or behaviour change (sales, discipline, counselling, performance appraisal)
> 3 problem-solving and decision-making (employment interviews, performance appraisal, medical interviews, counselling, grievance procedures, parent-teacher discussions)
> 4 research and discovery of new information (academic and social casework, market research, polls and opinion surveys, police interrogation, academic and writer research).

Most interviews, whatever their overall purpose, will be concerned with eliciting or exchanging information of various kinds.

6.4 Types of interview information

Six are common.

- *Statements of description* – The interviewee is required to provide information concerning something he has observed or experienced and may be questioned much as a witness is by a lawyer.
- *Statements of factual knowledge* – The interviewee is required to pass on an explanation of information he possesses (e.g. an interview with an expert or specialist).
- *Statements of behaviour* – The interviewee defines the previous, present and future behaviour of the interviewee.
- *Statements of attitude and belief* – Information of a more subjective nature revealing attitudes, personality, ambition and motivation; these statements represent the interviewee's evaluations (good/bad) and opinions of the truth and falseness about things, for example, 'I think that may be true but ...' 'I believe all staff should ...'
- *Statements of feelings* – These messages reveal physical and/or emotional levels which reflect the state of the individual, for example, 'I am fed up with always being ordered about by someone for whom I've no respect'; 'I'm thoroughly enjoying this new responsibility' and so on.
- *Statements of value* – These statements convey long-standing belief systems that are highly treasured by the respondent, for example, 'The essential quality in anyone is commitment – a willingness to see things through and stick at the job despite difficulties. Without that, all the qualifications in the world are useless.'

Many of these types of statement, particularly the last three, are concerned with subjective data rather than objective factual or biographical data. The interview has survived as an information-getting tool, despite the expense in terms of time and money, and despite criticism of its reliability, primarily because it is the only known means of getting certain subjective types of information, and because much of this information can be conveyed by non-verbal messages. Even the questionnaire designed to elicit attitudes, opinions and beliefs is more and more being administered by an interviewer who talks to the interviewee, using the questionnaire as a framework for the interview. The check-list which follows includes some of the more common business interviews.

Check-Points: Types of Business Interview

- employment
- performance appraisal
- counselling
- discipline
- termination
- induction
- consulting
- sales
- data gathering
- order-giving

Exercise 6.1

1 How does an interview differ from a spontaneous conversation?
2 What is the basic purpose of each of the following interviews?
   (a) selection/employment interview
   (b) market research interview
   (c) interview with the witness of an accident
   (d) performance appraisal interview
   (e) sales interview.
3 Which types of interview information would you expect to predominate in each of the interviews in Question 2?

6.5 How to plan an interview

Contrary to popular opinion, successful interviews do not 'just happen'. Successful interviews are the result of careful planning and preparation on the part of one or both of the participants. Good interviewers and interviewees are made, not born. They practise the skill until they appear to be able to do it without thinking, but their apparently easy, relaxed behaviour often belies the conscious analysis which has taken place beforehand and the careful monitoring of what is happening during the interview.

Obviously, while certain interviews allow for considerable preparation by the interviewer and by the interviewee, this is not always the case. A member of staff may suddenly surprise their supervisor by using their regular progress interview or performance appraisal session to air a string of grievances, and staff seldom have much advance warning to prepare carefully for discipline or reprimand interviews.

The conversational nature of interviewing precludes the kind of detailed planning which is possible for a public speech. However, at least one of the participants should carefully consider the usual *why? who? what?* and so on, questions before the interview. If you can discipline yourself to practise this routine regularly it will not only make the process of interviewing less stressful, but will also mean that when you are surprised by a sudden chance to interview someone or a sudden summons to see someone, you will be able to do some very quick but effective thinking as you walk along the corridor and during the initial stages of the interview.

Why?

- What broad type of interview is it?
- What exactly do you hope to accomplish?
- Are you seeking information or giving information?
- If so, what type of information?
- Is the interview seeking change in beliefs or behaviour?
- What is the nature of the problem to be solved?
- If you fail to persuade, have you a fall-back position with which you would be satisfied?

You should never enter an interview which you have initiated without thinking through what you hope to accomplish.

Who?

Analyse the other person. Find out as much as possible about the other person before the interview.

- What are their likely reactions/objections?
- Do they have the power to make the decisions you require?

Where and When?

Analyse the context.

- Where will the interview take place? In your office, their office? In a car during a journey?
- Is it likely to be interrupted?
- What time of day will it take place?
- What is likely to have happened just before the interview?
- What stage are you at in the matter?
- Will they need to be introduced to the whole matter, or merely reminded or brought up to date on the main events so far?

What?

Determine the topics you will need to cover and the types of question you will need to ask, or will be asked.

How?

Decide on the structure of the interview.

- How will you accomplish your objective?
- How should you behave?
- Would it be better to begin in a friendly manner or come smartly to the point?
- Are you going to have to tread carefully? Listen more than talk?
- Would it be better to begin with general questions, followed by more specific ones?
- Or should you get the detailed information first and then progress to the wider, philosophical issues?
- How are you going to arrange the furniture?
- How can you prevent interruptions?

Assignment: Now think of an interview you have taken part in recently. Imagine you could have your time over again, or that you are the interviewer this time, and think carefully about how you would answer all the planning questions above.

6.6　Structuring the interview

The opening

Regardless of the purpose of the interview, it is essential that the opening of the interview is handled carefully, for on the relationship established during the first few minutes will depend much of the success of the rest of the interview.

Without taking up too much time, you will therefore need to 'establish rapport' and introduce the main content of the interview. Obviously the opening will depend on the nature of the interview and it would be impossible to cover all the possibilities but here are some which are fairly popular. However it is essential that whichever one is chosen it is handled sincerely, or the interviewee will realise it is merely a gimmick.

- *Summarise the problem facing the interviewee and/or the interviewer* – This method is useful, when the interviewee knows vaguely that the problem exists but is not aware of the details.
- *Explain how you (the interviewer) discovered the problem* – Suggest he might want to discuss it with you. This helps to establish the idea that the problem is mutual, and encourages a cooperative, objective discussion.
- *Ask for advice or help regarding the particular problem* – This must be a sincere request, or it will be recognised as a mere gimmick and set you at a disadvantage.
- *Suggest a possible advantage to the interviewee of solving the problem by accepting your proposal* – Again, this must be seen as sincere and honest by the interviewee.
- *Open with a startling or striking fact* – Effective in a real emergency and when the interviewee tends to be rather apathetic.

- *Refer to the interviewee's known view* on the particular problem – Effective when the interviewee has taken up a position which is well known, has asked you to put forward proposals, or is likely to be strongly opposed to your ideas.
- *Refer to the background, cause, origin of the problem* without actually stating the problem itself – Effective when you suspect the interviewee may be hostile to your ideas but is familiar with the background.
- *State the name of the person who sent you to the interviewee* – Very useful when you need a 'way in' because you don't know the interviewee. But the 'introduction' must be genuine and the person must be respected by the interviewee.
- *State the organisation or company or the group you represent* – This can help your prestige, but again only if the organisation is respected by the interviewee. It may also provide an explanation for your visit.
- *Ask for ten minutes/half an hour of the person's time* – Be specific and don't sound too apologetic. Asking for a brief period of time is effective with the busy, impatient or intolerant interviewee.
- *Ask a question* – The question may be leading, anticipating agreement, or direct (see Section 6.7, 'How to question and probe'). It obliges the interviewee to answer and they automatically become involved.

Assignment

1 You have been invited to the wedding of an old schoolfriend, but you have used up all your annual leave and so need to persuade your boss to allow you to take the Friday off in order to travel. You have made an appointment to see them but have not told them what your purpose is. Which type of opening would you use? Write some notes on what you would actually say in raising the subject?

2 You have a temporary job selling 'executive desk-tidies' (containers for pens, pencils and paperclips). Always supposing you manage to get past the secretary and in to see the executive, how would you start the interview?

3 You are having problems getting on with a colleague. He seems to be avoiding you and no one seems to know why. You have mentioned the problem to your boss, who has suggested you first try to speak to the colleague yourself, during a quiet moment. How would you start the interview?

4 You are attending a course at a local college, but you and the other course members are very concerned about a particular member of staff's teaching. You have been advised to speak to the member of staff personally in the hope that an improvement will remove the need to take the matter further. **You** have been elected spokesperson by the rest of the course! How will you broach the subject?

The body of the interview

Whichever type of opening you adopt, you should make sure that it does not take up too much time: remember one of the typical problems is the interview that never gets to the point.

The major part of the interview should be reserved for asking and answering questions, seeking solutions to problems, or trying to persuade the interviewee to accept your idea or your product. A rough guide is to allow about 95 per cent of a 30-minute interview for this phase.

The extent to which you will want to structure the interview will depend on the purpose of the interview, the type of interview and any time restrictions. In a non-structured interview, the interviewer allows the interviewee to steer the interview (e.g. if the interviewee has a complaint or grievance or a personal problem). In a structured interview, the interviewer dominates and controls the interview (e.g. an information-getting interview with severe time limits). Interview structure is frequently described as 'non-structured', 'moderately structured', 'highly structured' or 'highly structured–standardised'.

- *Non-structured interviews* – These have no pre-arranged schedule or framing of questions. You simply think about the purpose and make a mental note of a few possible areas or topics which need to be covered. While this is a very effective strategy for certain interviews, particularly those of a counselling nature, you should beware of justifying poorly prepared badly conducted interviews on this basis.
- *Moderately structured interviews* – These involve planning and framing the major questions you want answered and perhaps some possible follow-up questions to probe deeper if necessary. These follow-up questions are only used if the interviewee doesn't volunteer the information required.
- *Highly structured interviews* – All questions are arranged and scheduled in advance. These questions are put to each interviewee in exactly the same way. Some questions may be open-ended but this type of interview tends to rely mainly on close-ended questions; useful when you want to compare interviewees' responses systematically as in market research or opinion surveys but also useful in some fact-finding/investigatory interviews.
- *Highly structured/standardised interviews* – All questions are again arranged and scheduled in advance but in addition the potential answers are preplanned in such a way that the interviewee has a restricted choice of answers from which to choose one, for example,

> If the price of this product were reduced, would you buy more, less or about the same as you do now?

In other words, all the questions are close-ended.

Exercise 6.2: Look at the Check-points list of types of business interview on p. 70. Which structure would you choose for each type of interview?

6.7 How to question and probe

The main body of the interview normally consists of questions and responses but in most interviews the aim of the interviewer is to conduct a conversation rather than an interrogation session. The way in which they frame their questions and the extent to which they talk and listen will directly influence the atmosphere of the interview, the feelings of the interviewee and thus the outcome of the interview. You, therefore, need to be familiar with the basic types of question and their uses.

The direct question or close-ended question

This kind of question permits the interviewee very little, or no freedom in selecting their response. There is usually one specific answer.

Examples

'What "A" level subjects did you do?' 'How long have you worked for us now?' 'Where were you when the accident took place?'

Self-Check

- What would the direct or close-ended question be useful for?
- What are the possible disadvantages of direct questions?

Uses

When specific replies are sought on a definite topic, direct questioning is most often used. It is particularly useful in seeking objective factual or biographical data, or where straightforward answers are required for comparison with other interviewees, that is, qualifications for a job, details about an event or accident, statistical or objective facts.

Disadvantages

In limiting the response, it does not encourage the interviewee to talk. An interview based exclusively on this type of question is a very cold, lifeless affair which makes the interviewee feel they are being interrogated (which they are) rather than consulted or invited to expand or discuss.

Bipolar questions or yes/no questions

If the interviewer wants to limit the potential responses beyond the limitations already imposed by direct questions, they can ask a bipolar question, which limits the answer to one of two possible answers, or simply 'yes' or 'no'.

Examples

'Were you actually there when the accident happened?' (yes/no) 'Did you come by train or car?' 'Are you happy in your job?' (yes/no) 'Would you be able to start work by the first of March?' (yes/no).

Uses

In a sense, bipolar questions are a form of direct question and therefore have the same uses. Used with a carefully considered purpose, they can be very effective in eliciting definite information quickly.

Disadvantages

Because they are so limited in the answers permitted by the nature of the question, when they are used incorrectly they force the interviewee to opt for one or other extreme answer, when the answer he really wants to give may be halfway between, for example, 'Are you happy in your job?' strictly speaking implies either a 'yes' or 'no' answer. A fairly talkative interviewee may answer truthfully and go beyond the limitations of the question, but a quiet person who lacks confidence will be inhibited by this question and feel unable to expand. The interviewer should be aware of these dangers.

The leading question or standard-revealing question

This is the kind of question which makes it so obvious what the answer should be, or what the interviewer expects, that the interviewer is in effect 'leading' the interviewee.

Examples

'Don't you think the weather's been awful lately?' 'Don't you think it would be a good idea if we ...?' 'There's no reason why someone earning your salary could not afford £10 per month, is there?'

These are examples of leads which are expressed in the negative. Usually they get a 'yes' response or, at any rate, are obviously intended to get a 'yes' response. However, the last example gets a 'no' response which is in effect an affirmative answer for the sales rep!

Uses

Leading questions which expect an affirmative answer in this way are, of course, the weapon of the sales rep. If they can prepare a series of questions in this way, they can lead the respondent, and they are well on the way to getting the respondent to accept their idea or product. This technique has been successfully adopted by countless sales reps. Used subtly it can be very effective when the purpose of the interview is persuasive.

Disadvantages or abuses

Used aggressively or thoughtlessly it can either make the interviewee feel under severe pressure and attack by revealing the standards by which the interviewer measures people:

'You didn't do very well at school, did you?'

or it allows the interviewee to give the 'right' answer even if they might have unwittingly answered differently if they hadn't been given a clue:

'The person we accept for this position will have to supervise a staff of twenty and be good at handling people and their problems. Do you think you would be capable of this?'

No one but an idiot would answer anything but 'yes' to this question! The interviewer has given away their own views or standards, thus helping the interviewee to give the 'right' answer.

Sometimes this type of question is simply a waste of time:

'Presumably you are keen to get this job?' 'I suppose you are ambitious?'

The loaded question

Sometimes the use of emotive words in the question indicates the response the interviewer wants:

'Do you think we should accept this crazy idea?' 'What do you think about this whole sorry business?'

Self-Check

Can you think of any possible uses for such emotively-loaded questions?

Uses

It is difficult to imagine a situation in which this type of question would be anything but useless in terms of eliciting people's *real* feelings and opinions.

However, such questions are sometimes used when the interviewer is trying to find out how able the interviewee is to resist being led, how strongly they hold their own opinions. Taken to an extreme it is also used to discover how an interviewee reacts under stress, and when the interviewer wants to see how far they have to go to get the interviewee to 'crack'.

'I don't agree with employing women. I mean they're a dead loss really, aren't they? They are always taking time off to look after the kids or leaving to have babies. You can't rely on them, can you?' (A question put to a woman applicant for a job and now obviously illegal under the Sex Discrimination Act.)

This may not be the true opinion of the interviewer. They may be asking it to see how the woman defends the role of women at work, whether she would be able to cope under genuine attacks like this, and *how* she answers the question – aggressively, or with dignity and calm, reasoned arguments.

The open-ended question

Unlike the previous questions, this type of question allows the interviewee maximum freedom in responding.

Examples

'Tell me about yourself.' 'How do you see the problem?' 'What are your feelings on this?' 'How do you think a course in business education or training can help you to do the job better?'

As you can see, these questions frequently begin with 'why', 'what', 'how' and 'where'.

Self-Check

What sort of information might be elicited by such open-ended questions?

Uses

When selected carefully, these questions can reveal a great deal about a person's attitudes, beliefs and motivation. They also reveal how well an interviewee can collect their thoughts, organise what they want to say, and express themselves without guidance or prompting.

Disadvantages

Although open questions may provide the interviewer with some measure of the person's ability to think, and may lead to worthwhile areas of discussion not perhaps anticipated by the interviewer, considerable thought should go into their selection and use, otherwise a lot of time may be wasted in gaining answers to only a few very general questions.

The prompting question

This question helps the interviewee who appears to have a mental 'block', or is not clear exactly what the interviewer is getting at.

Examples

'Tell me about yourself.' ... (pause) ... 'Well starting from your last couple of years at school, what have been the major milestones in your life, what do you see as the most important decisions you've had to make? That sort of thing.'

Uses

To help the interviewee who has 'gone blank'.

Disadvantages

It is easy to jump in too quickly with this type of 'prompt question'. The interviewer should avoid not allowing the interviewee time to think before answering, or prompting in such a way that much of the value of the original open question is lost.

The mirror question

This question 'plays back' to the interviewee the interviewer's understanding of the last response, or summarises several different statements made by the interviewee.

Examples

'So you're saying that, in general, you would support the idea?' 'If I've understood you correctly, you like the practical aspects of the work, but not the paperwork?'

Uses

This type of question is one of the most effective ways of ensuring that real communication is taking place. It provides the interviewee with immediate feedback as to how well they are communicating what they really mean, and it allows the interviewer to check their understanding. These two advantages improve the quality of listening in the interview and help to promote an atmosphere of empathy and trust.

Disadvantages

There is a real danger of 'putting words into the mouth' of the interviewee. They agree that that is what they meant even if it is not!

Example

'So you think you're being victimised?' 'Yes.' (Thinks: 'Well, I didn't really see it like that, but it sounds more dramatic, so now I come to think of it – yes!')

The probing question

Frequently, the initial response given to a question may be lacking in detail or may indicate the need for a follow-up question.

Examples

'Could you give me an example of what you mean by poor workmanship?' 'When you say you haven't been late very often, how many times would you say you've been late during the last month, say?' 'I'm not sure I really understand what you mean by that. Can you give me some examples?' 'Which of those causes is the most serious, do you think?'

Probing questions often begin with 'why'. In fact, the simple question 'Why?' is a useful question in itself, particularly if the interviewer doesn't want to run the risk of stopping the interviewee talking.

> **Self-Check**
>
> There are several specific uses for the probing question. How many can you think of?

Uses

To elicit more detail – example, illustrations, explanations; to encourage the interviewee to keep talking; to move the interview from the general to the specific; to steer the interviewee back on the predetermined route of the interview when it is getting off-course; to encourage the interviewee to stick to specific facts rather than generalisations.

Disadvantages

Used aggressively or too persistently this kind of questioning may make the interviewee feel they are in the witness box.

The hypothetical question

Examples

'Let's assume that you have discovered one of your subordinates is drinking heavily and that it is interfering with their work. What would you do?' 'Imagine I had to introduce a new piece of equipment or process which was going to affect the work routine of my employees. How would you advise me to go about it?'

> **Self-Check**
>
> Why might an interviewer use this type of question?

Uses

Effective for determining how an interviewee might handle some potential job-related situation, or for discovering how someone imagines his ideas might work out in practice. Also useful in discovering an interviewee's prejudices, stereotypes and other attitudes, beliefs and values.

Disadvantages

If the imaginary instance is too far-fetched it will reveal very little of any value about the interviewee and is more likely to say something about the personality of the interviewer!

Example of a bad hypothetical question

'Suppose a third world war broke out today. What would you do?'

Exercise 6.3: Examine the questions below and spot the errors involved. What types of question are they? Suggest a better alternative in each case.

1 'Did you have a good journey?'
2 'Do you realise that as the supervisor of this section I am here to carry the can for your weaknesses?'
3 'You say that you're persistent in the face of problems, but three jobs in four years doesn't indicate that you stick at anything for very long, does it?'
4 'Why did you take CSEs instead of "O" levels in 1986 or perhaps you didn't. (Looking down at the form.) Did you take CSEs in preparation for "O" levels the next year or because you were in the CSE stream? And did you improve your grade when you took them again – CSEs I mean, not "O" levels, or was the "O" level an improvement in each case?'

Sequencing the questions

When you have thought about the types of question you will use, it is equally important to give some thought to the sequencing of the questions in the interview.

- You may want to begin with broad, open-ended questions and then move on to increasingly specific questions. This is called '*funnel*' sequencing.
- Conversely, the '*inverted funnel*' sequence begins with close-ended specific questions and moves to more general, open-ended questions.
- The '*tunnel*' sequence, as its name suggests, is a series of similar questions. This type of sequence is particularly suitable when you want to get initial answers to each separate question without asking follow-up probes. For example, a series of questions aimed at discovering attitudes to a number of job-related experiences would be considered a tunnel sequence.

Closing the interview

When your time limit is up; when you have got the information you wanted; when you have managed to persuade the interviewee to accept your suggestions or buy your product; when the problem has been solved; or when it is obvious that continuing the interview will be unproductive, perhaps because more information is needed, or interviews with other people are necessary, you should close the interview.

Check-Points: Closing the Interview

There are three main things to be accomplished when closing the interview:

- briefly summarise the achievements of the interview, or the views expressed
- thank the interviewee for participating
- agree on the next meeting or the actions which will follow.

Summary – interviewing

If you follow the guidelines suggested in this chapter you should be able to cope with even the most difficult interview (and have learned a little about the reason for the methods which an interviewer may adopt when you are the interviewee). However, perhaps the most common type of interview is the fact-finding interview since fact-finding either forms the basis of most interviews or a part of a series of interviews with a more specific purpose. For this reason, you may find the following Checklist useful. Try it out when next you have to conduct any interview which involves determining the facts before anything else. You may also like to use the Interview Assessment Form at the end of this chapter to assess the skill of the interviewer when next you are interviewed!

Checklist: Fact-finding Interviews

1 *Purpose*
- To enable the individuals to air the problem
- To discover the causes of dissatisfaction
- To establish the facts of the problem situation

2 *Preparation*
- Consider individual to be interviewed; check previous record/history
- Endeavour to establish circumstances causing dissatisfaction (particularly attitudes, feelings)
- Be aware of company policy which may affect action which can be taken
- Ensure privacy and no interruptions
- Allow adequate time
- Arrange desk and chairs to create the right atmosphere

3 *Conduct*
- Put at ease – establish rapport
- State purpose of interview

- Don't try to solve the problem before you know what it is (there may not even be a problem)
- Allow individuals to state the problem from their point of view
- Get feelings as well as facts – feelings are usually more important though less likely to be expressed without encouragement
- Listen attentively
- Do not evade the issue or belittle it
- Probe in depth to ensure all relevant details are known
- Use 'open' questions
- Do not commit yourself too quickly or appear to take sides
- If possible get individual to suggest solutions
- Discuss implications of different solutions (if appropriate) ⎫

  ⎬ It is not always appropriate to arrive at a solution in a factfinding interview; other interviews may be necessary before a solution can be determined
- Agree a best solution (if appropriate) ⎭
- Agree course of action to be taken (if appropriate)
- Review ground covered
- Arrange next meeting

4 *Follow up*
- Investigate facts/information if necessary – interview others as appropriate
- Decide on action in light of investigation
- Check that results are as required – relationships, attitudes, performance
- Hold follow-up meeting.

Assignment: Try to persuade someone you know who does a lot of interviewing in the course of their job to allow you to sit in during an interview, as an observer. Look at the following assessment form before you go into the interview and then complete it after the interview is over.

Then, ask someone to observe you interviewing someone. Ask the observer to complete the assessment form and discuss it with you afterwards.

Interview Assessment Form

	Yes	No	Not sure
1 Was the interviewer prepared for the interview?			
(a) Had they done their homework?			
(b) Were they mentally ready?			
(c) Had they arranged to give their whole attention?			
(d) Had they arranged the room appropriately?			
2 Did they state the objectives of the interview at the outset?			
3 Did they use an appropriate opening technique?			
4 Did they make the interviewee feel at ease?			
5 Did they make their points clearly and concisely?			
6 Did they give the interviewee a chance to make his/her points?			
7 Did they listen to the interviewee?			
8 Did they frame questions appropriately?			
9 Did they give valid reasons for statements made?			
10 Did they make suggestions?			
11 Did they encourage the interviewee to make suggestions?			
12 Did they 'back down' under pressure?			
13 Did they structure the interview sensibly?			
14 Was the interview:			
(a) non-structured?			
(b) moderately structured?			
(c) highly structured?			
(d) highly structured–standardised?			
15 Did they allow sufficient time for the interview to run its natural course?			
16 Did they summarise what had happened for the interviewee?			
17 Did they end on a positive note of agreed action with the interviewee?			

Further reading

Keats, Daphne, *Interviewing: A Practical Guide for Students and Professionals*, Open University Press, 2000

Performance Appraisals, Bob Havard, Kogan Page, 2000

■ ⊻ 7 Being interviewed for a job

Under the inerviewing spotlight

Stuart Peat was a trainee civil servant in the fast stream for promotion to Principal grade. He was one of the oldest people still in the training grade, and felt he was ready for promotion; he had already been passed over two or three times, and had expressed his view that the promotion system was unsatisfactory. But when the next list for Promotion Board interviews came out, his name was missing. He was not even being considered.

Stuart decided to exercise his right to demand an interview. It took place on the day he always met his sister, Sue, for a lunchtime drink. Stuart walked into the pub looking ashen. 'I don't have to ask how it went', said Sue. 'No', answered Stuart, 'it was a disaster. They didn't ask a thing about why I thought I was ready for promotion or about my work, just why I thought the system was bad; as soon as I walked in, they kept on about it. What would I do if I were given a free hand to put it right? For a whole hour. I was at a loss for words – must have looked a complete idiot.'

Assignment: Where did Stuart go wrong?

This chapter is intended to help you in preparing for that all-important interview – the job interview. It should provide you with guidance in:

- thinking positively about the interview beforehand
- getting to know your strengths and weaknesses
- making the most of yourself at interview.

7.1 Preparing – the organisation

By now, you should be familiar with some of the main types of interview and the ways in which the interviewer can best use the time available to achieve their objective; whether it is to select the best person for the job; deal with a complaint or a problem of discipline; or make that appraisal interview more than just a superficial chat. But unless you have a job which happens to involve a lot of interviewing, you will probably be interviewed during your life many more times than you will ever be the interviewer. So let us look at the problems of being on the other side of that table.

Probably the most important interview you ever attend is the job selection interview – important because, whatever else you choose to do with your life, you will probably spend a considerable part of it working, so you might as well try to get a job you will enjoy. It is therefore just as important that you select the right job as it is that the interviewer selects the right person. For this reason, it seems sensible to use the job interview as a vehicle for exploring some of the techniques of the successful interviewee.

Dealing with nerves

Perhaps the major problem for most interviewees is 'nerves'. Almost everyone's heart sinks at the very idea of being interviewed, because the idea of being 'on trial' causes stress and not being sure what is going to happen causes apprehension. However, you should take comfort from four thoughts:

- Almost everyone is nervous before and probably during an interview as well, so you are in good company.
- 'Nerves' can in fact be beneficial – just as for the actor or the public speaker, a certain degree of nervous tension will make you more alert and better able to perform well; however, it is obviously necessary to learn ways of reducing anxiety to a level where it can be a help rather than a hindrance.
- The interviewer will probably expect you to be nervous, will make reasonable allowances, and will try to help you feel at ease; remember too, that they may be feeling just as nervous as you!
- 'Nerves' are usually made worse by being unsure of what is going to happen and of how you are going to cope, so the secret is to do some thinking beforehand – positive thinking not negative worrying – about the interview, and about you and your behaviour: in other words – be prepared!

Get some practice

Let us assume that all the hard work necessary to write many application letters has finally paid off, and you have been invited for interview. But suppose that, out of the jobs you have applied for this is the one you like the look of least. You should still go! You have nothing to lose and everything to gain: above all, the best way to become good at being interviewed is to go to lots of interviews.

Second, you cannot really judge whether the job is the right one for you until you have found out all you can about the organisation; and the best way is to visit the organisation, meet someone who actually works there (more than one, possibly) and get a feel for the place.

Any good interviewer recognises that although he needs to find out as much as possible about the interviewee, equally important is the need of the candidate to find out as much as possible about the company. It is therefore always a good idea to go for an interview if you are invited.

However, finding out about an organisation is not something which can be left entirely to the interview itself. In preparing for the 'big day', you need to do some research, so that you know as much as possible *before* you get there – about the job and the company.

Get some background information

Don't be like the interviewee desperately wanting a job with Rolls-Royce plc who, when asked by the interviewer about the company's products, replied: 'Well, you make cars, don't you?' Now you may be forgiven for not knowing that Rolls-Royce plc makes aero-engines, but the interviewee wanted a job with the company and should, at least, have taken the trouble to discover that since 1971 the car division has been a completely separate company from the one that makes aero-engines and in fact is now owned by BMW.

Above all then, you need to know, at the very least, what the organisation does. Is it in retailing, or manufacturing, or distribution, or does it provide a service? What does it make, sell or distribute? What service does it provide?

You will probably be applying for a particular job in a particular section or department, so you will also need to know roughly what the department or office does. Obviously, you will not be expected to know everything in great detail. However, there are some basic facts which you should be able to discover in advance.

Self-Check

Before we tackle the problem of how and where you might be able to find the information, try listing some of the things it would be useful to know about an organisation, in the form of questions:

Questions about the organisation

1 What does it do? (for example)
2
3
4
5

It will obviously depend on the particular organisation to which you are applying, but here are some check-points:

- Is it a big organisation or a small firm?
- Is it part of a group?
- Is it in the public or private sector?
- How many people does it employ?
- Where is it based?
- What is its annual turnover?
- Is it quoted on the stock exchange? If so, is the share price rising or falling?

- Is it an expanding or contracting industry?
- Does it have subsidiaries or branches? If so, which one(s)?
- Does it have a good employee relations reputation?
- Have any recent political or economic events been likely to affect it?
- Has it been in the news lately? If so, why?
- What is the name of the chief executive?
- Does it export goods? If so, where to?
- Does it take training and career development seriously?

Jotting down some questions like this is a good way of starting your research, but of course you could begin by thinking of sources of information which, on investigation, will give you not only the answers to questions like these, but also answers to questions that had not occurred to you.

Where to find out

You could already have discovered something about the organisation before you applied for the job. The advertisement itself may have held some clues:

- Was the address for applications different from the location of the job?
- To whom were you asked to apply? A personnel officer/manager/director? The manager of a particular department?
- Did it describe what the organisation does? And so on.

If you are a good detective and you know what to look for, you should already know a little about the organisation or at least have some questions which will start you off in your investigation.

When you first applied, the organisation may also have sent you some information for candidates, which you should read carefully and questioningly.

Bearing these facts in mind then, where can you get information about an organisation? Who can you ask? Who might know something of use?

Self-Check

List the possible sources of information about an organisation.

Sources of information

The Internet

Perhaps the most obvious source of information nowadays about almost anything is the Internet, and in the search for jobs it has become invaluable both in saving time and in making an infinite amount of information available to anyone who can get online. But, it is the very amount of information out there that makes it difficult to know where to start or how to find really useful information.

Keying in the name of the organisation is an obvious place to start for general information about organisations and companies, but a little book like *Choices: Jobs Through the Internet* (the online version is at www.choicesonline.com) not only provides an index of website addresses of hundreds of top employers but also contains useful tips on what is involved in the selection process (see also Chapter 15 – Applying for a Job in this book).

The organisation itself

You may well have been sent some information when you first applied, but if not, it is always worth writing to the public relations officer for anything they publish about their products or activities and, also, for a copy of the annual report, which should contain all sorts of useful facts (e.g. the name of the chief executive), as well as the usual financial information.

Local public or college library

The reference section of most libraries should provide many sources of information. For example, *Who Owns Whom?* will tell you what kind of company it is, who owns it, whether there are subsidiary companies and so on.

It is always worth spending time finding your way around the reference section of the library, but if you cannot find what you want, or do not know where to look, explain to the librarian what you want and why you need it. You should certainly be able to get all the hard facts about an organisation from reference books or from computer data bases that the library probably holds on CD-ROM.

Television and newspapers

When you are in the throes of applying for jobs, it is always advisable to read the newspapers regularly and listen to news broadcasts. These can be a valuable source of information on topical events and their effect on organisations, industries and groups of people like trade unions, for example.

In addition to the usual news report, you should also skim through the business section of newspapers and keep your eye open for articles in magazines like the *Economist* and TV programmes which report on various aspects of business and industry. Again, the local library should help with copies of current periodicals and magazines, but a college library will almost certainly have copies of all the daily papers, journals and magazines, both current and back copies on file.

Even if you are not a member of the library, there should be no difficulty in visiting the reference section, and your efforts will be well repaid if you can make informed comments about the organisation and its business during the interview.

Personal contacts

Mention the names of the organisation when you are talking to friends and relatives. It is surprising how often even a chance acquaintance may know something which will help you to build up a picture. They may have worked there, or know someone who does, and you may learn details which would be impossible to get easily from any other source. But be careful. Remember to keep a sense of perspective. For every one ex-employee who only remembers the darker side, there are many more currently employed who might paint a rosier picture.

Prepare some questions

As well as answering many of your questions and providing you with valuable background knowledge, research like this will probably also suggest further questions, which you should make use of, to ask at the interview when you get the chance.

The famous question 'How much will I be paid?' frequently causes interviewees embarrassment, but it is a very reasonable question and if the interviewer does not bring up the subject, they will not be at all surprised or offended if you ask. You may have some associated questions and can ask about salary together with other conditions and training opportunities, for instance.

Many people find that when they are asked if they have any questions, their mind goes a complete blank. For this reason, it is a good idea to jot the questions down on a card. Then if you cannot remember them, ask the interviewer if you might refer to it to remind you. Interviewers should regard this as an example of good organisation, and it all helps to show that you are sufficiently interested to have thought about the interview beforehand.

7.2 Preparing – know yourself

The next stage of interview preparation, and probably the most important, is to find out about yourself. This may sound obvious and perhaps you think you already know yourself pretty well, but how would you cope if the interviewer suddenly asked:

> *'What are your strengths and weaknesses?' or 'We have many applicants for this job. Tell me why we should take you?'*

Try it! Without any preparation for these questions, you may well suddenly be struck dumb. At best, and depending on your self-confidence, you may either overstate your strengths or exaggerate your weaknesses. Neither would be viewed very favourably by the interviewer. In a job interview you obviously want to make the most of your strengths and play down your weaknesses, but you can only do this effectively when you have given the matter some considerable thought.

Another reason for reviewing your good and bad points is to be able to consider, in advance, how to admit your weaknesses in as favourable a light as possible and balance them with compensating strengths. Of course, it is always possible that something you regard as a strength may be regarded differently by the interviewer, but of course it might happen the other way round too. In any event, since it is rather unnerving to discover for the first time, in an interview, that a particular characteristic or failure to achieve could be regarded by someone else as a black mark against you, it is far better to consider it beforehand and think about how you might cope.

Finally, then, it is really only possible to plan tactics for the interview itself when you are reasonably sure what your qualities and characteristics are and where your weak spots are. For example, let us take the interviewee who maintains they are 'no good at interviews'. They can do very little about improving until they have first determined why they are bad at interviews. One of their weaknesses may be that they suffer badly from stage fright in strange situations but are not prepared to admit it. Not until they have honestly admitted to themselves that they do get nervous can they start to plan ways of reducing their anxiety. They may then be prepared to try some of the techniques suggested in this chapter, like preparing properly for an interview, for example. But even these are no guarantee that stage fright can be completely conquered. Indeed, for many people extreme nervousness during stress is part of their lives. These people must analyse their nervousness and develop strategies for living with it. When they stop to think about it our fictitious interviewee may realise that they suffer more from stage fright at the beginning of interviews but gradually calm down. They would therefore be better off if they could try to keep the key points they want to make until later in the interview. On the other hand, they may realise that they can usually begin calmly but become progressively more nervous, and would be wiser to inject their better remarks at the beginning and then try to keep the interview as short as possible.

You can see now that by admitting a weakness and analysing it, you may be able to make the best of it.

Assignment: It is now time to take a long, hard, honest look at yourself. Don't be shy about your strengths and don't be blind to your weaknesses. Be honest!

- What do people like about you?
- What do they not like?
- What sort of things are you good at?
- What are you bad at?
- How would colleagues at work describe you?
- Are you different at home?

Make a list of as many strengths and weaknesses as you can think of. *Keep the list –* you may want to return to it later, perhaps to amend it, as you discover more about yourself.

Now comes the hardest part of all! Find a friend who seems likely to be cooperative but honest, to write a list of *your* strengths and weaknesses, as they see them. Then compare the two lists. Try not to be defensive about the weaknesses but get them to give examples and discuss the two lists objectively.

Someone who works with you at college or work who knows you fairly well would probably be the most suitable. It might be preferable not to choose someone you are too close to – they may see you through 'rose-tinted glasses' and not want to ruin a beautiful friendship.

If you can bring yourself to do this exercise conscientiously, it will probably be one of the most useful exercises you ever do. As Robert Burns said:

O wad some Pow'r the giftie gie us
To see oursels as others see us!

Awkward questions

The last assignment sprang not only from a sensible need to be prepared for an interview, but also from a particular question posed by many interviewers in one form or another:

'What are your strengths and weaknesses?'

In their efforts to discover as much as possible about you in the shortest possible time, they will have thought out carefully and developed preferences for particular questions which are designed not so much to elicit specific facts as to discover how you think, what motivates you, what kind of person you are.

Assignment: Here are some very awkward questions sometimes asked by interviewers which have felled many a candidate before you. How would you answer? Make a note of your answers, so that you can refer to them later.

Don't be put off by these questions. Unless you are applying for a fairly high-level job, most interviewers, however inexpert they are, will try to be kind and are unlikely to ask questions quite as blunt as these. However, if you are prepared to answer these, you should be prepared for almost anything and find the more conventional questions easier to answer.

- What has been your most valuable experience?
- Which do you prefer: money or status?
- Are you an aggressive person?
- When did you last lose your temper? Why?
- Describe yourself in three adjectives.
- What is the best idea you've had in the past year?
- What is the hardest thing you've done in the past 3 years?
- Have you got enough experience for the job?
- Tell me about yourself.
- What is your worst fault?
- What is your proudest achievement?
- What would you like to be doing in 5 years' time? In 10 years' time?

You should have answers ready for these questions and be prepared to recognise others with a similar purpose, bearing in mind that the interviewer is not so much interested in *what* you answer as *how* you answer.

Even if you are not asked specific questions, just having made yourself think about your answers to them will provide you with things to talk about and that is what the interviewer wants you to do.

Obviously there are no right or wrong answers to the questions – it will depend on you, the job, the organisation, the atmosphere of the interview and so on; but one woman, who was asked if she was aggressive, responded that she was assertive rather than aggressive. In other words, she went on, she always sought to be cooperative, but she was very keen to get on with her career. Thus she managed to characterise herself as neither contentious nor passive. Most questions which might seem 'awkward' to you need to be answered in this balanced way.

7.3 At the interview

Be yourself

Now we come to the interview itself.

- In order to give yourself a fair chance make sure that you find out exactly where the interview is to take place, and allow yourself plenty of time to get there early rather than late.
- The interviewer will probably start the interview with a few general questions about your journey and so on, designed to set you at your ease. Use the time to make yourself comfortable and take a few subtle deep breaths to calm you.

They will probably then turn to your application form or letter and ask you questions arising from what you have written.

Check-Point

Keep a copy of your letter and application form to refer to just before the interview.

There is nothing worse than finding that you cannot really remember what you wrote and getting flustered into saying something which does not really agree with what the interviewer is looking at in your paperwork.

Projecting a good image

As we have seen, the points you make in an interview have to do with what you say about yourself and what you say about the organisation and the job. In one way or another you have to show that you are responsible, hard-working and competent. In sum, that you care about yourself and are firm in your beliefs about your qualities. But you must also show that you are flexible and ambitious enough to learn new skills and gain new qualities. Moreover, you must show that you have performed both competently and creatively – the kind of person who has not only accepted responsibility but also sought it out.

The projection of this image of yourself may sound like a tall order. Perhaps you feel that this description does not fit you at all. But let's take a closer look.

- Supposing, for example, that you don't think you're hard-working, but basically rather a lazy person. Try to explain to yourself why this may be so.
- There must have been some occasions during your life when you have been hard-working. What were they? What were the particular characteristics of the situation that prompted you to work hard?

- Try always to think of examples of occasions when you have displayed the qualities the interviewer may be looking for. They will be looking for evidence, not bald statements like 'I think I'm hard-working.'
- Instead of reeling off a list of your characteristics, try using anecdotes which provide evidence of those characteristics: short stories about yourself which involve a demonstration of each quality as part of the story.

One young man, for example, described several experiences which he had had as a clerk with a professional football team. In one story his hard work had led him to develop an innovation; in another his flexibility and ambition had involved him in an interesting problem of personnel work. Your answers to the awkward questions will probably have prompted you to think of examples like these which you would be able to use in any interview.

Adopting this approach will ensure that, above all, you are yourself. If you are recounting an incident or experience in which you actually took part, you are likely to talk more naturally and easily. It is when interviewees start to invent things which they think will sound good that they come unstuck in interviews. They try to be someone they are not: they cannot produce the evidence and they cannot keep the act up. It is the resulting feeling of unease and discomfort that can cause nervousness.

Check-Point

Be yourself but make the most of what you have!

Be realistic

However, making the most of what they've got can lead people into the other trap: that of being over-confident and arrogant. The secret lies in showing your finest feathers in as modest a manner as possible. Demonstrate your ambition but within reason. Most interviewers will expect you to be fairly ambitious, so don't be afraid of admitting that, like many people, you would like to be managing director one day. However, show that you have a sense of perspective and have thought about your own strengths in relation to what you can reasonably expect from your career. Be prepared to say something about your goals, but relate them to time and the experience you hope to gain in five years and in ten years. The use of a time-span will demonstrate that you are organised and thoughtful.

Check-Point

Show that you know who you are, what you can do, what you want and where you are going.

Reveal your qualities in a way that allows them to speak for themselves without having to overstate the case. Be prepared to admit your weaknesses but express them in such a way that you show you are aware of them but having some success at overcoming them. Compensate for them by making the most of your strengths:

'I didn't really work as hard as I could have done at school, but my disappointing exam results really taught me a lesson. At the moment I'm trying to plan my time better, write out a daily checklist of things to be done, for example, and I'm finding that I not only get a sense of achievement at the end of the day, but that I am more self-disciplined than I thought I was.'

What to avoid

When speaking to an interviewer there are a number of things to avoid. Most important of all are those related to your style of delivery and your posture because, as we have seen, non-verbal communication can often speak louder than words (Chapter 1).

Monotonous delivery

A loud, domineering voice will make the interviewer feel threatened; a quiet, low, monotonous voice will bore them. They may lose interest in you; worse still, they may even think you are bored and uninterested. Anxiety can often cause people to speak in a lower, more monotonous voice than normal without their realising it. So, concentrate on projecting your voice in a dynamic, enthusiastic tone. Above all, aim at variety – variety of pitch, volume and speed.

Unresponsiveness

When people are nervous they are often also less responsive than normal. The interviewer wants to hear about you so if they should ask a question which appears to require only a 'yes' or 'no' answer, try to expand your answers beyond a simple 'yes' or 'no'.

Deliberate unresponsiveness

You may of course be asked a question which you really cannot or do not want to answer. Women, for example, may be asked questions which they consider embarrassing, or even illegal, like

'Won't you leave to have a baby before long?'

Always try to answer honestly if you can – this might be an opportunity to offer your opinion about women working, for example – but always avoid a direct refusal to answer or an argumentative answer. It is far better to adopt the 'political' response. Learn from politicians. They are frequently asked questions which they cannot or do not want to answer, but they reply by steering the question neatly round to a slightly different question which they are prepared to answer. However, this technique should only be used when absolutely necessary; it is no alternative to good preparation.

Inappropriate language

You should also try to avoid using slang or excessively casual language – 'brill', 'well pleased', 'OK', 'no way', 'it was all right', 'I mean', 'like … I was… you know…

chairman of ... ', 'fantastic', 'like I said ... Yeh', and 'me and my friend went ... '. Such expressions are not typical of a business professional.

Unnatural posture

Slumping or sitting like a stiff tin soldier are both frequent symptoms of nerves. The best impression is created by sitting up straight with legs crossed. This position looks good and allows you to lean forward a little towards the interviewer to make special points or to show special attention. It also provides a natural rest point for your hands but allows you to gesture naturally – without the sweeping movement required if your hands are in your lap or resting awkwardly on the chair seat. Practise sitting on different chairs until you can readily find a comfortable but alert position which looks good and feels easily maintainable without fidgeting.

A negative start

Watch the opening of an interview. Avoid making remarks that create a 'negative set' for the rest of the interview, such as

> *'I'm not really sure that my background is suitable for this job', or 'I'm afraid I haven't had any experience.'*

Check-Point

Be positive!

7.4 Tips to remember

When you are in a strange, formal situation it is easy to forget the obvious things which are second nature on more relaxed occasions.

Check-Points: The Job Interview

- Arrive in good time – not only because it is polite but because having to rush will leave you feeling hot and flustered, and therefore nervous.
- Be neat and fairly conservative in your appearance.
- Take cues from the interviewer on degree of formality – your sensitivity to non-verbal communication should help you with this. Perhaps be a little more formal than usual – not a stuffed shirt. Be cautious about jokes, sarcastic asides and so on.
- Don't smoke unless invited to do so, and then only if you must, unless the interviewer smokes. Never smoke if there is no ashtray in sight.
- Be prepared to take notes, if it is necessary to record information. But it might be best to ask the interviewer if they would mind if you did. Even then, don't scribble furiously all the way through.
- Be polite, but friendly and don't forget to *smile* (but only when it's appropriate).
- Leave promptly when the interview is over; don't hover. Smile, shake hands and thank the interviewer.

Summary – being interviewed for a job

Advice to prospective interviewees is often 'Be yourself', but if being yourself has been unsuccessful in interviews so far, perhaps it is time to analyse what you do and don't do before, during and after interviews. If you follow the suggestions in this chapter and get as much practice as possible and are prepared to be self-critical and accept feedback from others, your confidence will gradually increase until 'being yourself' means doing the right thing to get that job.

Assignment: Using a tape recorder, or better still a video recorder, your list of strengths and weaknesses and your answers to the awkward questions, imagine that the interviewer has just asked you the question 'Tell me about yourself'.

Try to speak for 3–5 minutes. (Note: In a real interview you may not have so long, as the interviewer may interrupt you. You would, anyway, have to use your judgement about when to stop.)

When you have finished, play it back, listening critically to the tone of your voice, the language you use, the evidence you provide to back up your statements and so on. Would you be interested, impressed, attracted if you were the interviewer?

If you're not happy with your performance, try again.

Exercise 7.1

Summarise the things you should and shouldn't do

(a) before the interview;
(b) during the interview.

Further reading

Studner, P. and McDonald, M. (Eds) *Super Job Search: The Complete Manual for Job-Seekers and Career-Changers*, Mercury Books, 1996

8 Communicating in groups

The meeting of minds

A meeting brings together a group of the unfit, appointed by the unwilling to do the unnecessary for the ungrateful.
A camel is a horse designed by a committee.
A meeting is a group of people who keep minutes and waste hours.
A meeting is a meeting of people to decide when the next meeting will take place.
A meeting is a group of people who singly can do nothing and collectively decide that nothing can be done.

Until now we have tended to treat communication primarily as an individual and/or interpersonal activity, but individual or personal communication is only one aspect of organisational communication. The group meeting as a method of informing and decision-making is as old as man, and has existed ever since people began to work in groups. However, during the last decade or so, it has become increasingly prevalent. This growth is due mainly to the fact that organisations have become larger and more complex, which has led to such a level of specialisation that all the information needed to make decisions in this increasingly complex business society can no longer be adequately assimilated, evaluated and decided by one person or specialised area, without reference to other areas in the organisation.

Furthermore, research studies into attitudes and motivation of people at work have shown that people need to feel involved and informed and able to participate in the decisions that affect them. The result has been, as one writer commented, that

'Meetings have become big business. Group participation is in vogue and the wheels of modern industry are turned by committees.'

And yet, according to one expert, of all the thousands of meetings which take place daily up and down the country, only 1 in 10 works efficiently. The other 9 out of 10 presumably cause the frustration and cynicism which are reflected in the statements quoted in the extract at the beginning of this chapter. In fact, many people view the appointment of a committee as a waste of time and energy and as a delaying tactic on the part of those who are willing to pay 'lip service' to an idea, but are unwilling to actually *do* anything. Perhaps you have experienced wasted hours in group meetings and agree with those who question the value of meetings, working parties and committees. Maybe you are among those who want quick action, not wasted hours of talking. Or perhaps you are one of those who wonder why other people are apparently prepared to spend hours of their time taking part in an activity about which they complain so volubly. But the problem is not so much the meetings, as the people who attend the meetings – the leader and the participants.

This chapter will look at

- the differences between individual and group communication
- the advantages of group decision-making
- why people join groups in the first place
- the factors which influence what happens in a group.

In short, we will look at the nature of the group communication process in the hope that an understanding of this process will help to explain why you or others have experienced non-productive meetings and to encourage you to become a more effective leader or participant.

Self-Check

First of all, from your own experience of belonging to groups and attending meetings, however informal, can you think of any advantages which groups have over an individual working on their own?

8.1 Advantages of groups

It is true that an individual analysing a problem alone may perform more effectively and efficiently than would a group. Sometimes after a group discussion it is easy to recognise that one or two people could have reached the same conclusion without the help from the others. The problem is, however, that it is usually impossible to determine in advance which particular members are skilled enough to solve the problem alone, or who will be the main participants in any discussion.

More commitment

Research studies have shown that people are more committed to a decision (i.e they are more positively disposed towards the decision and more likely to try to carry it out) when they are included in the decision-making process. This can be explained by two factors:

- involving a group in the process of determining a policy or decision ensures they are familiar with the nature, background and need for the policy; they are, therefore, more likely to understand why the policy or decision is necessary;
- attitudes tend to be more favourable because of the personal involvement in the decision.

Better decisions

Groups on the whole make decisions which are better than those of an individual working alone. It is true that sometimes for various reasons the interesting, bright ideas of one individual may be stifled by a conservative majority, as we shall see. However groups should be able to make better decisions for four reasons.

More available information

In trying to solve a problem, an individual normally has access to their own experience and observation and to the written reports of others. In a group, that individual can be exposed to the experience and observations of other people's personal investigation.

This increased information can make it easier to find the correct solution and allows members to select from a number of alternatives. The number of different ideas tends to increase with group size but levels off at about five or six participants.

It is possible to increase artificially the amount of information produced in a group – especially new, imaginative and creative information – by means of a technique known as 'brainstorming'.

Check-Points: For Brainstorming

- The **subject** or **problem** must be clearly and simply stated.
- **Adverse criticism is not allowed** and mental self-criticism should be resisted. This is a crucial rule since criticism or negativism inhibits thinking as well as communication. If you think of an idea but know that someone is likely to disagree with it, or criticise it, you are more likely to keep it to yourself. So, in a brainstorming session, evaluation of ideas is suspended until after the session is completed.
- **All ideas are recorded**. Every idea is recorded by a secretary or someone else appointed to the task, or by means of a tape recorder, as the ideas are put forward as rapidly as possible. However, it is a good idea to write the ideas up on a whiteboard or series of wall charts so that everyone can see them.
- **Free association** of ideas is encouraged. However 'way-out' the ideas may seem, all ideas are encouraged.
- **Quantity** of ideas is important. Members should be encouraged to keep ideas coming thick and fast, since at this stage it is the quantity which is important, not the quality.
- **Combining and building on** ideas is encouraged. One idea may trigger further ideas, or an idea which is a combination of others, or a development of a previous idea.

At the beginning of a brainstorming session, the leader should remind the group of the rules and possibly start with a warm-up session on some quite unrelated subject. The best-known subject is probably

What can you use a brick for (or a paper-clip, or a wire coat-hanger)?

This warm-up session overcomes the initial inhibitions and guarded poses that might otherwise exist.

Usually after about 10–30 minutes, depending on the subject, ideas dry up and the evaluation stage can be started, although it is a good idea to hold the evaluation session a day or two later, if possible.

The results of brainstorming groups in business indicate that through using this method, groups produce more ideas than they would otherwise and, for some problems, produce higher-quality suggestions. It not only increases original thought by participants but also teaches them to have greater empathy and tolerance for the ideas of others. It can therefore improve the morale of the group because interaction is increased and everyone feels they are making a contribution. For these reasons, it is often worth a try when the situation is appropriate.

More and better suggestions

Regardless of the task, groups in a good communication climate will produce more and better suggestions than an individual working alone. It is true that some tasks are not best carried out by groups, but there are others for which groups are uniquely qualified:

Check-Points: Tasks Performed Better by a Group

- those requiring some kind of division of labour
- those where manual rather than intellectual skills are required
- those for which creativity is desirable
- those where memory or recall of information is important
- those where the object of judgement is ambiguous.

Self-Check

Can you think of the reasons why groups are better at performing these five types of tasks?

Tasks requiring division of labour or manual skills are obviously best suited to a group: six pairs of hands are better than one, and usually faster. Groups are better at tasks requiring judgement, creativity and memory because six heads can usually make more accurate judgements and be more creative as a result of exploring more possibilities, and remember more things for longer than just one.

Groups also in this respect learn faster than individuals since there is less chance of bias disrupting learning. Human perception of experiences and viewpoints can produce a very individualised 'frame of reference' – a blinkered view, if you like. In a group these problems are offset by the different backgrounds and experiences of the individual group members, and this results in one member seeing aspects of the problem under discussion that were not perceived by others. By the time the collective opinions have been brought to bear upon the problem, a high-quality decision should be the result.

More courageous decisions

Another interesting difference between group and individual thinking and communication is that people seem to be more willing to accept a more risky decision in a group than they would alone.

Self-Check

In your experience, do you think this is true? What reasons could explain this tendency?

There are several theories to explain this phenomenon, but the two most popular are:

- People feel they can share the responsibility for their decision over all the group members, rather than just bearing it themselves.
- Groups somehow invest a risk with 'value': it can be regarded as brave and courageous, and then no one individual wants to be seen to be cowardly or conservative, or the 'wet blanket' or 'odd one out' by not agreeing with others to accept the 'risky' decision.

Whatever the reason, it is interesting to bear in mind that we can usually expect decisions reached in a group meeting to be more risky than the decisions of those same people if approached individually. For an organisation, of course, this could prove an advantage or a disadvantage.

Higher productivity

People join groups for very different reasons, as we shall see, but whatever their reason for being there, working together with others on the same task can act as a stimulant to greater productivity since group members often work to gain social approval.

Self-Check

In talking about the advantages of group decision-making I have hinted at some disadvantages. Can you remember them and think of any others?

8.2   Disadvantages of groups

All the advantages mentioned above result, of course, from a 'good' group working in a 'good communication climate'. As we know only too well, the problem with many meetings is that they do not reach these heights of excellence. Group decision-making can have disadvantages compared with the individual working alone, and many of these disadvantages are associated with the advantages.

Time

In terms of 'man'-hours, an individual working alone is far superior. One person does not have the problem of coordinating efforts with other individuals, does not have to listen to information already known, does not have to test the group climate before contributing, and runs no real risk of having their efforts duplicated by others.

Although we considered the different frames of reference as an advantage earlier, we must now see them as potential disadvantages, if we consider the time required to satisfy each member's desire to comment and react to the comments of other members.

The length of a meeting rises with the square of the number of people present. (Eileen Shanahan, quoted from Harold Faber, New York Times Magazine, March 1986)

This may not be an irrefutable law, but our experience surely tells us that it has an element of truth in it: there are times when the necessity of prompt action precludes the use of committees and meetings.

The length of time required to reach a decision would matter less if it weren't for the fact that much of that time is *wasted*.

Self-Check

Write down ways in which you have found time is wasted in meetings.

Check-Points: How Groups can Waste Time

- Too much time is spent pursuing one issue or train of thought, with the result that the agenda cannot be completed.
- Members insist on discussing irrelevant points.
- Members feel obliged to make a 'speech' even when they agree and are only repeating what others have said.
- Members spend so much time maintaining group morale and other human relations matters that time does not permit solving the problem assigned to the group.

Group pressure

Although the tendency to make more risky decisions can be a positive phenomenon in group decision-making, this 'mob psychology' may also result in poor decisions. The presence of others can produce a 'group pressure' which influences people to agree with a mediocre outcome. Group pressure need not necessarily lead to a mediocre decision, but groups do value compromise, and compromise can lead to mediocrity through the process of accommodation and consensus-seeking.

Talk rather than action

Groups sometimes substitute talk for action. Most people seem not to like making decisions and given half a chance they will avoid doing so. Some groups therefore tend to exhibit a willingness to discuss almost any problem but solve none. Certainly a considerable sense of achievement can sometimes be derived simply from discussing an important social or business issue and so some groups are so satisfied with their talk that they never get round to a solution.

Exercise 8.1

1 Give two reasons for the trend towards what might be termed 'management by committee'.
2 Give two reasons why decisions made by a group are likely to be better than those made by one individual working alone.

Effective groups, then, can have considerable advantages over the individual working alone. They can provide the individual member with a sense of satisfaction derived simply from being a member of the group, and they can produce higher productivity. But it must be remembered that not all groups have these results, nor do both results necessarily occur together, and although member satisfaction may result in productivity, productivity does not necessarily result in satisfaction.

8.3   Factors affecting group effectiveness

The outcome of the group is a result of a very complex set of interconnected factors and it is difficult to discuss intelligently any one factor in small-group communication without first knowing something about all the factors since they are all interdependent and influence one another.

As an example of the way in which these factors are all related, let's look first at an important characteristic of effective groups which will affect the outcome of any group's activity but which in turn can be affected by other factors.

Cohesiveness

Cohesiveness is the attraction that a group has for its members. It is sometimes confused with 'morale' but cohesiveness refers to one's desire to work towards a goal. Cohesiveness therefore represents an individual's attraction to a group and its members, while morale represents one's satisfaction with these as well as other major aspects of the task and the work situation.

Cohesiveness is circular in nature in that once established in a group it leads to many desirable outcomes, which in turn lead to even stronger cohesion.

There are many causes of cohesiveness. In fact, there have been instances where people are attracted to groups which have a history of failure. This probably occurs when an individual is more concerned with the group's membership than with its task.

A cohesive group will have a strong sense of loyalty both from its members and to its members. Obviously, the level of cohesiveness will exert a direct influence on individual members' determination to abide by group decisions. Groups that are high in cohesiveness will generally tend to enjoy one another's company, are interested in the well-being of other group members and tend to help each other with problems. Although highly cohesive groups do tend to develop rigid group standards (or norms) which everyone is expected to abide by, their members are more likely to feel able to disagree openly than are members of less cohesive groups.

Assignment

- You are almost bound to belong, or to have belonged, to groups – different groups at work, at college, in your leisure activities. Think about them: which ones did you enjoy belonging to, which ones did you join and why?
- You may belong to some groups whose cohesiveness is very weak. What do you think are the reasons for this?
- Make a list of the factors which cause this cohesion or lack of cohesion and compare your list with the many interrelated factors in Figure 8.1 which affect the way in which a group operates.

Look at Figure 8.1 and you will see that the ultimate outcome of a group – its productivity and member satisfaction – is affected by two main groups of factors or variables:

- uncontrollable (independent) variables
- controllable (intermediate) variables.

For example, a group may have been appointed to carry out a certain task. The individual members may have little control over who makes up the group or committee – who they may be working with, in other words; equally they may have little choice over the nature of the task they have to perform; nor will they have much control over the environment within which they act, which will impose certain constraints and conditions on the way they operate and which will also determine the physical location in which they meet. All these 'uncontrollable' factors, which in turn affect one another, will have an influence on what happens in the group – the extent to which people interact and participate, the level of motivation of the group, the style of leadership which exists or is adopted, the friendship relationships which develop in the group and so on. These factors are 'controllable' by the group. They are also known as 'intermediate' factors because although they are influenced by the uncontrollable or independent variables, as we have seen, they in turn will influence the performance of the group – the end result, in terms of group productivity and member satisfaction.

Uncontrollable variables

It is obvious that in one sense these factors are not totally uncontrollable in that group members could exert influence to change them, but usually only over a

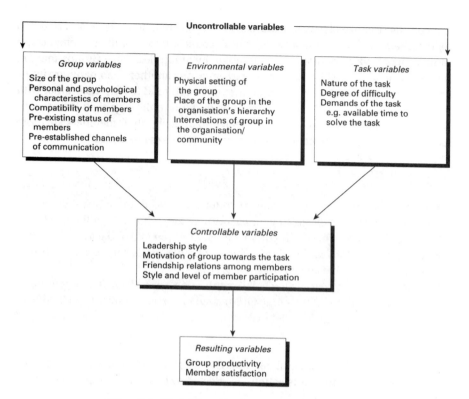

Figure 8.1 **Variables affecting group effectiveness.**

longer period of time than the group is in existence. As far as the group is concerned, at the moment it comes together as a group, it will have certain conditions imposed upon it. Let's look at the nature of the group itself.

Self-Check

- What is the optimum size of a group?
- Think about the groups you belong to.
- Which groups seem to work best and why?
- Do you think the size of the group is important?

The group

Size

We have already seen that the larger the group the greater the diversity of information, skills, talent, backgrounds and experiences available. On the other hand, the larger the group the less chance there is of an individual participating. However, the effect of size does not affect everyone in the same way. One person may find no difficulty in speaking in a group of 20, whereas another may find a group of 10 too large unless they have some official role or know the group well. In larger groups, more powerful or forceful individuals will tend to dominate the available communication time; and since studies show that those who participate most are perceived as having the most influence but do not necessarily have more knowledge or experience, this will tend to distort what happens in the group. The 'neglected resource' is a common feature of groups: the silent expert whose views are never heard because their participation is so low.

There must therefore be a trade-off between the optimum size for participation and the optimum size for breadth of available knowledge and experience. Groups of fewer than 5 will tend to be less cohesive as splits occur 3 : 1 or 2 : 2 and there is insufficient breadth of experience, variety and intellectual stimulus to produce good results. Over 10 begins to make face-to-face contact difficult; over 15, low participators will probably stop talking to one another altogether, and interaction and thus creativity are stifled. However, big groups can solve some types of problem more efficiently than smaller groups – for example, where there is a verifiable answer. The more people in the meeting, the more chance there is that it contains an expert who knows the correct answer.

The problem of size is particularly intense where a committee must include representatives of various interest groups, and this has given rise to the plethora of sub-committees and working parties which are often formed by a large committee, in an attempt to get the best of both worlds perhaps.

The optimum size is probably between 5 and 7 members but a size of 5–10 will allow people to talk almost as much as they want to while still providing a sufficient variety of talent and personality to tackle problems imaginatively.

Size tends to be related to cohesiveness. As the number of members is increased beyond 6 or 7, cohesiveness begins to decline. This is due mainly to the reduced interaction, the need to divide tasks, the need for stronger, more autocratic leadership to keep order and the number of cliques or factions which appear.

Member characteristics and objectives

When a group forms or is formed, the members do not arrive with characters like blank sheets. They come complete with different attitudes, values and beliefs and the ways these mix within the group process will again affect the level and style of participation and interaction in the group, and in consequence the productivity and member satisfaction. Effective groups will have a high level of compatibility between the members, but this does not necessarily mean that to be effective a group must have members whose attitudes, beliefs and values are all similar. While this kind of group (homogenous) tends to promote satisfaction, and heterogenous groups (groups where members are very dissimilar) tend to exhibit more conflict, heterogenous groups have been shown to be more productive than homogenous ones. The aim is therefore to get a mix of members, or help a group to develop, in such a way that both member satisfaction and productivity is high, and this will be very dependent on the personality and style of the leader. In fact, compatibility can often be achieved when there is agreement with and acceptance by the whole group of the leader.

In an effective group, all the members will accept the group's objectives and work to achieve the common goal. However, most people will come to a group with personal objectives of their own – sometimes called 'the hidden agenda'.

Since it is obviously not possible to satisfy all the individual objectives and group objectives simultaneously some sort of trade-off or give-and-take arrangement has to be arrived at. The extent to which each member is prepared to sacrifice personal objectives in favour of the objectives of the group as a whole will depend on many other factors, but it will be related to the degree of cohesiveness that the group possesses.

Status and roles

When a group comes together, they may all be equal members of the group, but they will also each have a pre-existing status in the eyes of the rest of the group. For example, a committee may have been formed to think of ways of reducing accidents and each member may have been picked because of the contribution they can make, but there will inevitably be differences in seniority in the group and some people, whether senior or not, will be regarded as influential by others, before they even open their mouths.

Each member will also see themselves as being there to perform a particular role: to stir up others and get some action; to pour oil on troubled water because there are conflicting interests present in the group; to be the logical thinker, and so on.

Another factor which is important is the existence of pre-established links or friendships. Almost inevitably there will be some people present who know one another from outside the group. The quality and extent of any communication which has taken place before will influence the way they behave inside the group.

In deciding either consciously or unconsciously how they are going to behave, each member has to ask themselves three questions:

Check-Points: Group Participation

- Who am I in this group? What is my occupational role? What role do others expect me to play? Am I to be a listener or a leader? Am I here to represent others or am I here in my own right? Who will be judging me on the way I behave?
- What is the pattern of influence? Who is likely to have influence? What kind of influence is it? Do I want to change the influence pattern? If so, how am I going to do it?
- What are my personal needs and objectives? Are they the same as the group's? Or, at least, compatible with them? If not, should they be? What shall I do if my needs and objectives don't fit with the group's? Will I be prepared to sacrifice this need, in order to achieve another one?

The environment

Physical location

The simplest of the so-called 'uncontrollable' factors is the setting of the group, but its importance to the way a group interacts and performs its task is often ignored.

Self-Check

In what ways can the physical setting of the group affect the group?

Physical proximity increases interaction. A large room where everyone feels rather distant from their neighbour will hinder cohesiveness. Seating arrangements which separate the leader or chair from 'the rest' will also discourage interaction, and encourage the leader to adopt a very autocratic style of leadership. Members are more likely to form alliances with those sitting near them and conflicts often occur across a table. Some leaders knowing this will actually arrange the seating so that potential opponents sit along the same side of the table rather than opposite one another.

The location of a meeting gives out signals. If the meeting takes place in the manager's office the pre-existing status relationships are likely to be reinforced, whereas a meeting on neutral ground may lessen the impact of these relationships and encourage everyone to feel they can be themselves.

Shared facilities, even shared discomfort, can encourage cohesiveness by helping group identity. Although the facilities should be suitable for performance of the task and things like lighting, seating, tables and so on can be quite significant, even when these are poor the 'we're all in the same boat' idea can often be helpful to a group in developing a sense of group identity.

Inter-group relations

The way a group is regarded by the rest of the organisation or community will affect its productivity, cohesiveness and morale. No one wants to belong to a group, or wants to spend hours sitting in meetings of a committee which is not regarded by the rest of the organisation as being important. The extent to which it is perceived to influence events in the organisation or outside; the influence it can exert on key figures in the organisation; the extent to which it is accepted as important, helpful, cooperative to the overall goals of the organisation will all affect the performance of the group and the attitude of individual members to the group.

A member who feels that the group is a waste of time because it is not regarded as being important may react in several ways.

Check-Points: The Dissatisfied Group Member

He or she may

- reduce the importance of the group to themselves; they may actually stop coming or at least 'withdraw' in the sense that they stop participating
- use 'negative' or 'nuisance' power by generally being difficult and uncooperative
- encourage the group to become a nuisance, so that at least people notice it.

Expectations of the group

The significance of the task for the organisation will have implications for the group, as we shall see, but in addition many organisations have a particular 'house style' for meetings. Things are expected to be done in a particular way. In other words, the organisation will have norms about ways of conducting meetings, methods of working, reporting and coordinating. Often a group cannot avoid conforming to these norms and expectations, even if they are not the most appropriate in a particular set of circumstances.

The task

The nature of the task, the degree of difficulty and any special demands of the task – for instance the time available to complete it – will all affect the attitude of the group members, the way they work and the decisions of the leader about the best way to structure (or not structure) the meeting. Tasks will usually fall into one or more of four main types.

Check-points: The Purpose of Meetings

- information-sharing (exchange of views and information)
- persuasive (recommending action)
- creative/problem-solving (generating ideas)
- decision-making (choosing the best alternative and planning action).

Of these four, 'information-sharing' and 'persuasive' are probably the most common, but meetings which have to solve problems will be concerned with generating ideas and planning action to carry out their decisions.

Information-sharing meetings can usually be larger and more tightly controlled, whereas problem-solving meetings will depend on a high degree of interaction and a looser structure which takes more time.

Different tasks will therefore require people to play different roles. To confuse two different tasks in one meeting will put great strain on the leader and the participants, as one minute they may be expected to contribute ideas in an uninhibited fashion and interact freely, and the next minute conform to a tight timetable and restricted interaction. For this reason, agendas for meetings should try to separate tasks by type rather than lumping everything together in the order it was received by the secretary.

Controllable factors

All the 'uncontrollable' factors will affect what actually happens in a group, and the leader and the participants need to be aware of the potential impact of these factors so that they can arrange their own behaviour accordingly, because the 'controllable' factors are just that: they can be changed and adapted to improve group productivity and member satisfaction. The leader is, of course, central to this adaptation. The leader may have been appointed from the outside, or may have emerged from within the group, chosen by them as the most appropriate leader in those circumstances and for that particular task. But whatever the reason the leader needs to be aware that there are different styles of leadership and that these styles will have different effects on the group, on their interaction and therefore on the productivity and morale of the group.

Leadership style

There are many ways of classifying leadership style but perhaps the three principal styles of leadership are:

- democratic
- autocratic
- laissez-faire.

Each style is likely to cause people to behave in a particular way and to cause certain things to happen.

Exercise 8.2: Look at the following statements. Each is a characteristic likely to arise in a group as a result of a particular style of leadership. Look at each one and decide whether it is more likely to occur in meetings with a *democratic* leader, an *autocratic* leader or a *laissez-faire* leader.

Clue: behaviour in meetings can be self-oriented (aimed at achieving personal goals), group-oriented (aimed at achieving group goals and group-member satisfaction) and task-oriented (centred mainly on performing the task, with little concern for members' satisfaction and human relations in the group). Generally speaking *democratic-style* meetings demonstrate *GROUP-oriented* behaviour, *autocratic-style* meetings demonstrate *TASK-oriented* behaviour and *laissez-faire style* meetings demonstrate *SELF*-oriented behaviour.

In each section there is one characteristic typical of each leadership style; except in section (d) Status, where there are *two* for each.

(a) **Activity planning**
   1 The activities of the group are planned by the leader; members are rather uncertain about what the next steps may be.
   2 The group plans its activities, technical advice being provided by the leader when necessary.
   3 Members of the group are given help by the leader in planning their activities only when it is requested.
(b) **Disciplines**
   4 Little stress is placed on discipline, unless imposed by the group; the leader's relation to the members is friendly, helping and tolerant.
   5 There is no concern for discipline; members develop self-assertiveness without regard for others.
   6 Considerable stress is placed on discipline and on getting the job done.
(c) **Responsibilities**
   7 Limited responsibility is placed on all members; members are chosen for specific tasks.

8 Leader places no responsibilities on members, who are left to develop activities if they wish.

9 Responsibilities are placed on all members.

(d) **Status**

10 Leader and members function as equals; emphasis on status decreases and emphasis on respect increases.

11 Considerable status differences exist between leader and members; aggressive status-seeking activities develop among members who need status.

12 Few contacts exist between leader and members; little friendship for the leader develops; status-mindedness develops, resulting in competitive hostility.

13 Status comes from praise from the leader, which is usually personal and subjective.

14 Comments by leader or members are infrequent; lack of development of feelings of unity, self-confidence or friendliness.

15 Status in the group is earned by the contribution made to the achievement of the group's goals; praise from the leader is objective and factually based.

(e) **Interaction and participation**

16 Listening improves, resulting in greater acceptance of the ideas of others.

17 Members listen carefully to leader's instructions; they may pay little attention to what others say, unless productivity is at stake.

18 Members focus mainly on their own concerns. Listening to the comments of others is infrequent.

Look at p. 420 to see how well you did.

Assignment: Now copy out the appropriate characteristics for each leadership style and you will have a useful checklist of the kind of behaviour to expect from each style of leadership. Looking at the behaviour typical of each of the three leadership styles how would you rate each leadership style in terms of group productivity and member satisfaction?

- **Democratic style** – Generally speaking since the leader only guides as needed, working on the fundamental belief that members can attain their own ends by using their own resources, members gain satisfaction from this confidence and making their own decisions. Group productivity is therefore usually fairly high.

- **Autocratic style** – The leader's behaviour is governed by a fundamental belief that constant direction is necessary to achieve the goals. The task is derived from achieving personal objectives not from achieving group goals.

- **Laissez-faire** – Since there is very little concern for goal achievement, the task may not be performed and member satisfaction will only be derived from achieving personal objectives not from achieving group goals.

However, despite the apparent advantages of a democratic style and the modern trend towards democratic management, there are times when it is inappropriate. The nature of the task, the limited time available, the characteristics of the members and so on may all suggest at a particular moment that another style of leadership is required.

Check-Point

The effective leader is the one who is able to be flexible, adapting their style to suit the demands of the occasion.

Group interactions and roles

Interaction patterns

The willingness of group members to interact verbally and non-verbally has a significant effect on the type of meeting that takes place. Earlier in this chapter, we discovered that group size and the time available could severely limit the members' participation. Many groups seem to assume that the only interaction that takes place is between the leader and the members. If ideas are to be discussed in depth, if the collective wisdom of the group is to be used to advantage, interaction between all the members is a must. In groups where the leader adopts a highly structured, autocratic style of leadership, the interaction is likely to be highly centralised, whereas in a freer discussion members' comments are directed in any one of many directions rather than exclusively to the leader (see Figures 8.2 and 8.3).

Neither way is absolutely right or wrong. Both will be appropriate in different circumstances, but you should realise that a tightly controlled discussion 'through the chair' which is often necessary in large meetings will considerably restrict a group's ability to deal with a task like solving an open-ended problem.

Group roles and behaviour analysis

In all human interactions there are two major ingredients – content and process. The first deals with the subject matter or *task* upon which the group is working. The second ingredient, *process*, is concerned with what is happening between and to group members while the group is working. Group process or group dynamics deals with such items as morale, atmosphere, influence, participation, conflict, leadership struggles, competition, cooperation and so on.

In most interactions most people tend to focus their attention on the content of the task and neglect the process even when, as is sometimes the case, it is the major cause of ineffective group action. Sensitivity to the process will enable you to diagnose a group's problems early and deal with them effectively. Since these processes are present in all groups, awareness of them will make you a more valuable and effective member of a group.

Assignment: Next time you take part in a meeting observe the way in which the group behaves in terms of things like influence, morale, conflict, leadership struggles, competition and cooperation, as well as the way it performs the task.

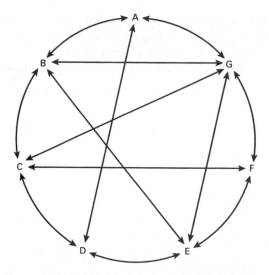

Figure 8.2 **Decentralised communication structure.**

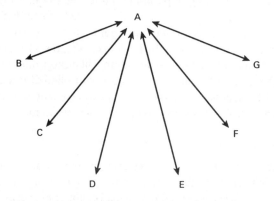

Figure 8.3 **Centralised communication structure.**

It is possible to analyse people's verbal behaviour and then group these different kinds of behaviour into two main groups – those concerned with performing the *task* and those concerned with *maintaining the group* as an effective group.

Many people interested in group dynamics have put forward their ideas on the way in which behaviour can be analysed. Most of these behavioural analysts have tended to try to classify behaviour into only 10 or perhaps 12 categories, which can then be used by observers to analyse the behaviour of groups. These categories are inevitably all slightly different and so the list below represents an accumulation of the ideas of various analysts.

Assignment: Consider the descriptions of the different kinds of behaviour given below and try to think of group meetings in which you have taken part in. Do you recognise these behaviours? In you? In others?

(a) **Task roles (functions required in selecting and carrying out a group task)**

  1 *Initiating activity* – Proposing solutions; suggesting new ideas, new definitions of the problem, new attack on the problem, or new organisation of material.

  2 *Seeking information* – Asking for clarification of suggestions; requesting additional information or facts.

  3 *Seeking opinion* – Looking for an expression of feeling about something from the members; seeking clarification of values, suggestions or ideas.

  4 *Giving information* – Offering facts or generalisations; relating one's own experience to the group problem to illustrate points.

  5 *Giving opinion* – Stating an opinion or belief concerning a suggestion or one of several suggestions, particularly concerning its value rather than its factual basis.

  6 *Elaborating* – Clarifying, giving examples or developing meanings; trying to envisage how a proposal might work if adopted.

  7 *Coordinating* – Showing relationships among various ideas or suggestions; trying to pull ideas and suggestions together; trying to draw together activities of various subgroups or members.

  8 *Summarising* – Restating suggestions after the group has discussed them.

(b) **Group building and maintenance roles (functions required in strengthening and maintaining group life and activities)**

  1 *Encouraging* – Being friendly, warm, responsive to others; praising others and their ideas; agreeing with and accepting contributions of others.

  2 *Gatekeeping* – Trying to make it possible for another member to make a contribution to the group by saying, 'We haven't heard anything from Jan yet', or suggesting limited talking time for everyone so that all will have a chance to be heard.

  3 *Standard setting* – Expressing standards for the group to use in choosing its content or procedures or in evaluating its decisions; reminding the group to avoid decisions which conflict with group standards.

  4 *Following* – Going along with decisions of the group; thoughtfully accepting ideas of others; serving as audience during group discussion.

  5 *Expressing group feeling* – Summarising what group feeling is sensed to be; describing reactions of the group to ideas or solutions.

Some behaviours serve both functions at the same time; they help the group to perform its task while contributing to the maintenance of the group as well.

(c) **Both group task and maintenance roles**

  1 *Evaluating* – Submitting group decisions or accomplishments to comparison with group standards; measuring accomplishments against goals.

  2 *Diagnosing* – Determining sources of difficulties, appropriate steps to take next; analysing the main blocks to progress.

For any group to be effective, these task and maintenance functions will have to be performed by some member or members of the group, at some time or another. Of course, it is the ultimate responsibility of the leader to ensure that they are performed, but although the leader will perform some functions, the extent to which the leader and the others share the responsibility for their performance will be determined by the leader's choice of leadership style. In some groups, all members may, at some point, perform each of these functions.

Of course, from time to time, people behave in non-functional ways that do not help the group and the work it is trying to do, and sometimes actually harm the group and its proceedings.

(d) Types of non-functional behaviour

1 *Being aggressive* – Working for status by criticising or blaming others; showing hostility against the group or some individual; deflating the ego or status of others.

2 *Blocking* – Interfering with the progress of the group by going off at a tangent; citing personal experiences unrelated to the problem; arguing too much on a point; rejecting ideas without consideration; difficulty stating.

3 *Self-confessing* – Using the group as a sounding board; expressing personal, non-group-oriented feelings or points of view.

4 *Competing* – Vying with others to produce the best idea, talk the most, play the most roles, gain favour with the leader.

5 *Seeking sympathy* – Trying to induce other group members to be sympathetic to one's problems or misfortunes; deploring one's own situation, or disparaging one's own ideas to gain support.

6 *Special pleading* – Introducing or supporting suggestions related to one's own pet concerns or philosophies; lobbying.

7 *Horsing around* – Clowning; joking; mimicking; disrupting the work of the group.

8 *Seeking recognition* – Attempting to call attention to oneself by loud or excessive talking; extreme ideas; unusual behaviour.

9 *Withdrawal* – Acting indifferent or passive; resorting to excessive formality; daydreaming; doodling; whispering to others; wandering from the subject.

You should be careful in using the classification above not to blame either yourself or someone else who demonstrates non-functional behaviour. It is more helpful to see such behaviour as a symptom that all is not well with the group's ability to satisfy individual needs through group-centred activity. You should also be alert to the fact that each person may interpret such behaviours differently. For example, there are times when what appears to be non-functional behaviour may not necessarily be so, for the content and the group conditions may also have to be taken into account. Sometimes aggressive behaviour may serve a useful purpose in clearing the air and stirring the group into action, for example.

Check-Points: Group Efficiency

Any group is strengthened and enabled to work more efficiently if its members:

- become more conscious of the role function needed at any given time
- become more sensitive to and aware of the degree to which they can help to meet the needs through what they do
- undertake self-training to improve their range of role functions and skills in performing them.

Summary – making groups and committees work

All too often people take part in group activities or committees which they find dissatisfying without stopping to reflect on the factors which can make or mar the achievements of the group. Understanding how these factors inter-relate and how together they affect what the group achieves and what each member gains from membership would help each group member, whether leader or not, to behave and influence others to behave in a way that would maximise the success of the group.

Exercise 8.3

1 Name two uncontrollable variables and two controllable variables which may interact and affect the resulting variables – group productivity and member satisfaction.
2 What is the optimum size of a group? Why?
3 For a group to be effective, is it essential for all the members to have similar personalities?
4 What does the 'hidden agenda' mean?
5 Which three main questions do members of a group ask themselves either consciously or subconsciously on joining a group? Suggest typical examples.
6 How can the physical setting affect the group?

Exercise 8.4: Using the role functions described on pp. 115–16 say what kind of function each of the following statements might perform in a meeting. Remember one behaviour may serve more than one function.

1 'What do you think about that for an idea, John?'
2 'OK, so let's just see where we've got to. Some of you think the best plan would be to ... but the others think that might be counter-productive.'
3 'I get the impression that deep down none of us is really happy about this.'
4 'Oh, that's a daft idea!'
5 'Remember, though, that whatever we do, we have agreed to have the report ready by November at the latest.'
6 'Well, I think, and I suspect the chairman will agree with me, that ...'
7 'In the last job I was in, we tried that, and it was very successful – it cut absenteeism by about 10 per cent.'
8 'Well, that may be all right for you but just imagine how my lot are going to react to that. It's always the same, you never think about the ones who actually have to implement your great ideas.'
9 'So, it looks as if our only problem is finding the space to put the machine until it can be properly installed. Perhaps we could persuade Jim to shift those crates in B warehouse. That's near the unloading bay and reasonably near where it will finally be used, so transporting it shouldn't be too difficult. What do you think?'
10 'Now that's a great idea. I hadn't thought of that.'

Further reading

Handy, Charles, *Understanding Organizations*, Penguin, 1993

⚆ 9 Running and taking part in meetings

Getting round the table

We have already discussed the three major styles of leadership and examined the ways in which people contribute to meetings. In this chapter let's look briefly at the responsibilities of group leaders and at the requirements for effective participation in group discussions, together with the requirements of conducting and recording fairly formal meetings.

Self-Check

From what you now know about the nature of groups, what do you think the responsibilities of the person who chairs the meeting are?

9.1 Chairing meetings

The role of a chairperson or leader at a meeting or conference requires that they should preside, maintain order and ensure that the group does a constructive job of work. They need to bear constantly in mind two things: the task to be done, and the kind of group they are dealing with. A sense of purpose needs to be quickly created. This can be achieved if they start the meeting on time and provide the group with its terms of reference for the meeting – in other words, spelling out the order of the business and the plan of campaign.

The objectives should provide the leader with a basis of control and the rest of the group with a sense of direction. Well-defined objectives, stemming from a carefully prepared and clearly expressed agenda, will provide a good foundation for teamwork. Ideally members of a group should identify themselves with the objectives so that they realise they have a responsibility and a real part to play. Remember that most people work better when they know what a job is about and that they have a useful part to play and can have a hand in making decisions. If a group's function is only an advisory one it is best to let the members know. It may prevent frustration later.

Controlling the meeting

The reason for the meeting should indicate the type of control and structure most appropriate, as we have seen. Control should be exercised with a view to setting standards of performance. Results should be checked against these standards and, where necessary, corrective action should be taken. The leader must accept the responsibility for ensuring that this is done because it is they alone who must accept the ultimate responsibility for the group's performance.

To be effective a person in the chair should follow five basic principles.

Check-Points: Responsibilities of the Chair

- Decide the item of business to be discussed.
- Define the limits of discussion.
- Keep people to the point and ensure that one person speaks at a time.
- Try to be as impartial as possible and at all costs avoid arguing with members.
- Make sure the rest of the group understand what is going on.

Guiding

However much the person in the chair intends to limit their own contribution, they will be obliged to start things off and make sure topics and problems are discussed in the right order. Members have an unfortunate habit of jumping in with solutions before they have understood exactly what the problem is, for example.

Check-Points: Introducing an Item of Business (problem-solving procedure)

When considering a subject there are four basic stages:

1 **Identify the subject/problem** – this should be stated clearly and if necessary repeated at intervals.
2 **Exchange and develop ideas** – get the evidence and interpret it before getting ideas for the solution to the problem.
3 **Evaluate the alternatives** – identify the range of choices available; predict the consequences of each (time, cost, resources, political considerations).
4 **Select a course of action** – preferably by consensus, decide 'who?', 'where?', 'when?', 'how?', and make sure everyone knows what their responsibilities are.

The chairperson should make sure that members stick to this order of events and may have to intervene in order to suggest new ideas, clarify previous statements, summarise and draw attention to possible consequences.

Stimulating discussion

In Chapter 8, we discussed 'brainstorming' as a technique for encouraging ideas and encouraging quieter members, but 'brainstorming' is not always appropriate.

However, the chairperson should from time to time stimulate members by asking appropriate questions. The types of question analysed in Section 6.7 can be used in discussions as well as interviews. The use of questions helps not only to stimulate members but also to control the discussion. This may require interrupting a too-talkative member and calling on the more retiring members for their thoughts. This can be achieved by commenting as you interrupt the too-talkative member: 'Now there's an interesting point. What do you think about that, Tony?'

Check-Points: How to Stimulate Discussion

- Phrase questions to avoid 'yes' or 'no' answers.
- Keep questions brief and straightforward.
- Use simple words.
- Use questions directly related to the topic.
- Use questions which cover a single point.

Coping with the 'hidden agenda'

The chairperson should also try to keep the discussion on an ideas level, rather than allowing it to slip into a conflict of personalities among members. Hidden agendas, competition among members and emotion-laden statements made by group members must be dealt with properly or else social and emotional concerns will become the major focus of the group, at the expense of task considerations. Asking members to give *examples* of sweeping generalisations is a good technique for encouraging members to keep to facts and ideas but you may need help with this task of 'maintaining the group'. Research has indicated that the socio-emotional leader may often be someone other than the officially designated leader.

Reaching a decision

So far as reaching a decision is concerned, in the absence of formal voting methods, the chairperson should either adopt the consensus method or, if appropriate, decide themselves which conclusion is the most suitable as an answer to the problem. The nature of the work and the composition of the group should produce a procedure most suited to the situation.

Self-Check

What are the main methods a group can use to make decisions? What are the advantages and disadvantages of each?

9.2 Decision-making methods

1 **Decision by authority**
   - chairperson makes the decision
   - efficient and fast
   - but members may not be committed or agree

2 **Decision by majority rule/voting**
  - generally recognised as fair
  - timing of the vote is crucial
  - may divide the group members
  - minority will not agree and therefore may not be committed
3 **Decision by consensus**
  - decision 'emerges' as the general feeling of the group
  - members highly committed
  - lengthy – necessary for all members to have their 'say' even if they do not eventually get their 'way'
  - preferable but not always possible
4 **Decision by unanimity**
  - everyone genuinely and wholeheartedly agrees
  - difficult to achieve, and usually not necessary anyway.

No way is the best way, since all have advantages and disadvantages but if possible the group should agree to the method adopted. In any event, whichever method is chosen, it is vital that the group should know what the final decision is, and the chairperson should make sure it is recorded.

Finally, once the meeting is over the chairperson is responsible for ensuring that minutes of the meeting are prepared and any action agreed during the meeting is followed up. This may involve writing a report or monitoring the progress of any action.

> **Exercise 9.1:** Name two techniques a chairperson can use to stimulate discussion.

9.3 Responsibilities of participants

> **Self-Check**
>
> What are the responsibilities of participants at meetings?

Attitude

One of your first responsibilities as a participant is to develop a healthy attitude to meetings – one of open-mindedness and consideration for others.

> **Check-Point**
>
> You should resist negative feelings about meetings.

Meetings are an essential tool of management and supervision, and they can have positive value for everyone – if everyone plays their role conscientiously.

> **Self-Check**
>
> How can you benefit from meetings and other small group discussions?

Meetings can provide you with several opportunities:
- benefiting from the knowledge and opinions of others
- gaining maximum information from the backgrounds and experiences of your colleagues
- feeling a part of a policy or decision under which you will be working
- developing a better understanding and appreciation of your colleagues and the teamwork that can be developed among you
- expressing and communicating your own thoughts to others
- evaluating your own opinions, beliefs and attitudes in the light of other people's.

(If you are a student, you might also like to consider that most of these benefits can also be derived from small discussion or tutorial groups.)

Preparation

Your second responsibility is to ensure that you are properly prepared and informed on the topic. This may require considerable time and effort, but the quality of a meeting can rise no higher than the quality of information possessed by the group members. (Again, students should take note of this responsibility.)

Knowledge of group process

As far as the meeting itself is concerned, knowledge of 'group process' and how groups function will both help you to develop the right attitude and make you a better participant. You should be aware of the problems and responsibilities of the leader, so that you can be more understanding of their methods of leadership and also be helpful in contributing positively towards helping them achieve the meeting goals.

Leadership is a dynamic phenomenon. During a two-hour meeting various leaders (you may be one) may emerge from time to time, even though the same person remains as the official chairperson.

You should realise that every other member sitting around the table with you is an individual who is different from you. They each have their own personal problems, their own self-centredness (which all of us should try to avoid in favour of being more 'you-centred') and their own way of thinking, which may be different from yours.

The goal of your development as a good meeting participant should include a constant study of other people, including a consideration of their basic drives, prejudices, emotions and thinking processes.

Your own actual participation depends on how good a communicator you are.

Check-Points: Characteristics of an Effective Meeting Participant

- a consideration of the other people involved
- a recognition that the interaction process must be two-way, flexible and tolerant
- an awareness of communication barriers and a desire to overcome them

- an ability and desire to speak clearly, to the point and in a language adapted to others
- a sense of proper timing both in terms of when and how to speak, and consideration for the setting and place of the meetings
- a desire to cooperate and conciliate in order to achieve group goals
- an understanding of the need for attentive listening.

Self-Check

When should you participate in a meeting?

The answer should be: when you have something to say. You should never talk just for the sake of talking, but nor should you be too diffident.

- Be ready to get involved on the spur of the moment. Contribute your ideas at the moment that group interest in your contribution will be strong. Don't sit back patiently until everyone else has had their say. There is some indication that members who contribute early in a discussion gain the initial respect of the whole group, and are perceived as credible sources as the meeting progresses. Another psychologically good moment to make perhaps another contribution is at the end of a section of discussion. It will of course depend on the subject and the group, but if you have a good argument to put with sound evidence, it can come at a very persuasive moment just as everyone else is drying up.
- It is also wise to talk a number of times, rather than try to say all you have on your mind at one time. Speak only to the point at hand, and do not fall into the pitfall of becoming a 'chain' talker, whose one thought leads to another and who does not know when to stop. Remarks of about 1 minute in length are usually sufficient at one time, or perhaps up to 2 minutes at most.
- You may find that several people want to speak as soon as the present speaker has finished, so you must come in with split-second timing. The slow and less alert members may want to say something but find themselves going all the way through a meeting saying nothing because they don't maintain constant alertness.

Of course, this does not mean that the group does not need attentive listeners. An animated, alert listener contributes a great deal. But listening alone will keep within you valuable information or opinion that should be offered so that the group can consider your contributions.

9.4 Duties of officers and members

Table 9.1 provides a useful reminder of the essential duties of the officers and members of meetings.

Table 9.1 Duties of officers and members.

Before meeting	During meeting	After meeting
Chairperson		
1 Establish and understand the items of business to be transacted	1 Start on time	1 Verify draft copy of minutes prepared by secretary or minute writer
2 Agree a draft agenda	2 Introduce topics clearly	
3 Ensure members are notified of time, place, purpose of meeting and issue agenda if possible	3 Obtain valid contributions	
	4 Maintain order	2 Monitor progress
	5 Get decisions effectively	
4 Ensure the room is properly arranged – seating arrangements, papers, water, etc.		
Secretary or minute writer	1 Attend before time	1 Draft minutes
1 Obtain the material from previous minutes or new sources	2 Get the room ready	2 Agree with chairperson
2 Draft agenda to a logical order of priorities	3 Have all necessary papers available	3 Distribute to members within 2 days of meeting
3 Agree with chairperson	4 Take note of the proceedings	4 Issue instructions arising from minutes and monitor if necessary
4 Circulate notice of meeting and agenda	5 Do not allow unclear discussion and decisions to pass	
	6 Assist the chairperson	
Members		
1 Notify secretary/chairperson of items for agenda	1 Attend on time	1 Read and verify minutes
2 Read all papers	2 Make disciplined contributions	2 Carry out any action required and if necessary report back
3 Prepare, if appropriate, own supporting papers		
4 Clear any points of correction with secretary	3 Take note of decisions made and action required	

Note. If there is no appointed secretary, the chairperson is responsible for ensuring that the secretary's duties are performed by someone, if not them.

9.5 The agenda

An agenda for a meeting should indicate the order in which items of business will be discussed. When appropriate, these items may have been obtained from contributors. Some care should be taken to ensure consideration of items in the most logical order. Another feature of agenda planning is the ability to appreciate what can be achieved in a given period of time. As a general rule, very routine items are placed at the beginning of an agenda followed by business arising from the last meeting. This information is then succeeded by new items requiring consideration. Where there are several fairly brief and/or urgent items on the agenda, attend to those first, allowing the rest of the meeting to be concentrated on more time-consuming matters. Remember the warnings in Section 8.3 about mixing different kinds of task on one agenda.

It is a mistake to compress major items from the previous meeting under the heading of 'matters arising'. These are far better placed under individual headings, but high on the agenda. This provides the chair and participants with a more realistic idea of the work that has to be done.

Don't be tempted to overload the agenda. This inevitably leads to over-running time, which in turn leads to inefficiency (hastily agreed decisions, for example) because members quite reasonably want to get away.

Order of agenda

We can now look at a comprehensive list of the most usual order of items at a formal meeting, but obviously not all these items will always appear.

Check-Points: Order of Items on the Agenda

1 Election of chairperson and officers (as necessary)
2 Notice of meeting – read by secretary (usually only at a very formal meeting)
3 Minutes of previous meeting – taken as read (or read by secretary) and then signed by chairperson
4 Matters arising from minutes
5 Correspondence received – read by secretary
6 Chair's opening remarks
7 Matters adjourned from previous meeting (if any)
8 Financial matters (treasurer's report, circulation of accounts, etc.)
9 Reports by committees and working parties
10 Motions showing wording where possible and names of proposer and seconder
11 Any further items of business previously notified and listed on the agenda
12 Date of next meeting
13 Any other business (sometimes referred to as AOB; only minor points should be permitted – significant items should have been previously notified and should therefore be held over to the next meeting)
14 Vote of thanks to the chairperson (not usually proposed at regularly held meetings)
15 Reply by chairperson (see above)
16 Meeting declared closed by chairperson.

Assignment: List the agenda items that are normally necessary at a work-group meeting.

Agenda preparation and supporting documents

Each item on the agenda should be numbered. If for any reason the sequence of items then needs to be altered, the chairperson should give the reasons clearly at the start of the meeting. This is important because members interested in other items may feel aggrieved if their business is deferred or even postponed.

When an item is continued from a previous meeting it is helpful to quote the minute number and date of the meeting. Cross-referencing is useful because it allows the history of an item to be traced and thus may prevent wrong decisions being made. This method is also helpful to new members who do not know what has gone before.

Another useful practice is to make a reference to essential supporting papers, either against the relevant item of business, or in the form of a short checklist at the end of the agenda.

In preparing for a meeting, you may want to remember that questions stimulate a greater variety of responses than do plain statements. This is particularly true if care is taken to structure questions in an open and unbiased manner. Your agenda, then, could consist of a carefully thought out series of questions.

Finally, the agenda should provide a reminder to fix the date, time and place of the next meeting. If a meeting is likely to be recurrent, it is helpful if a calendar can be agreed on.

Assignment: Produce a checklist for planning an agenda which you could use to remind you of the important things to cover and in the order you would do them, if you had to produce an agenda for any meeting.

Check-Points: Steps in Agenda Planning

1 Establish what is outstanding from previous meeting.
2 Identify new items of business through anticipating current developments and contacting meeting participants.
3 Select significant items.
4 Avoid overloading 'matters arising' (show significant items separately, high on the agenda).
5 Place routine items early on the agenda.
6 Arrange significant items in logical sequence (see Order of agenda in Section 9.5).
7 Relate these items to time available and people attending.
8 Number items consecutively.
9 Cross-reference items from previous meetings.
10 Ensure details of next meeting are asked for by placing 'date of next meeting' at the end of the agenda.
11 Specify what additional papers are required or included with agenda.
12 Discuss and agree agenda with chairperson (if appropriate).
13 Submit draft agenda for typing or, more likely, type it yourself.
14 Proof-read typed agenda.
15 Link to minutes of previous meeting and send both documents and any relevant papers to all those who should attend the meeting.

9.6 The minutes

Minutes of a Board Meeting held at the Registered Office of
REES AND GREENWOOD LIMITED
on Wednesday 10 December 2003 at 10.30 a.m.

Present: Mr Ashley (in the Chair) Ms. S. R. Gilroy
            Mrs B. Coultate   Mr N. W. Langham
            Mr T. A. Thorne   Mr R. G. Sheddon (Secretary)

Apologies for absence were received from Mr P. Green and Miss S. Shelton

162 **Minutes of the last meeting**
     Minutes of the meeting held on 13 August 2003 were taken as read, and signed by
     the Chairman.

163 **Matters arising from the minutes**
     163.1 **Minute 159.2**
            Mr Thorne reported that all supervisors had been issued with leaflets outlining the
            details of the Employees' Share Option Scheme.
            They had been asked to ensure that all employees receive a leaflet, and to explain the
            scheme to all members of their section. This should be completed by 15 January as
            requested by the Board.
     163.2 **Minute 160**
            Mr Sheddon reported that all the necessary alterations had been made to the Pension
            Scheme and that each employee would be seen personally by the Personnel Department.
            These interviews were scheduled to start on 16 January 2004.

164 **Reaction to the employee share option scheme**
     164.1 *Noted* that the only real opposition received had been submitted by employees absent
            from work during the week that the consultative meetings had been held.
     164.2 *Resolved* that these employees should be seen personally by their Department
            Managers, if this had not already been done.

165 **Staff restaurant alterations**
     165.1 *Noted* that the building work on the restaurant and snack bar would begin on 31 January
            and was expected to be completed by the middle of February.
            Resolved that both restaurants should be redecorated, in view of the architect's report.
            Redecoration would begin immediately the building work was completed.

166 **Flexitime**
     166.1 Ms Gilroy reported that flexitime terminal sites had been identified including one for
            the director's floor.
     166.2 *Resolved* that the new system should be rented rather than bought. P. C. Flexitime
            would be operating the system.

167 **Press cover**
     167.1 *Resolved* that the Public Relations Officer should draft a press release about the changes
            in time for the next Board meeting. The decision about the date of the press release
            would be considered at that meeting.

     167.2 *Resolved* that should the press wish to, they should be invited to interview any
            employee, who was agreeable, on the subject of the Employees' Share Option Scheme
            once the press release had been issued.

168 **Date of next meeting**
     The date of the next meeting of the board of directors would be Wednesday 15 January 2004. In
     the absence of any other business, the meeting closed at 11.45 a.m.

Signed
S. Ashley
Managing Director 15 January 2004.

Figure 9.1 **An example of formal minutes.**

Any meeting which makes decisions should certainly record how the decision came about, what final decision was reached and who is responsible for any action. But most meetings, whatever their purpose, benefit from recording the nature of their business. Minutes provide a useful reference on the history of a committee's business, reducing the possibility of disagreement over what exactly was discussed and decided, when and by whom. For this reason properly constituted meetings and legally based organisations are required to keep minutes.

Normally, taking minutes is the responsibility of the secretary, but whether or not you are ever prepared to take on this role officially, it is always possible that it will fall to you to record the minutes of a meeting, in the absence of anyone else either authorised or willing to do so.

Minute writing is not an easy task but there are some basic *do's and don'ts* which, if you can bear them in mind, will make the task much easier.

Check-Points: Producing Minutes

Before the meeting
1 Seek guidance and instruction on how to do the job; check with the chairperson if there is a particular house style, but anyway, familiarise yourself with the basic pattern of minutes (see the example in Figure 9.1).

During the meeting
2 Record the date, time and place of the meeting.
3 Record who has attended and from whom *apologies for absence* have been received.
4 Identify topics of discussion; if suitable, using the agenda as your guide.
5 Follow the convention of dealing with routine items first – minutes of the last meeting read and signed, matters arising from the minutes, correspondence received.
6 Plan your minute-taking on the basis of a short title which summarises the topic, a **brief** summary of the discussion, decision taken and action required, by when and by whom.
7 Give each minute a consecutive reference number.
8 Keep up with the thinking of the meeting.
9 Clear up outstanding or ambiguous points before it is too late.
10 Write in note-fashion, and unless required avoid verbatim recording.
11 Use short, clear sentences and paragraphs.

After the meeting
12 Draft the minutes clearly **immediately** after the meeting.
13 Check them through with another person – preferably the chairperson.
14 Type them using clear layout within two days of the meeting.
15 Proof-read the typed minutes **very carefully**.
16 Send the minutes to all who were or should have been at the meeting and to anyone else who needs to know what took place; send edited versions if necessary.
17 File the minutes carefully: organisations may have 'rules' about filing minutes which you should know and stick to.
18 Check that any action is monitored and followed-up.

Do not

- try to chair the meeting **and** take minutes; appoint someone else to take the minutes
- allow the pace of discussion to overtake you and so prevent accurate note-taking
- allow your own personal bias or point of view to creep into your interpretation of what has been said
- insert too many names of people into the minutes
- include unexplained abbreviations and jargon unfamiliar to potential readers
- delay the drafting of the minutes – you won't remember what took place
- be over-influenced by the status of members; just because your boss is there doesn't mean you have to record diligently every word they utter
- forget to ensure that the date, time and place of the next meeting is agreed.

Assignment: Volunteer to act as secretary next time you get the chance. Or, arrange a meeting and carry out the necessary tasks.

Exercise 9.2

Which of the following statements are true, and which are false?

1 Autocratic leadership is a type of leadership in which the leader plays a 'permissive' role sharing the functions of leadership with members of the group by encouraging their participation in goal setting, and in planning and directing the activities of the group.
2 Participation involves a willingness to assume some leadership functions and a willingness to contribute your comments spontaneously.
3 Items of business requiring very little discussion should be placed last on the agenda, in case time runs out and there is no chance to discuss everything.
4 Solutions to a problem should be invited immediately the chairperson has introduced the subject for discussion.
5 In knowing how to participate at meetings, your best advice is to follow the basic principles of effective communication.

Assignment

1 Attend a local council meeting, or a staff meeting, or some other meeting of a small group and observe what happens.
   Who are the high participators? Do they include the leader? Who are the low participators? Does participation change during the meeting?
   Which members are high in influence? (i.e. when they talk, others seem to listen attentively.) Which members are low in influence? (Others do not listen to or follow them.) Does the influence-pattern change during the meeting?

Is there any rivalry, competition, conflict in the group? How is it dealt with? Is there a struggle for leadership? Is there a willingness on everyone's part to share leadership functions?

Are the task functions and maintenance functions shared by all? Or do some concentrate on the task and others on the group?

Characterise each member of the group as predominantly self-oriented, group-oriented or task-oriented.

What were the major successes of the meeting? Failures? What factors seemed to account for these?

2 Examine carefully the cynical statements about committees and meetings at the beginning of Chapter 8. Suggest the breakdown or problem which probably prompted each of those statements.

9.7 Videoconferencing and audioconferencing

Nowadays it is possible to hold a meeting without the expense of time and travel that bringing people together would entail. *Videoconferencing* consists of a video link between two or more studios in separate locations. It is usually used to run a meeting of people from different locations without having to bring them together in one place. Many organisations run their own studios, and it is also possible to do videoconferencing from your computer as long as you have a fast connection like broadband and the right software, which can easily be downloaded.

Advantages

- *Cost* – An hour of videoconferencing in a rented studio will cost ten or twenty times less than calling a meeting of people from different locations.
- *Immediacy* – Meetings can be set up at comparatively short notice.
- *Realism* – Some people prefer it to audioconferencing because you can see people's expressions and body language.

Disadvantages

- *Atmosphere* – Other people think that much of the ability to 'sense' what others are conveying through body language and so on: is lost.
- *Contacts* – There is no scope for informal chat before and after the meeting, or to negotiate off-line.
- *Seriality* – In practice, meetings are more stilted because each participant has to take their turn to speak, allowing time for the camera to focus in.

In fact, *audioconferencing*, in which people anywhere in the country (even overseas) are simply connected by phone to one another, is often almost as effective. It costs substantially less, because the amount of data being transmitted is much smaller than for video, and is available to all organisations very easily.

There are several ways to organise an audioconference. If there are just three people participating, you can set up the meeting by using the Three-Way Calling option offered by BT's Network Services. Another way is to use BT's Conference Call bureau. Here, you leave it to the operator to make all the arrangements. Finally, you may be able to use your own company phone system, if it has the right facilities.

Multi-person conversations can be tiring, so don't try to cover too many issues or go on for too long. Because they are easy to set up and don't involve travelling, you can always have, for example, four short meetings once a week rather than one long meeting each month.

Check-Points: How to Hold a Successful Audioconference

Tips for the chairperson
- Fax or e-mail an agenda to everyone in advance, detailing the topics to be covered and who's in on the meeting.
- Also send ahead any documents or drawings that might need to be consulted; keep a note of everyone's fax number or e-mail address so that you can send additional materials during the meeting, if necessary.
- Hold a roll-call as soon as everyone is on line and announce any extra arrivals or departures as they occur.
- Always address participants by name to make sure your remarks are picked up by the right people.
- Sum up regularly to ensure that everyone remains in step.
- Keep track of who's been silent and draw them into the conversation.

Tips for all participants
- Don't talk at the same time as someone else; pause for a second or two before speaking to make sure the other person has really finished.
- When you're asking a question, make it clear whom you are talking to.
- If someone asks a question, always reply, even if you don't have an immediate answer.
- Don't hold side meetings with other people in the same room as you without telling the chairperson and switching on the mute or secrecy button on your phone.

9.8   Formal procedure

In very large meetings, over about 20 members, it is often customary to adopt a fairly formal method of dealing with the items on the agenda and controlling the conduct of the meeting. This formal procedure, sometimes called parliamentary procedure, is intended to help maintain a degree of order in what might otherwise be an unruly, unmanageable shouting match. However, as you will realise, any restriction on the interaction of participants is bound to affect the quality of discussion and decision-making. It is therefore advisable to keep the degree of formality to the minimum compatible with conducting the business.

However, many bodies are required by law to conduct their meetings according to established conventions, and these are usually indicated in the 'rules of the association', and are referred to as 'standing orders'. Even if you do not agree that meetings should be run on very rigid lines, it is nevertheless advisable to be familiar with this formal procedure or you may feel inhibited from speaking at all at such a meeting, purely because you don't 'know the ropes'. The danger of this is that the few people who seem to make a hobby of learning and then pompously adhering to these standing orders are able to take advantage of everyone else's ignorance.

Another danger of being rather ignorant of the formal conventions and procedures is that 'a little learning is a dangerous thing' in that it is possible for the formal procedure to end up confusing the issue rather than facilitating the discussion.

There is not space enough to deal with all the details of formal procedure in this book and anyway the subject has been eminently well covered in various books on the law and procedures of meetings. However, I would warmly recommend a book by Lord Citrine called *The ABC of Chairmanship* (Fabian, 1995). Although it was originally published as long ago as 1939, it is regarded by many people as well as me as the 'bible' on the subject. Despite being an extremely comprehensive reference to almost everything you are ever likely to want to know, and despite the author's considerable experience and reputation in the field, Lord Citrine has managed to explain the potentially dry principles and procedure in a lively and very readable style supported by plenty of realistic and practical advice.

However, to whet your appetite, I shall end this chapter with an amusing example of what can result when formal procedure is used in a rather half-hearted way in a meeting, by people who are not too clear about the meaning and implications of some of the terminology, nor about quite how to manage a meeting.

Assignment: Read through the extract below from *The Ragged Trousered Philanthropists* and try to define the terms which are in italics. You could then use these as a basis for your first dip into *The ABC of Chairmanship* to check your answers.

The Ragged Trousered Philanthropists, by Robert Tressall, (Flamingo Modern Classics, 1991) is a very readable novel about the 'reality of the subjection and destitution of working class life in the good old days of the Edwardian age – an age when everyone knew his place and because of it was supposed to be content'. It revolves around the lives and experiences of a group of housepainters, and the inspiration of a newcomer to arouse them from their acceptance of their lot.

This extract describes the events of 'The Beano Meeting' – a meeting called to decide if, when and where the annual outing – the Beano – should take place.

The Beano
1 It was just about this time that Crass, after due consultation with several of the others, decided to call a meeting of the hands for the purpose of considering the advisability of holding the usual beano later on in the summer. The meeting was held in the carpenter's shop down at the yard one evening at six o'clock, which allowed time for those interested to attend after leaving work.
2 When all those who were expected to turn up had arrived, Payne, the foreman carpenter – the man who made the coffins – was *voted to the chair on the proposition of Crass, seconded by Philpot*, and then a solemn silence ensued, which was broken at last by the chairman, who, in a lengthy speech, explained the object of the meeting. Possibly, with a laudable desire that there should be

no mistake about it, he took the trouble to explain several times, going over the same ground and repeating the same words over and over again, whilst the audience waited in a miserable and deathlike silence for him to leave off, for he continued, like a man in a trance, to repeat what he had said before, seeming to be under the impression that he had to make a separate explanation to each individual member of the audience. At last the crowd could stand it no longer, and began to shout 'Hear, hear!' and to bang bits of wood and hammers on the floor and the benches; and then, after a final repetition of the statement that the object of the meeting was to consider the advisability of holding an outing, or beanfeast, the chairman collapsed on to the carpenter's stool and wiped the sweat from his forehead.

3 Crass then reminded the meeting that the last year's beano had been an unqualified success, and for his part he would be very sorry if they did not have one this year. Last year they had four brakes, and they went to Tubberton Village. It was true that there was nothing much to see at Tubberton, but there was one thing they could rely on getting there that they could not be sure of getting for the same money anywhere else, and that was – a good feed. (Applause.) Just for the sake of getting on with the business, *he would propose* that they decide to go to Tubberton, and that a committee be appointed to make arrangements – about the dinner – with the landlord of the 'Queen Elizabeth's Head' at that place.

4 Philpot *seconded the motion* and Payne was about to *call for a show of hands* when Harlow *rose to a point of order*. It appeared to him they were getting on a bit too fast. The proper way to do this business was first to *take the feeling of the meeting* as to whether they wished to have a beano at all, and then, if the meeting was in favour of it, they could decide where to go, and whether they would have a whole day or only half a day.

5 The semi-drunk said that he didn't care a dreadful expression where they went: he was willing to abide by the *decision of the majority*. (Applause.)

6 Easton suggested that a special saloon carriage might be engaged, and they could go and visit Madam Tussaud's waxwork. He had never been to that place and had often wished to see it. But Philpot objected that if they went there, Madam Tussaud's might not be willing to let them out again.

7 The chairman then began rambling on again at considerable length. Having thus made another start, Payne found it very difficult to leave off, and was proceeding to relate further details of the last beano when Harlow again rose up from his heap of shavings and said he wished to *call the chairman to order*. (Hear, hear!) What was the use of all this discussion before they had even decided to have a beano at all! Was the meeting in favour of a beano or not? That was the question?

8 A prolonged and awkward silence follows. Everybody was very uncomfortable, looking stolidly on the ground or staring straight in front of them.

9 At last Easton broke the silence by suggesting that it would not be a bad plan if someone was to *make a motion* that a beano be held. This was greeted with a general murmur of 'Hear hear' followed by another awkward pause, and then the chairman asked Easton if he would *move a resolution* to that effect.

After some hesitation, Easton agreed, and *formally moved*. 'That this meeting is in favour of a beano.'

10 The semi-drunk said that, in order to get on with the business, he would *second the resolution*. But meantime, several arguments had broken out between the advocates of different places, and several men began to relate anecdotes of previous beanos. Nearly everyone was speaking at once, and it was some time before the chairman was able to *put the resolution*. Finding it impossible to make his voice heard above the uproar, he began to hammer on the bench with a wooden mallet. Some of them looked at him curiously and wondered what was the matter with him, but the majority were so interested in their arguments that they did not notice him at all.

11 Whilst the chairman was trying to get the attention of the meeting in order to *put the question*, Bundy had become involved in an argument with several of the new hands who claimed to know of an even better place than the 'Queen Elizabeth', the 'New Found Out'. He went there last year with Pushem and Driver's crowd, and they had roast beef, goose, jam tarts, mince pies, sardines, blancmange, calves' foot jelly, and one pint for each man was included in the cost of the dinner. In the middle of the discussion they noticed that most of the others were holding up their hands, so to show there was no ill-feeling they held up theirs also and then the chairman declared it was *carried unanimously*.

12 Bundy said he would like to ask the chairman to read out the resolution which had just been passed, as he had not caught the words.

13 The chairman replied that there was no *written resolution*. The motion was just to express the feeling of this meeting as to whether or not there was to be an outing or not.

14 Bundy said he was only asking a civil question, *a point of information*: all he wanted to know was, what were the terms of the resolution? Were they in favour of the beano or not?

15 The chairman responded that the meeting was unanimously in favour. (Applause.)

16 Harlow said that the next thing to be done was to decide upon the date. Crass suggested the last Saturday in August. That would give them plenty of time to pay in.

17 Sawkins asked whether it was proposed to have a day or only half a day. He himself was in favour of the whole day. It would only mean losing a morning's work. It was hardly worth going at all if they only had half a day.

18 Harlow proposed that they decide to go to the 'Queen Elizabeth' the same as last year, and that they have half a day.

19 Philpot said that, in order to get on with the business, he would *second the resolution*.

20 Bundy suggested – as *an amendment* – that it should be a whole day, starting from the 'Cricketers' at nine in the morning, and Sawkins said that, in order to get on with the business, he would *second the amendment*.

21 One of the new hands said he wished to move another amendment. He proposed to strike out the 'Queen Elizabeth' and substitute the 'Three Loggerheads'.

(For three more pages of the novel from which this extract is taken, the meeting rambles on through various motions, amendments, counter-amendments, heated arguments, quarrels, jeers and cheers, until they eventually agree to the original motion that they go to the 'Queen Elizabeth's Head'.)

Assignment

1 Write the notice and agenda for the Beano meeting, which Crass might have distributed before the meeting took place.
2 Write a brief set of minutes of this part of the Beano meeting.
3 Check Lord Citrine's definitions and explanations of the terms given below in 6 a–e and then find out what a quorum is, and what 'putting the question' and 'the previous question' mean.

Exercise 9.3

1 What do you deduce from paragraph 1 of *The Beano* about the principles governing where and when a meeting should take place?
2 What mistakes did Payne make in carrying out his role as chairman?
3 In paragraph 3, Crass makes a proposal. What was his reason for doing so? Is the reason justified?
4 Crass and his colleagues were obviously not sure about the difference between a proposition, a motion and a resolution. What is the difference?
5 What are the accepted rules for speaking at a formal meeting?
6 There seemed to be a fair amount of confused uttering of meeting terminology. Did the members understand the terms they were using? Do you know what the following terms mean?

   (a) a point of order
   (b) call the chair to order
   (c) a point of information
   (d) rule the point out of order
   (e) an amendment

7 Which points should the chairperson be aware of in conducting a vote?

Further reading

Barker, Alan, *How to Manage Meetings*, Kogan Page, 2002
Hayes, Manon, E., *Make Every Minute Count*, Kogan Page, 2000

☑ 10 Giving a talk

A captive audience

Claire had worked for the personnel department of Hossack Construction plc for three years and during this time she had learned a lot and was gradually being given more responsibility. The company had expanded recently and had won several large contracts. Each new contract involved recruiting hundreds of construction workers. The personnel department was beginning to feel the strain of taking on all these people.

Little by little, Claire realised that her responsibilities were changing. She was being asked to speak on company induction and training courses. She had never minded talking to people on a one-to-one basis, but when faced with large groups, she became terribly nervous, her stomach churned, her mouth went dry and her voice either dwindled to an inaudible murmur, or became shrill and breathless ... and she forgot what she had intended to say. She had always hated this sort of thing, even at school, and had managed to avoid reading or reciting in class.

Eventually, she decided she couldn't cope with the job any more. Fortunately she was able to find another position with another company as a personnel clerk but at a salary level considerably below what she had received at Hossack. In two minds whether to take the new job, she had decided to keep looking for a while, when her boss called her into her office.

'Good news, Claire, we've just won the Glenfrome contract but we've got to get 200 extra people within the month. The personnel director has decided to try regional TV and local radio in the north-east to see if we can attract enough people that way. Second piece of good news – we'd like you to be the one to make the radio and television announcements.'

Claire went back to her office and wrote two letters – one resigning from Hossack and the other accepting the new job.

Feeling the way she did, did she take the right action? Is it fair to ask people who may be very good at their job in other ways to take on the responsibility of talking to large groups?

It is true that unless you become a politician, an actor, a teacher, a television personality, or similar public figure, you may not be called upon to talk formally very often during your working life, especially early on. However, perhaps because we are living in an era when oral and visual communication are very common, many people prefer listening to messages rather than reading them; and because organisations realise the advantages of face-to-face communication, the number of occasions when you might be called upon to talk to a reasonably large group of people is increasing. For these reasons it may be difficult to avoid this task without jeopardising your reputation and the chances of promotion.

This chapter should help you tackle the task with more confidence – confidence born of knowing what you are going to do, when you are going to do it and how you are going to do it. It will provide you with practical suggestions on how to

- approach different kinds of talk
- open and close the talk
- design good-looking visual aids even if you aren't a graphic artist, and
- organise your 'stage' on the day so that you feel as confident as possible to meet an audience, who, after all is said and done, want you to succeed.

Knowledge may be useless unless it is communicated to others. In the case above, Claire clearly knew her company's business, especially her responsibilities in the personnel department. She could communicate this to her supervisor and to others in very small groups. But she became nervous and hesitant when talking to larger groups. The thought of going on television and radio with an audience of thousands looking at her and listening to her terrified her, so she left her job – a job with responsibilities, variety, a good salary and probably the chances of promotion.

What she obviously did not realise is that it is quite normal to be nervous before talking to large groups. Famous politicians, whose job consists largely of speaking in public, have confessed to feeling literally sick with nerves before making a speech. Lloyd George (Prime Minister during the First World War), who is still considered by many to have been the best orator and debater this country has seen, was said to have been like a cat on hot bricks before he had to speak in the House of Commons.

Perhaps, if Claire had talked to her boss about her fears, she might well have discovered that she had performed much better on those occasions when she had had to do it than she realised. We are often far more critical of our performance than others are. Perhaps because we know how we feel inside – and they don't.

Her boss might also have suggested that she attend a training course to help her gain the necessary confidence. Few people are born speakers. It is an acquired skill, and everyone is able to acquire it to some degree. Claire didn't give herself a chance – the chance to discover that skill and confidence come from two things: hard work and practice.

Even if your job does not involve talking to large groups of people, the day may come sooner than you think when you will have to. How well you can do this will affect your job success.

10.1 Techniques of public speaking

All the great speakers were bad speakers once.
(Emerson, The Conduct of Life, 1993)

So how do you go about the hard work and practice? Let's deal with the practice first.

It is true that no amount of reading and learning techniques from a book will turn you into a competent, confident speaker. Radio recordings spanning the long careers of famous speakers reveal that the practice gained over the years perfected their art. Early recordings of Lloyd George have none of the power and oratory that he later developed and in the early days Aneurin Bevan (who created the National Health Service in 1946) was greatly hampered by a stammer. But although he never mastered this completely (which perhaps proved that even difficulties like this do not prevent someone from being a successful public speaker), over the years Aneurin Bevan developed an enviably wide command of language which allowed him to avoid almost completely the words which he couldn't pronounce fluently.

Similarly, videos spanning Margaret Thatcher's career from selection as MP to Prime Minister and finally ex-Prime Minister reveal just how much coaching changed her appearance, her voice and her delivery. However, Tony Blair was as good when he was shadow spokesman for trade as he later was as Prime Minister.

Although political speaking is perhaps a very specialised form of public speaking and you may feel that it is irrelevant to the demands which speaking for business or social purposes may make of you, we can learn a lot and gain confidence from appreciating the effect of carefully mastered techniques and the rewards to be gained from practice.

'But how can I get practice?' you may say. Think back over your life. There are almost bound to have been occasions when you asked someone else to give a vote of thanks, or just 'stand up and say something!' when the occasion seemed to demand it? Have there been occasions when perhaps someone else has tentatively asked if you would say a few words to open a meeting perhaps, or thank a visiting speaker and you have hastily declined saying, 'No! I'm really no good at that sort of thing. Ask so-and-so. They've got the gift of the gab.' Have you sat through a public meeting on something you felt strongly about, dying to put your point of view, but resisting the urge to get to your feet? Well, these are the occasions which can provide you with practice. From now on, take every opportunity to get to 'say a few words'. Not only will you gain in confidence, but you will also find out what are your own particular strengths and weaknesses, and like Aneurin Bevan learn to exploit your strengths and avoid your weaknesses.

However, there are techniques which we can also learn from experienced speakers – and the most essential of these, as with every other form of communication transmission, is *preparation*.

Lloyd George prepared his speeches very thoroughly with the help of *Roget's Thesaurus* and often wrote them out beforehand and learned them by heart. But all the work that went into his speeches paid dividends. He was renowned as a brilliant phrase-maker. He once described the people of Monmouthshire as 'suffering from morbid footballism'. The House of Lords was simply '500 men chosen accidentally from the unemployed'. To that skill with the language it is true he added a dramatic talent and the voice to demand attention for the product of all that hard work. Many great speakers have the essential talent of making speeches sound informal. It seems as though they are thinking on their feet, but the work has been done long before they reach the platform.

Your platform may not be the House of Commons or the political rally, but you would do well to learn from these speakers the need for thorough preparation until your talk is so polished that you can deliver it with the enthusiasm and vitality that suggests it is impromptu.

10.2 Preparation

First questions

Yes, as with any other communication, it's back to Why? Who? What? When? Where? and How? Let's look at how they might apply to giving a talk, speech or presentation. When you are first asked to give the talk there should automatically be some questions to which you should seek an answer, then and there:

- *When* will it take place? Be sure you have adequate preparation time – for both written material and visual aids.
- *How long* are you to speak for? Is the time adequate for your subject? Remember that, contrary to what may seem the case, the less time you have to speak, the more carefully planned your talk must be.

> As one speaker said:
> If you want me to speak for five minutes – I need two weeks to prepare.
> If you want me to speak for an hour – I need a week to prepare.
> If you don't mind how long I speak, I'll get up and do it now.

- *Where* is it to take place? In surroundings familiar to your audience? Familiar to you? If not, try to visit the venue before you speak and in any case check beforehand the type and size of the room, tiered seating or flat floor, acoustics, lighting, equipment available (data projector, overhead projector, whiteboard) and so on. Don't be frightened to ask if particular arrangements are possible.
- *Who* are to be present? Number, age and type of people, male or female, intellectual level, their current knowledge of the subject, their reasons for attending and their attitudes (possible objections to what you have to say, for example). These will, of course, influence the ideas and the language you use.
- *Why me?* What special knowledge or position have you? What will the audience expect from you? This is not the moment to be falsely modest, but honestly realistic. If you have been asked to speak as a newcomer to the organisation, perhaps

to give your impressions or reactions to something, then no one will expect you to behave like a managing director with 30 years' experience.

- *How?* Are you expected to give a formal speech or lecture, or an introductory talk to provoke discussion? Will there be a question session? If there is to be a discussion or question session, you might like to leave some things unsaid so that you leave your audience with some questions to ask and yourself with something fresh to say in answer to them.

Adjust to circumstances

Of course, you may have control over some of these points, or you may be the one who has suggested the occasion, in which case you can regard it like a performance with you as the producer, able to determine the most suitable room, the ideal size of audience, whether there will be questions or not and so on.

But in either case there is likely to be a conflict between the *desired* circumstances and the *given* circumstances, since they usually don't match. In this case, some modification or compromise is necessary.

For example, you decide that the audience should be fairly small – perhaps a maximum of 20 people – because a high level of interaction between you and members of the audience is essential if you are to achieve your goal. But your boss, or perhaps someone else of high status even though unconnected directly with the proceedings, wants at least 60 to attend. Should you modify what you want to achieve, or offer to give the same talk three times? Supposing you want to keep the audience to 20. What arguments would you use in persuading your boss that this is the ideal number?

Take another example. You have decided that you need at least 40 minutes to do the job adequately but the organiser can allow you only 30 minutes. Will you modify your objective or convey parts of your subject matter by means of audio-visuals?

Assignment: Choose one of the subjects below. Imagine your audience and the circumstances in which you might be called upon to talk on that subject. Write down a description of the audience and the circumstances. Use this framework and your chosen subject to apply the suggestions which follow in this chapter.

- The place of humour in your life
- The advantages of foreign travel
- A speech to make on leaving your job
- On wanting to work
- Economic self-sufficiency
- The case for a shorter working week
- The freedom of the press.

Having adjusted to your circumstances you are now ready to consider the question 'why?' carefully.

- What do you plan to achieve with this particular group on this particular occasion? *Be as precise as you can.*
- What do you want to do to your audience?
- What do you want them to do/feel at the end?

Look at the following check-points showing how the purpose of your talk determines your approach to it.

Check-Points: What are You Trying to Do?

Purpose	Approach

To inform or describe

- Describing observations, background against which something happened, facts and details.

Know the audience's current level of knowledge; use appropriate language – if jargon is necessary and they are unfamiliar with it, you must explain the meaning of the words.

Use anecdotes, examples and illustrations to give life and colour. Use deductive, chronological or spatial order and carefully chosen words to describe things precisely.

Refer back to Section 1.7 for help with how to order your material.

To instruct or explain

- Explanations, directions, instruction.
- You are concerned with explaining **how** things work, **how** processes or procedures are carried out, **how** actions are performed, you may also want to include an explanation of **why** things are the way they are, **why** certain steps are taken in a process.

You should concentrate on **showing**, either by means of diagrams, pictures or demonstrations. In the last resort your words must be chosen to produce clear visual images that the audience can grasp.

Analogy can be helpful here. 'This process is rather like ...' (describing something they are all familiar with).

Usually deductive, chronological or spatial order is most suitable but if you are concentrating on **why** a procedure is necessary, or is the way it is, inductive order might be appropriate.

To persuade, convince or inspire

- Usually changing beliefs, attitudes or behaviour.
- Presenting a case, or an argument in favour or against.

Recognise how difficult a task this is: you must appeal to the heart and the head by quoting audience benefits and evidence to back up your arguments – statistics, authoritative opinion, experience of

---

others – but these must be accurate and relevant.

Avoid generalising and exaggerating, 'emotive' and 'coloured' language. If you base your arguments on assumptions, explain those assumptions.

Avoid, or at least admit, your prejudices. Give some reference to the other side of the story, or your case will be weakened.

Your structure must be **very** logical – and inductive order can be very persuasive (see Section 1.7, Stage 4 Putting the information into logical sequence).

Above all, (a) you must get the audience's attention, (b) find out what the audience's needs and interests are, (c) show how you can satisfy those needs, (d) ask for an appropriate reaction or approval.

To entertain or amuse
- Vote of thanks, 'after dinner'.

This kind of speaking is, more than any, an art to which some people seem born; however, since we all have to do it sometime, it is worth learning.

The general guidelines are: be brief; ration the humour (quotations, i.e. other people's humour, can be very useful here); relate your speech to the audience's interests and to the occasion – be personal and particular.

10.3 Developing the material

Start by breaking the main theme/objectives down into key ideas and work out how these might best be presented, illustrated and put together. This process can take place over quite a long period of time. It is a process of incubation when the ideas can be developed in your mind, in different ways and along different routes.

Stage 1 – think

You have selected your subject, now give the talk time to grow.

- Take time to gather and arrange your thoughts.
- Think about the talk at any convenient moment; a good time often presents itself when you are doing some other, usually manual job, like digging the garden, or decorating your flat, or perhaps travelling to work or college.

- Discuss the theme with colleagues and friends.
- Carry a note book or card, on which to note ideas as they occur to you.

Stage 2 – read

Read as much as time permits. Gather more material than you can possibly use, not only on the subject itself but also, for example, possible quotations. (*The Penguin Book of Quotations* and *The Penguin Book of Modern Quotations* are both very useful sources which can provide not only quotations but ideas for ways to tackle your theme.) Collect anecdotes and stories from newspapers and magazines. The Internet has made this process of research so much easier, but it has made it easier for everyone, so make sure you've checked things.

Stage 3 – construct your outline

As with any carefully presented message, it will require an *introduction* and a *conclusion*.

Check-Points: Outline of a Talk

- Introduction
- Presentation of one main point:
    illustrations
    reasons   } repeated as necessary
    dealing with objections.
- Conclusion (appeal for action?)

However you do it, it should be logical and systematic (look back at Section 1.7).

Even if you use the outlining facility on your computer at this stage to produce the basic outlines, you may still want to write each main point and its development on a card. You can then shuffle them around to get the best order, as with writing a report, but this method has the added advantage in speech-making that, once you are really familiar with what you are going to say, you may be able to use these cards and their headings as keyword notes during the delivery of your talk.

A famous piece of advice that has an element of truth in it is:

Look after the beginning and the end … and the middle will take care of itself.

Of course, the middle needs to be well structured if you are to achieve your goal, and another saying runs:

Men perish because they cannot join the beginning with the end.

But you need not worry so much about the actual words; whereas how to start and how to finish usually hold the most terrors for the beginner – justifiably so, perhaps, since a good speech can be made or marred by its opening and its close.

Assignment: Before we look at some suggested ways of coping with these essential parts of a talk, think back to talks, speeches and lectures you have listened to. If you can't remember any in sufficient detail, break off at this point and spend the week listening carefully to radio and television lectures and talks – the Open University programmes are a good source of material for this sort of observation, or you might go to a public lecture or meeting.

- What does the speaker say and do which makes the beginning and ending successful or unsuccessful for you/for the audience as a whole?
- Make a note of the opening and closing remarks and then analyse them in the light of comments that follow in this chapter.

10.4 Opening the talk

For three reasons, it is crucial to be absolutely sure in your own mind exactly what you are going to say and do in the first few minutes:

- You may have to follow a speaker who, through the attractiveness or strength of their personality or by reason of their subject, have achieved great acceptance by the audience; or you may have to follow some other activity which has been extremely entertaining, or the high-spot of the occasion.
- You may be the first or only speaker on that occasion and you have to cut the ice, so to speak: make the audience feel immediately that their attendance is worthwhile.
- You may, like most other people, feel far more nervous during the first few minutes.

For any of these reasons, you have to create an impression and gain the attention and interest of your audience at once and to do these things you need to know exactly what you're going to say.

Check-Points: Creating a Good Opening Impression

- Remember, your presentation is only complete once the talk begins. Arrange the 'stage' on which you are to perform. Take a little time before you start speaking to position your notes and visual aids so that you can use them comfortably. Make sure you have room to move between the table or lectern and the board or OHP, that your notes are high enough for you to see without continually dropping your head.
- Don't hesitate; start as soon as the audience is settled, but take a few seconds to survey the audience and let them take stock of you.
- Don't open with clichés or hackneyed expressions, for example 'it gives me great pleasure ...' You may want to thank your audience, or express pleasure in the occasion, but do this a little later, or even towards the end of your talk.

- Don't apologise. You may not feel that your knowledge, subject, ability or even presence is up to the occasion but the audience will be confident, if you start with the confidence that stems from being well prepared.
- The opening must be something original and interesting enough to make them want to hear what you have to say.
- Avoid too early a climax – interest will fall if the high standard of the opening cannot be sustained.
- Remember it is only an opening – an introduction. Don't make it too long. Keep it in proportion to the total length of the talk.

Check-Points: A Dozen Ways to Start

- **Statement of subject or title** – not very inspiring: they probably know your subject anyway.
- **Statement of your objective and the plan of your talk** – a good safe way to start if you have adopted a deductive sequence (see Section 1.7) but if you are trying to persuade, you don't want to give the game away too early. Even where it is appropriate to include the objective and structure of your talk in the introduction don't make this your opening remark – try one of the more interesting ideas which follow.
- **Informal** – for informal occasions.
  'Only a few days ago Tim (Brown) and I were discussing the problem of...', Tim (Brown) is on your side at once, and you have avoided giving the impression of 'making a speech'.
- **Question** – anticipate the sort of questions your audience might want answered in connection with your subject:
  'Are the days of a Great Britain finished for ever?' 'Must we sacrifice the essential quality of life if we are to take full advantage of the benefits that high technology can bestow?'
  The audience instinctively tries to arrive at the answer and you can go on to give yours.
- **Mind reading** – similar to the use of the question. Anticipate the audience's preconceived ideas; bring these into the open and correct them if necessary. 'If I were a member of the audience tonight, I might be expecting just another 'pep-talk' on safety at work. But this evening I have something more valuable to propose ...'.
- **Anecdote** – must be well told, relevant to the subject, brief and, if possible, personal (the willingness to laugh at yourself will usually win an audience).
- **Joke** – if your experience tells you that you can do this well, then it may be worth risking it. But people's sense of humour differs radically, and if the joke falls flat you are worse off than before. Again, it must be well told, relevant and brief.
- **Facts and statistics** – used sparingly they can get the audience to rise to the occasion. Most business or technical subjects offer many facts which will interest and inform your audience. Choose them carefully, make sure they

are accurate and keep them simple. Contrasting facts can be particularly interesting:

'Annually, during the 1970s, the average number of working days lost through strikes was 6 million, yet the average number lost through industrial accidents and sickness was 300 million.'

Don't be too specific – no audience can take in numbers like 6 454 100, without plenty of time and reinforcement from visual aids. Even then rounded figures and percentages are easier to grasp.

- **Quotation** – perhaps the easiest method to use and often most effective. The quotation should be from a well-known person or author known to the audience, and strictly relevant to your subject.
- **Shock** – not just the gimmicky opening, firing revolvers or letting off explosions, which can often go wrong and are always difficult to sustain. Shock can be created through the effective use of words:

'Training is a waste of time and money...'
pause to allow the shock to take effect, then:
'unless, of course, it is aimed at developing the team rather than the individual.'

- **Topical story** – as opposed to the humorous story. Everyone likes a story – but only if it is skilfully chosen and told. Ideally it should have an intriguing twist and must lead into the subject.

Choosing an opening to a talk will depend, of course, on your personality but be flexible and imaginative. Polish the opening until you have got it off to perfection and are sure what you are going to say and how it will flow into the main body of the talk.

Assignment: Now keeping your imagined audience and purpose firmly in mind, write out openings for your talk using each of the 12 suggestions above, if they are at all appropriate. Use your imagination and actually carry out any research that is required, for example for quotations, statistics and so on.

10.5 Closing the talk

Just as you need to attract the interest of your audience at the beginning of a talk, so you must finish on a high note. The effect of a speech which is otherwise good can be damaged by its close.

Check-Points: Pitfalls to Avoid

- Avoid 'wandering' towards the end. End on a high note which is relevant to all that has gone before.
- Don't make a 'second speech'. Even if you suddenly think of something else which is relevant don't be tempted. It is very easy, as the tension relaxes, to

start developing a new line of thought which was not developed in the body of the talk.

- Avoid repetition. In summing up the main points you have made, don't repeat details or labour over points again. If you have finished before your allotted finishing time – sit down. Don't pad it out.
- Don't give too many closing signals, for example, 'and finally', 'in conclusion, then', 'one other thing before I finish'. In fact, it is probably best to avoid a closing signal altogether. Your closing remarks should round off your talk, and therefore by implication your audience will know that your talk is complete.
- Avoid having to rely on your notes for your final remarks. Learn your closing words so that you can look at your audience as you reach your climax.

To avoid these pitfalls, you need to have a closing plan which is an integral part of the development of your whole speech. In this way you won't get lost at the end of your presentation. Here are several suggestions for rounding off your presentation.

Check-Points: 10 Ways to Stop

- **Summary** – a fairly standard way to finish but nevertheless effective. A brief review of the important points leaves no doubt in the minds of your audience.
- **Questions** – send the audience away to think of an answer.

  'This then is what we have to do. The question now is, how can we best achieve it?'

- **Quotations** – as with the opening, a quotation can indicate wide knowledge, and can therefore lend credibility to your performance. The quotation must be relevant and not just tacked on for its own sake.
- **Alternative** – offer a choice of alternatives, or different solutions. The one your want accepted should be obvious from the way you have constructed your presentation and you can give this one more weight than the others in your summary.
- **Dramatic** – if you carry it off by dramatic use of your voice, or dramatic content, this method can certainly end things on a high note.
- **Action** – you want action now, not later. So ask for it. Many of your audience will respond.
- **Incentive** – if you can suggest ways in which the audience can benefit, some sort of reward or incentive, they are even more likely to respond. An audience is less likely to forget your message if you offer a reason for taking action.
- **Fear** – use of fear to gain action is risky because it can alienate the audience. But since it is often difficult to provoke the audience to action, you may be justified in introducing an element of fear if the end result is worthwhile. 'You must act – now! Before it is too late!'
- **Conscience-pricking** – this can have the same effect as fear, but it is less risky. By appealing to their honesty, you may make your audience realise that they have been lazy, apathetic, too busy, or ostrich-like in the past, to do what they know they should do.

Whichever way seems appropriate, above all don't go on! Remember the old adage on effective public speaking:

Stand up, speak up, shut up

Assignment: Carry out the assignment on p. 147, only this time dealing with the close of the talk.

10.6 Visual aids

You do not have to be a graphic artist but it helps! At this stage you might like to look at Chapters 11 and 18 for more detailed guidance on the use of visual aids, but the following check-points should be borne in mind.

Check-Points: How Can Visuals Aid my Talk?

- Hand-outs and/or visual aids during the talk?
- Use pre-prepared visuals for: or after
  (a) complex interrelated ideas
  (b) persuasive communication
- Words alone are *not* visual aids – where you do use words make them provide visual impact by means of graphic devices:
  - underlining and boxes or circles
  - bullets and dashes (as in this example)
  - careful lay-out
  - use of space
- Don't use overcomplicated visual aids – everybody in the audience must understand every aid you use by the time you have finished with it.
- Visuals must complement what you say.
- You should have a visual for everything you want your audience to remember.
- Don't have a visual aid which you don't need – and, anyway, don't have too many.
- Make sure there are no spelling mistakes.
- You don't have to be a professional to produce good visuals.

Many computer packages make laying out OHP slides fairly easy, and colour printers are now cheaper than ever.

However, if you do not have access to a computer, you can still do a fairly professional job.

Check-Points: How to Make Effective Visual Aids

- OHP transparencies allow you to write using guidelines underneath and to trace shapes, cartoon figures, even letters.
- Don't write letters too small (they won't be seen) or too big (your hand will wobble).

- Use a stencil, or press on letters, if you can't write neatly.
- Achieve a good balanced layout. Above all, visuals should be pleasing to the eye.
- Use coloured felt-tip pens – but use bold colours not wishy-washy ones. Don't use too many colours on one visual, and let them reinforce the verbal message (e.g. red for danger, stop, debit, problem; green for go, credit, favourable).

Mark on the outline of your talk where you are going to use visual aids and which ones.

At this stage, if you are unsure of yourself, then it is probably advisable to write out your talk in full so that you can become really familiar with it, but write in spoken English not written English, and don't rely on using this script on the day.

10.7   Use of notes

Why use notes?

Even the best and most confident speakers use notes because:

- memories are faulty
- they guard against omissions
- they help to develop a complicated close-knit argument
- they prevent loss of sequence.

Written and read

Even if you have written out your talk you should not use it as a script on the day, because a 'written and read' speech, by any but the most experienced speakers, produces a normally dull and stilted speech which lacks vitality and prevents you looking at your audience.

Exceptions: If the speech is highly technical, liable to be quoted or concerned with policy matters, it should be typed and double-spaced and marked for stress and pauses.

Check-Point

Type or write most of your notes in lower case not capitals: lower case letters are easier to read.

Written and memorised

Many speakers learn to do it as though they are speaking impromptu but for the rest of us it has pitfalls – it produces the effect of a 'canned speech', and forgetfulness in a supposedly memorised speech spells disaster.

Summary headings or keyword notes

Cards or sheets (numbered or fastened with a tag) containing main points and key arguments and illustrations is the best method providing you are really familiar with your material.

Check-Point

If your nerves show through shaking hands, use cards rather than paper notes, and preferably place your notes on a lectern (or a pile of books if there is no lectern handy).

10.8 Practising the talk

Two activities can keep 'butterflies' within reasonable bounds:

- thorough preparation
- plenty of practice.

So practise the whole talk

- out loud
- in a similar-sized room
- using a tape recorder
- checking the timing.

Mark on your notes how much speaking time should have elapsed by the end of each key area in the talk.

Consider a 'dry run', with an audience of colleagues – if you can bear it, and if it is a very important occasion.

Remember that you may well feel more self-conscious and less relaxed because of the artificiality of a rehearsal.

10.9 Room and platform layout

Room

Examine it at leisure, when empty. Consider:

- *seating plan* – audience more responsive when close together; semi-circle better than a 'classroom' layout
- *windows* – balance need for fresh air with the need to avoid draughts! Check blackout arrangements
- *lighting* – know the position of the switches; avoid lights behind the speaker.

Visual aid apparatus

- *overhead projector* – plugged in; on/off switch; acetate pen; how to focus; spare bulb

- *whiteboard* – check pens (number and colours) and rubber/duster
- *data projector* – check that it really is working, and run through your slides really carefully.

Platform layout

- room to move (but not too far!)
- supply of clean, covered water and glass
- microphone?
- will you sit or stand?
- will you obscure the screen/board?

10.10   Delivery of the talk

Be yourself! And look at your audience! For every book on the 'do's and don'ts' of delivery techniques, there is a very successful speaker who breaks the rules. So if you are at the beginning of your career as a public speaker, you should concentrate on thorough preparation, the basic skills of speaking outlined at the beginning of this book and the four qualities listed below, but above all *maintain interest.*

You can break almost every rule in the book, but don't break this one. The audience will listen with interest if you have four essential qualities.

Summary – being a good speaker

Check-Points: Essential Qualities of a Speaker

- **Conviction/sincerity** – The audience wants facts (and they must be accurate) but more than that, they want to know your attitude towards those facts; they need to feel that you have a sincere belief in what you are saying and a sincere interest in them – the audience.
- **Enthusiasm** – Real conviction breeds enthusiasm: If you are listless and half-hearted, so will they be; if you are enthusiastic, they will catch your enthusiasm.
- **Power of speech** – Speak with controlled power. Be positive – avoid weak phrases like 'in my humble opinion', 'please bear with me', 'forgive me'.
- **Simplicity** – Speakers frequently do not recognise the complexity of the idea that they are expressing and falsely assume that it is clear to the audience. They are suffering from what is known as the 'COIK' fallacy – 'clear only if known'. We can make the unknown clearer by expressing it in terms of the known (familiar ideas and familiar language).

In fact these four qualities are the basic ingredients of all effective communication.

Further reading

Bradbury, Andrew, *Successful Presentation Skills*, Kogan Page, 2000

▼ 11 Using visual aids

A picture's worth a thousand words

Mark had been asked to give a five-minute talk on one of the company's products, to a group of new employees as part of their induction course. Aware that even a five-minute talk requires careful preparation, he had been hard at work, on and off all week, writing his notes and getting his material together and now he was as confident as you can be when you have to stand on your feet and keep the show going on your own, even for five minutes.

His subject was 'the nose-cone of a satellite' – well, I think it was, but then I can't really remember, because for the next five minutes we, the audience, worked extremely hard. In the space of the next five minutes, as well as talking at breakneck speed, he showed us eight overhead projector transparencies all beautifully drawn in minute detail (which we couldn't have seen from the back of the room, even if he had given us time to look at them); he also directed our attention to two wall posters, both of which looked, from where I was sitting, like aerial views of London taken from the moon; and while all this was going on he circulated six photographs which we were expected to pass round the room.

Any speaker faced with the task of giving a talk or presentation is nowadays spoilt for choice. They can select from an impressive array of imaginative and technologically sophisticated devices, as well as the more traditional methods for providing their audience with visual aids. It doesn't seem surprising then that many people like Mark, will go overboard trying to use as many of them as possible or, bewildered by possible methods which they don't really know how to use, will rely entirely on the spoken word, as if they don't even know the blackboard has been invented.

So what exactly is available? What are they each particularly suitable for? What are the advantages and disadvantages? And how can you best use them so that they 'aid' you as well as your audience? This chapter is intended to

- guide you through the 'hardware' of visual-aid methods currently available
- provide some tips on how to use them effectively, but above all

- point out what can go wrong, how to avoid the more obvious traps and what to do when things do go wrong.

Whether or not you have ever given a presentation, talk or lecture, you will no doubt have experienced different methods of visual aids and been aware of some of the problems. At the very least, you will inevitably have suffered at the hands of the teacher who spent the entire lesson scribbling furiously in illegible handwriting on the blackboard and only turned to face the audience as they left the room.

> **Assignment**: List as many different kinds of visual aid as you can think of, together with the problems for the speaker or the audience associated with the use of each one.

Obviously the number of aids available is enormous, and your list may well contain examples that I've missed. My list includes:

- whiteboards
- flip charts
- magnetic boards and other 'build-up' visuals
- physical objects
- models and experiments
- overhead projector
- data projector
- slide projector
- videos
- closed-circuit TV and video-tape.

We'll go on to look at these in more detail – but first some general principles.

11.1   General principles

The most important thing to remember is that visual aids should be just that: *visual* and *aids*:

- *visual*, in that they make use of the most effective channel of communication of all, the sense of sight, not just be providing the audience with something to look at, but wherever possible providing them with pictures rather than words to look at;
- *aids*, in that they should help, not hinder, the speaker in getting their message across, and help, not hinder, the audience in receiving and understanding the speaker's message.

All too often, audiences are subjected to a never-ending stream of very similar, boring Powerpoint slides or what Antony Jay called 'visible verbals'; in other words, flip charts or slides covered in words, and fairly indigestible words at that: 'costs', 'benefits', 'advantages', 'disadvantages', 'reliability', 'creativity'. However, whereas some authorities would argue that visual aids should very rarely contain words, there is a danger that in an attempt to find a pictorial or graphical representation of everything, many speakers would find it so difficult that they would give up altogether and not use any kind of visual aid at all. As with most things, it is a question of judgement and compromise. Certainly, speakers in planning their visual aids should aim for pictures of some kind or another, and even abstract concepts can be turned into pictures of sorts – diagrams, charts, cartoons and so on – with a little imagination. However, visual aids can use words very successfully to reinforce the speaker's message, and to remind the audience of the key ideas being presented, but they need to be *designed* not just written out in untidy writing as if the speaker has merely jotted down a few of his thoughts, while awaiting his turn to speak.

Many speakers give the impression that the visual aid equipment they are using provides more of an obstacle course than anything else; and the visual aids themselves seem 'designed' to cloud the issue rather than help communicate the message. Using two media of communication is almost always more effective than one, but *only* if the two are complementary.

- *Used badly, visual aids are time-wasting, distracting, expensive, inflexible, at best confusing, at worst catastrophic and humiliating.*
- *Used well, visual aids are time-saving, essential, interesting, entertaining, memorable, and invaluable.*

So if you are to avoid the traps and make them work for you, rather than against you, you need to know what is available, what are the problems, what are the most suitable applications and how to manage them effectively.

11.2 Whiteboards

The traditional blackboard, or chalkboard, has now been replaced by the whiteboard or marker board, which is usually a plasticised laminate surface on which you can write with felt-tipped pens. Whiteboards are clean to use, allow a varied use of colour and tend to show up visuals clearly, but they can reflect the light and sometimes retain traces of the pen colours. A more modern version of the whiteboard can also produce paper copies for handing out to the audience after use.

Uses

- Building up a fairly simple visual message.
- Spontaneous use with small informal groups.
- Display of permanent background information.

How to manage

- Use strong-coloured marker pens.
- Use 'dry' markers for dry boards, which can then be wiped clean with a duster.
- Always have spare markers in case one gives up.
- Check beforehand that the board is not reflecting the light, and move it if possible.
- Plan in advance what you are going to write or draw.

- Keep drawings bold and simple (if a drawing is complex, trace it faintly on the board beforehand using dotted lines).
- Restrict writing to key words or short, memorable sentences.
- Practise writing clearly, quickly and in straight lines.
- Use capital letters, unless your handwriting is very clear and beautiful.
- Don't talk to the board: stand aside; face the audience with the board on your left if you are right-handed. Try to write or draw in short bursts and then turn to talk to your audience.
- When referring to the board, try to use a pointer.

Advantages

- Usually available – although often replaced by the overhead projector.

Disadvantages

- Temptation to use board as a scribbling pad – result: illegible hieroglyphics.
- Tedious for audiences to watch speaker laboriously spell (or misspell!) words they have just spoken.
- Interrupts eye contact/rapport with audience.

11.3   Flip charts

These are often pre-prepared on large sheets of paper or card and then used, either singly or in sequence, to present information to small groups of people. The term is also used to describe the large sheets of paper, clipped together on a stand, used to write up information provided by the audience which can be referred to later, or removed and stuck on the walls for reference purposes. However, because the effect can be rather untidy, the speaker should try to obey the rules for whiteboards.

Uses

- Providing background information during a presentation when used singly.
- Building up an increasing amount of information or revealing the successive stages of a story, when used in sequence.
- Recording group discussion or decisions.

How to manage

- Keep lettering and diagrams simple, bold and colourful.
- If you are using a single chart and want to reveal information gradually, use hinged flaps of card or paper to mask parts of it.
- A flip-chart sequence can be very effective but needs a lot of preparation – it might be better to use an overhead projector.
- As with other visual aids, a picture left up after it is finished with can be very distracting; the answer is to have a plain sheet after every picture or sequence of pictures.

- You need to be very familiar with each of the charts and the order they are in, so that you know what to expect.

Advantages

- Useful way of preparing a complete presentation which is to be repeated.
- Visuals are not rubbed off each time as with whiteboards, so they can be kept for future reference.
- Sheets can be torn off and stuck up round the room for continuous reference.

Disadvantages

- Whatever the mechanism for clipping the sheets together at the top, there is a problem when folding each sheet back: they can start falling back after about the sixth sheet, so you need to be familiar with the particular flip chart you will be using and you should rehearse the sequence right through.
- Temptation to make drawings and lettering too small for audience to see detail.
- Cumbersome to use: you need some method of propping up the charts, either your own home-made version or the conventional stand, but either can topple over easily.
- If you are using a flip chart as a whiteboard you can't erase each drawing so you need to get rid of the previous sheet each time. Either you have the fold-back problem, or you can tear off each sheet and drop them, but this may leave the stage looking rather like a football stand after the match is over. Have a cardboard box for the purpose, or have an assistant who can retrieve the sheets inconspicuously.

11.4   Build-up visuals

These include magnetic boards and pin boards where you can build up a picture as you go along and add things and take things away at will. This adds movement to your presentation which is not possible with whiteboards or flip charts.

Pin boards are usually made of cork or fibreboard on to which you can then pin cards with drawing pins, although ordinary sewing pins can be used and are less obvious to the audience.

Magnetic boards are often available, as modern whiteboards have a metal backing, but if not, you can always use the back of a metal filing cabinet or cupboard. All kinds of display items can be used by glueing them to a flat magnet or a piece cut from plasticised magnetic strip which can be obtained from do-it-yourself or hobbies shops. Alternatively you can always use Blu-tack to attach cards to any flat surface.

Of course, computers are tending to replace these methods but computer slide presentations (usually Powerpoint!) can become rather samey, so a more original method could add that special touch to your presentation.

Uses

- Building up a simple visual presentation.
- Moving display items about the board.
- Complex visual presentations: better on a magnetic board because items can be moved more easily.
- Achieving a dramatic effect, for example, the services have used magnetic boards for demonstrating ship movements and changing formations.

How to manage

- Limit the range of items or the number of items in each range, otherwise you will get confused trying to hunt through too many items to find the one you want.
- Make display items large and colourful and make sure everyone can see really well.
- Unless you are absolutely sure that you will always be able to use a magnetic board, it is not worth going to the trouble and expense of making magnetic items; use cards and Blu-tack.

Advantages

- Allows movement and dramatic effect.
- Pieces, once prepared, can be used over and over again.
- Less conventional visual aid, so immediately interests the audience.

Disadvantages

- Confusion over pieces to be added.
- Takes time and effort to prepare well.
- More expensive than using a whiteboard or flip chart.
- Magnetic board would be heavy to carry around, especially if it is used for a complex display.

11.5 Physical objects

Real examples of what you are talking about can be extremely effective in capturing the interest of the audience and turning an abstract word or concept into something concrete and easily understood, but it is a method which tends to be under-used. This may be because it is all too easy when you are speaking about something with which you are extremely familiar, to assume that your audience is too.

Small objects produced at the right moment from your pocket or even larger ones hidden under the desk or in a bag can turn a fairly conventional lecture into an entertaining and dramatic presentation.

Uses

- Providing an example of a product or concept which the audience has heard of, but never seen (not perhaps so much now, but a few years ago many people had never seen a silicon chip).
- Providing an everyday example of the more unfamiliar and complex process you are talking about.

How to manage

- Picking the right moment to produce the item needs careful judgement and some rehearsal; the climax of a statement or at the end of an introductory section can be quite successful. If you leave it until the very end of your presentation, it must be good or it will produce an anti-climactic effect.
- If you have enough to pass round the audience this is ideal, but in that case, allow enough time for everyone to receive their example or it will cause distraction as everyone watches the box being passed from hand to hand.
- If you have only one example it must be big enough for everyone to see, or alternatively you must keep it back until the end and then invite people to come up and look at it when you have finished. If you produce it too early with an invitation to look at it at the end, people will be frustrated and distracted by their curiosity.

Advantages

- Introduces interest and vitality.
- Provides real examples of what you are talking about.

Disadvantages

- Can create frustration if people cannot see what you are showing, or have to wait until the end to satisfy their curiosity.
- Fumbling around in your pocket or struggling to get something out of a bag may create the opposite effect from the one you intended.

11.6   Models and experiments

These, if they work and are really relevant to the presentation, can be absolutely captivating and the high spot of any presentation. But if they are not really relevant, the audience may feel they have been conned by showmanship; and if they don't work, they are almost always a complete disaster, so beware!

Uses

- Explaining abstract or scientific concepts and processes, where they are almost essential despite the dangers.

- Transforming a potentially dry subject into an involving and fascinating demonstration.

How to manage

- It is absolutely essential to know exactly where the model or experiment is to be used and to check for space, table height, power supply, ventilation and possibly even fire regulations and measures to control fire, should the need arise.
- Make sure you have everything you need to do the experiment or make the model work – remember, water is not usually on tap in the ordinary lecture room: you may have to bring your own supply.
- Practise: everyone involved in an experiment should practise over and over again until they can play their part without thinking.
- Don't be put off from using models and experiments by the potential problems – just prepare extremely carefully and rehearse very conscientiously: the value of a successful demonstration is worth the risk of disaster! But if the success of your whole talk rests on a working model or experiment, either have a standby or a prepared diagram or visual which would do instead.

Exercise 11.1: So far we have looked at mainly non-mechanical aids. Before we go on to look at the group of aids which might be classified as 'projected' aids, try these questions:

1 As office manager you are responsible for office organisation which includes deciding who occupies which office, the efficient location of furniture and people and the best use of space generally. A new extension to the office block is about to become available and you have called a meeting of 30 staff representatives to discuss the way in which the old and new offices should be reorganised. You have several alternative plans which you intend to present at the start of the meeting before opening it up to discussion and you recognise that people may have their own ideas as well. Which visual aid method would you choose to support the presentation of your suggestions if money and effort were no object? Why?

2 When you are using a whiteboard or flip chart, on which side of it should you stand and why?

3 Can you think of two reasons why producing some physical object during a presentation might be useful?

4 You have been asked to give a talk which will require a detailed explanation, based on a rather large complicated visual aid, or a piece of equipment. Which visual aid would you use and what would you need to bear in mind when preparing it?

5 You have been asked to conduct a discussion on a subject about which you know quite a bit, but about which the audience will also be able to contribute quite a lot. The main points of the discussion are to be reported in the organisation's newspaper. Which visual aid would you use and why?

11.7 Overhead projector

Known as OHP for short; if you don't know what it is or what it does, now is the time to find out.

The OHP is a device for projecting prepared transparencies, or writing or drawing done at the time of the presentation, on to a screen which is above and behind the speaker. A light is projected up through a horizontal transparent plate on which the speaker places his prepared transparencies. Alternatively, the speaker can write down or draw on blank acetate film which is rolled over the plate. The resulting image is transmitted to the screen by the optical system erected over the plate.

The OHP is intended to remove the problem of subjecting the audience to a view of the back of the speaker as they write on a board or flip chart. The speaker can face the audience throughout the presentation even while pointing to the visual, on the transparency rather than on the screen.

In theory, it has all the advantages and flexibility of many other methods and in the hands of an experienced speaker it is effective and easily controlled; but in practice it has numerous traps which await the inexperienced amateur. However, practice will pay dividends in that you will inevitably have to use it sooner or later because it has become so popular, and familiarity will enable you to take advantage of its possibilities and operate it in a confident and controlled manner.

Uses

- Almost everything that can be portrayed on transparent film.
- Complex visuals: quite complicated effects can be created with the use of overlays. Coloured acetate film can be stuck to the basic transparency, and masks, paper sheets, placed on top of the transparency and removed to reveal additional transparencies which can be laid one after another on top of the original transparency to produce a changing picture.

How to manage

- Start off with simple transparencies until you can use the machine with ease and confidence.
- Position yourself in such a way that you can reach the machine naturally as well as your notes, without standing in the audience's line of sight to the screen – apart from obliterating your picture, you are likely to find yourself dazzled by the light shining full in your face. In practice, some speakers seem to get so bemused with concentrating on operating the machine that they are totally unaware that the light is shining in their face and that furthermore, much to the amusement of the audience, their head is silhouetted on the screen.
- Your transparencies should be carefully prepared beforehand (see 'Visual aids', pp. 149–50. Arrange them carefully in the right order, preferably with blank sheets of paper in between, so that you can see them clearly as you pick them up.
- Don't get into a panic about which way round they should be in order to be projected properly – OHP slides are not like 35 mm photographic slides which

have to be put into the machine in almost any way other than the one you would have expected! Simply pick a transparency up and if it looks the right way up to you, put it down like that onto the plate. By the miracles of optical science, it will appear on the screen as it appears to you, looking down at the machine.

- Glance once at the screen just to check that the whole of your transparency is being projected and that it is straight – a crooked picture with bits cut off can be very distracting to the audience and you will wonder why they are fidgeting or sniggering.
- Some authorities suggest that you should not switch the light on until your transparency is in position and then switch it off before the transparency is moved away. However, if you are using quite a lot of slides, the effect of the light going on and off continually can be more distracting than watching the slide positioned while the light is left on: again, it is a case for practice and judgement.
- Point to the transparency with a pencil if you want to refer to a detail on the screen. A pointer is better than a finger because just as the screen magnifies your picture so it will magnify your finger ... and your hand; and if you are shaking because you are nervous try to avoid pointing at all.
- Follow the rules for whiteboards if you want to write or draw on the blank acetate film. It is possible to prepare a roll of this film beforehand, with all the visuals that you need for the whole presentation but, of course, this gives no flexibility and you are stuck with the order of visuals on the roll.
- Always check that the projector has a spare bulb that works; bulbs have a horrible knack of blowing in the middle of presentations.

Advantages

- Allows complete control and greater flexibility by the speaker.
- The speaker can face the audience throughout the presentation.
- Although the OHP is a projector, it can be used in normal lighting.
- Provided the screen is properly positioned, nothing can obscure it; the best screen position is behind the speaker, slightly above and to their right.
- Adds vitality and movement – allows considerable variety, through use of masks and overlays, and changes in sequence of slides.

Disadvantages

- Difficult to use expertly and casually – this can be overcome by practice.
- Many rooms have permanent screens which are poorly positioned making it almost inevitable that the speaker will obscure part of the screen for part of the audience.
- Most projectors are fairly heavy and bulky, though portable 'briefcase' ones are available.
- Many speakers use the acetate film roll as a scribbling pad.
- Most speakers do not take enough care in producing their transparencies, although it is possible to get good results using computer software like Microsoft Powerpoint without using the services of professional graphic artists.

11.8   Data projector

Very popular in recent years, data projectors have become light and relatively portable – although still not cheap. They appeal to many because of their apparently high-tech nature and because they save having to make or print out slides; however, in some ways they are less flexible than an OHP.

Uses

- Projecting anything from an electronic source: computer, video-tape player, DVD player, digital camera, specifically:
- Slides from a laptop computer's slide programme, typically Powerpoint.
- Video-tapes and clips.

How to manage

- Check carefully that you know how to use the particular projector available. Follow its instructions to the letter: these often require you to switch the projector on before you switch on your source computer or other machine.
- Check that you have the correct cable(s) to link to your source machine: these usually come with the projector in its bag.
- Take care to get the angle and screen size right: some projectors can be switched between different image sizes, and between front and back projection.
- Check the lighting level: mostly you can keep lighting at normal levels.
- If you're using a computer source, you can toggle (using a function key, usually f8) between image on screen, image on computer, or both, so that you can set your presentation up without participants seeing it, then switch to showing it on screen.
- Allow plenty of set up time: these electronic gizmos often play up!

Advantages

- Saves printing out OHP slides or making 35 mm slides.
- Allows still and moving images to be used sequentially or combined.
- In Powerpoint presentations, allows the use of sophisticated facilities such as having words or pictures 'fly in' or build up, move across the screen, fade and so on.
- Allows you to transport your material in a very light-to-carry format: CD-Rom, diskette, or video-tape.
- Allows you to stand away from the computer and projector and use a remote control or mouse.

Disadvantages

- Prone to go wrong, and sometimes difficult to sort out without technical help – especially if you rely on a projector someone else is providing, and you run even more risk if you also rely on a laptop computer provided by someone else.

- If you use your own projector, things are less likely to go wrong, but you have to lug it about – and your laptop computer too, if you want to play safe.
- Resolution, although good on modern machines, can be less sharp than from a good OHP or 35 mm slide, especially for video-tape presentations.
- For Powerpoint and similar software, forces you to go through your slides in sequence – although you can skip fast – but you can't easily miss slides out, as you can with an OHP, nor switch quickly back to exactly the slide you want, unless you are using very few slides.

11.9 Slide projector

Very commonly used and frequently misused, it can be used on its own or in conjunction with a tape recorder, where the slides are changed either by means of a remote control button controlled by the speaker or an assistant, or automatically by means of a synchronised sound tape which has been electronically pulsed. Commercially-produced tape/slide presentations can be bought ready-made but the speaker can, of course use their own slides.

Uses

- Showing real photographs (35 mm) of people, places or objects.
- Showing visuals of diagrams, plans or charts which would be too complicated to produce on boards or be seen on flip charts or an OHP screen.

How to manage

- Always use a magazine-loaded projector, if possible; you can then load the slides beforehand and ensure that they are in the right sequence and up the right way.
- Since slides are usually only worth the expense and trouble of making them if they will be used more than once, store them carefully, preferably in their own magazine, so that you don't have to load and unload them every time.
- Never use poor quality slides however relevant or interesting you think they are; there is nothing worse than being subjected to a series of shadowy, unrecognisable photographs, or pictures of people or things with bits cut off by poor photography, which is accompanied by repeated apologies from the speaker. If you feel the need to apologise for a slide, don't use it.
- Either use a synchronised tape/slide presentation which you have checked and double-checked to make sure it is synchronised correctly or, if you are providing the commentary, use a remote control lead which you control. Never let someone else change the slides unless it is absolutely necessary, which it may be if you are showing slides in a large room because the throw of projectors which you can operate yourself would be too short. In this case, you will need a projectionist who knows as much about your presentation as you do, who is willing to work to your script and cues, who is quick-thinking and intelligent; you must agree the sequence and cues with him and then stick to them – never change the order or

make cuts once you have had the final rehearsal – and you must agree to a breakdown procedure, for example what to do if a slide sticks.

- Arrange cues for raising and dimming the houselights.
- Prepare a commentary which links the slides so that the continuity is smooth and fluent; there is nothing worse than a presentation in which virtually all the speaker says is 'And this is a picture of…'
- Know your projector – they tend to be extremely temperamental, prone to breaking down, overheating, changing focus and so on. In fact they are probably the most potentially disastrous of all visual aids.
- Be hypercritical in preparing or selecting your slides. Antony Jay lists seven main faults of slides: too verbal; too comprehensive; too complex; too crowded; too colourless; held too long; not explained.
- Bear these potential faults in mind when you are preparing your slides and then get someone to sit through the rehearsal and criticise them frankly and honestly.

Advantages

- Slides provide the clearest and most colourful reproduction of any projected aid.
- They add reality to your presentation.
- If you are good at photography the slides are fairly cheap and easy to make compared with using video, for instance.
- They can magnify details which is impossible with non-projected aids and the OHP.

Disadvantages

- The potential problems are almost too numerous to mention.
- Normally the room has to be darkened or blacked out – so unless you are prepared to give your whole presentation in a darkened room, you need to arrange to show slides in fairly large batches rather than scattered throughout.
- If you want to point to a detail on a slide, you have to point to the screen, and you will therefore be in danger of obscuring it.
- Slides are easily damaged or lost.
- Unless you are using a preloaded magazine, it is very easy to get slides the wrong way round or upside down (of the eight possible ways of inserting a slide, only one is right!).

11.10   Videos

Videos can be hired from distributors, whose addresses can be found in the library, but some addresses of those distributors which produce films suitable for business and training purposes are included at the end of this chapter.

Uses

- Bringing the real living world into your presentation.
- Providing an entertaining as well as instructive dimension to your presentation.

- Showing processes which would be impossible to reproduce by means of any other visual aid.

How to manage

- Check how to dim the lights and lower blinds.
- Check that your video-tape will run on the machine to be provided. Although the system most people use at home is the most commonly available in organisations, there are other systems in existence!
- Allow enough time before you start your presentation to find out how to operate the video recorder. Check how to insert, stop, start and pause the tape – the most intelligent of us can be reduced to an incompetent, clueless idiot by the sight of a strange machine, so beware!
- Select your film or video carefully; preview as many as possible and measure each against your objective. Can you use one complete or should you use only parts of it?
- Run through the video several times until you are completely familiar with it; it often helps to write notes on the main sections and the sequences of events so that you have something to refer to during any discussion afterwards.
- If you only want to use selected sequences of a video, stop it at the beginning and end of each sequence. Use the counter to make a note of your stop and start points.
- Have a contingency plan ready, in case you find the distributor has put the wrong video in the box!

11.11   Closed-circuit television and video

At the moment we are living through a technological revolution which means that the speaker will have access to an increasingly sophisticated range of television recording apparatus. Just as the range and sophistication is increasing, so the expense of this equipment is tumbling and it is becoming common practice for individuals to make their own video-tapes comparatively easily and cheaply, just as almost everyone has access to television.

Since the rate of change in price and choice of equipment is so fast it is difficult to be very specific about exactly what is available and how best to use it. However, video cameras are now fairly simple to operate because they allow instant control of picture and lighting, for instance, and you can see the picture you are filming while you are filming it. In addition, you can check instantly how successful you have been (cf. waiting for slides to be developed) and therefore do a retake immediately if necessary.

Moral: If you can get access to a video camera, use it. Experiment with it; it is a lot easier to use than it looks. It is all too understandable to be put off by the apparent complexity and mystique which surrounds the 'video and television business' and it is certainly true that you will need quite a lot of practice and advice to produce really good videos yourself, but – and this is my real message – you can cope with the mechanics and you can really only discover the pitfalls and secrets of success if you are prepared to have a go.

11.12 Points to remember about visual aids

The audience can't do two completely unrelated things at once

They can't read your visual aid while you talk about something else; and they certainly can't look at your visual, listen to you and pass things round and look at them, all at the same time.

Do not use too many different types of aid

If you try to include use of an overhead projector, a slide or data projector and a whiteboard or flip chart, you will find it very difficult, if not impossible, to schedule it all smoothly enough so that each piece of equipment is ready at the right time and in the right place. The result is more likely to be a complete shambles.

Decide exactly what aids and equipment you are going to use

Check that equipment (e.g. projectors and screens) is available before you start working on the visuals themselves. Don't assume anything – there may not even be a board, let alone a projector of the type you want. If a piece of equipment you need is not normally in the room you will be speaking in, it is really safer to take care of the arrangements for booking it and actually collecting it yourself. There is nothing worse for your confidence or your reputation, than to turn up having based the whole of your presentation on a video, only to discover that something has gone wrong with the arrangements and there is no video recorder, or that *your* video-tape and *their* recorder are not compatible.

Organise the layout of your 'stage', yourself

First, find the time and the opportunity to get into the room and familiarise yourself with the position of everything you are likely to need. Is that table going to be big enough to get all your notes and material on, without your having to stack things in piles? Is that screen in such a position that you won't obscure it when you're talking? If not, can it be moved? If not, plan your presentation accordingly – perhaps it would be better not to use the overhead projector at all, for example.

Second, get into the room at least a quarter of an hour before you are due to speak. Work out how you want the area you will be working in arranged so that you will be able to move easily and naturally in the space provided, and then move the furniture so that it feels right for you. Obviously, you should do this tactfully, but do not feel that you must use the room in the way it happens to be laid out. It may have been set out that way for a previous speaker who had different needs; it may have been set out by the organiser working purely on intelligent guesswork – it may even have ended up that way because that was the way the cleaner left it!

So check

- the television, screen and projector are correctly positioned
- the flip chart will be on your left when you face the audience if you are right-handed or on your right if you are left-handed

- the table or lectern is near enough to the OHP so that you won't have to keep skipping about between them to look at your notes
- there isn't an electric cable stretching right across the area in which you will want to move
- you know how to operate the blinds quickly and smoothly when you need to
- you know how to operate that particular machine and that it works.

Visuals should not be too detailed

First, because your audience will probably not be able to assimilate the information quickly enough, and even if you vow to allow enough time for reading, in the heat of the moment you are almost bound to forget; and second, because you will either have to plough through detail and they will get bored, or worse, you will probably get yourself confused.

Visuals should be big enough for everyone to see

The slide must occupy the whole of the screen; the slides must be clear enough and big enough for someone in the back right-hand corner to see. Prepared slides, flip charts or transparencies always seem big enough to you, when you are up close, preparing them: they have an unfortunate habit of 'shrinking' to the illegible or even invisible when viewed by your audience, even in a fairly small room.

Be careful using pointers

While it is always better to use some kind of pointer than just your hand or your finger, it does tend to accentuate any movement in your hand, so if you are nervous it may show more. An old telescopic radio aerial is ideal as a pointer, since it can be extended to reach quite large distances and then contracted when you don't need it, but if you are nervous the end will tend to flutter. Similarly, a laser pointer can produce a very distracting dancing, red light that never seems to be pointing at what it should.

Don't leave visuals up too long

Visuals left up after they have ceased to be relevant to what you are talking about are distracting.

Always be prepared for disaster

However well prepared you are, things can, and frequently do, go wrong. What will you do when the OHP bulb blows half-way through the second of your ten essential transparencies? When the video-tape breaks? When you open the box and find the wrong video? When Blu-tack is not allowed by the venue owner? When the experiment on which the whole of your lecture depends does not work? When the felt-tip pen dries up? When your whole presentation is in your laptop and it crashes?

11.13   Video and DVD hire and purchase

Ashgate and Gower Publishing Company Ltd
Gower House
Craft Road
Aldershot
Hants GU11 3HR
Tel. 01252-331551
www.ashgate.com

Fenman Training
Clive House
The Business Park
Ely
Cambridgeshire CB7 4EH
Tel. 01353-665533
www.fenman.co.uk

BBC Worldwide Learning
Room A3040
80 Wood Lane
London W12 OTT
Tel. 0208 4331641
Fax. 0208-4332916
www.bbcworldwide.com/business

Capita Learning and Development
(Previously owned by The Industrial Society now know as The Work Foundation)
49 Calthorpe Road
Edgbaston
Birmingham B15 1TH
Tel. 0870-400-1000
www.capitald.co.uk

Video Arts Ltd
6-7 St Cross St
London EC1N 8UA
Tel. 0207-7400-4800
Fax. 0207-7400-4900
www.videoarts.com

Summary – being in control of visual aids

More than anything, success with visual aids is about being prepared – planning in advance how you're going to use them and what they're going to say... and what you'll do if things do go wrong.

Think now about all the disasters that you've seen happen to other people; recall how they dealt with them. Then, let your imagination run riot and think of worse things still. Now, don't panic. Instead, spend your mental energy on thinking up a contingency plan for every possible disaster, or ways in which you could deal with them. A good speaker always anticipates the problems, then minimises the chances of their happening by thorough preparation, but above all, when they do happen (and they do – to the best of speakers) the good speaker thinks very quickly and copes ... somehow!

Exercise 11.2

1 If you want to show some photos developed as transparencies, which kind of projector should you ask for?
2 You have decided to limit yourself to two kinds of visual aid. Which ones would you try to avoid using together in the same presentation because the 'stage management' might present problems?
3 You want to explain a complex process which involves various machines and complicated operations. Which visual aid(s) would be ideal for the purpose?
4 The overhead projector bulb suddenly blows, the spare in the projector also doesn't work – and you've only just started. What do you do?

Further reading

Bradbury, Andrew, *Successful Presentation Skills*, Kogan Page, 2000

☑ 12 Faster reading

The information is probably here ... somewhere

From: Head of Department
To: You
Date: Monday

I have to attend a meeting on Wednesday afternoon at which I gather there will be a discussion on the possibility of introducing a new performance management system. I gather there are several magazine articles reviewing the effectiveness of P M Systems, but I shan't have time to read them as I shall be away at the planning conference and won't be back until late on Wednesday morning.

Can you read through them and let me have a summary of the main points and your comments so that I can read it through quickly just before the meeting? I'll get Jo to give you copies of the articles.

Your reputation is at stake here: you are ambitious and keen to get on. This gives you the chance to make a good impression by showing you can handle any situation, so it's not just a case of skimming through the articles and handing them back with a short note. You will need to read them carefully, analyse them and make valid comments, but today is Monday and you have your own job to do as well, so you haven't much time. How would you react to this task? How would you go about it?

Perhaps you feel that this is an unlikely assignment to be given, but even if you feel this now in your present circumstances, things change; and one of the purposes of this book is to provide you with skills in communication, so that when the opportunity to use them arises, you will be well equipped not only to cope, but to do well.

Even without a task quite like this, for many of us the problem of reading a great deal of material in too short a time is fairly common; we seem to be living through an information explosion or a 'paper avalanche'.

For students on courses, it is a problem of tutors recommending books and articles faster than they can read the ones already recommended. Many students do not read quickly or retain what they read, so reading becomes a chore and their courses become more difficult than they need be.

For people at work, it is often a problem of finding the time to read all the things they know they ought to read – minutes of meetings, piles of letters and memos, too many e-mail articles which might be helpful, copies of this 'for information', copies of that 'for information', as well as wanting to keep up with newspapers and perhaps the occasional novel.

So what's the problem? After all, most of us have been reading since we were five or so, and for many of us that is quite a long time. But despite all this experience few people read as well as they might. They read too slowly, they cannot concentrate and they don't retain what they've read.

Check-Point

The average adult reads at a speed of between 200 and 300 words per minute (w.p.m.) but some people read at 600 w.p.m. and John F. Kennedy is reputed to have been able to read at 1000 w.p.m.

Why do people read at different speeds? How is it that some people are three times more effective than others when it comes to reading?

It certainly doesn't appear to have anything to do with intelligence, or education, or status, or occupation or sex. There are many wives whose jobs require little reading, who infuriate their husbands by being able to read much faster than their husbands, despite less experience and less practice. Similarly, there are many brilliant men and women who are outpaced by their subordinates.

No one seems to know why faster reading comes more easily to some people than others. What we do know is that more effective readers read in a different way from slower readers.

If you feel you do read more slowly than you would like, perhaps it isn't your fault. Certainly, the best of readers can be slowed down by things like:

- the complexity of the material
- the author's style
- a typeface which is hard to read
- monotonous layout and presentation (e.g. 'solid blocks of print weary the eye')
- unfamiliar words and expressions.

However, these may be just excuses. It is equally possible that it could be your fault, in the sense that we do know that slow readers tend to have developed some bad habits, whereas effective reading calls for certain techniques. These techniques can be learned and practised. You could very probably read at least half as fast again as you do now and still understand as well; many people who either attend an 'effective reading' course or are conscientious enough to teach themselves with the aid of a book like *Breakthrough Rapid Reading* by Peter Kump (Prentice Hall) a programme like www.acereader.com are usually able to double their reading or speed without any drop in comprehension. Some people's comprehension level actually increases.

In this book it is not possible to allow enough space to give you a structured training course. What we can do, though, is:

- explain why people read slowly and ineffectively
- find out how you read at present
- suggest some techniques which, if you really want to improve your reading, you can practise perfectly well on your own.

12.1 How do you read?

Self-Check

The first thing to discover is how you read. As with other exercises in this book, it is important to answer questions honestly. You will gain nothing by trying to guess what you think the answer should be. In order to assess how effectively you tackle serious reading, put a tick ('usually true') or a cross ('seldom true') against the points below.

1 I skim over reading material before studying it.
2 I tend to go back over words and phrases I have not understood, before going on.
3 I find it difficult to pick out the main idea of a passage.
4 I read different types of reading material at different speeds.
5 I pronounce words to myself when I read.
6 When I have a lot of reading to do, I try to stick at it for as long as possible before having a break.
7 I always skim over the entire questionnaire, exam paper and so on, before starting to answer the questions.
8 I have a tendency to daydream when trying to study a report, article or section of a report.
9 I prefer to read slowly and carefully through a fairly difficult article, rather than read it quickly two or three times.
10 I find it easy to understand and remember what I read.
11 Generally, I am a rather slow reader.
12 I skimmed quickly through all these questions before I started to answer any of them.

If you put a tick for 1, 4, 7, 10 and 12 then you have probably already been through an 'effective reading' course, or you have developed good reading habits naturally, or you cheated yourself by trying to guess the right answers!

If, however, you put a tick against any of the other points, you have developed some bad habits and could probably improve your reading considerably by practising conscientiously some of the techniques suggested in this chapter.

Different material – different speed

At the moment, it is very likely that you read practically everything you read in much the same way and at much the same speed. A moment's thought will tell you that you are spending too much time on the easy material, which doesn't leave you enough time to spend on the more difficult stuff. Improving your reading speed is, therefore, mainly intended to increase the range of reading speeds available to you, so that instead of reading everything at the same fairly slow speed, you can be more flexible. With practice you will probably end up reading everything rather faster than you do now, even the very difficult material.

Reading is rather like driving: when you are learning and rather lacking in confidence, you drive fairly slowly and you don't get much above second gear. When you are more experienced, you can change up and down through all the gears at will, almost without thinking about it, in order to suit different road and traffic conditions. So it is with reading. If you can gain confidence by employing advanced techniques, you will be able to adapt your approach to reading to suit the material and your purpose, at any given moment.

Purposes of reading

There are three basic reasons why we read:

- *Pleasure* – Many people read for no other reason than the sheer pleasure they gain from a good story or the sound of the words.
- *Information* – This type of reading is perhaps the most basic reason. Whether we like reading or not, most of us have to read in order to get facts – about our job, our interests, our lives in general: it covers everything from recipes to nuclear physics; from instructions on forms, to guidance on operating machines or gadgets.
- *Judgement* – In this type of reading, you are interested in people's ideas and opinions, in order to come to your own opinions and conclusions; you therefore need to be able to evaluate critically the arguments put forward, and be alert to the presence of prejudice or bias, or the use of emotive arguments intended to manipulate you.

This book is not intended to enable you to change your style of reading for pleasure or to help you get through a novel in one sitting, since much of the pleasure of reading comes from savouring the words and images the author uses to create particular effects. What we are concerned with is making the serious business of acquiring information and reading for judgement purposes a more efficient process; in other words, making better use of your time.

Comprehension and speed

Reading *faster* is not the only problem. Although it is obviously important to eliminate bad habits and increase your reading speed, this is only part of developing a more effective approach to reading.

The other dimension is, of course, concerned with understanding, for it is no good simply increasing the rate at which you read if in doing so you gain less from what you read. In fact, these two aspects of efficient reading are inextricably linked, as we shall see; it is certainly true that many people discover that their comprehension improves as their speed increases.

12.2 The physical process of reading

Eye movements

Many people read inefficiently because of faulty eye movements, of which they are not even aware.

When you read, your eyes do not move smoothly across the page from left to right without stopping. If they did, all you would see was a blur. Try moving your eyes from one side of the room to the other without letting them stop. What did you see? A blur? You can only keep your eyes in focus while they are moving smoothly without stopping if the object you are looking at is also moving. Since the words on the page are stationary, your eyes can only focus on the words when your eyes are stationary. So when you read, your eyes stop to take in a word or phrase and then move on to the next. These stops are called *fixations*. It is estimated that each fixation that our eyes make lasts approximately 1/4 or 1/2 second and then the eyes move on. At each fixation, the eyes read a word or perhaps several words.

The number of words you focus on and take in or recognise at one fixation is called the *recognition span*. Some people appear to be able to read straight down a printed page. In other words, they fixate only once each line and, at each fixation, take in or recognise the whole line. Their recognition span is large.

Now it is obvious that the bigger your recognition span, the fewer fixations you will need to make, and so the faster you will read – since it is the fixations that take up the time. Poor readers tend to make a large numbers of fixations and have a small recognition span, but they also tend to have other habits associated with the eye movements and the brain's activity while reading.

Regression

This is the tendency to backtrack while reading. Poor readers, who tend to focus on each word, are actually making life more difficult for themselves than they realise, because individual words do not convey very much meaning until they are joined to other words. So, as the slow readers plod steadily from word to word, trying to join the idea of one word to the idea of the next, they find it difficult to grasp an overall meaning from the individual words. After three or four words they probably find they have forgotten what the first was and have to go back to the beginning again, rather like Figure 12.1.

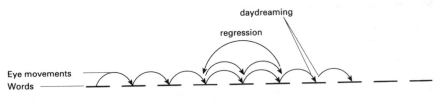

Figure 12.1 **Eye movements.**

Because this process is slow, much slower than their brain can actually perform, the brain finds something else to do. In other words, they get easily sidetracked or distracted by what we tend to call daydreaming or thinking about something else. Let's look at an example.

Self-Check

Read the sentence below very slowly word by word, using a finger to cover the word in front each time, but gradually uncovering each word.

Though ... there ... are ... no ... doubt ... some ... people ... who ... think ... words ... must ... be ... read ... one ... at ... a ... time ... they ... are ... wrong ... because ... meaning ... tends ... to ... come ... from ... groups ... of ... words.

Like this: 'Though' ... 'Though there' ... 'Though there are' ... 'Though there are "no"' ... 'Though there are no doubt' ... and so on. At each stage the words do not convey very much meaning, do they? Not until we get to 'people' does it begin to make some sense.

A good reader, then, with a bigger recognition span and fewer fixations, not only reads faster, but also makes the business of comprehension easier, and is less likely to be distracted because their brain is being pushed to keep up with the eye movement.

A good reader's reading pattern might look like Figure 12.2. So the good reader tends to select recognition spans on the basis of their meaning. They read thought-groups rather than single words.

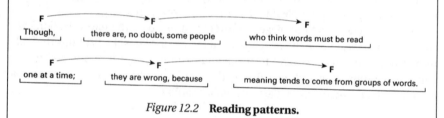

Figure 12.2 **Reading patterns.**

Self-Check

Find out the pattern of your eye movement. Ask a friend to stand behind you while you read from a book, holding a mirror in front of your face so that the friend can see your eyes. Then ask whether your eyes tend to regress from time to time, whether they stop to focus many times along a line or only two or three times.

Sub-vocalisation and visualisation

Another habit of the slow readers is the tendency to register the sound of the words as they read, either by physically mouthing them, or internally acknowledging the sound of the words in their head.

This is often a legacy from the days when we learned to read, first aloud and then 'to ourselves'. Small children can certainly be seen mouthing the words as they read and, though this is less common in adults, either externally mouthing or internally acknowledging the sound will inevitably slow down your reading speed.

Reading aloud, the average reader can only read at about 125 w.p.m. Mouthing the words or acknowledging the sounds inside your head would be bound to limit your reading speed to something below 200 w.p.m.

This habit also has consequences for the idea of reading for meaning, which we have just looked at. If you mouth the words or hear them inside your head, you are concentrating on the words themselves, not on the meaning of the ideas you are reading.

Self-Check

There is a simple test which you can try, to check whether you mouth the words. Place your index finger vertically over your lips while you are reading. If your lips are moving, you will feel them moving with your finger. This test is also a cure because if you do find your lips are moving, all you have to do is to press your finger harder against your lips and they won't be able to move!

Finding out whether you tend to register the words separately by *internally* acknowledging the sound of each word, is more difficult. There is no real test other than just consciously thinking about the danger, perhaps while you are reading this, and trying to discover whether you tend to do it or not. If you are a slow reader, the chances are that you are almost bound to be doing it. If you push up your reading speed you won't be able to mouth the words or visualise them – it will become physically impossible.

Comfort

Physical discomfort can also affect the ease and fluency with which you read. But too much comfort can reduce your concentration:

- *Position* – A comfortable (but not too comfortable!) chair, which is the right height, at a table, is probably the most suitable position for a serious reading task.
- *Lighting* – Good lighting is essential. Although desk lights are commonly accepted as the best form of lighting, a light source falling over your shoulder is best, since it reduces glare.
- *Eyesight* – Have you had your eyes tested recently? Your eyes can deteriorate without your realising it, since the muscles work harder to compensate for any deficiency in vision. Similarly, the lenses in spectacles can become unsuitable. Pride often prevents people going to the optician, but even if you aren't suffering from any physical effects like tired eyes or headaches, your reading could still be suffering.
- *Rests* – While you should avoid being distracted by noise, other people, hunger or thirst and should give yourself a chance to get stuck into a reading or studying task, you should allow yourself reasonable breaks. Short frequent breaks are probably more helpful than a longer break caused by exhaustion, after trying to stick at a reading task for hours without a break.

Vocabulary

Obviously if you are having to go back to words or ponder over them because your brain can't assimilate them because they are unfamiliar or you do not understand them, your reading speed will inevitably be held back. Although writers should try to avoid using unnecessarily complicated and unfamiliar words, if your own vocabulary is weak you should work to improve it.

Quizzes designed to test your wordpower are a useful method of measuring your vocabulary from time to time.

Exercise 12.1: Test your vocabulary in the list below. Underline the word or phrase you believe is nearest in meaning to the keyword. Answers are in the 'Answers to Exercises' at the end of the book.

1 NEFARIOUS	a dangerous	6 PREMISE	a basic assumption
	b suspicious		b a building
	c evil		c foreword
	d distant		d abstract idea
2 CENSURE	a suppress	7 CREDIBLE	a superstitious
	b reject		b sceptical
	c blame		c praiseworthy
	d delete		d believable
3 NEBULOUS	a transparent	8 INVALIDATE	a overwhelm
	b vague		b cancel
	c fat		c injure
	d luminous		d verify
4 SALUTARY	a beneficial	9 BIZARRE	a odd
	b courteous		b a market
	c respected		c comical
	d restful		d colourful
5 TORTUOUS	a arduous	10 DEFUNCT	a wicked
	b cautious		b forbidden
	c slow		c extinct
	d winding		d hopeless

How did you get on? If you got 9 to 10 correct, your vocabulary is excellent. You probably need no encouragement to continue learning new words.

8: good – a very creditable score, but make the effort to look up the odd word you come across that you're not sure about.

6/7: you have a fairly good vocabulary, but try some of the exercises suggested below.

5 and under: your vocabulary is rather limited and this will inevitably slow down your reading. Make a resolution to practise the exercises suggested below.

12.3 Ways of increasing your vocabulary

Read widely

Apart from reading tasks for work or study, you should try to read as much as possible: books and articles on subjects other than your own; a newspaper regularly (preferably one of the 'quality' newspapers, which tend to use a more varied vocabulary than most of the popular newspapers – but any paper is better than none). You might also try reading magazines like *New Statesman, the New Scientist, The Economist* and *The Spectator*.

Word of the week

Try choosing one word each week, which you have come across but don't know or would not naturally use. Then use it in speaking and writing as much as possible throughout the week. Your friends may find it amusing but will soon envy your wide vocabulary.

Get the dictionary habit

If you hear a word you are not familiar with ask the user what they mean and/or make a note of it and look it up in a dictionary later. If you don't possess a good dictionary, that is at least two inches thick, buy one now. *Chambers English Dictionary* and the *Concise Oxford English* are both good but any good bookshop will help you choose one. And, get a good dictionary and a thesaurus as a software package for your computer, or better still on CD-ROM.

Latin and greek roots

Many English words, even those that come from other languages, are formed from Latin and Greek words. Although very few people now learn Latin and Greek at school, it is well worth learning some of the more common affixes (parts of words which usually appear at the beginning or end of a word), for example, 'auto' comes from Greek and means 'self', giving us words like 'automatic', 'autobiography' and 'autograph'.

Self-Check

How many of these Latin(L) and Greek(G) roots and affixes do you know? (You should know all of them. If not, learn them – now is as good a time as any.)

Root of affix	Meaning	Example
ante (L)	before	antecedent
anti (G)	against	antibiotic
amphi (G)	around, both sides	amphitheatre
aqua (L)	water	aquarium
audio (L)	hear	auditorium
bene (L)	well	benefit
bio (G)	life	biography
circum (L)	around	circumference
corpus (L)	body	corporate
dia (G)	across, through	diameter
graph (G)	write, record	photograph
hyper (G)	over, excessive	hypertension
hypo (G)	under, inadequate	hypotension

Summary – faster reading

The purpose of rapid reading is to get your eyes used to moving quickly and smoothly across the page, and your brain used to searching for the meaning of what you are reading, rather than concentrating on single words.

Most of the practice exercises that follow will feel awkward at first, and you may well find that you are concentrating more on the mechanics of the exercise than the meaning of the words. However, as with any skill, you will find that actions that seemed awkward to start with soon become automatic.

You may find that one or two of the exercises don't work for you at all, but give them a really good try before you reject them.

Assignment

Pointer

Follow the words across the page with your finger or a pen: try to move the finger or pointer at a steady speed along each line.

At first, you will find that you are tending to concentrate on the pointer rather than taking in the words, but gradually with practice you should find that you are forgetting the pointer.

Now gradually increase the speed but keep the movement smooth and regular. Then try following only the alternate lines; then every third; then every fourth line.

You may feel foolish doing this exercise, but it is one of the good habits which unfortunately children are taught to drop. In fact, this method of using a finger or pointer is only a simpler copy of the method used in more sophisticated rapid-reading training courses, which use some form of moving light on film to encourage your eyes to move at a smooth but increasing speed.

Tapping a rhythm

Since the aim in rapid reading is to obtain a steady rhythm, it is helpful to use a rhythmic sound as well as the sight of a moving pointer. This can be achieved by tapping the page lightly with a finger or pen down the margin at the end of every line, or every alternate line or less often. Practise for a while until you find a sound and frequency which is comfortable for you. Then, when you have found a comfortable speed, gradually increase slowly, as in the previous exercise with the pointer.

The sound and sight of the tapping finger act rather like a musician's metronome in improving your rhythm.

Read everything faster

Practise reading everything you read that much faster.

Further reading

Buzan, Tony, *Use Your Head*, Harper Collins, 2000
Buzan, Tony, *Speed Reading*, BBC, 2001
Kump, Peter, *Breakthrough Rapid Reading*, Prentice Hall, 1998
Wainwright, Gordon, *Read Faster, Recall More*, How to Books, 2001

▓ ⊻ 13 Better reading

Imagine you are faced with more e-mails than you can count, and an in-tray containing an assortment of letters, memos, articles, reports and so on. Some of it will be important, requiring urgent attention; some of it will be interesting but could afford to wait. Some of it will be easy to read; some of it will be difficult and very time-consuming. Or imagine that as a student you have been told to read a certain book and have just settled down to start the task. In both cases, particularly if time is short (and it usually is!), the temptation is to start reading and keep going until you run out of time or stamina, which is usually before you have finished the pile of paperwork or e-mails or reached the end of the book.

13.1 Determining reading priorities

- Some of what you read turns out to be *essential*, perhaps only a small fraction of the total amount but nevertheless the vital stuff without which you can't do your job – but it may be halfway through or even at the very end of the pile or the book.
- Some of it is *useful*: it includes interesting background information, not absolutely essential, but useful to know. It needn't be read immediately and could probably wait until you are less busy.
- The rest is *irrelevant*: this type of material may have been sent to you in error, or incorporated with the useful and essential stuff, or it contains things you already know. You don't want to waste time reading this at all. A lot of e-mail junk may fall into this category, as people are often not very discriminating when sending on e-mail copies.

Ineffective readers not only read everything at the same speed, but they also tend to wade straight into their reading at the beginning – which in this case is not necessarily the best place to start. This tendency to jump straight in – either at page 1 of the book or at the top paper on the pile in your in-tray – leads to two problems:

- you don't read things in the most sensible order
- you don't know what to expect when you start reading: walking over a strange track is always more difficult than walking along a track you're vaguely familiar with.

In this chapter we will look at how you should approach your reading tasks so that you do read things in a sensible order.

Check-Point

You should devote just as much time as, and no more time than, the nature, difficulty, and your purpose in reading the material requires.

You should read material only after you have gained an overall idea of what it is about and how it is structured; this will make reading not only easier, but also faster. The suggested approach is dependent on two essential skills – scanning and skimming – which are both a form of reading, as we shall see, but which allow you to alter your reading speed in relation to your purpose at any given moment.

But let's go back to that overflowing tray, or the weighty recommended textbook with which you are confronted. If you do have a tendency to start reading at the beginning and work steadily through material, the trouble is that you have to read right through everything before you find out what is *essential*, what is *useful* and what is *irrelevant*. But all this material takes the same amount of effort and concentration to read. A moment's thought will make you realise that this is obviously inefficient. But how can you find out how valuable the material is until you've read it?

13.2   Scanning

What you need is a method of reading which allows you to get a broad view of the whole piece of reading material *before* you read it properly, so that you can assess its value to you and get some idea of when you need to read it and how much effort it will require.

Scanning is one of the techniques of reading which allows you to do just this. Strictly speaking it is not really reading at all, but it is an essential part of the reading process.

In fact, you probably do it occasionally now: when you are looking for a number in a telephone directory, for example. Certainly, having the names in alphabetical order helps, but if you are looking for a friend's name amongst a lot of Browns, you will probably scan the list looking first for the right initials and then the right address. You don't *read* every address, but because you know what you are looking for, the address you want seems to stand out on the page when you get to it.

You would probably look first of all on the front page, to see if there was a list of contents. Your eyes would range over the entire front page in a rather random fashion, not really reading anything, but looking for the one area relevant to your purpose. Your eye and brain would register only those words which seemed to contain clues to what you were looking for: 'TV', 'radio', 'programmes'. Your eyes might be attracted to the word 'TV'. Your eyes would stop ranging, or scanning, far and wide, and come to rest focusing on that word. You might then discover that the word following 'TV' was 'reviews' – not what you're looking for. Your eyes would then start ranging again, until they found what they were looking for. If the 'contents list' then directed you to a particular page, you would ignore all but the page number on each page until you came to the one you wanted, and then begin the ranging or scanning process on the relevant page until you again found what you wanted.

This process of scanning involves blotting out everything but the few key words related to your purpose, and a constant coming-in and narrowing-down to what you need.

Scanning has two main advantages in helping with the process of all your serious or work-related reading:

- *Assessment* – Allows you to 'read' rapidly through a text looking for key words, which will give you enough of a taste of the whole thing to assess its value to you.
- *Introduction to the structure* – Provides you with a rough idea of the material, and how the author has structured it, and therefore you will know what to expect when you come to read it properly.

Categorisation

If your purpose has been to gain an overview of the material in order to assess its value to you, and determine whether you need to read it at all, only part of it, or all of it in some depth, you should now be in a position to assess it against these three categories:

- *essential* – to be read with maximum attention
- *useful* – to be read when you have the time, after you have read the essential stuff
- *irrelevant* – in this case, if you are at work, one writer has suggested that you file it in the wastepaper bin!

Warning! If you are a student and have judged as irrelevant something recommended by a tutor, you will still need to read it through critically in order to be able to support your judgement with well-argued reasons and evidence. Alternatively, you should consult your tutor and discuss your initial reaction with them. But be prepared to accept that since you are learning, the tutor may know better than you at this stage and their advice to read it conscientiously should be taken, particularly if it is essential reading for the course. In this case, you are going to have to think hard and find the relevance.

You will find this process of scanning is needed on and off throughout the process of reading, not only when sorting through material. It is rather like the highest gear imaginable on a very fast car – not useful when you are negotiating steep hills or difficult winding roads, but very useful when you want to get from *A* to *B* as fast as possible.

Getting an overall idea of the material

If we continue the analogy of the car, you know that it is far more difficult to travel along a route which is totally new to you. In view of this, most people before setting out on a journey which is unfamiliar will attempt to find out where they are going and how they are going to get there, by either seeking directions or looking at a map. In just the same way, reading any new material is made considerably easier by having an *overview* of what the material is about and how the author has structured or organised their ideas.

In scanning the material in order to carry out an initial assessment, you will already have picked up some clues and you are now ready to start reading – but still not in the conventional sense of the word. First you need to become familiar with the route, where you will have to make changes of direction, where you will have to slow down and where you can expect to find signposts to help point you in the right direction. Gaining this overview will require another rate of reading, in which you are not concerned with taking in all the words and all the detail, but only the author's major ideas so that you can get a feel for their structure and treatment of the material.

13.3   Skimming

Skimming is one of the techniques of reading which allows you to do just this. It is a kind of rapid reading *par excellence* where you are reading right at the top end of your range, as fast as you possibly can, gaining a broad outline and ignoring the detail. It is probably the ability to skim well which accounts for the sometimes incredible speeds at which some people are reputed to be able to read. They skim through large chunks of the material, only slowing down for the bits which they need.

Since skimming is a technique intended to help you pick up the main ideas and the structure of the material, the process is considerably helped if you are aware of the way in which English writing is structured and where you might expect to find the main ideas; in other words, the way in which sentences are put together to form paragraphs and the way in which 'signposts' are used to help the reader know what's coming. So before we discover more about the technique of skimming itself, let's look at these two aspects of structure.

Self-Check

In a paragraph of technical or business writing (i.e. not fictional writing) where would you expect to find the main idea?

Paragraphs and topic sentences

Most paragraphs in factual, explanatory or discursive writing contain *one main idea*. Normally, one sentence contains this idea and is, therefore, known as the *topic sentence* in the paragraph.

- *First sentence*: the author uses it to state a main idea and then the rest of the paragraph is devoted to material which illustrates, supports or elaborates on this main idea (see Figure 13.1 The Paragraph).
- *Last sentence*: the author uses the first part of the paragraph to lead up to the main idea in the last sentence.

Exceptions:

- sometimes the first sentence is used as a link with the previous paragraph or as an introduction, and the topic sentence is the second sentence;
- occasionally the topic sentence is in the middle of the paragraph;
- fiction or descriptive writing is produced for very different purposes and will, therefore, be structured differently;

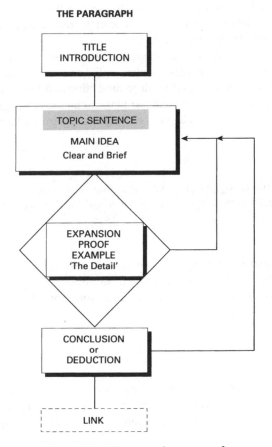

Figure 13.1 **Diagram of a paragraph.**

- poor writing: you may well come across badly written material which does not obey the rules of clear writing (and, of course, the best of writers will go astray from time to time); this will just make your job that much harder.

Self-Check

Look at each of the following paragraphs and find the topic sentence:

1 'Getting an overall idea of the material'. paragraph 1, p. 184.
2 'Getting an overall idea of the material', paragraph 2, p. 184.
3 'Skimming', paragraph 1, p. 184.
4 'Skimming', paragraph 2, p. 184.

In both the paragraphs under 'Getting an overall idea of the material', the topic sentences are the last sentences, though you may have been tempted to think that they were the first. However, even if you had, in skimming through the paragraphs you would have paid some attention to both the first and last sentences and would therefore have picked up my main ideas. In the two 'Skimming' paragraphs the topic sentences are both the first sentences, with the rest of the paragraphs providing elaboration and details of the main idea.

There is no specified length for a paragraph. It can be one sentence or over a page long! However, very short successive paragraphs, as found in advertisements or popular journalism, can have a rather disjointed effect; while very long paragraphs can give the impression of heavy material that can be read through only in a slow laborious manner. The most effective writing usually mixes longer and shorter paragraphs.

Assignment: Look through other sections of this book and see if you can find the topic sentences in paragraphs. If you find it very difficult too often, it is probably my fault, not yours!

Once you get used to spotting topic sentences, you will see how joining topic sentences together can be a useful method of summary-writing. To make the summary flow well you may have to add a few other words, but the method works well in principle.

Self-Check

An author can use various devices – some visual and some verbal – to indicate to the reader which direction their line of thought is taking and which ideas they consider are important. Can you think of any examples of these 'signposts'?

Signposts

Visual signals

Most textbooks and writing for business purposes will make use of headings and sub-headings which indicate to the reader what is to follow. Other devices which act as visual signposts are:

1 Words and phrases underlined
2 Words written in **bold face type**
3 Words written in *italics*
4 Lists using numbering, as in this example, or alternatively, lettering (a, b ...)
5 Lists using bullets (see below for an example).

Verbal signals

In addition to visual signals, there are also signal words to look out for, which suggest to the reader what is to follow; for example 'first' should prompt you to be on the look-out for the 'second', 'third' and so on later in the text; 'for example' will introduce some supporting detail which, at the skimming stage when you are only aiming for a broad picture, you can afford to skip over rapidly; and 'therefore' may introduce an important conclusion of what has gone before, so at the skimming stage you would want to read a sentence with 'therefore' in it.

These signal words act rather like traffic signals telling you to slow down or speed up and can therefore be classified accordingly:

Check-Points: Signpost Words

- **Slow-down words** – These words signal that you should slow down because a change in ideas is about to occur:

however	but	nevertheless
although	despite	rather
yet	in spite of	on the other hand

- **Keep-going words** – These words signal that there is going to be more of the same:

furthermore	and	moreover
also	more	more than that
in addition	likewise	similarly

- **Here-it-comes words** – These words signal that a summary or conclusion is about to be stated:

therefore	consequently	thus
in conclusion	so	then
accordingly		

All these words help you through your reading like signposts. It is worth learning them and watching how they are used from now on. Then use them clearly to help you read faster and better (and to help you to write more clearly).

Bearing in mind the importance of topic sentences, and visual and verbal signposts, there are seven rules of skimming which you should always follow when faced with a pile of paperwork to read or before starting to read a textbook.

Check-Points: The Skimming Method

1 Use your *fastest possible reading speed* – this is one of its main purposes; since you are concerned with gaining an overview you can afford to go fast; you can read the detail later – if you need to.
2 Don't stop when you get to an *interesting bit;* it will only destroy your concentration on evaluation of the text; in any case, you will understand it better later on after you have formed a general view – keep going!
3 Read the *title, contents list* and *summary* where they exist; if the document or book has headings and subheadings, skim rapidly through it reading them all before you go back to the beginning and continue with the rest of this method.
4 Read the *first paragraph* of the document or chapter; this will introduce the main topics and will state the assumptions on which later information is based; if the first paragraph is very general, you may need to read the second – use your judgement.
5 Read the *first sentence*, and only the first sentence, of each subsequent paragraph; this should state the topic of the paragraph and should give the basic information about it; don't read the paragraph itself – that's where the detail is, and you'll be coming back to it later if you need it.
6 Normally when taken in order, the first sentences of consecutive paragraphs should follow one another logically, without gaps; if they don't, try the last sentence of the paragraph you're on; if that doesn't work, go on to the first sentence of the next paragraph. Though you may be left wondering – no writing can consistently stick to the rules – it is usually better to go on.
7 Near the end, read the *last two or three paragraphs* completely at a slower speed; they should contain deductions, conclusions and results from the preceding material; they may also contain a summary of the whole document or chapter, even though there is no heading to that effect.

Just as scanning is a technique of reading which you need to be able to call upon whenever it is appropriate to your reading purpose, so the ability to skim efficiently, when reading in more detail is not required, will extend your range of reading speed. Depending on your purpose and the nature and difficulty of the material, you should be able to slow down and speed up at will.

Assignment: Turn to a chapter in this book which you have not already read. Skim through the chapter following the procedure recommended above. Remember – your purpose is merely to get an overall idea of the way the chapter is structured and a rough idea of what it is about. Keep your speed up and don't stop to consider detail or to carry out any of the self-checks or assignments.

How did you get on? Don't be disappointed if you found that from time to time you were slipping back to reading at a fairly slow speed. Like everything else, it takes practice. It also takes a fair amount of self-discipline to drive yourself on, and constant reminding that if your purpose does not require you to get a good grasp of the detail, then why hang about?

Now let's assume that you have scanned through the material in your in-tray, or found a book or an article which you now need to read thoroughly. Let's see how the skills of scanning and skimming can be used along with other techniques to approach your reading task in a systematic and active way, so that you will get the most possible from the material, in the shortest possible time, and in such a way that you can remember what you need to remember after the task is finished.

One method of effective reading that pulls together some good reading habits is called the *SQ3R method.*

13.4 SQ3R method of reading

The approach has five stages and is called the SQ3R method after the initial letters of each stage.

First stage of reading – SURVEY

If you only want to read a particular section of the document, you will need to scan the table of contents and possibly the index, if there is one, to find the particular reference you are interested in. If you are reading the whole document then you will need to survey the whole thing using the method suggested for skimming. This is an essential first stage in reading any fairly lengthy or complex material. Don't be tempted to skip sections like the preface or a synopsis, as they will usually contain valuable clues to the purpose of the document, the way it is organised and the overall idea of the whole document.

Second stage of reading – QUESTION!

In order to read actively and purposefully, you need to think continuously about what you are reading – in other words, concentrate. One of the best ways of concentrating and thinking about what you are reading, rather than just being like a piece of human blotting paper sopping up ideas in a completely passive way, is to question what you are reading, just as you might question a speaker. Since the author is not with you, you must ask yourself questions:

- What is all this about?
- In the Preface (or Introduction) the author said the book/document would cover such-and-such an area. It doesn't seem to appear amongst the main headings. Have they linked it with something else under a different heading? The author said at the beginning that they would make four points. I can only find three. What is the fourth point? Do I agree with these points?
- That seems to be rather a far-fetched conclusion. Have they got the evidence to support that view?

Many of these questions should occur to you while you are doing the initial survey, and will provide you with a basis for reading the text more actively and critically. But when you come to the actual reading, you should continue this questioning:

- Did the author really back up what they said?
- That opinion seems to conflict with my opinion/my tutor's opinion/another author's opinion. Is the author's evidence better than that of others? Why?
- Is that what they really mean, or are they being sarcastic or ironic?
- How many people did they interview to arrive at that conclusion?
- They seem to be using emotive arguments here. Are they trying to manipulate me?

Active participation in the reading process like this will help you to understand and retain what you are reading. It is therefore one of the most important reading skills and although it is suggested here as the second stage, you should constantly practise it throughout the whole process of reading something – just as skimming is a skill which, though used particularly at the survey stage, you should be prepared to use whenever it is appropriate.

Third stage of reading – READ!

'At last', you may be saying, 'we are going to get down to the real business'. Yes! But like every other skill, it is not enough just to wish you were a more effective reader. It is necessary to analyse what good readers do, and be prepared to try out the various stages and techniques in the process – at first very slowly and then, as you become more skilled, the whole process becomes automatic.

Your initial survey will have provided you with some questions to which you are probably seeking the answer, and also an outline of the whole document or the first chapter which has suggested the main ideas the author is trying to communicate. As you now start to read, you will be looking to confirm the main ideas of each section, and find the main ideas at a lower level than you found in your survey. For instance, if you are reading an article or a short report, you will have skimmed through at the paragraph level looking for the main ideas in each paragraph. You will now be reading to confirm these ideas and to search for the supporting detail, the examples and illustrations which you ignored during the survey.

If, however, you are reading a book, your first survey will have been of the entire book, reading the chapter headings and section headings, the first and last paragraph of each chapter, and the whole of the preface and the last chapter to get a good general view of the whole book. You would then have to do a slightly closer survey of the first chapter along the lines suggested in the method of skimming; now you would be ready to start reading the chapter properly, looking for the supporting detail.

At this *first* reading, don't take notes – it will only break your train of thought and you would probably end up copying out large chunks of the author's original prose anyway.

If what you are reading is fairly complex it is better to read it twice fairly fast rather than once slowly. At this *second* reading, provided it isn't someone else's book, *underline the main ideas* and the supporting detail, if you want to, but still don't take notes.

Fourth stage of reading – RECALL!

Now you can take notes! But not by copying. Try to recall the main ideas and the supporting detail contained in the section you have just read. 'Ah', you say, 'but I can't!' If, after really trying, you can't remember what you've read, then you haven't been reading effectively. Go back and try again. This time, knowing that you are going to have to recall what you are reading will probably help you to concentrate and read more effectively. There is nothing that concentrates the mind so well as a test!

If retaining what you have read is your problem, then this is the most essential step for you – you can't afford to skip it. If, however, you find this step easy, then it won't take you long.

Fifth stage of reading – REVIEW!

This is the final stage – the chance to check that you haven't missed anything essential, that you have found the answers to the questions you've been producing, that you have been able to recall and make a note of all the main ideas and the important supporting detail without missing anything.

The review stage consists of going back very rapidly over the previous four stages:

- *Survey* – Quickly survey the whole chapter or report again, checking that you are completely clear about the way the author has structured his material and that there aren't any loose ends, that you haven't explained. (There may still be some that the author hasn't explained!)
- *Question* – Remind yourself of the questions that you had after doing the survey and while reading the text, or should you make a note of them to get the answer elsewhere!
- *Read* – You may need to read through the text again. This is where your skill at rapid skimming will again be useful. Have you noticed something important this time, which you hadn't made a note of before?
- *Recall* – This is your chance to check your notes. Fill in any gaps and make sure that your notes reflect the balance that the author gave to the material. Have you got very lengthy notes on a section to which the author devoted very little space? You may have a very good personal reason for this being so, but at least think about it!

Summary – better reading

Explained in detail like this, the process of reading better may seem time-consuming and off-putting. But remember, like any skill, reading takes longer to write about than to actually do. Learning to ride a bike can be rather painful at the beginning but now you can't remember what it felt like *not* to be able to do it. So it is with effective reading – hard at first but worth it in the end.

Assignment: Carry out a *chapter survey*. Using an article or the chapter of a textbook, fill in the following survey outline:

1 Title of the journal or textbook:
2 Title of the article or chapter:
3 List at least *three* questions the title suggests to you:

   (a)
   (b)
   (c)

4 Skim through the article reading the first paragraph, the headings and sub-headings, the topic sentence of each paragraph and the whole of the last two paragraphs. What is the article/chapter about?
5 How much do you know already about the subject?
6 What reading aids do the article/chapter contain?

bold print	headings	summary
italics	introduction	bibliography
graphs, charts	clear topic sentences	questions
pictures	lists	other:

7 How valuable is the article/chapter to you?

   essential
   useful
   irrelevant

8 How long will it take you to study it properly?
9 If you will need to divide the article/chapter into sections to study it, where are you going to divide it? (Name page numbers)
10 List at least four questions you need to find the answers to:

   (a)
   (b)
   (c)
   (d)

Assignment: Carry out a *complete survey*. Using this book, another textbook or a fairly long report, fill in the following survey outline:

1 Title:
2 List at least *three* questions or thoughts which the title suggests to you:

   (a)
   (b)
   (c)

3 List at least *two* major points the author makes in the Preface/Introduction/Foreword

   (a)
   (b)

4 Take at least *five* chapter or section titles listed in the table of contents and turn them into questions:

(a)

(b)

(c)

(d)

(e)

5 If there is an appendix, what does it contain?

6 Does the book/report contain a glossary? An index? If the answers are 'yes', look over the glossary and/or the index looking for familiar names, places or terms. How much do you think you are going to know about the contents?

7 Look through the first two chapters and tick any of the following reading aids used in them:

headings	introduction or objectives	footnotes
subheadings	lists	pictures
graphs, charts	boxes to highlight	italics
bold print		bibliography
study questions		other:

Exercise 13.1: If you were normally in the habit of skimming through a book *before* you started to read, then you would probably have come across the following questions before you started reading this chapter. In that case if you didn't know the answers already, you would have been looking out for the answers as you read through the chapter. This would have meant you would have been reading actively, and will mean that you will now find the questions very easy to answer.

If, however, you started at the beginning and this is the first time you have come across the questions for this chapter, then you may find them a little more difficult to answer, but now is your chance to assess your comprehension of this chapter.

1 What are the *three* categories into which you could group your reading material, in terms of its value to you?

2 Suggest at least *one* advantage of skimming.

3 Apart from fictional writing, where would you expect to find the main idea of a paragraph?

4 Give an example of a 'slow-down' word, a 'speed-up' word and a 'here-it-comes' word.

5 List the *five* stages of reading.

6 At which of these five stages should you start making notes?

Further reading

Buzan, Tony, *Use Your Head*, Harper Collins, 2000

Fairbairn, G.J. and Winch, C. *Reading, Writing and Reasoning*, Open University, 1996

Kump, Peter, *Breakthrough Rapid Reading*, Prentice Hall, 1998

Wainwright, Gordon, *Read Faster, Recall More*, How To Books, 2001

▪ ☒ 14 Writing business letters

Written communication

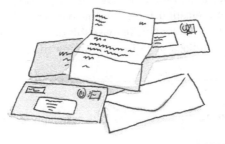

Apart from using the products and services of a business organisation and reading advertisements, the only direct and individual communication contact many people have with a company is a business letter. You, as the writer of a business letter, have a tremendous opportunity to help your organisation to meet its objectives and help a customer or client, while at the same time building goodwill.

This chapter looks at:

- the advantages and disadvantages of written and oral communication
- how you can write letters which achieve their purpose – to convey your message and maintain goodwill
- the mechanics of letter writing and letter layout so that the finished product will complement your message
- some tips on dictating.

Self-Check

Which is cheaper: a letter, a fax, or a telephone call?

14.1   Why good letter-writing matters

One county council calculated that if every employee whose job involved writing letters made only one mistake a week which either required the letter to be rewritten or retyped, or made an extra letter necessary, the total annual cost would be about £750 000.

A local authority exists to provide a service at the lowest possible cost. A business organisation depends on making a profit. Communication costs are a part of the total expense of doing business or providing services. So what is the cost of a business letter? A piece of paper, an envelope and a postage stamp? How did the council mentioned above arrive at the astronomical cost of £750 000 then?

The real cost of a letter involves not only the cost of sending it, but the costs of handling the letter through the internal post system, filing time, filing equipment and space, and the biggest item of all – the salaries of the letter writer and word-processor operator. It follows then that the higher these salaries, the higher will be the cost of their letters.

Some organisations estimate the cost of a business letter at about £25, even if it is dispatched electronically. Knowing this, you may discover that it is cheaper to make a telephone call, and in some very delicate and/or important matters requiring face-to-face communication, it may be cheaper to travel (even fly!) to deal with things personally. You are better able to make this decision if you know some of the advantages and disadvantages of written communication.

Self-Check

Make a list comparing the advantages and disadvantages of written and oral communication.

Check-Points: Written and Oral Communication Compared

WRITTEN	ORAL
Advantages	
• Better for facts and opinions.	• Better for feelings and emotions.
• Better for difficult or complicated messages; can be reviewed.	• More personal and individual.
• Useful when a written record is required for reference purposes.	• Provides far greater interaction and feedback.
• Can be both written and read when individuals are 'in the right mood'.	• Can make more impact.
• Can be carefully planned and considered before transmission.	• Generally less costly.
• Errors can be removed before transmission.	• Allows for correction and adjustment of message in the light of feedback and non-verbal cues.
Disadvantages	
• More time-consuming.	• More difficult to think as you speak.
• Feedback is either non-existent or delayed.	• Something once said cannot be erased.
• Lacks non-verbal cues which help interpretation.	• People may look as though they are listening but may not be receiving you – difficult to check with a large audience.
• Some people cannot or do not like to read.	
• You can never be sure the message is read or even received.	• Things said will often get forgotten.
• Lacks warmth and individuality.	

14.2 Backing up the phone call or meeting

It often pays to send information ahead of, or following a phone call. Examples include: diagrams, maps, graphs, tables of figures, price lists and technical specifications. This way the phone call can concentrate on reaching agreement rather than going over detailed information, and sending a fax or an e-mail is a good way to follow up a phone call while the matter is still fresh in the other person's mind. It doesn't have to be a literary masterpiece, but of course it should still obey the six Cs of effective communication:

- Clear
- Concise
- Courteous
- Constructive
- Correct
- Complete

For legal reasons, and when corresponding with the public, the letter sent by post (sometimes called snail-mail) is still a business necessity. But whether the letter is sent by post, fax or e-mail it still has to be composed. And yet, many people either do not communicate well in writing or think they do not communicate well in writing.

14.3 Planning a letter

Letters that get results do not just 'happen'. Like every other form of effective communication they have been thought about: why? who? what? how? where? when? and so on.

To plan your letter well you will need to review the background that has led to the *need* for a letter. This will often mean reviewing previous correspondence, and it is helpful to underline key points in incoming correspondence and make notes in the margins which will ensure you cover everything necessary in your own letter.

As you review the background, the reader and the reason for writing, the nature of the problem you have to solve will become apparent. You can then determine the type of letter you must write in order to solve the problem. For instance, if you have received a letter from a customer claiming some reparation for what they see as a fault on your part ('claim' or 'adjustment letter') and you are unable to satisfy the claim ('adjustment refusal') a certain type of letter, with a certain type of structure, will be indicated. If your purpose in another letter is to send a credit note or refund cheque, another type of letter will be suggested. Most of the letters that you have to write will fall into one of the standard categories.

In all these letters you are acting as an ambassador for your organisation, trying to maintain or build goodwill. In some of these letters, this task will be easy, in others more difficult, depending on the *anticipated reader reaction*. It is this which you should keep clearly in your mind, as it will help you to determine how to write the letter.

<table>
<tr><td colspan="3">**Check-Points: Principal Types of Business Letter**</td></tr>
<tr><td>**Purpose**</td><td>**Letter classification**</td><td>**Area**</td></tr>
<tr><td>• To seek information, opinion, confirmation</td><td>Query</td><td rowspan="5">General</td></tr>
<tr><td>• To give information, opinion, confirmation</td><td>Acknowledgement, information</td></tr>
<tr><td>• To seek reparation for some fault or deficiency</td><td>Complain/claim</td></tr>
<tr><td>• To accept the claim, provide reparation</td><td>Adjustment</td></tr>
<tr><td>• To place an order for goods or services</td><td>Order</td></tr>
<tr><td>• To confirm acceptance or an order</td><td>Confirmation of order</td><td rowspan="4">Ordering and estimating</td></tr>
<tr><td>• To give an estimate of price, time, etc.</td><td>Estimate</td></tr>
<tr><td>• To give a final price, time, etc. (contractual)</td><td>Tender</td></tr>
<tr><td>• To sell goods or services</td><td>Sales letter</td></tr>
<tr><td>• To remind of sales offers</td><td>Follow-up sales letter</td><td rowspan="3">Sales and advertising</td></tr>
<tr><td>• To advertise goods or services</td><td>Non-solicited sales letter</td></tr>
<tr><td>• To authorise advance of credit</td><td>Letter of credit</td></tr>
<tr><td>• To check or comment on credit-worthiness or rating</td><td>Credit reference inquiry – reply</td><td rowspan="2">Financial and credit management</td></tr>
<tr><td>• To obtain payment of a debt</td><td>Collection (various stages – usually 1, 2 and 3 – getting more and more threatening)</td></tr>
</table>

Anticipated reader reaction

- *Favourable* – You agree to do something: send goods, services, money, will speak at a meeting and so on. Fairly easy to write.
- *Neutral* – Neutral messages are neither favourable nor unfavourable. Many business letters fall into this category, for example, writing a letter of recommendation for a former employee or providing a credit reference.
- *Unfavourable* – You have to refuse to do something. Difficult to write because saying 'no' runs the risk of losing goodwill; your letter must therefore use every possible method of softening the blow and building goodwill in other ways.
- *Persuasive* – You have to sell an idea or product, turn the reader from being disinterested, or even uninterested, to being interested enough to do what you want – accept your position or proposal, buy your product or service.

Your analysis of your reader's reaction and the type of letter you must write will suggest the approach you should adopt and the most appropriate organisation or structure of your material.

Obviously there is no hard and fast rule, and many letters defy classification since their subject matter and purpose often cut across the boundaries between different types of letters. However, the check-points on a suggested approach to writing business letters may give you some help in tackling a particular letter.

Check-Points: Suggested Approach to Writing Business Letters

Broad type of letter	Particular type of letter	Suggested approach	Structure (parts or paragraphs
• Favourable	Order Confirmation of order Acknowledgement Information Claim (expecting 'yes') Adjustment Credit offer or acceptance	Deductive	I Pleasant idea in 'yes' letter or main idea in routine 'neutral' letter II Details or explanations
• Neutral	Credit reference Personal reference Letter of credit Estimate Tender Resignation	Deductive	III Closing thought
• Unfavourable	Adjustment refusal Credit refusal Order refusal Favour refusal Information refusal Solicitor's letters	Inductive	I Neutral statement that leads to reasons II Facts, analysis, reasons
• Persuasive	All sales letters Claim (expecting 'no') Collection letters Application for job, loan, etc. Estimate Tender	Inductive	III Unpleasant message or unsolicited suggestion IV Related idea that takes emphasis away from the unpleasant or asks for action

Assignment: In each of the cases below consider what kind of letter you would have to write, given the likely reaction of the reader to the basic message you have to convey.

Now consider how you want the reader to react. What therefore is your real purpose? What do you want them to do/feel/believe? How then are you going to structure your letter? What are you going to say and how are you going to say it?

1 Your department of Floridan Airlines is responsible for dealing with customer complaints. You have received a letter from a woman who reports that she was served a live frog in her meal on a flight from Nassau to Mexico. She realises that there is nothing you can do about it now, since the event is in the past, but she does feel that you should know about it and avoid this sort of thing happening again. How would you reply?

2 You work for a rather traditional firm in the credit control department and have received a routine request for a credit reference on behalf of a small company with which your firm has never had any debt collection problems. How would you reply to the company requiring the reference?

3 Your boss has been asked to speak at a company communications seminar but will be unable to do so as he will be involved in his annual visit to regional offices to discuss plans for the coming year. He has to be away from the office today and asks you to draft a letter for him to see on his return. As he leaves the office he mumbles something about 'perhaps I could get Dave Wainwright to do it for them'.

4 You have so far failed to pay £25 for a Green Card (insurance confirmation necessary for travelling abroad) which was issued several months ago. You have felt disinclined to offer payment until the insurance brokers asked for the money and intend now to offer only £15, since you were put to considerable inconvenience by the insurance company (for whom the brokers act). They were extremely inefficient, failing to produce the card on time despite adequate notice, and only supplying one eventually at the eleventh hour after you had made several telephone calls and personal visits. What sort of covering letter would you send with the cheque?

Now look at the suggestions below. They are all genuine letters (even the first one!) with only the names changed. The parts of the letter may coincide with your paragraphs as in the following suggestions but a 'part' of a letter may consist of more than one paragraph.

I Favourable letter

Dear Mrs Linklater,

Our Catering Superintendent for North America, Ian Taylor, has reported that a live frog was served with your meal tray on the flight between Nassau and Mexico on 19 June. I hope you will accept our sincere apologies for this, which I very much hope has not lost us a valued customer.

Needless to say, this kind of thing is taken up very seriously with the airports concerned and their contractors, but despite every effort to ensure that this type of incident will not occur, very occasionally we must admit to a failing in our very stringent quality procedures.

We greatly appreciate your liberal approach to the incident, but hope not to stretch your goodwill in the same way again on a Floridan Airways flight. Thank you for flying with us.

Yours sincerely,

Simon Temple-Combe
Customer Relations Manager

Part I   Opens with a positive reaction to complaint and reference to 'you' as a 'valued customer'.

Part II Gives explanation of action taken by the company.

Part III Ends with a note of goodwill.

2   Neutral letter

Dear Sirs,

In reply to your letter of 4 July, we have always regarded Rees and Greenwood of Winterdown as a very reliable firm.

We have supplied them with our goods for many years. Indeed, many of the orders we have received have been greatly in excess of £500 so that we feel there should be little danger in granting them credit for £500.

If you need any specific details, please contact us again.

Yours faithfully

M Wisbech
Credit Control Manager

Part I   Identified the subject quickly and offers some information about the firm immediately.

Part II Gives further details (length of time over which business has been transacted) and justified confidence in the subject (many orders in excess of £500).

Part III Ends on a helpful note – confirming goodwill.

3   Unfavourable letter

Dear Mr Leverton

I was very interested to hear of your plans for a Company Communication Seminar – an initiative which I'm sure will be welcomed by the impressive number of firms taking part.

Spring is always a hectic time of the year for me because I make my annual visit to each of our regional offices to discuss plans for the coming financial year. As you can imagine, it is quite a task fitting all these visits in and, having made the arrangements so far ahead, I must stick to the time-tables. Unfortunately, on the date you have asked me to speak, I shall be in Scotland.

However, may I suggest my colleague David Wainwright, who would make an ideal alternative speaker. He has 10 years' experience in Employee Communications during which time he has himself initiated several successful ventures and would, I am sure, be happy to speak on 'Tell or Listen?' if he is free. Let me know if you find this an acceptable suggestion and I will ask him to contact you.

Best wishes for a successful seminar.

Yours sincerely
Richard Sharp

Part I	Using inductive order (see Section 1.7), the letter leaves the unpleasant element until later, and opens with a pleasant and sincere comment on the idea of the seminar.
Parts II & III	Presents explanation and reasons for being unable to say 'yes' without saying 'no' bluntly or directly.
Part IV	Offers an alternative and then ends with a goodwill idea.

4 Persuasive letter

Sure-All Insurance and Mortgage Brokers Ltd
Sharp Hill
Sheffield SD37 4BS

Dear Sirs,

Thank you for the statement indicating that I still owe you £25 for the Green Card issued at Easter. I seem unable to trace an invoice for £25. However, I accept that as yet I have not settled the bill.

You will probably recall the considerable problems I encountered trying to extract this card from Sure-All Insurance in time for my departure. Despite having given the required notice for the issue of a Green Card, I had still not received it 24 hours before I was due to leave. I was therefore forced to make two special trips into town to fetch the card, both without success, although I had been told it would be ready on both occasions; two telephone calls to you and one to the ferry company to enquire about my position if I sailed without it; and finally another trip into town to fetch a specially issued card – all at my expense in terms of money, time and unnecessary anxiety.

Since I regard £25 as an excessive charge for the work involved in issuing a certificate to demonstrate that I am already insured, and since I incurred considerable expense in trying to obtain the card, I am therefore enclosing a cheque for £15.

Unless you tell me otherwise I shall assume that Sure-All agree with me that under the circumstances £15 is more than adequate.

Yours faithfully,
Helena Smailes (Ms)

The main idea of this letter is that the writer is sending a cheque for only £15 in settlement of a bill for £25, but by careful use of inductive order for both paragraph sequence and the sentence structure of the last but one paragraph, she only presents the reader with the unfavourable idea at the end of paragraph III – very near the end of the letter. This is achieved by presenting the reasons for not paying any more, in paragraph II, without actually saying so directly.

Part I   Neutral idea first – agreeing that the bill is not yet settled despite not having received an invoice before.

Part II   This main paragraph leads up to the idea of the writer's expense (inductive order).

Part III   Introduces a further justification for thinking £25 too much, and summarises main justification (inconvenience and expenses) before announcing unfavourable message.

Part IV   Related idea that takes emphasis away from the unpleasant idea, assumes success of the persuasion, and puts the onus on the recipient to do something if they have not been persuaded.

Each of those letters began by clearly *identifying the subject* of the letter in the first paragraph and ended by *suggesting what happens next* so that the reader is quite clear *who* has to do something next, or whether the matter is now complete. In between the introduction and the conclusion goes the detail which should be set out in paragraphs – one main idea to each paragraph. Within this basic framework you can use your skill at choosing words to create goodwill whatever the nature of your message.

Exercise 14.1

1 Why is a letter not a cheap method of communication?
2 What is the purpose of each of these letters?

• Adjustment
• Credit reference enquiry
• Collection.

3 Letters can be classified in many ways, but most letters fall into four main categories depending on how their message will be viewed by the reader. What are the four main categories?
4 What is the psychological effect on the reader of a business letter when negative elements are introduced early in the letter? How does proper organisation help the writer to deal with this problem?
5 What are the advantages of using a question as a technique for beginning a letter?
6 Can you think of four ways to end a letter effectively?

Assignment: Collect examples of different business letters, perhaps one sent to you personally as a consumer or householder from firms or public organisations you deal with.

- Classify each one: was it a favourable, neutral, unfavourable or persuasive letter for the writer to tackle?
- Did the writer assess the reader reaction correctly and organise the letter accordingly?
- What structure did the writer use?
- What techniques for beginning and ending the letter have been used?
- What metacommunications elements are present in the letter?
- What reaction did you have to the letter? Do you think it was the one intended by the writer?

14.4 Layout and style

A letter begins its job as an ambassador of the organisation immediately it arrives, and however well the message has been planned and written, the reader cannot help but be affected by the overall appearance of the letter (and even the envelope).

Most organisations, appreciative of the significance of conveying the right 'corporate image' and creating a favourable impression from the first moment, devote considerable effort to the design of their packaging and advertising material, and this attention to design is reflected in the printed stationery and the appearance and lay-out of the document. Consequently, you will probably find that your organisation has a particular 'house style' which everyone is expected to follow. This 'house style' is often reflected in templates provided on the computer system.

Assignment

- Find out whether your organisation has a house style or presentation and lay-out guidelines
- Does your department or section follow this house style or does it have its own?
- What are the rules for laying out a fax, letter, memo or e-mail and the envelope?
- What impression does it create?
  - reliable? efficient? modern?
  - old-fashioned? traditional?
  - uncaring? untidy?
- What factors contribute to this impression?
- Do you like the layout? Why?

You should not ignore these aspects of letter-writing, even if you feel they are the preserve of the office resources staff, for the following reasons:

- You may one day, if not now, be in a position to influence or help create a house style

- You will probably have to prepare letters for yourself, and a poorly laid-out letter, whether keyed or handwritten, will convey metacommunications – 'I'm not really interested in what impression I create', 'I am untidy and careless', 'I am not concerned with details', 'I am not sensitive to the many ways in which "messages" can be conveyed.'

Check-Points: Preparing Letters

- The neat appearance of the type or handwriting is important
- Careful use of space, balanced paragraphing and positioning of the various parts of the letter can create a visually pleasing effect.

Shape

You may have come across the older lay-out style known as 'fully indented' (see Figure 14.1). Both addresses and the close and signature are progressively indented, each paragraph is indented and the heading is centred. This layout is now very uncommon – can you think of two reasons why this layout is no longer preferred?

Take a ruler and, placing it vertically down the page at the beginning of each indented line on the page, draw a vertical line. How many have you got? I calculate that there are about a dozen different vertical lines. Anyone keying this letter would have to centre the heading and the close and signature ('subscription'), use a tabulator key to line up the paragraphs, and work out how to make the sender's address and date fit into the top right-hand corner without overflowing into the margin. This all takes time. One reason for abandoning full indentation layout, therefore, is inefficiency. But a second reason is that all those imaginary vertical lines produce a cluttered effect. For these reasons the layouts in Figures 14.2, 14.3 and 14.4 are currently preferred.

Fully blocked (see Figure 14.2)

Everything starts at the left-hand margin – one vertical line.

- *Advantages* – efficient, very modern, most commonly used
- *Disadvantages* – it has a rather lopsided look which would be even worse if the sender's address had to be written on the left above everything else (when non-headed paper is used).

Semi-blocked (see Figure 14.3)

The date and the subscription are on the right, the heading is centred and everything else starts at the left-hand margin. Paragraphs and so on are blocked.

- *Advantages* – fairly efficient, and produces a more balanced look.

Semi-indented (see Figure 14.4)

Like semi-blocked but the paragraphs are indented.

- *Advantages* – slightly less cluttered and easier to key than fully indented – but not much.

RUNAWAY AND BOLT, LTD

Thorn Mills,
Bradford,
BD3 7RS,

① **Letterheading**

3rd May 20..

② **Date (in full)**

③ **Ref. No**

Our ref:

Your ref:

④ **Recipient's name, position and address**

The Chief Accountant,
Rees & Greenwood, Ltd
Winterdown Road,
SHEFFIELD SH3 4B4.

⑤ **Salutation**

Dear Sir,

<u>Alan Francis Lines</u>

⑥ **Heading**

Replying to your letter of 30 April, we are pleased to inform you that Mr. Alan Lines has served this firm faithfully and well for the last five years.

He is a thoroughly efficient, honest and capable member of our staff. If he considers leaving us, we shall indeed be sorry to lose him, even though we realise his qualifications and experience must enable him to gain promotion.

⑧ **Body of the letter**

We have therefore no hesitation in recommending him to you and wish him well at the interview.

Yours faithfully,

⑤ **Complimentary close**

Edward Q. Bolt,
Company Secretary

⑦ **and Signature**

Figure 14.1 **Fully indented layout – now old-fashioned.**

Assignment: Which of the layouts in Figures 14.2, 14.3 and 14.4 do you prefer? Which would suit a hand-written letter?

You will probably come across other variations of these three basic models and the one you choose will depend on (a) your organisation's house style or (b) your

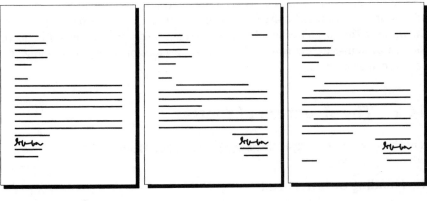

| *Figure14.2*
Fully blocked layout. | *Figure 14.3*
Semi-blocked layout. | *Figure 14.4*
Semi-indented layout. |

personal preference. But whichever you adopt, be consistent. For example, don't block some paragraphs and not others.

Open punctuation

This is the practice of omitting punctuation marks (Mr not Mr. for example) from everything in the letter *except the main body of the message*. It is perfectly acceptable and is almost universally adopted nowadays – again it makes your life easier. It does not necessarily have to be used with fully blocked layout. However, use it with care. Again, be consistent and pay particular attention when writing the initials of names to leave sufficient space, so as not to produce absurd or incomprehensible 'words', for example, PEAGREEN Esq, Mr ITIsis (people with names like that probably have enough problems already!).

Stationery

Decisions concerning the design of the letterhead and choice of layout will depend on the size of paper used.

Paper

The most popular sizes of paper currently in use are:

- A4 – 297 mm × 210 mm
- A5 – 210 mm × 148 mm (half the size of A4).

A short single-spaced letter on A5 paper would look better than double-spacing on A4.

Envelopes

There are various envelope sizes available. The *Post Office Guide* gives those that the Post Office prefers, but choose an envelope which will not force you to fold the letter more than twice.

When window envelopes are used, you should take care to key the recipient's address in exactly the right place on the letter so that it can be seen clearly through the window. The *post code* should always be visible and *last* in the address, either on its own or alongside the county. In the case of cities or large conurbations, the county can be omitted.

14.5　The structure of a letter

A business letter normally consists of *eight* parts (see Figure 14.1).

1　Heading or letterhead

On business letters the name and address of the sender are printed: the name usually in much bolder type. The letterhead usually spans the whole page approximately 2–3 inches deep, or is positioned in the top right-hand corner. It usually includes the company's trading name, address, post code, telephone and fax numbers and web address. As a result of legislation it must include certain other information.

Check-Points: Statutory Requirements for Letterheads

Company's trading name
Its status as a limited company (if appropriate)
List of company directors if
   founded after 23 November 1916 (showing
   nationality in certain circumstances)　　　　Usually placed at the
Address of its registered office　　　　　　　bottom of the page
Registration number of company
Location of registration

Logo

Most organisations now use logos in the design of their stationery and packaging. A logo is a visual symbol or identification mark which is usually directly related to the company, its products, or its services; or simply a design that has become associated with the company over time. The logo is closely linked with the image the organisation wishes to convey and so some marks are updated while others remain the same over the years. Look at the logos that Palgrave Macmillan and the Open University use on the title page of this book.

The sender's address

On non-business letters, the sender's address (which should not include the name) is usually placed in the top right-hand corner.

2 Date

This is usually placed two or three spaces under the last line of the sender's address Ideally it should finish flush with the right-hand margin (or placed against the left-hand margin if fully-blocked layout is used). The recommended method of writing the date is day, month, year. Increasingly the 'th', 'st' and 'nd' are omitted, as is the comma between the month and the year.

	20 February 20..	European practice
or	20th February 20..	
but	February 20 20..	United States practice

3 References

So that letters can easily be filed and traced for reference purposes, it is advisable to provide a reference code: 'Our ref: NL/JM CF2'. When replying to a letter which itself includes its own reference, both references are typed:

Our ref: NL/JM CF2 (outgoing letter)
Your ref: SB/sjt (incoming letter)

References are usually entered above the date or level with the date on the left-hand side and are composed of:

- first: initials of letter writer (in capitals)
- second: initials of secretary (sometimes in lower case)
- if relevant, third: reference to a particular file ('Conference File 2').

In all cases, they should be quoted when replying to a letter.

4 Recipient's name, position and address

Usually placed two or three spaces below the reference(s) blocked (see Figures 14.2 –14.4), with open punctuation:

Mr R A Jones
British Engineering plc
20–27 Wansdyke Road
SHIPLEY
Yorks SY3 1QS

Where possible, the address should be confined to three or four lines to avoid starting the body of the letter too far down the page.

The name and address should never be omitted from a business letter as, without it, the copy preserved for reference would be useless.

Names and forms of address

How do you address a knight? When should you use 'Mr' and when 'Esq.'? How do you write to a company if you do not have a person's name to use? How do you address a woman if you don't know whether she's married or single?

These and similar questions have caused untold problems for letter writers and secretaries, and justified the writing of countless books on 'etiquette' over the years – and it is still difficult to remember the rules.

Self-Check: Try to work out the rules from the following examples. If all the following forms of address are correct, what are the rules governing:

(a) 'Mr' or 'Esq.'?
(b) Women?
(c) People with titles?
(d) People with degrees, diplomas, decorations, orders and membership of professional bodies?
(e) Companies and partnerships?

1 Mr. R. Smith
2 John Smith
3 John Smith Esq. VC MA MIPD
4 Rev. S. Martin, LIb
5 Miss V. Ryan Msc
6 Mrs S. Taylor BA Dip Ed.
7 Ms Lisa Thompson BEM AMIMech.E
8 Lady Abigail Smythe
9 Lord Chalstead
10 Sir Alex Groves
11 Dame Anna Smailes
12 Messrs Hamlyn and Cook
13 Sir Matthew Dunn & Sons
14 The Company Secretary, Marsdyke Shipping plc
15 Sir Frederick Tinsdale Ltd

(a) *'Mr' or 'Esq'* (1, 2 and 3) Originally the term 'esquire' was only given to people of high rank in society; in more recent times it has been used instead of 'Mr' for members of the professions – solicitors, doctors, engineers, architects and so on, while 'Mr' has been used for aldermen, councillors, trades-people and others of lower rank! However, the 'Mr' prefix is now more popular and can be used when addressing everyone but those of higher rank in society.

Note: the two should never be used together; if 'Mr' is used 'Esq.' should be omitted.

The forename is given in full when 'Esq' is used, but initials are sufficient when 'Mr' is used.

Check-Point: It is now increasingly acceptable to omit the 'Mr' or 'Esq' altogether. In this case a forename must be used, e.g. John Dunn. However, if in doubt, use 'Mr'.

(b) *Forms of address for women* (5, 6, 7, 8 and 11) The most commonly used styles are: Miss, Mrs, Ms, Lady, Dame. Women in business are tending to use 'Ms' since many regard it as irrelevant to their job whether they are married or single. If you do not know which style is preferred (or indeed which is appropriate) you have to take a chance between Miss and Mrs, but since many women are rather sensitive about the implication associated with both, you probably can't win! As with men, you can now omit the style altogether, for example, 'Faye Brooks'. In the case of titles the forename is used for wives of knights (Sir Reginald and Lady Abigail Smythe) and for Dames, but not for wives of lords (Lord and Lady Chalstead).

(c) *Titles* (8, 9 and 10) Note that the forename is used with 'Sir' but not with 'Lord'. Other titles currently in use are 'Dr' which is used both for a medical doctor and someone who has been awarded a doctorate of philosophy (Ph.D). A surgeon consultant and a dentist are both addressed 'Mr' and 'Reverend' is abbreviated to 'Rev'.

(d) *Letters and qualifications after the name* (3, 4, 5, 6 and 7) Many people who have earned academic degrees, military decorations and membership of professional bodies are understandably proud of their achievements. They may therefore be gratified if these letters are used as part of their style of address (some may even be offended if you don't). The problem of writing them correctly and in the right order is not always as difficult as it may seem. The simple rule is that they should appear in the following order:

1 decorations (military and civil)
2 degrees and diplomas
3 membership of professional bodies.

If in doubt, you will probably have access to a letter or other document from which you can copy. Failing that, a phone call to the secretary or another official in the organisation will probably provide the information you need.

(e) *Companies and partnerships* (12, 13, 14 and 15) Writing to organisations does not normally cause a problem as the correct title usually appears on their stationery. However, the word 'Messrs' does appear to cause problems and in fact has been used inaccurately (perhaps through ignorance) by many companies. The word *'Messrs'* is derived from the French word messieurs meaning 'gentlemen'. It is now rather dated but would be correctly used when writing to an *unlimited company* or *partnership*, unless another title (e.g. 'Sir') is already included, or the partnership is registered under another name. However, it should never be used before the name of a *limited company*.

Letters to a limited company are normally addressed to the Secretary, or some other official, for example,

Messrs Hamlyn and Cook	Unlimited companies
Messrs John Fielding & Sons	or partnerships
Sir Robert Dunn & Sons	
'Just Boats' Hire Company	
Sir Frederick Tinsdale Ltd	Limited companies
The Secretary, Marsdyke Shipping plc	

How well did you work out the rules? It is possible here to deal with only the most general rules and the most common problems, and you would be well advised to check in a reference book whenever you are in doubt.

5 Salutations and complimentary closes

These refer to the formal opening and closing of the letter's message and there are certain conventions which should be followed. With the increasing relaxation of formal business-writing style, it may seem odd that these rules of propriety still exist, but exist they do and many people still feel so strongly about these conventions that they are provoked into writing to *The Times* about the frequently found mistakes in this matter, particularly incorrect pairings of salutation and complimentary close.

Self-Check

Which of these is right and which is wrong?

(a)	Dear Sir	Yours sincerely
(b)	Dear Mr Brown	Yours sincerely
(c)	Dear Ms Jones	Yours sincerely
(d)	Dear Madam	Yours sincerely
(e)	Gentlemen	Yours sincerely

Now look at the check-points below.

Check-Points: Complimentary Closes Appropriate to Various Salutations

Salutation	Complimentary close
Dear Sir	
Dear Sirs	
Gentlemen	Yours faithfully
Dear Madam	
Dear Mesdames	
Dear Mr Smith	
Dear Ms Jones	Yours sincerely
Dear Mrs Bennett	
Dear Reverend Cavendish	
Dear Dr Smythe	
Dear Sir Lionel	
Dear Lady Julia	Yours sincerely
Dear Lord Chalstead	
Dear Lady Chalstead	
Dear Jane	Sincerely *or* Best Wishes *or*
Dear Robert	Kind Regards *or* Love

Note particularly that where the name is not used 'Yours faithfully' is the only correct complimentary close ('Yours truly' as an alternative to 'Yours faithfully' is really unacceptable now) and note also that 'faithfully' and 'sincerely' both start with *lowercase* letters when written after 'Yours', which starts with a capital letter.

The conventional linking of a salutation with a particular complimentary close is based on the degree of relationship between the writer and recipient:

Dear Sir *Yours faithfully* (writer and recipient have not met, name of recipient is not known, relationship is fairly formal)

Dear Mr Brown *Yours sincerely* (more friendly, name known – commonly used in business even where correspondents have not met).

Other than these two conventions, the rules are becoming more relaxed and where the relationship is fairly familiar, writers can choose what seems the most appropriate to them and the circumstances, for example,

Dear Charles/Dear Susan/My dear Charles/Mr dear Susan/My dear Brown, etc. with
Sincerely/Kind regards/Best wishes/Yours affectionately/Affectionately, etc.

6 Subject heading

Strictly speaking every business letter should deal with one subject (it makes filing easier) and it should therefore be possible to sum up the subject of the letter in a brief but helpful heading which assists the reader in knowing immediately what the letter is about. It should be placed between the salutation and the body of the letter and is either centred over the typed area (semi-blocked layout) or started at the left-hand margin (blocked layout).

Assignment: Devise clear brief headings for each of the letters on pp. 200–3.

7 Signature

The practice of typing the name of the organisation immediately under 'Yours faithfully' has almost disappeared:

Yours faithfully,
ARNOLD J. BROWN & Co.,

S. Stevens

S. Stevens (Mrs)
Company Secretary

but it is good practice to type the name of the sender in lower-case letters (or in capital letters when the letter is hand-written) in case the signature is illegible, and many people's are! The designation of the writer is then written immediately below the name:

Yours faithfully,

S. Stevens

S. Stevens (Mrs)
Company Secretary

8 The body of the letter

The body of the letter should be written in clear and concise English with correct paragraphing and punctuation.

Paragraphing

Each paragraph should express a separate item in the letter and may therefore consist of only one sentence; but too many short paragraphs can spoil the appearance of the letter. Look back at Section 13.3, 'Topic Sentences', for help in constructing good paragraphs.

Subheading. If the message can usefully be divided into sections, do not hesitate to use subheadings (within reason).

Lists. Similarly if a paragraph contains points which could be usefully presented in list form, do so. Use numbers or bullets to highlight the list.

Punctuation

Even where open punctuation is chosen for the addresses and so on, the body of the letter must still be punctuated.

Punctuation should be used to help understanding. Too many commas liberally sprinkled about a letter are not necessarily helpful to the reader and usually suggest that the writer is really not too clear about the purpose of the various punctuation marks (see Appendix A).

Check-Points: Well-presented Letters

- reference to previous correspondence where necessary.
- indentation or spacing between paragraphs (see Figures 14.2–14.4);
- punctuation to help understanding.
- the use of subheadings and lists where helpful.
- clear and correct English (check Appendix D and Appendix H).

Moral: anything that helps the reader to understand the message quickly and easily, and improves the visual appearance of the letter, is usually permissible.

Margins

The most important guide is visual appearance. Generally a margin of about 2.5 cm on both sides of the sheet looks good, but it will of course depend on the length of the letter and the position of the letterhead. Organisations often provide templates or macros (pre-designed lay-out) on their computer systems to help staff stick to the house style.

Spacing

Nearly every business letter is laid out in single spacing with a double space between paragraphs. Some organisations, however, prefer that very short letters (up to say 10 lines) be typed in double spacing with wider margins. The recipient's address (and the sender's address, if it is not already printed) should always be typed in single spacing.

Enclosures

The fact that a letter contains enclosures is indicated by the letters 'Enc.' or 'Encs 3' at the foot of the letter, or by '/' placed in the margin alongside the reference to the enclosure in the text.

Follow-on sheets or continuation sheets

These are used where the letter extends beyond one page, but you should avoid using them if fewer than two lines of the letter would appear on the sheet and you should never use a continuation sheet which would contain only the complimentary close and signature. The printed letter heading is not required, but the continuation sheet should bear the name of the recipient, the page number, and date:

G Mainwaring & Co Ltd   –2–   22 February 20..

Copy/copies

When a copy of the letter is to be sent to a third party, this is indicated by: 'copy to', 'copies to', or 'c.c', usually written near the bottom of the letter with the relevant name(s) listed.

Warnings

If the contents of a letter are confidential, private or personal, this should be indicated prominently on the letter (usually above the recipient's name and address) and on the envelope.

> **CONFIDENTIAL** or **PRIVATE AND CONFIDENTIAL**
> **PERSONAL** or **PERSONAL AND CONFIDENTIAL**

Note: if a letter is marked 'Personal' it will be opened only by the person to whom it is addressed.

Another method of ensuring that a particular person in a company deals with your letter is to write the words:

> **For the attention of:**
> followed by the name and address.

14.6 Dictating

Increasingly, people at work have access to WP equipment and are expected to prepare their own letters but if they do not have a portable computer and work away from base, using a dictaphone can be a useful way of making notes or using up waiting time. Yet many people who have access to typists and dictating machines still go to great lengths to avoid dictating where possible.

We are all finding our roles increasingly affected as more efficient methods of communication are introduced, and we need to be familiar with the modern electronic information-processing equipment which is now increasingly available at all levels in organisations.

Amongst the many new skills needed, more and more emphasis is being placed on the specific skills in oral communication which are essential when using modern equipment, where clarity in enunciation and precision and unambiguity of expression are particularly important.

So whether or not you have occasion to dictate material to a secretary or a tape recorder at the moment, practice in the skills involved will stand you in good stead for leaving messages on answer machines or voicemail systems and, of course, for using voice-input WP systems.

Preparation for dictation

Good dictation is only good writing out loud; and good writing is only good thinking well expressed. In other words, so long as you give your messages preparation time, and plan in advance what you are going to say, it should make very little difference whether the final draft is handwritten onto paper, dictated to a telephone or dictated into a machine. The fear that dictating holds for many people results either from their unwillingness to plan the message carefully before they start or simply from their fear of the unfamiliar; so as usual it is a case of practising. Practise at home using a small cassette recorder, if you have one, until you have the knack of stopping and starting.

Check-Points: Preparing to Dictate

1 **Prepare yourself** – forget everything else; clear your mind and your desk – concentrate; clear your mouth – pencils, cigarettes, anything in your mouth interferes with speech.
2 **Prepare your material** in just the same way as you would if you were going to write the draft, that is, as far as the skeleton outline stage.
3 **Prepare the priorities** – If you have more than one letter or message to dictate, list them by priority; you may be interrupted.
4 **Prepare the WP operator** (it may be you!) – Brief them fully, whether face-to-face or on the tape recorder. Tell them:

- who the letter is to
- who the letter is from.

If you need to keep hard copies for filing tell them:

- the reference
- how many copies you need
- who the copies are for.

If you need the WP operator to see letters you are replying to, for addresses and so on, tell them clearly which original goes with which letter.

Dictating practice

Check-Points: Dictating

1 Say it simply – in brief sentences – one idea to a paragraph.
2 Punctuate as you dictate, say: 'paragraph' (new paragraph), 'stop', 'comma', 'indent', 'list' and so on.
  Natural pauses when speaking are a good clue to the need for punctuation marks, but don't go overboard.
3 Concentrate on speaking clearly and more slowly than usual. Mumbling is expensive – it leads to mistakes and frustration for the typist. But don't speak too slowly – this will disrupt your natural fluency and the typist's natural speed.
4 Spell names of people, roads, towns and technical terms when they are not obviously simple.
5 If you dry up – stop. It happens to everyone and it doesn't matter. What does matter is trying to plough on when you've lost your thread.
6 Play it back, collect your thoughts and then carry on.
7 When you've finished, check. Have you been clear, correct, complete and concise?
8 Every so often, listen back to your dictated material. Although it may be a painful experience, it will help you to improve.

Remember: most typists type what you say

- not what you think you say,
- not what they think you wanted to say.

Assignment: Bearing in mind the principles covered in this chapter on organising a letter, creating the appropriate tone, and laying out the letter well, write a letter suitable for sending to the *unsuccessful* applicants for a position of personnel manager with your company.

- Remember that as well as needing to convey your message you will also want to maintain goodwill – that is, leave the disappointed applicants with a good impression of your company and with their self-respect intact.
- Before you write the final draft, try dictating the letter into a tape recorder.
- Then write out the letter and compare your written letter with your dictated letter.

Now look at the letter below, written with the same objective as yours. It is an example from real life. What do you think of it? Why? How does it compare with yours? Which do you like best? Which would you prefer to receive?

Dear Mr Thompson,
Personnel Manager – HOU 163

This letter is to let you know the latest position regarding the recruitment of a personnel manager for our Swindon branch.

I am about to see some candidates whose overall background and experience appear very close to our requirements. In view of this I do not suggest that you come for an interview at this stage; but should the position alter, I shall write to you immediately.

However, if I am not able to take matters further on this occasion, I hope that you will let us know if one our future advertisements appeals to you.

Your sincerely

G.B. England
Personnel Director

14.7 Standard letters

Your organisation may provide you with standard letters for the main occasion when you have to write letters. But beware! You still need to think – especially if you are joining standard paragraphs together. Make sure they really do 'fit' together and that you have not left in things that do not apply, or left things out which need saying *in this particular situation.*

Summary – writing business letters

A business letter, whether a personal communication or a sales letter, is an ambassador for you, your department, your profession, your organisation. You cannot allow it to let you down.

Assignment: Choose a typical situation in which your organisation would send a letter. Write the letter you would write and then compare yours with the real one(s) that your organisation would send.

Further reading

Maitland, Iain, *Write That Letter!*, Kogan Page, 2000

☒ 15 Applying for a job

The 'job letter'

One of the most important letters you are ever likely to write is the one applying for a job. But sometimes in the excitement or desperation of the moment it is easy to start writing without giving the matter too much thought, and without realising that writing the letter is only one part of the whole process – a process which although it is pretty demanding can actually be rather interesting, because it is like a detective hunt for clues to help you find out what kind of job you really want and to help you work out what kind of person they really want.

The intention of this chapter is to help you find out

- *what sort of job suits you*
- *what is available*
- *what employers are looking for.*

In addition it should provide you with some tips on how to

- *complete application forms*
- *write application letters*
- *generally increase your chances of getting an interview, which is really the first major objective of the application process.*

It will obviously only be useful if you are looking for a job at the moment or about to start the process. So if you are happily settled and not thinking of moving for a while you might prefer to skip this chapter and return to it another time when it is more immediately useful. However, remember to refer to it well in advance – the process of applying for a job is not one to be hurried, as we shall see.

More haste – less speed.

You may have seen an advertisement and simply want to apply; you may be trying to get promotion; you may be at college in the final year of your course and in the unenviable position of needing to write to organisations 'cold' (i.e. enquiring from many organisations whether they have any vacancies, rather than applying for a particular job that has been advertised); or you may be well on in your career but thinking about a new start or even a change of career. These are at least four of the possibilities which exist and which will require special treatment appropriate to the circumstances.

Whichever position you find yourself in, and even if you are desperate, don't be in too much of a hurry at first. The process of getting a job can be a long drawn-out and sometimes exhausting business and you should certainly start to think about beginning the process in plenty of time, rather than optimistically leaving it until the last minute. If you are at school or college you should certainly not leave it until the last year. If you are already working, then you should already have given some thought to the matter of your career. But if you have never stopped to think about it too deeply before, then now is better than never. However, as with most things to do with communication, some careful thinking and planning will avoid costly mistakes, disappointment and frustrating time-wasting.

15.1 What sort of job do you want?

For many people the unemployment figures in their area may make it tactless to suggest that you should start out being choosy, and it is true that it is very often the employer who can afford to be choosy, not you, the applicant. But for two very good reasons, however desperate you may feel, you should think carefully about what sort of job you want.

- *The situation may change.* By the time you apply for a job, the picture may be looking slightly less bleak, and however bad employment prospects may seem, there will always be some areas where the situation is reversed, where it is a seller's market and the employers are crying out for applicants.
- Unless you think carefully about the sort of job you want and are qualified to do, you are likely to apply too hastily for jobs for which you are *not suited*, and will probably therefore be unsuccessful.

Even if, more by luck than judgement, you happen to succeed in getting a job, then you may well turn out to be not very good at it, in which case you may eventually start the process all over again.

So, first of all – **what sort of person are you?**

In order to find out what sort of job would ideally suit you, you need to think about what kind of person you are, what your particular likes and dislikes are, what sort of things worry you, where and how you like working and so on.

In doing this, you should not necessarily be prejudiced by the kind of job you are doing now or the particular course of studies you are taking. First, you may be in the wrong job, or on the wrong course. Second, it is easy to be over-influenced by the nature of your present or previous jobs or courses into believing that you must search for a job in that, perhaps rather limited, field. For example, if you are taking a business studies course at the moment you should not feel too restricted to the traditional areas of business and industry, for you should remember that these are not the only places where you can make good use of the skills and knowledge you are acquiring. Doing office work can mean anything from working quietly on your own doing a tidy routine job, to working as part of a large team where one day is never like the next; from working in a large commercial firm doing a specific job like wages clerk or accounts clerk, to being a jack-of-all trades in a farm office or for a football team, for example.

At this stage you should *think imaginatively*. It is true we cannot all land the exciting glamorous jobs and you may not be lucky enough to find exactly the sort of thing which would suit you immediately, but it is all too easy to limit the scope unnecessarily.

Of course, you may feel you are in the opposite position – aware that there are so many jobs in existence that you do not know where to start. In either case you need to think carefully first of all about *yourself*.

Assignment: Here are some questions to ask yourself, but don't be limited to these; try to think of some of your own. Don't answer these questions too quickly. Think about things you have done in the past and work out why you liked or disliked them. Ask other people what they like doing and why. Keep your answers for future reference.

- Do you like working with people, or animals or things?
- Do you like being part of a team, or working on your own?
- Do you prefer being indoors, or outdoors; in the town or in the country?
- Do you welcome responsibility, however modest, or do you feel happier if someone else 'carries the can'?
- Do you like solving problems? What sort of problems: Practical? Theoretical? Numerical? Mechanical? Intellectual? People Problems?
- Are you creative or practical?
- Do you like working under pressure, or do you do your best work when you can set your own more leisurely pace?
- Do you like to be closely supervised, or do you prefer to be left to get on and sort things out for yourself?
- Are you self-disciplined, or do you need to feel there is someone driving you on?
- Do you want a quiet sedentary job, or an energetic job that takes you out and about?
- Do you like jobs that involve marshalling facts, juggling figures, a lot of writing?
- Do you prefer talking to people, selling your ideas, persuading people?
- Does it matter where you work? Near your home, friends and family?
- Would you be prepared to move?
- Would anyone else be affected adversely if you did move? Husband, wife, parents, children? What are their views?
- Could you settle down easily, make new friends quickly if you moved to a new area?
- What matters most to you? Pay? Conditions of work? Job satisfaction? The people you work with?
- Would you be prepared to undergo more training?

Personality tests and vocational guidance tests

There are tests available which can help you to discover what sort of person you are and what your real interests, likes and dislikes are. Ask the careers officer at your local careers office or college.

Assignment: Now armed with your answers to these questions and any others you have thought of, think about how strongly you feel about these things and which of them are absolutely essential in any job you apply for. These will form your criteria against which you will then be able to measure the suitability of any job. Produce three lists headed 'Musts', 'Wants' and 'Would be nice', for example,

Musts	**Wants**	**Would be nice**
Working with people	Training opportunities	Good pay

This might be the beginning of the list if you have decided you would be miserable working on your own; want to get further training but would be prepared to get more training/qualifications in your own time, for example, evening classes, if the job itself does not provide training opportunities; and are prepared to settle for low pay while you are getting further qualifications, training or experience.

Thinking about questions like these will:

- help you to narrow the field
- help you to apply for suitable jobs rather than waste time going up blind alleys
- provide you with material both for your application letter/form and for the interview stage.

So, keep your answers to these last two for future reference.

Assignment: Now, using this information, try to analyse the sort of job you want. How many different jobs would measure up to your criteria? Which would you prefer? Have you got the necessary qualifications or will the organisation help you get them?

To help you think of possibilities, get a copy of the local daily/evening paper and one of the quality national papers and go through every advertisement thinking about each carefully in relation to your criteria. Put a cross against each one which really does not measure up and a tick against each one that you would be prepared to consider (even if you would never have thought of it as a possibility before).

Now list all the jobs you have ticked. How many have you got?

More than you thought possible. In this case, subject them to really careful examination.

- Have you been realistic?
- Have you aimed too high, been optimistic about your own ability to do the job, included jobs which you might be able to do in a few years' time with a bit more experience but which may be outside your reach for the moment?

- Even if you exclude these, you should still be left with quite a few which are in areas you might never have thought of before.

On the other hand, you may have set your sights too low, causing you to include jobs for which you are really overqualified. Although there are some employers who seem unwilling to take on people with more qualifications than the job needs, it may not be a bad thing, at this stage, to be prepared to consider starting right at the bottom if necessary. For some occupations it may be the only way in and if you have talent and enthusiasm for whatever you do, you should not find it difficult to be promoted fairly quickly. There are more than a few managing directors who started out as office juniors.

If, however, your list is disappointingly short, again think carefully about the reasons.

- Have you been rather narrow-minded in considering possibilities?
- Are you short of qualifications in your chosen field?
- Are you being too demanding in what you expect from a job?
- You may of course have been too modest about what you have to offer, in which case you may not have aimed high enough or considered a wide enough range of possibilities.

So be realistic but do not go in for false modesty. If you do not have faith in yourself, no one else will. Know what you are aiming for and be prepared to do what is necessary to get it.

15.2   What is available and what are they looking for?

You should by now have a fairly good idea of the sort of job you are looking for. I say 'sort of' because at this stage, you should not be too specific, but considering as wide a range of jobs as possible. Now begins the real search for vacancies.

Keep your eyes and ears open

You need to explore every possible source of information and be constantly on the alert for job opportunities. Likely sources of information will obviously depend on the type and level of job you are seeking but here are some suggestions you should explore energetically. Unless you have a guardian angel, the jobs will not come to you. You will have to go out and search for them.

Self-Check

Where can you find out about job vacancies? List all the sources you can think of.

The Internet

This is by far the largest source of job information but it can be daunting. A good source of company website addresses can be found in *Choices: Jobs through the*

Internet. However not all organisations use the Internet for recruiting, so you must still use other sources.

Newspapers

The obvious source of job vacancies, but because they are so obvious and a comparatively easy source they reach a very wide readership, and there will be a large number of applicants for most jobs, so you will have to move fast and be prepared to follow up other sources.

Local newspapers are a useful source if you want to stay in a particular area, but if you are happy to move then national newspapers may provide a greater choice. Most of the quality newspapers tend to run special features from time to time on particular areas of employment and some devote space to particular areas of employment on the same day each week, so get to know your newspapers. If one particular newspaper looks like being a particularly good bet, it is probably worth buying it every day, but you must also make it a daily routine to visit the local public or college library, otherwise you will be in danger of missing advertisements which may be in for only one day.

If you want to move to a particular area elsewhere in the country, then you will increase your chances by getting hold of the local newspaper for that area. If you do not know anyone who can send you copies regularly, then write to the newspaper office asking for copies to be sent to you daily until further notice. If you do not know the name of the newspaper, address your inquiry to 'The Local Paper' followed by the name of the town.

Finally, read the advertisements of an appropriate specialist paper like *Computer Weekly*, the newspaper of the computing industry, or *Marketing Weekly*, the Sunday papers; and lastly do not forget the professional journals which usually appear monthly. Ask friends who belong to professional or trade organisations if you can borrow copies of the journals immediately they come out. Or, look them up on the Internet: you can read some of them online without subscribing, especially the sections on jobs.

Careers office

Visit your local careers office (address in the phone book). Some people often assume that careers officers are only there to help school-leavers, but careers counselling is now a well-established profession which requires extensive training in helping all manner of people with all sorts of problems: from getting a first job to changing jobs and careers; from helping people deal with the problem of redundancy to advising people on how and where to obtain further training or qualifications. So whatever your particular problem, it can do no harm to visit a careers officer – they are paid to help.

If you are at college, you will almost certainly find that there is some form of careers advisory service or appointments board within the college. Get to know it, preferably during the first year of your course.

If you are already working but feel that perhaps you are not in quite the right job for you and would like a change, then do not forget your own company's personnel department. There may be possibilities for change, not necessarily promotion, within your own organisation. The personnel staff cannot be expected to guess that you would welcome a change unless you approach them to discuss your ideas and inclinations.

Job Centres and employment agencies

Most towns now have Job Centres which act as a clearing house for vacancies in an area and can therefore link employers with applicants.

However, now that Job Centres are so well known, you will have to move fast if you find a vacancy which you think you would like, as there will be plenty of competition for most of them. In addition to these government agencies, there are also now plenty of private agencies which specialise in finding applicants for office and clerical jobs, and executive search companies (or 'headhunters') which specialise in recruiting senior staff for organisations.

Attack on all fronts

Above all, it is important once you get to this stage to follow up as many possibilities as you can at once. Don't apply for just one job and then sit back and wait to see what happens. You may be unlucky, in which case you will have wasted valuable time when you could have been applying for other jobs. So explore all the sources mentioned above and apply for as many jobs as possible, and keep at it. Most people have to make many applications, sometimes hundreds, before they are offered the right job.

What are they looking for?

It is very tempting and unfortunately quite common to skim through a newspaper, catch sight of the kind of occupation which applies to you and pick up your pen and start writing: so long as the job is the kind you are looking for and the advertisement mentions a few other things that seem relevant to you, like pay, area, the level of the job and so on, then why not apply? Well, look at the two advertisements in Figure 15.1. They are for the same kind of job – or are they?

Both the advertisements seem to be looking for the same sort of person with the same sort of qualifications and experience to do apparently the same sort of job. But if you look carefully you will see that there are some clues in the advertisements which suggest that the jobs may actually be rather different and that the two companies are looking for rather different people.

Self-Check

Underline the words in both advertisements which seem to you to be key words which communicate rather different messages.

In the first advertisement, words like 'old-established city firm' and 'the facility for day-release' seem to conjure up an image of rather staid old-world respectability, and the advertisement itself is fairly straightforward and unspectacular both in its layout and style and the information it conveys. It is also not 'with it' enough to

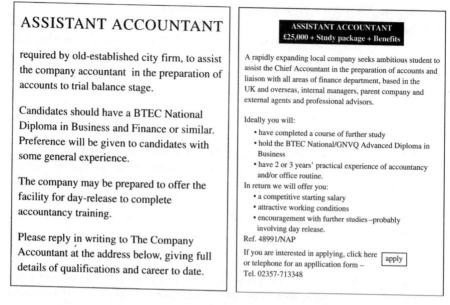

Figure 15.1 **Two similar job advertisements?**

have realised that the old BTEC National Diploma in Business and Finance has been replaced by BTEC National/GNVQ Advanced in Business. The second advertisement conveys a rather more modern and exciting image not only in the style and lay-out of the advertisement but also through adjectives like 'rapidly expanding', 'young ambitious', 'competitive' and 'attractive'. The younger, more progressive image of the company is also conveyed by the fact that it offers rather more than the basic information about the job, and invites application online rather than just in writing, which reinforces its go ahead image by the very mention of it.

Look, too, at the way the two companies deal with the issue of further training opportunities. The second company provides 'encouragement' whereas the first 'may' offer the facility for day-release. There is another important difference between the two advertisements. The first is written in the third person – 'candidates should have ... the company may be prepared ...' while the second manages to create a more lively personal relationship between the company and the reader (its potential employee?) by using the personal pronouns 'you' and 'we', and reinforcing the idea of an equal relationship by balancing what it requires of the candidate by what it will offer 'in return'.

Check-points: The 'Hidden Agenda' of Job Adverts

- It is important to be alert to these subtle clues, not just because they may tell you quite a lot more about the company than would at first seem possible in a small number of words, but because they can tell you a lot more about the kind of person they really want.
- At first sight we decided that the two advertisements seemed to be looking for fairly similar people. Now, however, we must reconsider that first impression.

If the second company conveys an image of a young, modern, go-ahead company then it is more than likely it is looking for someone with a personality that will fit. Similarly, the first company is consciously or unconsciously asking for someone who is solid, dependable and perhaps less demanding, who would be happy working in a rather quieter, less ambitious environment.

- Of course, we should not take these conjectures too far, for conjectures are all that they can be without any more evidence. However, at this stage of the application process this is all we have to go on and our impressions do seem to be based on reasonable evidence, whether the companies intended to convey these impressions or not. Of course, the advertisements may only be telling you something about the companies' advertising agencies!

Which job suits you?

Having carried out this kind of analysis, you should then compare the result with the personal analysis which you did in Section 15.1 to see whether either of these jobs would suit you and, perhaps more importantly, whether *you would suit* either of these companies. You might then feel that it would be better to apply to one and not the other. Whichever you choose, you must bear carefully in mind what you have learned from looking at the advertisement, when you come to write your application. How are you going to prove that you will fit into an 'old-established city firm' or that you are 'ambitious' and just what a 'rapidly expanding' company is looking for?

But perhaps you feel that you would be happy working in either firm and that bits of your personality would adapt well to the image of both. In that case you must still bear in mind the two very different personalities of the companies because you will need to write two very different letters and if you get that far, adapt your behaviour appropriately for each interview.

15.3   The application itself

Now at last we come to the application letter. Did you notice another difference between the two advertisements? The first asked for an application in writing giving full details, but the second asked for the applicant to apply online or telephone for an application form. Many organisations still ask applicants to write a letter setting out their qualifications and experience, as this provides the company not only with this essential information but also with a chance to see how the applicant writes; how they set out and order the facts about themselves; and even what their handwriting is like, something which some firms consider so important that they employ the services of a handwriting expert to give them additional information about a candidate's personality. This kind of application obviously poses more problems for the candidate as they are left to decide exactly what the company wants to know and how best to set it out. So let us deal with the method employed by the second company first.

More and more companies, particularly the larger ones, ask applicants to complete an application form, as it ensures that they get all the information they need in a standard lay-out to which they can refer easily. If this is online you don't have to worry about neatness and legibility so much, so some of the following tips wouldn't apply. However, you always have to worry about accurate spelling and punctuation.

'*Please apply for an application form to ...*' If an advertisement merely says 'Please apply' you can choose whether to write or phone to ask for the form.

'*Write for an application form to ...*' In this case it is not necessary to write a long letter giving all your qualifications and experience with your reasons for applying for the job. A brief letter referring to the advertisement and the post for which you are applying is all that is required:

Your address
Date

Name and/or position of person to whom
your application is to be made
Company name and address

Dear Sir (or name if given in the advert)

Job title and Ref. no. (if given in the advert)

Please send me details of the job (or appointment or vacancy) advertised in the *Evening Post* of 23 May 20 ... , together with an application form.

Yours faithfully, (or *sincerely* if you have used their name)

JANET BROWN (Ms or Mrs as appropriate)

Even though this letter seems to be a mere formality, it should be written neatly and correctly, as it will be put on your file and will therefore contribute to the total picture that the company has of you.

'*Please telephone for an application form.*' Although this may seem the simplest way to apply, you should be on your guard. When you telephone, you cannot be sure how much influence the person you speak to has, and if you are vague or discourteous or unfriendly or even too familiar, this might well be reported to the person who is responsible for selecting the person who is to get the job. So, remember your best telephone technique – be prepared: be clear about what you want, and about what they will need to know in order to help you (e.g. title of the job vacancy and reference number if there is one); speak clearly, especially when giving your name and address; and be friendly and courteous without being overfamiliar or presumptuous.

Application form

Remember that even though you should send a covering letter with your form, the application form will be the main thing on which the company will base its decision whether to invite you for interview. *So before filling in an application form you should*:

- read the whole form through very carefully so that you are clear about exactly what information it asks for and where you are required to put it

- make sure that you have plenty of time to complete the form carefully and completely
- make a rough draft of your answers to the questions so that you can ensure that you can get the information into the spaces provided and that you do not make any mistakes on the real form.

Check-Point

If possible make a photocopy of the blank form before you start. Use this to make your rough copy and then you can be sure that the final version is laid out as neatly as possible.

Hints on completing an application form

Dates
Dates become increasingly difficult to remember as you get older and there are more of them. Start keeping a file now which includes dates of school, exams, jobs and courses attended plus copies of any certificates and testimonials you may have.

(A testimonial is an open – as opposed to confidential – letter given to you to pass on to anyone you like. Because you are able to see what is said, the comments tend to be rather general and complimentary and are therefore not valued very highly by employers, who usually prefer to ask for names of referees from whom they can seek a confidential assessment of you.)

Presentation
Presentation must be faultless. You should write with dark ink, as the form may later be photocopied, and avoid a pen which runs even slightly on the particular quality of paper on which the form is printed. A ballpoint pen may therefore be safer than a felt-tipped pen but a very careful experiment in one corner of the back should be enough to tell you which to use.

Obey the instructions
If the form says BLOCK CAPITALS write in BLOCK CAPITALS, if it says write in ball-point pen then do as you are told. The company will have good reasons for these instructions even if you do not appreciate them.

Some forms are very specific about the information required, providing sub-headings and columns, for instance, under main headings so that you know where to include dates of exams or the responsibilities of the jobs you have done. However, some forms are much more general, merely indicating main headings (like the form shown in Figure 15.2).

In this case you must think carefully about which details to include under each heading and present your information under your own subheadings and in columns if it will look clearer.

Education.   Give the names and addresses of schools and colleges you have attended together with the dates.

Qualifications.   Give the subject, grade and date of examinations – 15 GCSEs taken on five different occasions are not as impressive as 8 taken and passed at one sitting,

```
┌─────────────────────────────────────────────────────────────────────┐
│ . . . . . . . . . . . . . . . . . . . . . . . . plc    APPLICATION FOR:        │
│                                                        (state position applied for)    │
├──────────────────────────────────┬──────────────────────────────────┤
│ SURNAME (BLOCK CAPITALS)         │ FIRST NAMES                      │
├──────────────────────────────────┼──────────────────────────────────┤
│ ADDRESS                          │ TELEPHONE NUMBER                 │
│                                  │ HOME              WORK           │
├──────────┬───────────────┬───────┴──────────────┬──────────────────┤
│ AGE      │ DATE OF BIRTH │ PLACE OF BIRTH       │ MARITAL STATUS   │
├──────────┴───────────────┴──────────────────────┴──────────────────┤
│ NUMBER, AGE AND SEX OF CHILDREN                                    │
├────────────────────────────────────────────────────────────────────┤
│ EDUCATION AND TRAINING (schools and colleges attended since the age of 11) │
├────────────────────────────────────────────────────────────────────┤
│ QUALIFICATIONS (in chronological order)                            │
├────────────────────────────────────────────────────────────────────┤
│ EXPERIENCE (All employment and military service in chronological order. │
│             Include positions held and reasons for leaving)         │
│                                                                     │
│ (Use additional sheets if necessary)                               │
├────────────────────────────────────────────────────────────────────┤
│ ADDITIONAL INFORMATION you would like to give about yourself or    │
│                        your experience                              │
│                                                                     │
│ (Use additional sheets if necessary)                               │
├────────────────────────────────────────────────────────────────────┤
│ HEALTH (Give details of any physical disabilities or serious illnesses) │
├────────────────────────────────────────────────────────────────────┤
│ PRESENT SALARY                                                     │
├────────────────────────────────────────────────────────────────────┤
│ REFEREES (Give the names and addresses of two people from whom we may │
│            seek references)                                         │
├────────────────────────────────────────────────────────────────────┤
│ If selected when could you start?                                  │
├────────────────────────────────────────────────────────────────────┤
│ Signed:                                          Date:             │
└────────────────────────────────────────────────────────────────────┘
```

Figure 15.2 **Typical application form (condensed, to show headings).**

and 1 'A' level taken and passed while you were working may be more impressive than 2 taken over two years while at school. Do not include short courses under this heading unless they resulted in some kind of terminal examination, or unless there is nowhere else on the form to put them. (Another reason why it is important to read through the form carefully before you start writing.)

Experience. Unless the form says otherwise, list any jobs you have had, starting with the most recent and then going backwards in time (chronological order in reverse). Include the title of the job, the name and address of the company, and the dates you were employed as accurately as possible. If there is room, you should also add a brief description of the main *responsibilities* involved in each job. If in doubt about what to include, concentrate on those things which are relevant to the job for which you are applying. But remember that previously insignificant parts of jobs can take on new importance if you think hard and realise their relevance.

No experience? If you have just left school or are still at college, the section headed 'experience' can present some problems because you probably feel you haven't any. However, if you have done any part-time or holiday jobs or if you held any positions of responsibility at school and have not put them anywhere else on the form, then use this space to give brief details – it can't do any harm, and although you may think that your holiday or gap year job are unimportant or irrelevant, the employer will at least be able to see what you have done with your time.

Present salary. Don't forget to include additional benefits like bonus or company car.

Referees. You will usually be asked to give the names of at least two people who would be prepared to supply a reference. If you are still at school or college then one referee should be from education and the other can be either someone who has known you privately for several years or preferably someone for whom you have worked if only for a short time. If you are already working then it is essential to give names of people for whom you have worked. Remember that although you will obviously want to choose someone who will speak well of you, it is also important that your referees are themselves able to communicate effectively, so think carefully before you put down the first names that come to mind.

Note: it is courteous to ask your referees for their permission before giving their names. Apart from giving them rather a surprise when they suddenly receive a request for a reference, they may find the task difficult if you have not given them some idea in advance of the nature of the job for which you are applying. If you do not want your referees approached before you have been offered the job, you should indicate this on the form. This is an understandable request and will usually be quite acceptable.

Supporting statement. Most application forms will include a space headed 'Supporting statement' or 'Other relevant information' or some other form of words inviting you to give additional information not covered elsewhere on the form. *Never leave this place blank.* Apart from the fact that it represents an opportunity to add to your case for being considered, it is often regarded by the employer as the most significant section on the form, for it is here that you give some indication of what kind of person you are, not by bald statements claiming that you are 'energetic', 'ambitious, hard-working and reliable, etc.' but by the way in which you deal with this section, select what to include and express yourself in continuous prose.

So always use the space, but plan what you are going to say very carefully. Occasionally you will find that under the main heading of this section there is some additional guidance, for example, 'You should use this space to describe your leisure activities and any other activities which you feel are relevant to your application', or 'Please give your reasons for applying for this position'. Where guidance is given, stick to it and don't go off the point. However, sometimes the heading is vague and no guidance is provided. Probably the best advice in this dilemma is to provide a short *autobiography*. This should not be a repetition in prose of the facts given on the previous pages but rather additional information which, taken with the facts, provides a fuller picture of you as a person and a personality. For instance, you could explain why your career to date has taken the course it has, mentioning things which have influenced you, the main interests you have developed, the achievements you particularly remember and your ideas and ambitions for the future, if you have any. Above all, it should be written in continuous prose, not notes, and in correct and clear English. This section more than any other must be drafted in rough so that you can work out how best to use the space provided.

How much should you write? As much as and no more than will fill the space provided. Although you may be invited to add another page if necessary, you should bear in mind that the company may have provided what they consider to be enough space. If you need more, it may be because you are not writing concisely enough and are tending to ramble on at great length on things which are not relevant. So work out what you want to say and then edit and rewrite it, over and over again if necessary, until you have found the precise wording to say what you want to fluently but concisely. Only as a last resort when you judge it absolutely essential should you add an additional sheet. If you are applying online you will also probably have to judge how much to say.

If there is no space provided or if this section asks for specific information and still leaves you with things unsaid which you believe support your application, then you should include them in the covering letter to send with the application form.

Make a photocopy

Photocopy the form or print off a hard copy once you have completed it and take this copy to the interview. It is surprisingly easy to forget exactly what you have said on the form several weeks before.

Assignment

1 Using the basic application form in Figure 15.2 design a more detailed one which will ensure the company gets the information it wants under suitable headings, and which will help the applicant complete it clearly, by dividing the

sections into subsections with suitable subheadings. (It will probably have to be larger than the one illustrated.)

2 Using your own data, complete the form as if you were applying for the job advertised in the second advertisement in Figure 15.1. (Keep this completed form, as it will provide you with a useful reference copy and checklist when you come to apply for a job. It will also be useful as a record of your data when we come to the problem of writing an application letter where no application form is provided.)

3 What problems did you have in redesigning the form? See 'Designing forms and questionnaires' in Chapter 17.

4 What problems did you have in completing the form? Make a brief note of these problems to remind you of the difficulties when you come to do the real thing.

The full application letter

'Please apply in writing to ... giving full details of your qualifications and career to date'. Although application forms are very common, many companies still prefer to ask for details in writing and even Internet applications may simply say, 'Insert a covering letter or text version of your CV'.

- Application forms are standard and although this has advantages for the employer as we have seen, it has disadvantages too: each candidate is different and what may be enough space under one heading for one candidate will not be enough for another and vice versa. Similarly, either a form must be designed to allow for every possibility in which case it will probably be far too long and for many applicants will end up full of blank spaces; or alternatively, as in the simple version illustrated in Figure 15.2, it will probably not be detailed enough.

- In controlling the way the applicant presents the information, the employer does not really get a chance to see how the applicant can select and order information for themselves – a skill which is in itself an essential prerequisite for many jobs.

- Following on from the last point, if the applicant is given no real guidance about what information to include, then they must use their judgement, and in doing so will tell the employer a great deal about their judgement and personality.

Assignment: Look at the following examples (a)–(n) taken from letters replying to a request for details in writing. What would they tell you about the applicant if you were the employer?

Complete letter

(a)

Dear Sir,

I am writting about the job in your advertisment. I have ten years experiance in buisness as well as the qualifications you want, so I would be glad if you would consider me.

Yours Sincerely

Beginnings

(b)

Please will you consider me for the job of accounts clerk. I am afraid I don't have any formal qualifications but I do have some experience and I need the job very badly as my wife and I are expecting our first baby next month, and at the moment I am unemployed following an accident...

(c)

I noted with interest your advertisement for a Production Assistant in today's Daily Times...

(d)

Further to your advertisement for a computer operator in last week's 'Dataweek'.

(e)

My name is Jaqueline Matthews and I am 19. I left school last year and since then I have been working for J.G. Telford and Sons. I am very hard-working and quick with numbers so I am sure I would be able to do the job to your satisfaction...

(f)

With reference to your advertisement for a management trainee advertised in yesterday's paper I would like to apply for the position as I have a BTEC GNVQ Advanced level in Business and one year's experience as a sales clerk and am now taking a course leading to the HNC in Business and Finance which amongst other things includes Accounting, Statistics and Production Methods all of which you have mentioned in your advertisement...

Middles

(g)

I am 32 years of age, and I am currently working as a Production Control Assistant. Before this I worked as a Progress Chaser at Bellings Ltd and then I got a similar job with Selco Fittings. I am responsible for making sure that the right components are being produced at the right time, which means that I have a lot of experience of organising and planning. I have just got married and I went to Chillingworth Comprehensive which is on the outskirts of Manchester near Bletchton. I enjoyed art and woodwork but I was not very good at games. I have a clean driving licence and I am in good health. If you need more information I shall obviously be happy to provide it. Also I have 5 GCSEs and would be available for interview at any time.

(h)

You will see from the attached curriculum vitae that I have five years' experience of various aspects of office work. In particular, my last job gave me the opportunity to gain some valuable practice in interviewing and the chance to discover that I should like to specialise in personnel work.

(i)

I enjoyed my course very much. It was very good and we studied all the business subjects so I have the qualifications which you are asking for.

(j)

I am very ambitious and for a long time now have been looking for the right job which will use my talent to the full. I am not prepared to do a monotonous or routine job and feel that perhaps the job you are advertising is the one for me.

(k)

I want to work for your company because I have checked up and found you are a very successful company. You produce a wide range of products and have a good export record.

Endings

(l)

Thanking you in anticipation. Yours faithfully,

(m)

If you consider that my qualifications are suitable, I could be available for interview at any time.

(n)

I would be grateful if you could let me know as soon as possible as I have a lot of applications in progress at the moment.

Comments on Examples

We can make some detailed points about all of these.

(a) Far too short and uninformative in answer to a request for details in writing. This together with the poor spelling (writing, advertisement, business, experience) and careless presentation would not help their application for any job which involved writing and would be likely to prejudice their chances even for a manual job unless they were the only applicant. 'Dear Sir' should be followed by 'Yours faithfully'; 'Dear Mr Smith' should be followed by 'Yours sincerely'.
Note: both 'faithfully' and 'sincerely' should start with small letters.

(b) The tone of this letter is inappropriate. It is far too humble and pleading. An application letter is not the right place to seek sympathy.

(c) 'Noted with interest' is a good way to make the first, rather ordinary sentence in an application letter sound a little different and attract the attention of the reader. In addition the sentence states clearly exactly what job is being applied for and where the advertisement was seen. Apart from wanting to know what job is being referred to, the employer will be interested to know which of perhaps several advertisements is attracting applicants.

(d) This opening contains the very common error of an incomplete sentence (see pp. 354–5).

(e) No mention of which job is being applied for nor of the advertisement or publication. The employer may never have heard of J.G. Telford and Sons and even if they have will be still none the wiser about what sort of work the applicant did while she was there. The applicant fails to give any evidence to support her assertions that she is hard-working and so on. It is not enough to state that you are sure that you can do the job; the employer needs reasons.

(f) One long sentence! The reader will have forgotten what the first bit of the sentence said by the time they get to the end.

(g) This long paragraph, which contains far too many ideas in a confusing jumble, is not guaranteed to convince the reader that the applicant is good at organising and planning, as he claims to be. The paragraph moves backwards and forwards in time and deals with qualifications, experience and personal details all mixed up together. Much of the information appears to be irrelevant and any sentence which starts with 'also' is likely to sound like an afterthought, which in this case it is. The applicant has obviously just started writing without any attempt to group related information or plan the sentences of his letter.

(h) A curriculum vitae is a good way to communicate the facts about yourself in a clear easy-to-refer-to manner. Where a curriculum vitae is sent, it should be accompanied by a covering letter which does not just repeat the facts but explains and interprets them, as in this example. The employer reading this letter is likely to be impressed by the applicant's method of presentation which in turn implies a tidy, well-organised mind. The letter also allows the applicant to explain why she wants the job and how her experience relates to the requirements of the vacancy.

(i) Apart from possibly implying that the applicant likes studying, this letter tells the employer very little else. What does 'very good' mean and which business subjects did he study? How can the employer tell that the applicant has the right qualifications? The applicant's assurance is not enough.

(j) The tone of this letter is likely to put off the most tolerant of employers. It sounds arrogant and over-confident, and therefore implies that the applicant is far too sure of himself. He sounds very demanding and unlikely to be willing to do anything he does not want to. In other words he has succeeded in reversing the traditional relationship of the employer and the applicant, leaving the employer with an uneasy feeling that he is being selected rather than the other way round.

(k) This letter also conveys an idea of over-confidence by using the words 'checked up'. While most employers would be impressed by an applicant who has taken the trouble to find out something about the company, this is not the way to communicate it. Furthermore the applicant seems to have discovered very little of apparent relevance and has merely succeeded in telling the employer what they presumably know already.

(l) Just as it is easy to use a hackneyed expression to open a letter (see (d)) and leave the sentence incomplete, so the same trap awaits the unwary at the end of the letter. 'Thanking you in anticipation' has no main verb. It is therefore a phrase, not a complete sentence (see pp. 354–5). The crime is made worse by the tone of this phrase, which either implies creeping humility or sounds over-sure that the application will be successful.

(m) This is quite a neat ending. It hints at the possibility of an interview without sounding over-confident.

(n) This ending sounds rather too demanding. Unfortunately it is the applicant who must wait patiently for a reply because in the application process it is the employer who is in control. Furthermore, even though most employers will be fully aware that this is not one's only application, it is hardly a good idea to communicate one's desperation, nor state the truth of the situation quite so bluntly.

Writing the full application letter

Now that you have had the chance to 'be the employer' you should be well aware of the reasons why some employers prefer the unstructured request for information, and what they will be looking for. You should keep this constantly in mind when writing your own application letters.

What is the best way to present your information? We have seen from examining the application form the basic information which you must include in any application letter:

- Surname
- First names
- Telephone number (home and work, if relevant)
- Marital status (married, single, divorced, separated)

- Education and training
- Qualifications

- Employment experience

- General interests.

The long letter
You could write a rather long letter incorporating all this information but this method has disadvantages:

- Being written in continuous prose without headings and so on, the essential information will be hidden and difficult for the employer to pick out.
- This method presents problems of style for the writer. It is difficult to avoid a rather monotonous catalogue of 'I did this … and then I did that; … and then I did that'. Notice the number of times the word 'I' is used in the examples.

The curriculum vitae with short covering letter
With this method you list all the facts on a separate sheet of paper (see example in Figure 15.3). In effect you invent your own application form, more or less. This list of qualifications and experience is traditionally known as a 'curriculum vitae' (CV for short) which literally means 'the course of one's life' and is usually headed CURRICULUM VITAE. Make sure you spell it correctly. This method of combining a business-like list with a covering letter has the advantages of the application form without the disadvantages, and above all gives you, the applicant, the chance to show that you are neat and well organised without being prompted by the employer's application form.

> Note that in the CV in Figure 15.3 the applicant has not given 'O' level/GCSE and 'A' level grades. At her age with other experience behind her, grades cease to be very significant. However, if you are a school or college-leaver, it is advisable to show grades.

CURRICULUM VITAE

Sarah Louise Leverton
34 Pike Street
Birmingham BM10 4EW

Tel: 01981-307062 (Home)
    01981-234987 (Work)

Age: 33

Date of Birth: 27.02.70
Status: Single

EDUCATION

Fairlawn Comprehensive School, Bristol	Sept. 1980 - July 1985
Brindley Sixth Form College, Bristol	Sept. 1985 - June 1987
Lanchester Polytechnic	Sept. 1987 - June 1989

QUALIFICATIONS

GCE O Level: English Language, English Literature, Maths, Biology, Chemistry, Economics, French	1985
GCE A Level: Economics, Politics, Maths	1987
BTEC Higher National Diploma in Business and Finance	1989
GCSE Spanish (Evening Class)	1989

EXPERIENCE

Management Trainee	Sealco plc	Coventry	1989 - 1990
Commercial Assistant	Sealco plc	Coventry	1990 - 1993
Finance Supervisor	CD Electronics	London	1993 - 2000
Commercial Manager	Ellwood Services	Birmingham	2000 - present

Experienced in financial accounting, contract negotiation and general administration, including computerised office systems. Several years' experience of man-management with a special interest in staff development.

OTHER ACTIVITIES

Pianist with a local jazz group.
Plays Squash and Badminton regularly for local team.
Committee member of CMI

REFEREES

Brian J Cameron	Ms Jan McKechnie	Ms Jane Crompton
Managing Director	Finance Director	Personnel Manager
Ellwood Services	CD Electronics	Sealco plc
Triangle Court	14 Ryecroft Street	Psion Business Park
Brigstock Street	London EC3 4LY	London Road
Birmingham BM3 9QA		Coventry CY3 1JZ

Figure 15.3 **Specimen curriculum vitae.**

Method

- *Order* – The information should be set down in the same order as the application form: personal details first; then education and experience; then other interests like spare-time activities, membership of clubs, part in school, college and community life, and so on; finishing up with the names of referees.

- *Presentation* – Each piece of information should be written under appropriate headings, with subheadings and columns where necessary; the appearance should be neat and systematic and well spaced out – do not overcrowd the page.
- *Style* – It is not necessary to write in complete sentences, but be consistent.

Advantages of using a CV

- The information set out under headings and columns is easy to pick out.
- Provided it is set out clearly and neatly in straight lines and columns, it will convey an impression of efficiency and attention to detail.
- It will avoid the problems of style noted above.

The covering letter

You will still need to include a short letter with your CV which should include:

- a formal application for the position (including job title, reference number, and source of the advertisement, for example, the name and date of the newspaper or magazine)
- your reasons for wanting the job
- your reasons for feeling you are qualified and competent to do the job.

Self-Check

In connection with the last point, which of the following ways of proving competence would you find the more convincing?

'I am good at supervising people and feel sure that I would be able to manage the department successfully'.

'While in my last job, I was promoted to section head in charge of three other staff. This responsibility gave me the opportunity to discover the problems of managing people and to gain some experience of allocating work fairly, motivating people, and dealing quickly with problems'.

The first example is merely an assertion. The reader has no real evidence for accepting that the writer's confidence in themselves as a successful supervisor is justified. However, in the second example the writer manages, without explicitly saying so, to imply that they are quite likely to be successful. They do this by

(a) quoting real evidence – they were promoted in their last job, so someone must have confidence in them;
(b) revealing that they are at least aware that managing people can have problems;
(c) showing that they recognise the opportunity they were given;
(d) using the word 'some' to describe their experience, which does not overstate the case and shows an appealing humility by subtly recognising that they still have something to learn;
(e) demonstrating that they know something of what being a supervisor involves – quite a lot packed into two sentences!

Finally, a covering letter provides you with the opportunity to show that you can write well, to emphasise those aspects of your experience which are particularly relevant to the job for which you are applying, and to demonstrate an understanding of and an enthusiasm for the responsibilities of the job.

Handwritten or typed?

Probably the best advice is a combination of the two. Type the CV but handwrite the covering letter. This will allow you to present a neat, businesslike approach while allowing the employer to see a sample of your handwriting. If your handwriting is appalling and you cannot do anything about it, then type both the CV and the letter.

If you don't have access to WP equipment yourself, get your CV typed by a bureau. There are always adverts in the paper offering WP or CV services.

15.4   Job-hunting on the Internet

Career websites

Because of the fast changing nature of the World Wide Web even by the time of printing a number of these websites may be obsolete or have changed in their level of usefulness. They are given as a guide however to aid you and, if not immediately relevant, may include links to other useful sites.

The websites listed below offer career advice, news on your industry and listings of positions available either advertised directly by employers or recruitment consultants. In addition, most offer a service where you can post your CV and be sent email notification of positions that suit your skills. There are a great many more than this but these are a good starting point.

www.workthing.co.uk
www.stepstone.co.uk
www.totaljobs.co.uk
www.topjobs.co.uk
www.monster.co.uk

Posting your CV on a job website

This is a matter of personal choice and its usefulness is debatable. The advantages are that you will receive notification of suitable jobs via email from the website and that employers can search the CVs posted for suitable candidates. There are unfortunately also the disadvantages. You could well receive notification of a great many unsuitable positions, which will serve no greater purpose than to clog up your inbox, so be careful when stating your requirements. You could also find that your current employer may stumble across your CV when looking for new staff! Check carefully the procedure that the website follows but many offer their CV databases for searching by employers.

If you do decide to post your CV on a job website, it is important that you include in it as many of the 'buzz' words associated with your industry and level, since all searching is done via electronic database using keywords, and if those keywords do not appear on your CV then your CV will not appear as a result in the search and you will be lost in the electronic wilderness.

Recruitment agencies

In recent years there has been a massive rise in the number of recruitment agencies setting up to skim off the crumbs that employers are willing to pay to find the right staff. There is a huge number of recruitment agencies to be found on the web specialising in every type of employment or industry and the easiest way to find them is usually just surfing and following web page links.

Signing up with a lot of recruitment agencies may seem like a good idea initially but can eventually be very time-consuming. Most will want to interview you before they forward your details to any employers and this can become time-expensive. Also, many will promise you the world and then only come up with unsuitable positions. The best advice is to look at their job listings and only register those with job listings that closely match the type of position you are looking for.

Website applications

Many large companies and most universities and colleges, charities and public sector organisations now have dedicated careers websites exclusive or attached to their main websites. These are an excellent source of information about the company and often have interviews with existing staff, breakdown of the organisational structure, training information and so on.

Many will also have an online application form. These usually take between 30 minutes and 2 hours to do and ask similar questions to those you would be asked on a printed application form. It can be tedious completing these forms but most big companies are not interested in a CV and will only accept their own application forms.

Since it is so much quicker these days to apply for a job, the competition is fierce. If it only takes a few minutes to send out an e-mailed application, people will apply for a huge number of jobs that may or may not be suitable. Hence, firms are now receiving an inordinate number of applications per position, particularly if they are advertised on the Web or invite e-mail applications. For this reason, it is all the more important to make sure that your application stands out; it is also, therefore, completely unacceptable to have any spelling or grammar errors. All PCs have checkers

---

Check-Point

Keep your CV up to date. Then each time you apply for a job, all you have to do is compose an appropriate covering letter and attach a copy of your CV or use it to apply online. This will reduce the time spent on applications and also the tedium caused to do the same thing over and over again.

for weeding these out, so most employers believe that there is no reason for mechanical errors to exist in your documents, despite the fact that these checkers are by no means foolproof yet – but that's another story.

Summary – applying for a job

Give the organisation the information *they* need in the format *they* want, but include information which you want to tell them about yourself, providing it is relevant. Present the information in the most perfect way you can. Above all, *take time and trouble.*

Exercise 15.1: Indicate whether each of the following is true or false.

1 The first stage in looking for a job involves replying to as many advertisements as possible.
2 In replying to newspaper and Internet advertisements, promptness is a key factor.
3 You should not 'read between the lines' when looking at advertisements.
4 You should take as much care with a telephone call asking for an application form, as with writing a complete application letter.
5 If you can't think of anything to say under the heading 'Other relevant information' or 'Supporting statement' on an application form, you should leave it blank.
6 Instead of two separate sheets, it is better to combine all the factual information in your letter of application. It is easier to write and the employer does not have so much to read.
7 When you are applying for an office job, you should omit from your CV any experience which involved manual work, since it is irrelevant.
8 If the traditional headings like 'Education' or 'Qualifications' in CVs seem too general to indicate the particular relevance of your education and qualifications to the job you are seeking, you should produce your own headings as appropriate.
9 The covering letter represents the chance to express in good, fluent prose what is contained in note form in the CV.
10 Typical errors made by applicants include: copying a letter written by some other person; using the present employer's stationery to write the application letter; and making disparaging remarks about the present employer.

Assignment

- Try replying to the first advertisement on p. 226.
- Now try writing a curriculum vitae and covering letter which would be suitable for the company in the second advertisement.
- Compare the two letters. Are there any differences? If so, what?

- How did you convey the impression that you were capable of fitting into an old-established city firm, for the first letter, and young and ambitious, eager to join the rapidly expanding second company?

Useful information and further reading

Choices: Jobs Through the Internet, www.choicesonline.com

Studner, P., McDonald M. (Ed.), *Super Job Search: The Complete Manual for Job-Seekers and Career-Changers,* Mercury Books, 1996

Yate, Martin, *The Ultimate CV Book,* Kogan Page, 2002

■ 〹 16 Writing reports

'Pity the computer can't actually write the reports.'

'Write a report' – the very thought fills people with horror. Reports seem to be the thing people dread writing more than anything else. If you feel like this then you are in good company.
This chapter will:

- *discuss 'the report' in general, the different types of report and the essentials of a good report;*
- *show how reports, whether long or short, simple or formal, have the same fundamental structure;*
- *describe the 'signposting' system that reports use to guide the reader along the route;*
- *explain the topping and tailing of longer reports.*

Then, with a clearer overview of what you are aiming for:

- *provide a step-by-step guide to preparing and writing a report;*
- *give you some tips on producing the final document*

Even if you feel that it is unlikely you will need to write a report in the very near future, you should still find the following pages useful, since the basic structure of a good report is very similar to the structure of any fairly long piece of writing – an essay, or an article, for example; reports come in many shapes and sizes as we shall see.

But first, let us go back to the dread and horror which writing a report seems to produce for even the most capable of writers.

Self-Check

Write down your reactions to being asked to write a report? What feeling do you experience at the very idea? What exactly is it about reports which makes you feel like this?

Perhaps it is because reports seem less common forms of communication. Writing letters, going to meetings, talking to people in all sorts of informal situations are more common activities for most people, and therefore seem less frightening. We don't have to write reports very often and so when we do have to, we aren't very practised at it and we don't know how to go about it.

Perhaps another reason for dislike of report-writing is that 'reports' seem to be so large and unmanageable. We conjure up a vision of many sheets of closely printed words in a rather official-looking binder and the prospect of producing something like that seems very daunting. But let us look at the facts.

First, we have discovered that to perform even the apparently simple communication activities efficiently and effectively we need to do a lot more thinking and planning than we realised.

Second, the principles we have explored in relation to communication in general and writing in particular apply in exactly the same way to writing a report as they do to letter-writing. Armed with those principles and techniques you should be in a position now to write a very effective report, even if there are a few special techniques to bear in mind of which you may not yet be aware and which this chapter is designed to cover.

Third, the problem of size; not all reports are long, complicated affairs, as we shall see. Without realising it, you probably produce reports on all sorts of things in the course of the day, because reports come in countless shapes and sizes. Furthermore, the long, complicated report has basically the same elements as the short simple report – it is only a question of scale, and coping with a large-scale project is only a question of disciplining yourself to stick to the steps in the process and above all having the courage to start.

16.1 What is a report?

A report is a communication of information or advice, from a person who has collected and studied the facts, to a person who has asked for the report because they need it for a specific purpose. Often the ultimate function of a report is to provide a basis for decision and action.

> **Self-Check**
>
> Using this definition of a report, think back over the past week and make a list of all the 'reports' that you have produced, or helped to produce.

If you have accepted the wider implications of this definition, you will have realised that you have produced 'reports' on all sorts of things during the week. For example:

- a report on a film for someone who was deciding whether to see that particular film or not
- a report of what happened in a lecture or meeting for someone who didn't attend
- a report of your knowledge of the facts or of your opinions on a particular situation or issue at work for your boss to help them arrive at a decision, or in taking some action or other

- a report of some figures or facts on a form which when completed goes elsewhere in the organisation, to enable someone else to take action or make a decision
- a report in the form of a letter or memo telling someone what you know about something, or giving them advice about what to do.

In other words, there are probably as many different types of 'reports' – as there are occasions which call for a report, from a casual conversation to a two-inch-thick government report which would act as a door-stopper.

16.2 Types of report

Reports can be transmitted in the form of:

- conversations
- demonstrations or presentations
- letters
- memos
- fill-in forms
- many-page documents

They can be classified according to:

- length (short/long)
- tone (informal-semi-formal/formal)
- subject matter (engineering/financial/marketing/accident)
- timing (daily/weekly/monthly; interim/progress/final)
- importance (routine/special/urgent)
- style (narrative/descriptive/expository/pictorial/statistical)
- distribution (inter-office/company/public/private).

Whatever form a report takes it must always be planned and communicated in a way which suits the receiver (reader or listener) and their purpose. Consequently some reports will require very little planning, others will require more; some reports will be spoken, others written; some will be short, others will be long.

Since this chapter is intended to encourage you to tackle what may seem to be the more difficult report – the written report – we will concentrate on this viewpoint, but you might like occasionally to consider how the principles and techniques suggested in this chapter can apply, with appropriate modification, to any reporting.

16.3 Essentials of a good report

Check-Points: The Good Report

- The report should be unified – about only one subject; it should contain nothing that the reader does not need, nothing that is off the subject.
- It should be complete; it should exclude nothing that the reader does need.
- All the information should be accurate and all the reasoning from the facts must be valid.

- It should present the subject matter according to a plan based on a logical analysis and classification of the material.
- The manner of presentation should make the plan clear, so that the reader is never in doubt as to where they are in the report and why they are there.
- The report should be written in a simple, concise style that is easy to read and impossible to misunderstand.
- The report should be readily intelligible to all who are likely to read it even though they may not know the technical and other details of the subject.

16.4 What is the purpose of the report?

It is essential to make sure when you are asked to write a report that you know exactly what you are supposed to be covering and why. These instructions, often called 'terms of reference', should define the scope and limitations of your investigation. They should be clear and agreed before you start as they will provide you with your *objectives* and guide you in carrying out your investigation and writing your report. Frequently, as in the case of committee inquiries, the terms of reference are quoted at the beginning of the report. If you are given formal written instructions which, as they stand, are suitably worded, they can be written into your introduction. If your instructions are clear but rather long-winded you may have to make them more concise before including them in your report.

If you aren't clear what your 'terms of reference' are, you must go back to the person or committee that has requested the report and ask for clearer instructions:

- Why is the report required?
- Who exactly is it for?
- What do they want it to do?

The terms of reference for the Auditor General (Head of the National Audit Office) in *Evaluating the Applications to Run the National Lottery*, are an example of formal terms of reference but notice how the objectives are clearly stated using verbs: 'to review', 'to establish' and so on.

Study scope
1.9   The National Audit Office study focused primarily on the evaluation process leading to the award of the Section 5 licence to run the National Lottery, ie the work that took place between the closing date for Section 5 licence applications (14 February 1994) and the announcement of the successful applicant on 25 May 1994.

1.10   *The objectives of the study were:*
- to review whether the Director General had established a proper and appropriate evaluation procedure for the examination of applications for the licence to run the National Lottery under Section 5 of the Act, in accordance with the statutory objectives set out therein and in a way which ensured a consistent and fair treatment of all applications;

- to establish that the final choice of the preferred applicant was arrived at in a rational and proper way, by reference to the established evaluation procedure and any properly documented modifications to it, whilst allowing the Director General to exercise his judgement properly in the context of the statutory objectives set out in the Act; and
- to establish whether the Section 5 licence granted by the Director General reflected the relevant commitments in the successful application.

We will look more closely at setting report objectives later in the chapter when you are clearer about what the various parts of a report are and what they might look like.

16.5 Fundamental structure

Parts		Elements
Introduction	{	Terms of reference or objectives
		Procedure or Method
Body of the report	{	Findings
Final section		Conclusions
		Recommendations (if requested)
		Appendices (if necessary)

This structure must be evident in any report, however short. A longer report might contain in addition to these essential elements what might be called 'accessories', as we shall see.

Self-Check

List what you think the introduction of a report should include.

The introduction

The function of the introduction is to prepare the reader for the report proper – the body of the report. The structure generally follows a standard plan which has been found in practice to be the best way of avoiding incoherent, badly proportioned and wrongly emphasised openings:

(a) a clear unambiguous statement of the real *subject*
(b) an indication of the *purpose*, together with any background information necessary to the clear understanding of that purpose
(c) a brief description of the *methods* used to obtain the information
(d) a summary of the *conclusions*, findings and recommendations and so on in their briefest form
(e) an announcement of the *plan* on which the body of the report is arranged.

Within this structure the introduction should:

(a) be as brief as is consistent with clarity
(b) correctly focus the reader's attention on your real theme and purpose

(c) harmonise with what follows, that is, it should promise nothing that is not done later in the report, and it should not appear in any way inconsistent with the final section.

The body of the report

The body of the report is the report proper, that is the several sections that lie between the introduction and the final section. In it are set out all the *facts* (e.g. the character of the investigation, a detailed explanation of the methodology used, the procedure followed, the results obtained), and an analysis of these facts leading the reader logically to the conclusions and recommendations in the final section that are justified by the facts. We will look at how to organise this information later in the chapter.

The final section

The function of the final section is to present briefly, clearly and finally, the conclusions reached, the recommendations to be made, or whatever the logical conclusion of the matter in hand. The characteristics of a good final section are:

(a) it introduces nothing new
(b) it harmonises with the introduction and with the body of the report
(c) it leaves the reader with the final impression that you want to make.

16.6 Format, layout, headings and numbering

Reports, as we have seen, can come in a variety of formats, but providing that the report does not have to be written on to a form, or to a particular style, you will have a choice of layout.

Letter/memo format

Perhaps the simplest form of short report is the one written in the form of a letter or memo. The essential elements are there though they are not necessarily headed as such (see the letter report in Figure 16.1).

Schematic format

This report could have been presented as a short separate report with a covering letter. The report would use sections and headings but would still contain the essential elements.

> **Assignment:** Using the information contained in the 'letter report' write a short report using 'schematic format', i.e. sections and headings.
> Now compare your report with the example in Figure 16.2.

The Managing Director,
Bolton and Foster Ltd,
31 Merrydown Lane,
BRISTOL BS17 2BT

Dear Sir

Introduction { Following the instructions of the Board I have visited the Coldharbour Business Park to assess whether the company should acquire a site for new offices there. I now have pleasure in submitting my provisional report. } *Terms of Reference & Procedure* / *Subject*

Body of the report {

The Business Park is a purpose-built enterprise situated about two miles from Speymouth, with which it has excellent road communication. Water, light and power supplies on the estate are excellent and the rate charges compare favourably with those in similar industrial areas elsewhere in the country.

The particular site offered to the Company is well drained, is adjacent to the main road which passes through the estate, and within half a mile of the M94.

I have interviewed a number of building contractors in the district and there would appear to be no difficulty in getting the building work carried out locally. The necessary planning permission should be readily obtainable since the Government has scheduled this as a 'development area'.

Supplies of skilled and semi-skilled staff are fairly plentiful and the local office of the Department for Education and Skills would naturally welcome new offices employing 600 personnel. It would, however, be necessary for the Company to bring in a number of skilled operatives and technicians. The accommodation of these key-workers would present a serious problem, as the housing shortage in the area remains acute. It would be possible to build temporary hostel accommodation on a site available near the offices or use hotel accommodation, as an interim solution to this problem.

} *Findings in paragraphs*

Final section { Despite this problem, the site at Coldharbour in all other respects appears to suit the Company's requirements ideally, and in my opinion the Company should accept the site and proceed with the building of the offices without delay. } *Conclusions* / *Recommendations*

Yours faithfully

J Longman

J. Longman
Development Manager

Figure 16.1 **Example of a letter report.**

REPORT ON PROPOSED NEW OFFICE SITE

1 TERMS OF REFERENCE

In accordance with the instructions of the Board, to report on the possibility of acquiring a site for a new office on the Coldharbour Business Park and make recommendations as appropriate.

2 PROCEDURE

This report was compiled following a visit to the Coldharbour Business Park and interviews with the Estate Manager, local building firms and the local office of the Department for Education and Skills.

3 COLDHARBOUR BUSINESS PARK

(a) Location and facilities

The Business Park is a purpose-built enterprise situated two miles from Speymouth, with which it has excellent road communication. Water, light and power supplies on the estate are excellent and the rate charges compare favourably with those in similar industrial areas elsewhere in the country.

(b) Proposed site

The particular site offered to the Company is well drained, is adjacent to the main road which passes through the estate, and within half a mile of the M94.

(c) Building and planning permission

(i) There would appear to be no difficulty in getting the building work carried out locally.

(ii) The necessary planning permission should be readily obtainable since the Government has rescheduled this a 'development area'.

(d) Staff

(i) Skilled and semi-skilled

Supplies of skilled and semi-skilled staff are fairly

plentiful and the local office of the Department for Education and Skills welcomes the establishment of new offices employing 600 personnel.

(ii) **Skilled/technician**

It would be necessary for the Company to bring in a number of skilled operatives and technicians.

(iii) **Accommodation**

The accommodation of these key workers would present a serious problem, as the housing shortage in the area remains acute. It would be possible to build temporary hostel accommodation, or use hotel accommodation, as an interim solution to this problem.

4 CONCLUSIONS

The site has:

- good access to roads and motorways;
- adequate facilities;
- competitive rate charges;
- local supply of skilled and semi-skilled staff;
- ready availability of building contractors; and
- no planning problems.

Despite the problem of accommodation, the site appears to suit the Company's requirements in all other respects.

5 RECOMMENDATIONS

That the Company accept the site and proceed with the building of the offices without delay.

Signed: *J Longman*

Development Manager

Date: 9 March 2003

Figure 16.2 **Example of report using schematic format.**

You may feel that this is a case of taking a mallet to crack a hazelnut, but it does demonstrate how the same information can be presented in different formats. Schematic format does help the reader to find the information they need at a glance but, of course, the headings should not normally outweigh the subject matter (as perhaps they do in this case).

Mixed format

Of course, a compromise between these two formats might be a letter, but with a few simple headings for the body of the letter/report: 'Business Park', 'Proposed Site', 'Staff' and so on. This is called 'mixed format' and is very common, since it follows good practice for setting out a letter of any length, that is, subheadings if they are helpful.

Good arrangement alone is not sufficient. The subject matter is often heavy going when compared with other kinds of reading, and the inherent design must be made immediately apparent to the reader. There are two main ways of helping to make the structure clear:

Sectional headings

Headings are an aid to the eye and hence to the understanding. There is no one right system and you may often have to follow the system adopted in your organisation or department, but here are some principles to guide you.

- The typography and spacing of the headings should reflect the inherent order of the report.
- Fussiness should be avoided: headings should help, not irritate, the reader.
- The text should remain independent of the headings, which are additional to, not part of, the text.
- Headings are useless if they are not illuminating and self-explanatory.
- Headings should consist of words or phrases, never of sentences.
- Headings should be precise, but concise.

Headings in Word-processed Reports

MAIN HEADING IN CAPITAL LETTERS IN BOLD CENTRED

CAPITAL LETTERS IN BOLD or Mixed Letters in Bold

Leave a double line space **before** the heading and a double or at least larger than normal line space (or indent 0.5 ins) **after** the heading before starting the paragraph.

Small letters in bold

Leave a double line space **before** the heading, and a double or at least larger than normal line space (or indent 0.5 ins) **after** the heading before starting the paragraph.

Small letters in bold and with a full stop. The text begins immediately after it on the same line.

These are the four main methods of indicating a heading. However, it is also possible to indicate different levels of heading using:

- underlined headings: <u>Underlined Headings</u>

- different font sizes: 12 POINT   14 POINT   18 POINT

- different fonts: **HELVETICA OR ARIAL 14 POINT BOLD**

    TIMES 14 POINT BOLD

    CLOISTER OPENFACE or
    CASLON OPENFACE (12 point)

- or spaced headings: **S P A C E D   H E A D I N G S**

Most word-processing packages now contain a range of different fonts which can be very tempting for the amateur, but take a tip from the professionals: don't use too many fonts in one document. Two different fonts in the normal business communication document are more than enough. Similarly, you should try to limit the number of different levels of heading, or it will become confusing for the reader.

Coherence

The aim of all paragraphing and sectionalising is to separate and yet at the same time to bind together the elements of the whole. A logical arrangement is the primary means to coherence. But it is often necessary to help the reader to pass smoothly from section to section by the use of *linking words and phrases* and *reference back and forth.*

Similar in purpose, on a larger scale, are 'functional' paragraphs. These are short paragraphs which do not add information but introduce, conclude and effect transition between sections.

Reference numbering

Numbering of headings is a matter of taste. If the appearance of the headings is clear enough, then numbering is not necessary. However, some writers prefer the level of importance of the headings to be reinforced by a numbering system which repeats the visual effect of the varied headings. It is based on an *alternation of numbers and letters* in descending order of importance:

A,B,C; 1,2,3; (a),(b),(c); etc.
or 1,2,3; (a),(b),(c); (i),(ii),(iii); ● (bullets); etc.

Similar is the so-called 'decimal' system:

1.
   1.1
   1.2
2.
   2.1
   2.2
      2.2.1
      2.2.2

This system can be particularly useful where a report is to be discussed at meetings. Reference to individual sections is made easier by the decimal system, for example 'point **3.2.1**' is easier to find quickly than 'point **(i)** in subsection **(b)** of section **3**'.

However, if your plan is sound and the headings clear, an alternative system which aids ready reference is simply to *number each paragraph sequentially* throughout the report, whether it forms part of a major or minor section, for example '1,2,3,4,5 ... 25' and so on.

The house style of some organisations requires this paragraph numbering in any document that is longer than two pages.

Self-Check

- What elements should be included in a report, however short, and in whatever form?
- What would be the minimum number of sections required?

To check your answers, see the letter report reproduced in Figure 16.1.

16.7 Long formal reports

A typical structure of a long formal report might look like this, but bear in mind that you may modify and adapt the following components to virtually any type or length of report.

(a) *Preliminaries*

  1 Title page
  2 Authorisation (terms of reference, scope, objectives)
  3 Table of contents
  4 List of tables and figures (if appropriate)
  5 Foreword/preface
  6 Acknowledgements
  7 Summary

(b) *Main report*

(All reports will need, as a minimum, these three sections)

1 Introduction
2 Findings and discussion
3 Conclusions (and, when appropriate, recommendations)

(c) *Supplements*

1 References and bibliography
2 Appendices
3 Index.

Preliminaries

The title page

The title page is the reader's first contact with the report and it is worth taking some trouble over its layout.

It answers questions in the mind of someone who might be going through a pile of reports looking for a particular one and those questions would probably be:

- What is it about?   (Subject of report)
- Who wrote it?   (Author(s))
- For whom?   (Name of person or group for whom it was prepared)
- From where?   (Full postal address of organisation on whose behalf it was written)
- When?   (Date, including month, when report was completed)

An example of a title page is given in Figure 16.3.

Although the title should be short enough to be read almost at a glance, it should still be definite. *The title should be centred in the middle of the page.* If the title runs into two or more lines, you should group significant words together in centred lines. The end of a line should never break a significant group of important words. Avoid:

The Incidence of Bark
Infestation in Apple
Trees in the Channel
Islands

Better:

The Incidence of Bark Infestation
in Apple Trees
in the Channel Islands

Authorisation

This may be an instruction expressed as a committee resolution stating the purpose of the report. In business reports the authorisation and instructions are usually run together in summary form under a title such as 'Terms of reference' (or Scope of the Report or Purpose of the Report or Aims or Objectives), as we have seen.

BOLTON AND FOSTER LIMITED

Report on Proposed New Office Site
Coldharbour Business Park

For: The Board of Directors,
Bolton and Foster Ltd,
3 Merrydown Lane,
BRISTOL BS1 2BT

Tel. Bristol (01272) 732210

By: John Longman, M.Sc.
Development Manager

9 March 2003

Figure 16.3 **Example of title page.**

Table of Contents

This aids reference, and makes possible selective reading by those who are interested in only parts of the report. By bringing all the headings and subheadings together it shows clearly the logical structure of the report. A few moments' study of the contents page by the reader helps rapid understanding, provided the layout really does show the structure clearly, and if the titles and subtitles are concise and explanatory, and identical with those used in the text. For an example, look at the Contents pages of this book.

It should also include the page numbers and should therefore be prepared last of all, when the final page numbers are known. Most WP packages include a facility for producing a Table of Contents.

List of tables and figures

This list not only aids the reader, but also helps to provide a valuable check against inaccurate collating (assembly) before stapling or binding.

Foreword or preface

This is sometimes found in a large general report, perhaps issued for a whole profession or for the general public, rather than a particular body. It briefly explains why the writer or the organisation wanted to carry out the investigation or to write a report about it, and explains why the report was produced in the way it was.

Acknowledgements

It is customary to thank by name those who have helped in the investigation and compiling of the report, both within your own organisation and in other organisations. This does not mean listing every single person who had anything to do with it, only those of particular significance: 'The Managing Director, Mr ..., and his staff', 'my colleagues and in particular Andy Neil and Gemma Taylor.'

Where money has been provided from outside funds, this must be mentioned but without any indication of the actual sums involved. You should also mention any help by secretarial staff and technicians.

Summary

The summary (see Figure 16.4) is a miniature version of the report, summarising the purpose of the report and the general character of its conclusions or recommendations. Its function is to give the busy reader quickly a good idea of what they may expect to find in the report even before they have read the probably much longer introduction. The summary (sometimes called 'Executive Summary') is now very common in all but the briefest report. Where a summary is not included, its function is often fulfilled by placing the conclusions and recommendations sections early on in the report instead of in their more usual position at the end. Either method helps the reader gain an overview of the report before reading the details.

For guidance on summary-writing look at Chapter 13, Section 13.3.

Supplements

References and bibliography

If you have used other people's work or writing to compile your report, you should acknowledge this in the text and then list the references at the back of the report. This is particularly important in academic dissertations or theses.

You should strictly observe these five rules:

- *All items which are not your own original work should be clearly shown as such*: this should prevent allegations of plagiarism (copying without acknowledgement).
- *Put any quotation within quotation marks*: even a single word might have to be treated in this way if it expressed a major aspect of another writer's opinion.
- *Every reference in the text and illustrations to other work should appear in the list of references.*
- *Every item in the list of references must have a reference in the text (or a figure)*: it is good practice for the text to make some mention of any reference quoted or a figure as a source of data.
- *Every figure and photograph must have a reference in the text.*

Normally the numbering of references should correspond to the order of mention in the text and should give the author, the title of the book or journal, the publisher and the date of publication. Example:

Gowers, Sir Ernest, *Complete Plain Words*, Penguin Books, 2003

A bibliography is optional. It provides a guide to suitable background reading around the subject of the report.

Appendices

An appendix (plural – appendices) should be used whenever statistical data or lengthy quoted material (e.g. passages from books, other reports, letters) would congest the main text, hold up the argument or otherwise hinder the reader. The main text itself must make quite clear the exact part played by the information given in the appendix. It is not sufficient to say simply 'see Appendix A', and hope that all will be clear from a first glance at the appendix. If an appendix is constantly referred to at many places in the text, it could be made to open out for easy reference. Mounted photographs, maps, or other flat examples should be placed in a pocket of the back cover.

Index

An index is really only necessary for very long, detailed reports. Key topics are listed alphabetically providing easy reference for the busy reader who wants to find a particular point. Look at the Index of this book for an example.

16.8   House style

I have already emphasised that the lay-out, the way in which the report is divided into sections and the kinds of heading are all going to depend on the nature of the report, its purpose, its reader(s). You will therefore have considerable freedom to choose how to present your reports. Don't be alarmed by this freedom. The typical sections described above are intended to give you ideas from which to choose the most appropriate and, although they may contain some strange terminology (e.g. 'Terms of reference'), you should now be able to see how you can use more familiar words (e.g. Objectives) to suit you and your particular circumstances.

In practice, many organisations produce typing and design guidelines for staff which help them select broadly the right structure and lay-out for the reports (and letters, emails and memos) that are typical of that particular organisation. You may even find that the word-processing package in your organisation has been customised to provide you with templates, styles and macros.

While this kind of 'house style' can often be very helpful and the organisation can be confident that all staff are presenting documents in a unified style, there are disadvantages which you will discover as you become more experienced and therefore more confident. The house style may turn out to be too rigid to allow you to produce the document in the way you feel is most suitable. You should always have the courage, therefore, to consult your boss on ways in which the house style might need to be adapted to suit your purpose. But, you should always ask permission: the house style has been developed to overcome the problems of everyone 'doing their own thing'.

Summary and conclusions

Background

1 Eight applications for a licence to run the National Lottery, to be issued under Section 5 of the National Lottery etc. Act 1993 ("the Act"), were submitted to the Director General of the National Lottery by the closing date of 14 February 1994. Following their receipt the Director General, with the assistance of expert advisers, evaluated the applications and, on 25 May 1994, announced that Camelot Group plc was the successful applicant. The relevant licence was issued on 29 July 1994, effective until 30 September 2001.

Procedure/ Method and Objectives (expressed here as questions to be answered)

2 The National Audit Office first reviewed the process by which the Director General reached his decision and then focused on two questions they considered central to the process:

- did the Director General select the application appearing most likely to provide the maximum return to the National Lottery Distribution Fund (the "Distribution Fund") and if not were the reasons for choosing a lower yielding application sound?

- had the successful applicant fulfilled the key commitments made in its application – and if not could and should the Director General have foreseen this during the evaluation process?

Conclusions

3 The National Audit Office's main conclusions were that the evaluation process was comprehensive, consistent, logical and properly controlled; that throughout the process the Director General acted in accordance with the statutory duties placed upon him; that following the completion the licence was awarded to the applicant who was shown by the Director General's evaluation to offer the highest return to the Distribution Fund; and that the key commitments offered in the successful application were incorporated in the Section 5 licence issued.

4 The National Audit Office's other main findings were that:

- the Invitation to Apply for a licence to run the National Lottery was widely publicised and generated significant public interest;

- the way in which applicants were required to structure their applications effectively guaranteed that, as sales increased, an increasing proportion of the revenue generated accrued to the Distribution Fund, thus ensuring the Fund benefited from any unexpected success in the lottery;

- the evaluation process was carefully thought through and codified in a manual drafted before the applications were received. This manual was logically sound, was applied rigorously, and proved robust in practice;

Findings

- the security arrangements designed to protect the confidentiality of the applications and of the evaluation process were rigorous and appear to have achieved their objective;

- the calculation of the present value of applicants' proposed contributions to the Distribution Fund was a huge task, involving not only thousands of arithmetical calculations but also the exercise of judgement in certain key areas. The National Audit Office are satisfied that the arithmetical calculations made were correct in all material respects and that the judgements made were exercised properly in the context of the statutory objectives set out in the Act;

- the contest for the licence was a remarkably closely fought one, suggesting that, within the framework set by the relevant legislation, it produced the best possible result for the Distribution Fund;

- the licensee launched the on line game on time, met the licence commitments relating to outlet numbers and (to a large extent) their geographical distribution, and achieved sales to 31 March 1995 that were some 40 per cent ahead of forecast (NB. The extent to which key licence commitments have been met in practice will be considered in more depth in a separate National Audit Office study of the monitoring and regulation of the lottery); and

- the launch of the first instant scratch card type game on 21 March 1995 was initially affected by computing problems which resulted in the suspension of instant ticket services to the lottery's retailers for most of the first day. The launch of the second instant game on 2 May 1995 was accomplished without any such problems.

5 At a detailed level, this report identifies some stages in the evaluation process at which, in the National Audit Office's view, the available information was capable of different interpretations. Indeed, given the complexity and sophistication of the evaluation it would be surprising if that were not the case. But the reservations are minor technical ones and:

- fall well within the normal range of variation in professional opinion and, more important;

- are not sufficiently material to affect the outcome of the process.

Appendices

6 The National Audit Office invited all the applicants to comment on the evaluation process. Some of the comments received (see Appendix 1) raised issues relating to the way in which the selection process was carried out, others addressed perceived deficiencies in the legislation and were therefore outside the National Audit Office remit, while the remainder focused on specific aspects of the evaluation. Where appropriate, the points raised were taken into account in the relevant parts of the National Audit Office examination and in the findings and conclusions, as summarised above.

Figure 16.4 **Example of a report summary.**

16.9   How to get started

We have already explored in Chapter 1 the preparation and planning stages of creating any message, be it a letter, an essay, a report or a talk, and so on. However, it might be useful to revise what's involved in the process of writing, in this case, a report, before we look at the process in a bit more detail. Think particularly about what you should do *before* starting to write anything.

Self-Check

Before reading on, try designing your own checklist of points/questions to remember under these six headings:

- **Stage 1**   Setting your objective
- **Stage 2**   Researching and assembling the material
- **Stage 3**   Organising the material and planning the report
- **Stage 4**   Writing the first draft
- **Stage 5**   Editing the report (criticisms and review of first draft)
- **Stage 6**   Producing the report.

Now, if you are actually writing a report

- estimate how much time you need for each stage and write out a time-table
- think about your 'terms of reference'.
  How clear are they? Do you really know what is expected of you?

16.10   Setting your objective

The success of your report will stand or fall on how well you do this. More reports have gone wrong because the writer thought they knew what the report was for (their 'terms of reference') but ended up writing their own report rather than the one that was really wanted. You need to establish very clearly at the outset exactly what the purpose of the report is and refer back to it again and again throughout the process of compiling the report.

> *Be warned: Instructions which begin 'Write me a report on ...' are often dangerously vague!*

Reports tend to fall into two main categories:

- regular reports
- one-off reports.

Regular reports

These probably represent the majority of reports produced in business: monthly, weekly reports providing historical performance-related information – financial, sales, production. If you have to take over production of a regular report the sources of information will probably already be identified, the information even provided for you. Your job will be to present it in a report to an agreed format. Sounds relatively easy? The temptation is to do it in much the same way as everyone else has done it before you. But, you need to ask three fundamental questions:

1 Why was this report first produced?
2 Does the report still serve any useful purpose?
3 Could the report (its information or format) be changed to make it more useful?

One-off reports

These are produced for a specific purpose and therefore present more of a challenge. However, it may be that your organisation has produced similar reports before that might provide you with some guidance. But, don't be too quick to follow the same approach without asking searching questions: you may be following a bad example.

While every report has a unique purpose, (and it is essential that you understand exactly what it is supposed to achieve before you start researching the material), it is possible to categorise the general aims of reports and the particular questions you need to answer:

The spectrum of report aims (and the questions you should ask)

- **To provide information**
  How much detail should be included?
  Who will receive the report?
  At what level should the information be pitched?
  Will the report be kept for reference purposes or simply be read once and then thrown away?

  Is the information cleared for circulation?
  Is this a one-off report?
  What value will the information be to the readers?

- **To provide a record**
  Why is it important to record this information now?
  Why might people want to refer to this information in future?
  Does the wording of the report need to be approved by anyone else?

  Who might want to refer to this information in future?
  Is the report likely to be used in any legal proceedings?

- **To answer a question**
  Is the question expressed clearly and unambiguously in the terms of reference?
  How does the recipient want to use the report?
  Does the recipient think they already know the answer to the question? If so, what?

  What kind of report does the recipient want?
  How much does the recipient already know about the topic of the report?

- **To recommend a course of action or decision**

    Why is the action/decision needed?

    Who will be involved in discussing the recommendation?

    What evidence will be needed to support the recommendation?

    Should the report include the implications of the recommendation?

    Do the recipients want one clear recommendation or a choice of options?

    Do the recipients already have their own preferences?

    Have the implications/effects of implementing the recommendation been considered?

- **To influence opinion**

    Which people is the report seeking to influence?

    Why do we want to change their opinions?

    What information must the report contain and in how much detail?

    In what other ways can the report be made more influential?

    What is their current opinion?

    How should the report deal with adverse opinions?

    What are the strongest arguments and how can they be presented most effectively?

- **To gain publicity**

    Why do we want publicity for the subject of the report?

    Is there a danger of a negative backlash?

    Which kinds of news organisation are likely to publicise the report?

    How will the publicity help the organisation?

    Is the content of the report newsworthy?

    How can style and format of the report make it more newsworthy?

- **To meet a statutory obligation**

    What exactly does the statutory body require?

    What other useful information could be included to give the report wider appeal?

    How should the information be presented to meet the statutory body requirements?

    How will the statutory information be distinguished from the other information?

Check-Point

Why are You Writing a Report?

You must be absolutely clear, before doing anything further, that you understand exactly:

- why your report is being written
- who it is for
- what they want you to cover
- how they want it presented
- when they want it,

If you're not sure, go back and ask

Now – write down your main objectives in the form of a 'thesis sentence'.

A 'thesis sentence' is similar to a topic sentence (see 13.3) but it states the main idea or argument of your whole document, written in one clear sentence, for example, 'To explore the different ways in which the ABC problem might be solved and recommend the best solution in terms of efficiency rather than cost.'

Keep the thesis sentence in front of you throughout the process of researching and writing your report.

16.11 Researching and assembling the material: *period of synthesis*

Your next task is to obtain the information you need for the report. You may have some already; it may be provided for you if it is a regular report; but if it is a one-off report, you may have to do some careful research. Take careful notes; don't rely on your memory. (See Figure 16.5, p. 266, for an example of one form of notes – mind-mapping.)

Sources of information

- Primary source: *People* (interviews/questionnaires/telephone calls)
                          Networking (friends, colleagues, other companies)
- Secondary sources: *Libraries* (in-house as well as public)
                          Databases (as well as numerical data, increasingly large amounts of text are stored on databases)
                          Customers and suppliers
                          Trade associations
                          Professional associations
                          Conferences and exhibitions.

Research techniques

Don't be lazy: don't only use the Internet

Desk research

- Best for facts – books, magazines, newspapers and journals, computer databases – all of which can possibly be found on CD-ROM or the Internet.
- Get help from a librarian.
- Use the techniques of *skimming* and *scanning* recommended in Chapter 13.
- Pick up an information trail – use the references in one book or article to take you somewhere else; if someone can't help you, ask them to suggest something or someone else.

Questionnaires and surveys

- Look at Chapter 17 for help with questionnaires.

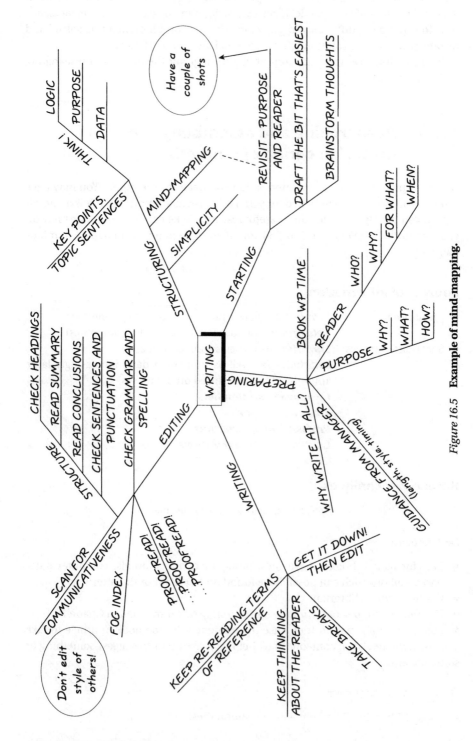

Figure 16.5 **Example of mind-mapping.**

Interviews (essential for attitudes, feelings, emotions)

- face-to-face
- telephone – works best when you know the person and the interview is no more than half an hour
- consider using a structured interview or a questionnaire as a basis (see Chapter 6 on Interviewing and Chapter 17 on Questionnaires)

Observation and recording

- ranges from complex scientific experimentation to simple counting of information from a single source (e.g. cars at road junction)
- can be costly to carry out
- could the information already exist from another source?

Always choose the sources of information and research techniques most appropriate to your task

Now measure all your information against your purpose and objectives:

- determine the relative value of details
- reject the obviously irrelevant
- fill in the gaps where details are lacking.

16.12 Organising the material and planning the report: *period of analysis and classification*

Either

1 *List* on cards or pieces of paper, one for each item, the topics that it appears from your investigation you will have to cover.

Or:

1 Draw up a *'mind map'* by writing your topics on a large sheet of paper on lines branching off from the centre (an example of a mind map is shown in figure 16.5).

Or:

1 Use the *Outlining* facility on your word-processor to list and move the topics.
2 *Check* these topics against your objectives and 'thesis sentence', paying particular attention to the purpose and the limitations (scope) of your report.
3 Look for the natural main *divisions* of your whole subject, or for some way of classifying the topics into groups; arrange all your topics under these main groupings. If you are working with topic cards, the floor is a good place to work at this stage. The main groupings will be the main sections in your report.
4 *Label* each group; these will probably become the headings in your report.
5 *Organise* the material within each of these main groupings into logical sub-groups – second and possibly even into third (order) level groups (see Figure 16.6).

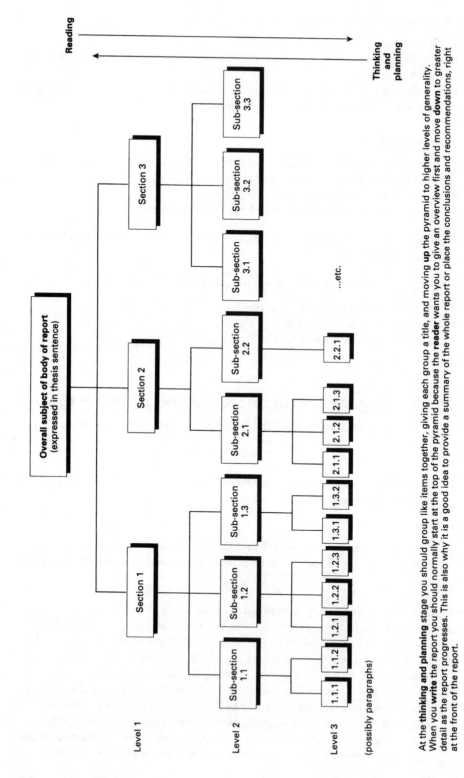

At the **thinking and planning** stage you should group like items together, giving each group a title, and moving **up** the pyramid to higher levels of generality. When you **write** the report you should normally start at the top of the pyramid because the **reader** wants you to give an overview first and move **down** to greater detail as the report progresses. This is also why it is a good idea to provide a summary of the whole report or place the conclusions and recommendations, right at the front of the report.

Figure 16.6 **The author's plan: pyramid of ideas.**

6 Arrange each of these main and sub-groups in the best *logical* and *psychological sequence* (see Chapter 1, Section 1.7, stage 4 on putting the information into logical sequence).

7 *Draft* the working plan. If you have been working with cards, draft the plan on a separate sheet of paper. This plan or outline will form the basis of your table of contents. Use all the devices of lettering and spacing to indicate what are main and what are subordinate and sub-subordinate headings.

8 Decide which areas of your report may need *visual aids* (for guidance on the use of visual aids and the visual presentation of information see Chapters 11 and 18).

16.13 Writing the first draft

This is the period in which the first draft is written. Forget that blank white sheet of paper – start writing! If you are really 'hung up' about starting, make yourself write something – anything – it doesn't matter at this stage and it will get you going.

Produce the first draft as quickly as possible, the whole or at least the whole of one section at one sitting. Don't worry about style or expression or about the details of construction. Leave these until the final critical stage.

Ideally this first draft, whether handwritten or typed, should be laid out in double spacing on one side only of the paper. It is essential to leave plenty of room for such things as your after-thoughts and editorial corrections for later reproduction.

1 Write the introduction

● State the subject; stress its value, or other important features to arouse your reader's interest.
● Indicate the purpose of the report, with any explanatory background information which may be necessary.
● Summarise briefly the results or findings, the conclusions and recommendations (if you are not writing a *separate* 'summary').
● Describe the sources and methods of your investigation.
● Announce the plan of the report (not necessary in a short report).

Note: Some people prefer to write the introduction *after* they have written the body of the report and the final section. Even though it will appear first in the report it is often easier to write it when you know what the report has covered.

But there is a danger in doing this, of twisting your report away from your real purpose and then having to modify your objective. This may be justified but it will depend on your terms of reference, so at least be aware of the danger.

2 Write the body of the report

● Explain what procedures you followed.
● Analyse and interpret the results and indicate the inferences to be drawn from them.

3 Write the final section

- Summarise the discussion, drawing out the main points of the report and presenting a considered judgement of them. Only draw conclusions which are justified by the evidence and the facts contained in the body.
- Make recommendations based on your discussion and conclusions.
- Don't introduce any new material or line of argument.
- Close with emphasis on the final impression you want to leave with your reader.

Now, if your report is a long, detailed one, prepare the 'accessories'.

4 Write the summary

- Summarise the entire report into a substantial paragraph (or two).
- Check it against your 'thesis sentence' to see that you have kept strictly to your original conception and intention.
- Check it against your introduction.

5 Prepare the table of contents, appendices and so on as appropriate

Now leave the report for a day or two and then come back to it to criticise it ruthlessly and objectively.

16.14   Editing the report

1 Take a general look at your draft as a whole

- Is the design of the report obvious?
- Is your system of headings consistent with your purpose?
- Are there any causes of confusion?
- Are the balance and proportion of the facts appropriate?

2 Consider the title, table of contents, introduction and conclusion in relation to one another

- Do they harmonise and agree with one another?
- Do your headings agree with your table of contents?
- Have you carried out your working plan?
- Have you emphasised the correct points?
- Have you stated your subject, purpose and plan?

3 Examine the text

- Have you provided clear transitions from one topic/section to another?
- Are paragraphs too long? Too short?

- Is the sentence structure of every sentence clear and grammatical?
- Is the average sentence length reasonably short (18–22 words)?
- Is the choice of words effective? Too many long words? Unnecessary technical terms?
- Are there any spelling or punctuation errors?

4 Read the text aloud to yourself, or even better, to someone else

- Does it read easily and smoothly?
- Can your listener follow you?
- Are there any 'echo' effects – repeated words, repeated ideas which are unnecessary?
- Have you left anything out? Or failed to mention something early enough to ensure understanding?

5 Check your visual aids

- Does each convey its message clearly enough?
- Have you linked illustrations with the text clearly enough?
- Have you taken advantage of visual aids to avoid long-winded explanations?
- Have you given each visual aid a caption or title?
- Are the captions precise and informative?

For guidance on visual communication and the use of visual aids look at Chapters 11 and 18.

6 Final critical comments

Finally, and if possible, get someone qualified to give constructive criticism to look through the report.

Change anything that needs changing – your reputation is at stake!

16.15 Producing the report

Whether you have already typed your report into your word-processor or will get someone else to do it for you, you should always allow yourself plenty of time from the moment when your final draft is completed to the moment when your report is required, to allow for typing, proof-reading, correcting, copying and binding.

There is never enough time left to type, edit, and proof-read!

Overall spacing and appearance

While you are putting the finishing touches to your report pay special attention to the overall visual appearance and layout of the pages.

Solid blocks of print weary the eye.

The use of white space is almost as important as the choice of typefaces. Normally the text is in single spacing with double spacing between paragraphs and the equivalent of line-and-a-half spacing between a heading and its following text. But plenty of space should be left all round lists, figures, diagrams, tables and so on. Word-processing packages now provide wide scope for breaking up blocks of print with different typefaces, bullet points, boxes, shading, and so on as in the examples on these pages. Don't go mad, but do experiment with what is available.

If you are not typing your report yourself, talk to the WP staff before you complete your final draft so that you can design the headings and layout in the light of all the possibilities and limitations. The WP staff will also explain how you should indicate your requests without confusing them with the text.

Simple WP or desktop publishing?

Assuming that your report now exists on a word-processor, you now have the choice of producing it as it stands in fairly conventional pages of text, or using a desktop publishing (DTP) program to produce a more sophisticated format. Many programs available on computers can produce written material to book-publishing standards. However, having access to a DTP program is only half the battle. They require a lot of skill to handle well, take a fair amount of time to learn and more importantly, however sophisticated the program, it cannot do the designing for you. Unfortunately, design sense, although sometimes innate, normally has to be learned and, even if understood, must be applied to this new discipline. There are now plenty of books to help you, for example *Desktop Design* by Brian Cookman (also on CD-ROM) and *Designing for Desktop Publishing* by Diane Hudson, but a report is probably not the best place to start learning the wonders and complexities of DTP and design.

The alternative is to use a specialist in your organisation or one of the many DTP bureaux which now exist in most towns. However, don't just hand in your copy and leave it to them. You will need to spend time discussing with them what you want your report to look like: which typefaces and type sizes look best, what kind of illustrations you want and so on.

Correcting the typed draft

If someone else has typed your report, check with them what symbols they would prefer you to use to indicate corrections. The list in Figure 16.7 represents a suggested selection, but *Copy Preparation and Proof Correction* (BSI 5261: Part 2: 1976 (1990)) should always be used for making amendments on work which is to be printed. (You should be able to find a copy of the Standard in reference books such as *The Writers' and Artists' Year Book* in your library; a discount on the price is available for students wishing to buy the Standard from the British Standards Institution.)

The marginal mark usually goes in the nearest margin. Make all corrections very clearly.

Instruction	Textual Mark	Marginal Mark	Notes
Leave unchanged	– – – – – – under characters to remain	✓	
Refer to appropriate authority anything of doubtful accuracy	Encircle word(s) affected	(?)	
Insert in text the matter indicated in the margin	⋋	New matter followed by ⋋	
Insert additional matter identified by a letter in a diamond	⋋	⋋ Followed by for example ◇A	The relevant section of the copy should be supplied with the corresponding letter marked on it in a diamond e.g. ◇A
Delete	/ through character(s) or ├─────┤ through words to be deleted	ℐ	
Set in or change to italic	———— under character(s) to be set or changed	⊔⊔	
Set in or change to capital letters	≡≡≡ under character(s) to be set or changed	≡	
Set in or change to bold type	∼∼∼∼ under character(s) to be set or changed	∼∼∼	
Change capital letters to lower case letters	Encircle character(s) to be changed	≢	
Change italic to upright type	Encircle character(s) to be changed	⊔	
Substitute or insert character in 'superior' position	/ through character or ⋋ where required	⌐ under character e.g. ²⌐	
Substitute or insert character in 'inferior' position	/ through character or ⋋ where required	⌐ over character e.g. ⌐₂	
Substitute or insert full stop or decimal point	/ or ⋋ where required	⊙	
Substitute or insert colon	/ or ⋋ where required	⊙	
Substitute or insert semi-colon	/ or ⋋ where required	;	
Move matter specified distance to the right	⌐enclosing matter to be moved to the right⌐→	⌐	

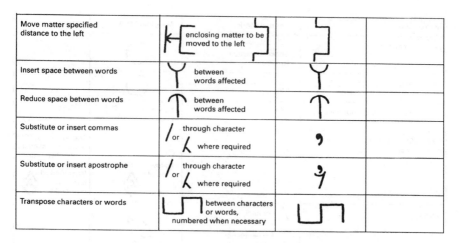

Move matter specified distance to the left	enclosing matter to be moved to the left		
Insert space between words	between words affected		
Reduce space between words	between words affected		
Substitute or insert commas	/ or ⋏ through character where required	❜	
Substitute or insert apostrophe	/ or ⋏ through character where required		
Transpose characters or words	between characters or words, numbered when necessary		

Figure 16.7 **Proofreading marks.**
Extracted from BS 5261: Part 2: 1976 (1990), reproduced by permission of the British Standards Institution, 2 Park Street, London W1A 2BS, from whom a copy of the complete Standard may be obtained.

Producing the copies

At the simplest level you will produce just two copies off your computer printer – one for yourself and one for the person who requested it, but if you need more copies you need to decide on the most effective way to produce your required number. Your decision will depend on three things:

- the size of the report
- the number of copies you plan to produce (the 'print run')
- whether your report contains pictorial matter.

Methods

	Advantages	*Disadvantages*	*Cost*
Run the copies off your computer printer	Copies are produced quickly; all the same quality. Good for short reports in small numbers.	Cumbersome if report is more than 50 pages. Quality depends entirely on quality of computer printer.	Depends on cost of printer materials. Laser printers are probably best but expensive. Good inkjet printers, which are considerably cheaper, can now produce very high quality both in black and white and colour.

	Advantages	Disadvantages	Cost
Run a master copy off the WP or DTP system and then photocopy	Quick and good for large runs, especially if high-speed copying services are used. Some copying services can take the text straight from a floppy disk.	Quality not as good as printing.	Usually cheaper than printing.
Run a master copy off the DTP system and print professionally	Very high quality print. Best for photographs and diagrams, and large print runs.	Total reproduction time slower.	Most expensive, but for large print-runs of any size report can be the most economic method.

Methods of binding

	Advantages	Disadvantages	Cost
Stapling	Simple for small reports in small numbers. Very acceptable for most internal reports. Some photocopiers can staple in the same process as copying.	Ineffective for large reports: staples won't go through all the sheets.	Cheap and cheerful.
Treasury tags	Can hold up to 200 pages.	Reports are not easy to handle: pages slip and tear loose. More time-consuming than stapling.	Cheap.
Ready-made folders/ring binders	Good for small reports and small print run. Easily available in a variety of formats.	Slide-type folders are not always effective: when pages are opened wide, report can fall apart.	Quite expensive – £1+ each.
Heat-sealing or Thermal-binding	Good for small report – up to 100 pages – and small print run.	Slow to make up. Seal is easily broken when pages are opened wide.	Machines are £50–£150. Instant print shops can usually provide this service.

Comb-binding	Good for reports of 20–500 pages. Report opens wide easily.	Slow to make up. Combs come in a variety of sizes: choose a big enough size. Heavy wear and tear on a big report can dislodge the pages from the teeth of the comb.	Machines are £50–£700 manual or electric. Combs are fairly cheap. Instant print shops usually provide the service.
Binding (stapled or saddle-stitched down central gutter)	High quality for printed report up to about 80 pages.		Expensive.
Perfect binding (pages are glued or stitched in groups at the spine)	Very high quality for printed reports more than 35 pages long.	Generally impractical below about 35 pages.	More expensive than saddle-stitching.

Summary – report-writing

Ending this chapter on report-writing with a discussion of the best methods of binding your report is not perhaps a good way to make report-writing seem *less* daunting. However, it should remind you that presentation is as important as the content – each should complement the other. But, if you still find the task rather terrifying, remember, that breaking a task down into steps and tackling it one step at a time can make even the largest task seem feasible.

Assignment: Faced with writing a report for someone else, list at least 20 questions to which you would need to get the answers before you start.

Assignment: Write a report, with a brief summary, to your board of directors who want to celebrate 5 years in business by taking the whole company (30 employees of varying ages but all fit and healthy) on an unusual day trip. They've asked you to come up with three suggestions and recommend the one you think best.

Assignment: You have to write a report on a subject about which you know very little. List as many ways as possible by which you could find out whether there are any central issues which you haven't already uncovered.

- For internal readers (such as the Board, your boss, the other directors, or the college principal and senior management team): a proposal to install a crèche.
- For external readers: a proposal to take over the catering/security/window-cleaning currently being done by other firms who are competitors of your firm.

Assignment: Summarise briefly how you might persuade the reader to accept each of the following proposals:

- A proposal to an electrical retail outlet to persuade them to stock your new range of electric household cooling fans.
- A proposal to the marketing director/the principal of your local college to launch an innovative marketing campaign.
- A proposal to a small local firm to be their computing consultant/'doctor', or to carry out their word-processing requirements from your home.

Exercise 16.1

1 What does 'terms of reference' mean? Why do they matter?
2 What are the main elements of any report?
3 What is the minimum number of sections a report should contain?
4 What is a summary? What purpose does it serve?
5 What is a 'functional' paragraph in a report?
6 What are the main stages in writing a report?

Further reading

Buzan, Tony, *How to Mind Map*, Harper Collins, 2002
Buzan, Tony, *Mind Map Book*, BBC, 2001
Forsyth, Patrick, *Powerful Reports and Proposals*, Kogan Page, 2003
Hudson, Diane, *Designing for Desktop Publishing*, How To Books, 1998
Inglis, John and Lewis, Roger, *Clear Thinking*, Harper Collins, 1993

▼ 17 Memos, messages, forms and questionnaires

'Geoffs's out today. Send him an email and let him know tomorrow's meeting's off, but we'll still need his figures first thing…'

'Can you send a memo to the purchasing department confirming our order for three new filing cabinets? I have phoned him so he knows all about them.'

'Draft a circular about the new catalogue, to go to all our current customers. Oh, and include some sort of reply-paid card to go with it, so that they can let us know if they want one.'

'We'll have to send a fax or scan it in and email it.'

'Can you have a go at devising a questionnaire…'

'Apparently Sue's gone home ill. Can you take the minutes…'

Letter-writing and report-writing tend to get a great deal of attention in most books on business communication – the one because it's such a common activity both in and outside the workplace, and the other because it is regarded as a fairly onerous job by most people. However, the barrage of instructions above is fairly typical of the many writing tasks which you might very easily be called upon to tackle. Do you know how a memo differs from a letter? Have you ever sent an email? Could you devise an effective questionnaire which creates goodwill rather than ill-will?
In this chapter we will look at these other writing tasks:

- writing memos which serve their purpose
- sending faxes and e-mails
- devising reply cards
- designing forms and questionnaires.

You will find some guidance on writing minutes of meetings in Chapter 9.

17.1 Memos

Originally the word 'memorandum' came from the Latin *memorare* – to remember – and meant literally 'a thing to be remembered'. However, memos now have a rather wider use in business than simply a memory aid as, together with the telephone, they have become the main method of internal communication. Their use, instead of a telephone call, retains the idea of a memory aid, in that they do, of course, have the advantage of written communication in providing a written record. They are used to communicate information, enquiries and instructions and in a longer form (memorandum) can serve the function of a report. (See 'Writing reports', Chapter 16, Section 16.1.) Incidentally, in the Civil Service a memo is known as a 'minute'.

Memoranda (or memorandums – both are acceptable) are the internal equivalents of letters and can be sent electronically (by email), in hard copy or handwritten. However, because they are *internal* letters there are one or two minor differences.

Check-Points: On Memos

- The salutation and the complimentary close can be dispensed with, since normal politeness is assumed; it is also not necessary to sign a handwritten or typed memo, although longer memoranda often are signed. However, in email versions it has become the convention to type your name and precede it with 'Regards' or something similar.
- The memo message should be kept as short as possible and should usually deal with only one item.
- Most organisations provide memo pads of headed message forms or computer templates, but whether a headed form is used or not, a memo usually has a four-part heading:
  'To (the recipient's name), 'From' (the sender's name), 'Date' (day, month and year and sometimes time, if appropriate), and 'Subject' (a brief summary phrase).
- Sometimes it also includes the sender's office number or department, fax number, telephone number and email address.

A typical memo would therefore look like the one in Figure 17.1.

Self-Check

What do you think of the style of this message? What does it tell you about the relationship between the sender and the recipient?

Memo

TO: Nick Bromhead – Personnel Director

CC: Ian Brixton – Induction programme Tutor

From: Denise Taylor – Training Manager

Date: 17 January 20...

Subject: Induction Training Programme

I am enclosing the draft programme of the proposed course that you asked for.

You'll see that the MD is down for Wed afternoon. Since I ought to get the whole thing buttoned up by Friday, can you check with her that Wed is OK and also let me have your comments before then.

Figure 17.1   **A typical message to a close colleague.**

Style

There can be no fixed rules about the style of language which is appropriate for an internal memorandum. It will depend on several factors.

Nature of the message

Information, enquiry, request, reprimand, congratulations and so on.

Context of the message

Potential reaction of the reader, what has gone before, how much the recipient knows already, urgency of the situation and priority of any action required – routine, emergency, crisis, follow-up instructions to all staff and so on.

Status and personality of the recipient

Position in the organisation, known tastes and attitudes on written style and methods of working, technical/practical background, education level and so on.

Relationship between sender and recipient

Friendly, distant, informal, formal and so on. (A neutral tone may be necessary where there will be several recipients.)

Assignment: Supposing you had to write to the managing director about the induction training programme because she had asked to see a copy of the draft programme. Using the same information, write the message required.

The style of writing will obviously vary a great deal. Directives and instructions from a very senior executive to all personnel may well be written in very correct

TO:	MANAGING DIRECTOR
FROM:	DENISE TAYLOR, TRAINING MANAGER
SUBJECT:	INDUCTION TRAINING PROGRAMME
DATE:	17 JANUARY 20..
CC:	IAN BRIXTON, INDUCTION PROGRAMME TUTOR

Following your secretary's telephone call, I am enclosing a draft programme for the Induction Course we are proposing to hold from 15 April to 20 April.

You will see that following your agreement to speak to the new staff, I have provisionally arranged for your session to start at 2.00 p.m. on Wednesday 17 April.

I would like to be able to finalise the arrangements fairly soon and would therefore be grateful if you could confirm that Wednesday is still convenient for you, and let me have your comments on the programme by Friday of this week if possible.

Figure 17.2 **A typical message to a more distant colleague.**

language whereas a hastily written message to a colleague may be written in extremely conversational English complete with 'in jokes' and slang expressions.

Messages written to people further up the organisation ladder will possibly be more cautious in style than those written to people further down.

You therefore need to be extremely sensitive to people's likes and dislikes, their attitudes to things like status and position, and to your position and relationship *vis-à-vis* the people you communicate with. Always be alert to clues, but cautious in their interpretation. A very senior manager may write chatty, familiar messages to you, but they might be offended if, following their example, you felt free to do the same!

If your position in the organisation were fairly low compared with the managing director's and you had never met her personally, or perhaps only on very formal occasions, your message might look like that in Figure 17.2.

The tone and style are more dignified but without being pompous or subservient. Specific dates are mentioned in case the MD is not sure when exactly 'this training course' is taking place, and to enable her to confirm her availability.

You might argue that since you occupy a lower position in the hierarchy you should not give her a 'reply by' date. However, since the message has been organised on an inductive basis with the call for action at the end, after presentation of the reasons for some urgency, it would seem reasonable to give her some idea of when you need her answer. The apparent demand for action 'by Friday' is somewhat softened by ending with 'if possible'. This hints that you are aware of the other more important demands on her time, but without leaving the matter completely open.

17.2 Email and netiquette

Strictly speaking emailing, like sending a fax, is a means of sending a message – almost any message (memos, letters and reports as well as those 'oh! so ubiquitous incomprehensible notes' so popular with real addicts!). The message still has to be composed bearing in mind the principles we have been exploring for all other forms of communication. But the email has become so popular in business that it has developed its own particular characteristics – both good and bad.

Advantages

- It is very cheap, normally only the cost of a local telephone, even when the message is sent to international recipients.
- You can send a message to several people at a time for the same cost as one message.
- It is very quick, providing that the recipient is online.
- The messages are sent normally in plain text, so you don't have to worry too much about layout, typefaces and the other metacommunication, but can just concentrate on wording the message.
- Its simplicity, convenience and independence of time and time zones is tending to make it more popular than telephoning.
- In the early days of email, Tom Peters quoted William Esrey, head of United Telecom (and therefore US Sprint) who recommended email 'for opening a "dialogue" with employees at all levels, from all over the firm. [They] feel that they are dealing directly with me', he said, 'and speak differently than if the communications were being screened by staffers'. Esrey even urged users not to take even a second to go back and fix misspellings or other glitches. 'The idea is that you communicate with no fuss'. Nowadays, many people would disagree about accuracy.
- Although an email can be simple and informal, it is possible to *insert* (enclose) or *attach* a more complicated document in another format – a letter, report, or even photo and graphic material previously sent by fax.

Disadvantages

- Because of its very advantages cited above, it has become almost too popular: some people report getting literally hundreds of emails a day! And, because people take the informality to extremes, many emails have so many misspellings and missed out words, that they become incomprehensible and reflect badly on the writer!
- Email does not allow you to show tones of voice and so on; misunderstandings can arise and emails can come over as blunt or aggressive, even unintentionally. So, courtesy is at least as important as in face-to-face communication.
- Although it is a form of written communication, it encourages people to behave very impulsively and thoughtlessly, resulting in sending into the ether things that cause regret or embarrassment – but by then it's too late!
- Its ease and convenience mean that notes, memos and letters are seeing a rebirth, and telephoning and face-to-face communication are dying. Anyone who is not an addict may be irritated by this and certainly regretful.

Things to remember, or netiquette

- Email has about the same security as a postcard! Any email could be read by anyone else – not least from an unattended or visible screen – so always treat it as public and write accordingly, even if it is sent to specific people; similarly an email could be forwarded to anyone else or even to huge numbers of people in an instant without the writer's permission or even knowledge – as has happened in a few celebrated cases recently costing several people their jobs! You may be able to prevent this by pressing the *confidential* button on Lotus Notes and some other systems, but don't rely on it too much.

- Nicknames and indiscretions, personal remarks and plagiarisms could be open to the laws of libel, defamation, obscenity, copyright, fraud and discrimination. And, of course, you should also remember that information about people that is stored and communicated electronically is liable to data protection legislation.
- Don't send copies of emails indiscriminately to long lists of recipients – your 'copy for info' can become someone else's junk email. Many people, in order to cope with the vast numbers of emails they receive, have resorted to reading only those emails with subject headings that make them appear relevant, and even to 'smart' filter systems which alert the manager to read only emails considered essential on the basis of the subject or field summary alone. The moral of this is to become known for being selective about sending emails, and skilled at composing them. The key skill in emailing is therefore summarising – first in the header and then in the message itself.
- Don't show other people's email addresses.
- If you need to send mail regularly to a long list of people, create a mailing list to avoid long lists of recipients at the top of everyone's copy.
- Use humour and sarcasm with care. Smileys (☺ ☹ :-D and so on), which can be useful in indicating that you are happy, sad, laughing and so on, can make you look very silly and immature, so be sparing in their use.
- Like smileys, too many abbreviations (BTW – by the way; TIA – thanks in advance; IIRC – if I remember correctly, and so on) can make your emails at best difficult to read, and at worst incomprehensible.
- If you are including the original message in your reply, edit the text to remove irrelevant material.
- Signatures should be limited to about four lines; lengthy signatures full of graphics irritate.
- Don't send people attachments unless you know that they can cope with the format.
- Try sending photos (and also short documents) inserted into the body of the email rather than as attachments. They are easier to deal with.
- Don't send large attachments. A good rule of thumb for any email and/or attachment is 'No more than 10 kb'. Warn people in the header (subject) if the attachment is big.
- Unless really necessary don't use 'rich text' because an old computer won't receive it.
- Make sure your email is going to the right address. Check and recheck. It is easy to use the wrong email address by mistake.
- Check your reply settings; it is easy to use 'Reply-all' by mistake. Again this could be very embarrassing, as well as annoying for your recipients.
- Remember to download your emails and then go offline to compose your replies.

- Clear out your mailbox regularly: if your mailbox is full, your mail may not get delivered.
- Know and obey the netiquette rules of your organisation.

DON'T FORGET ABOUT FACE-TO-FACE COMMUNICATION!

Summary – email and netiquette

So – email is immediate, instant and informal. Conciseness is paramount. Although it is a basic technique in this medium to compose quickly, almost as quickly as you consciously think, accuracy is still important. Spelling and grammar errors may *possibly* be different in magnitude in this form than they are in a formal letter but inaccuracy, as always, can lead to misunderstanding and cause distraction. Moreover, it will not add to your 'cool' image or reputation as a proper observer of netiquette! Although it is difficult to define exactly what email is, it may be worth bearing in mind it originates as a written document, then begins its journey on the telephone – the best of all possible cyber-worlds?

Assignment: Choose a project that you and your colleagues are involved in. In pairs – one be the project leader and one be the project manager – imagine that if the project manager has 10 team leaders who each send up to 10 emails a day, the manager would have to read 100 emails on the subject of the project alone! 'Smart' filter systems have now been developed that alert the manager to read only those emails considered essential, on the basis of the subject alone.

Project leader: compose 5 emails and write a subject header of no more than 4 words per email to ensure your emails survive the filter and are read.

Project manager: decide from these headers which emails you would read and in which order.

Afterwards, if you are working as part of a training group, show the full texts of all the emails and decide if the priorities were correct. How could they be improved? Brainstorm key words which might be dramatic and unambiguous. Try reducing each header to only 1 word.

Assignment: Look at a relevant article from a newspaper or magazine. Summarise it in 6 (or 3, or 1) bullet point(s). Look at the headline to the article. Turn it into a subject header of no more than 4 words.

17.3 Fax

Until the advent of email, the fax machine was probably the most successful business innovation of the past decade, as it became a much faster, usually cheaper and more efficient means of mailing than the post. As its name suggests (fax is short for *facsimile*), it is still a quick way of sending original documents – diagrams, maps, business documents and so on, and for many people is an easier way than scanning documents into a computer for dispatch by email. The only limitations are the facilities of the sender's and receiver's fax machine (size of paper etc.) and the need to put some form of header on the document or as the first sheet, showing:

- the name, organisation and fax number of the sender
- the name, organisation and fax number of the receiver
- the sender's phone number in case of problems
- the number of sheets including the header sheet so that the receiver knows how many to expect, and
- as with any other business communication, it is also useful to include a subject heading.

ABC COMPANY PLC §§§

To:	Annie Singleton		From:	Tony MacKay
Fax:	08671 345167		Tel:	03521 738991
Phone:	08671 345166		Cc:	
Re:	Directions to ABC Company plc		Pages:	2

☐ Urgent ☐ For Review ☐ Please Comment ☐ Please Reply ☐ Please Recycle

•Comments:

See you on Friday.
Call me when you're close and
I'll talk you in.

Regards
T.

Figure 17.3 **A typical fax header**

A simple handwritten note can quickly be sent by fax with a fax header label attached and many WP packages include a fax header template that you could use to type or handwrite a fax or attach to another document.

Other than that, the actual message simply needs to adhere to the conventions of a letter, memo or report whichever is the chosen medium. But remember that as it tumbles out of the fax machine at the other end it could be read by anyone so it is not an appropriate method for sensitive or confidential information.

Although the fax seems to have been predominantly replaced by the email for many business people, the fax still serves a useful purpose and for someone who does not sit at a computer all day it is as invaluable as ever for speed and convenience.

17.4 Postcards and reply cards

Since postcards and reply cards are relatively fast and inexpensive methods of sending business messages to the public they are worth bearing in mind. They save the cost and time of writing an unnecessarily long message, of folding, sealing and stamping a message.

They are usually pre-printed to suit standard situations – acknowledgement of receipt of a letter, order and so on – or, in the case of reply cards, to encourage the recipient to respond by doing the work for them (see Figures 17.4 and 17.5). The postage on reply cards is often paid by the originator by means of the Freepost system. This further increases the incentive to reply.

The heading and the salutation both appear on the message side of the card. The sender's address can be omitted as the address on the stamped side is sufficient.

The message needs to be fairly neutral in tone since it will go to a variety of recipients, but it needs to be courteous and friendly to compensate for the fact that it is a standard message and the recipient knows this.

Figure 17.4 **Reply-paid postcard.**

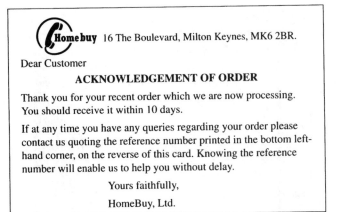

Dear Customer

ACKNOWLEDGEMENT OF ORDER

Thank you for your recent order which we are now processing.
You should receive it within 10 days.

If at any time you have any queries regarding your order please
contact us quoting the reference number printed in the bottom left-
hand corner, on the reverse of this card. Knowing the reference
number will enable us to help you without delay.

Yours faithfully,

HomeBuy, Ltd.

Figure 17.5 **Pre-printed postcard.**

17.5   Text messaging

Text messaging, also known as SMS (Short Message Service), using mobile phones
to send written messages is no longer the preserve of children, students and people
in night clubs who couldn't talk because the music was too loud.

In June 1999, just under 600 000 text messages were sent in the United Kingdom.
Just a year later, there were 500 million sent (Figure 17.6).

- an estate agent now sends a text message to house buyers, alerting them when a
  new property has come on the market. It will also send landlords a message
  when rent has been paid into their account, and keep vendors up-to-date with
  how their conveyancing is going
- a recruitment agency sends messages to its clients to see if they are interested in
  new vacancies
- a CD store sends messages to registered customers, telling them of new releases.
  Customers are then able to ring the store and hear clips of the album played to
  them, then place an order over the phone if they like what they hear
- an exam board sends candidates their exam results by text message
- a network operator sends sports results and weather forecasts and news flashes
  and tips on losing weight and ...

Companies can communicate with their own staff. A company can integrate a text
message system with its email system so if needed, its workers can be reached
wherever they are. Some might not regard this as a progressive move!

Messaging has, of course, been around for years: Japan and the spiritual home of
the mobile phone, Scandinavia and Finland, were well ahead of the rest of the
world. But it did not develop in the United States to the same extent because of the
competing mobile platforms.

The growth in SMS has occurred without the weight of advertising and hype
which accompanied the launch of WAP (Wireless Application Protocol) and this is
probably due to its simplicity. In a world where the technological possibilities seem
to be expanding every day, SMS is something people understand. You type a message;

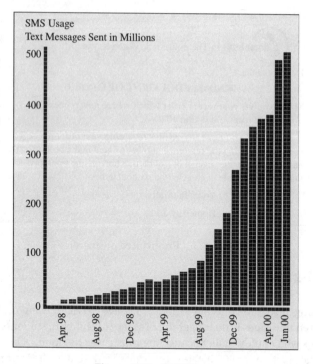

Figure 17.6 **SMS Usage.**

you receive a message … without looking like one of those people who talk loudly on mobiles at inappropriate moments … and, it's a nice way of contacting people when you don't want to disturb them. An additional attraction for users also appears to be that expenditure is controllable: without having to talk on the phone and risk getting a bigger bill than you want, you can get your message over. Although, at anything up to 12p for a short paragraph (30p with a picture), it can still be expensive, but as with everything technological the cost is decreasing by the month.

But, organisations need to be wary of using messaging as a promotional device: careless targeting of customers by businesses could be counterproductive. If customers sign up to receive information, then they will be happy to receive messages. But if they haven't signed up, it could be quite intrusive because people see the mobile phone as a very personal item. In other words, sending unsolicited messages by text messaging (as with email) known as *spam*, is severely frowned upon, and companies who are guilty of *spamming* may find there is a backlash effect.

Do u spk txt? The chncs r, if u dnt, u wll b4 lng.
2 jdge by ads 4 mob fns, txt msging hs ct pples imagntn, cos thyre all pshng it lk crzy.
1 sys u can snd pix, anthr sys u cn snd msgs to 15m pple in UK alne.
Bt lts gt smthg str8. Ths is jst the strt ;->

See below for translation!

This strange language millions of people are now reading and writing fluently, which looks like a cross between shorthand and an invented East European

Txt msging: Th shp of thngs 2 cm?

Figure 17.7 **Txt msging: Th shp of thngs 2 cm?**

language, stems from the fact that the word limit for a text message is normally 160 characters, so the art of summarising has never been so useful. Although children and students were generally the first to become fluent, many senior citizens who were brought up in the age of the telegram could probably beat them in a race to reduce a message to its absolute essentials and then miss out redundant letters. However, as with any other communication, the moral is 'Know your reader'. Will they think you simply can't spell or type? Will they be able to read and comprehend your message easily? If not, stick to recognisable words (which the Dictionary facility enables you to type almost as quickly as the texting language) but just as with emailing, you will have to write as concisely as possible and use punctuation to aid understanding.

Who knows what the inventors and market developers are dreaming up now? Already, the next generations of systems, which sound like more examples of 'txt' – WAP (Wireless Application Protocol), GPRS (General Packet Radio Switching) and UMTS (Universal Mobile Telecoms Service) mean that with more bandwidth to transfer data, handsets have turned into 'microbrowsers', capable of taking and sending photos, dealing with the web, receiving and sending email, and acting more like personal digital assistants.

In other words, the day is already here when you really can surf while you're at the beach and conduct much of your business from wherever and whenever it is convenient, all with the aid of a handheld gysmo.

But, so far, none of these developments has done away with the need to think about what you are communicating and make sensible judgements about what fits your purpose, the situation and your recipient.

(**Translation from above:** Do you speak text? The chances are, if you don't you will before long. To judge by adverts for mobile phones, text messaging has caught people's imagination, because they are all pushing it like crazy. One says you can send pictures, another says you can send messages to 15 million people in the UK alone. But let's get something straight. This is just the start.)

Assignment: Try 'format-hopping', using different media for different purposes. For example, invite friends to a social event by email, telephone, text message and letter. Compare the responses you get in each format!

Use symbols, abbreviations and smileys or 'emoticons' where appropiate, if you can manage them on the keyboard, but don't use capital letters in your emails or PEOPLE WILL THINK YOU ARE SHOUTING and you may get 'flamed':- (If you are not sure what flaming means look it up in a dictionary).

17.6 Forms and questionnaires

Perhaps like many people, you think that we have too many forms; that hardly any situation can occur without someone designing a form which we have to complete to get what we need, or do what we want, or merely help someone else to do their job. Your frustration may be justified, but forms do have their uses, and very frequently the cause of our irritation is not so much the need to complete a form, as the form itself – its *design*.

Self-Check

Can you think of four good reasons for using a form to gain information?

---

1 It enables you to get the *same* information from *different* people.
2 It enables you to get that information in the *same way*.
3 This means that it is easier to *compare* information.
4 It also makes it easier to get and refer to *specific items* of information.

Forms, in fact, provide a vehicle for asking for particular information in a way that ensures that you get the information you need and exclude what you do not need. When a form has been badly designed, problems arise for everyone who has to use it.

Assignment: Think back to forms you may have filled in recently, for example application forms for jobs, for money, for services perhaps, or to questionnaires you may have been asked to complete, and to forms which perhaps you use at work. What were the problems with these forms? Make a list.

The problem with forms ... !

1 The form is too long and asks for too much information.
   Result: people get bored or irritated, give incomplete answers or even fail to answer some questions at all.
2 The form tries to cover too many possibilities.
   Result: the form is confusing to follow and difficult to complete correctly. It is unclear in its purpose, or even has too many purposes so it fails to do any job properly.
3 The form is badly designed.
   Result: the language and the form itself are complicated and ambiguous. The instructions only add to the confusion and the form contains contradictions, or apparent contradictions, for example,

(i)   Do you have any children?

(ii) Do you intend to have any children?

The first question must presumably have been expecting the answer 'no', otherwise the second question is nonsensical, but worded as it is, what happens if the answer is 'yes'? This may seem an absurd example, but it is typical of the kind of nonsense which can appear in a badly designed form or questionnaire.

4 The form is badly laid out.

   Result: it provides too much space for some answers and not enough for others.

5 The form asks the wrong questions.

   Result: even if information is obtained, it's the wrong information or information which is produced in an unusable way.

Designing forms

Designing forms is quite an art and certainly not something to be undertaken lightly. With the increased use of computerised data processing, the task can be one requiring special training. However, it is more than possible that you may be called upon to 'have a go at designing a form' or at least help someone else with the task, or you may find that your experiences of using a form at work bring to light its deficiencies and prompt you to try designing a better one. Bear in mind the following brief essentials. The section on questionnaire design which follows contains principles which apply just as much to form design.

Layout

- Make it as attractive as you can
- Make it as brief as you can
- Ensure that it is functional:

   1 provides the information you actually need

   2 provides sufficient space for each answer

   3 can be filled in as easily as possible.

Arrangement

- Arrange your questions and instructions in logical order
- Avoid cross-references and explanatory notes where possible
- Beware of internal contradictions or apparent contradictions.

Style

- Direct questions and instructions are generally better than headings
- Use simple, clear and direct English.

Test

- Always test the form before you finalise it
- Test it on the same sort of people as it is ultimately intended for.

1 Design a form suitable for your organisation's (or college's) suggestion scheme, on which people can submit their suggestion. In the instructions section give them some ideas of what kind of suggestion might be acceptable, how to submit their suggestion, and what will happen next.

2 Start a collection of different forms. Try filling them in and note any problems or difficulties you experience.

Keep the forms – you never know when they may come in handy as examples of layout, question planning, instructions and so on.

Questionnaires

A questionnaire survey is a formal way of obtaining first-hand information. It is commonly used for research but has become the subject of a fair amount of criticism, mainly because it imposes on people: taking up time and asking difficult questions that may not be easily answered. Questionnaires are also frequently criticised for asking vague questions or asking people to commit themselves on issues on which perhaps they do not feel it is possible to be definite one way or the other without considerable qualification, or for asking them to commit themselves in a permanent way on paper.

Certainly as a method of obtaining information there is much to commend the questionnaire but indiscriminate use by amateur research workers tends to bring a great deal of discredit on the method, and to the validity of the results under certain conditions.

If, therefore, you do want to use a questionnaire, you should ideally seek expert advice, and in any case construct it with considerable care.

Check-Points: Preparing a Questionnaire

- Make sure that the questionnaire is the best method for getting the information you are seeking.
- Frame the questions in a neutral fashion so that you will not influence the answers.
- Write short questions; avoid long, complicated questions.
- Be sure that your questions are direct; avoid ambiguity.
- Be specific in the information you are seeking; consider how you intend to collect, analyse and present the information received.
- Frame your questions, as far as possible, so that only simple ticking of yes/ no answers will get the information; make the answers you receive easy to work with.
- Arrange your questions on the questionnaire in a logical manner.
- Select your sample – those to whom you are going to send the questionnaire – with care and attention to recognised sampling techniques (see the sections on sampling in Roger Cartwright, *Mastering Marketing Management*, Palgrave Master Series, 2002).

- Test your questions on a pilot group (a small group of people similar to those you are going to question but who are not to be included in your actual survey).

    This is an essential step in form and questionnaire design; however well you have anticipated the respondent's answers you are almost bound to have missed something and what seems clear to you may seem confusing to someone else.
- Use an attractive but straightforward layout so that your questions can easily be read, answered and returned.

Summary – other writing tasks

Many people when asked what they write at work claim never to write letters or reports but do write lots of other things, peculiar to their organisation and its activities. It is therefore difficult in a book like this to include everything. The best advice therefore is always to go back to first principles – why?, what?, who?, how?, where?, when? – for guidance.

Assignment: You have been asked to carry out some research and prepare a report which will require you to write a letter questionnaire requesting information from several organisations in your locality. You have had no previous contact with these organisations and will therefore have to write 'cold' letters. In other words your letter will arrive out of the blue and, in effect, will be asking busy people to work for you free of charge or reward, in order to supply you with the information you need in answer to several questions.

You will have to consider the tone and style of the letter very carefully, so that it will create a favourable impression and persuade the recipient to provide you with the information you need, willingly. You will have to make it easy for the recipient to answer your questions, arouse interest in the problem and motivate them to a positive action on your behalf.

1 Consider this situation very carefully and then write a list of the 'don'ts' which you will have to bear in mind as you plan and draft the letter.
2 Invent a reasonably realistic research project (a real one would be even better, if you have one in progress at the moment); decide which organisations you would write to and then draft the letter, bearing in mind the letter-writing techniques of Chapter 14 and the specific 'don'ts' governing the writing of request-for-information letters, which you have just listed. When you have finished the letter and would be absolutely happy to send it, criticise it against the list of 'don'ts' suggested below.
    When writing 'request-for-information' letters,

DON'T

- ask for information that might be confidential
- make your letter hard to understand

- send your letter to the wrong person (i.e. someone who can't or won't help you)
- ask too many questions
- make your questions too involved or complicated
- ask people to do 'research' work for you (i.e. don't ask them for information they cannot easily give you)
- expect people to drop everything just to answer your questionnaire
- expect anything; be grateful for what you do receive, and if possible, be prepared to write back thanking them (goodwill)
- make a pest of yourself by writing again asking for explanations of their answers: to the best of your ability, work out what they mean
- try to kill too many birds at once; narrow down your range of questions.

Exercise 17.1: Comment on the wording of the following question from a staff attitude survey:

Is pay in this organisation good enough?   Yes ☐   No ☐

Re-write it to overcome your criticisms.

Further reading

Cartwright, Roger, *Mastering Marketing Management*, Palgrave Macmillan, 2002

Crystal, David, *Language and the Internet*, Cambridge University Press, 2001

Rinaldi, Arlene H., *The Net: User Guidelines and Netiquette*,
   www.fau.edu/netiquette/net/netiquette.html, 1998

Flynn, Nancy and Flynn, Tom, *Writing Effective E-mail*, Kogan Page, 2000

■ M̌ 18 Visual communication

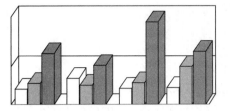

While it is true that there are occasions when pictures can stand alone, it is perhaps safer to regard visual communication as a complement to verbal communication. In this chapter we will look at the way we can use pictures of one kind or another to

- *reinforce our message*
- *make it easier to take in and understand*
- *or simply to make the receiver's task easier by providing variety.*

18.1   When to use charts and graphs

Look at the following extract from a written report:

10 newsagent shops in the Bristol area were selected to test the effectiveness of two different display stands in generating sales of greetings cards. For the purposes of the survey the shops were designated with the letters A–J (see Appendix for address of each shop).

During the period 15 March to 20 March the total sales for three items were recorded:

Two different stands were used to display these items for sale. Five of the stands were the traditional sloping top 1.5 m wide made of Formica with Perspex division while the other five were the metal revolving type; 75 cm in diameter. Shops A, C, D, G, I used the traditional stands and shops B, E, F, H, J used the revolving stand.

Total sales of the items during the 6 days test period (Monday to Saturday inclusive) were as follows: shops A, B, C, and D sold 175, 410, 220 and 187 respectively. Shops E, F, G, H showed sales of 435, 475, 286 and 575 cards and Shop I 275 with Shop J at 525.

There is an obvious correlation between sales and type of display stand. This correlation is reflected in similar studies carried out in Manchester and Aberdeen ...

This material is taken from a survey report. How well have you been able to assimilate the information? Was the correlation between the sales and the type of display stand quite as 'obvious' as the author suggests?

Assignment: Draw the most effective visual aid to represent this data, before reading on.

Statistical information

Much of the business of communication in organisations is concerned with *presenting facts* in order to enable *decisions* to be made. Many of these facts are in the form of numbers or statistics, and yet as we can see in the example above, these statistics are frequently presented in a way which appears to be designed to confuse rather than to clarify the facts.

The function of this statistical information may be

- 'historical' – to show what has happened in the past
- 'comparative' – to enable comparisons to be made between different things or between different periods of time
- 'predictive' – to forecast and predict what may happen in the future.

In other words the statistical information has to be used, but to be used it needs to be understood, and it is the function of the communicator to present this information in such a way that the person who needs to present the information is able to abstract from it the most pertinent ideas and concepts which it contains. In order to serve its purpose, then, the oral or written report must give the receiver its information quickly, clearly and completely.

Someone once calculated that:

1 Of each £10 spent on voluntary reading for employees, £3 was wasted
2 Of each £10 spent on copy for customers and the public, £4 was wasted
3 Of each £10 spent on writing to shareholders, £4 was wasted
4 Of each £10 spent on required reading for management, £8 was wasted.

Although this may be a rather exaggerated guess, there is a very real danger that much of the material presented, particularly for reading, is never used in the way it was intended, and that the cost involved in producing the material outweighs the value of the information conveyed.

This is particularly true of organisations which, through the introduction of dataprocessing equipment, may be tempted to produce such a mass of information that the user is unable to 'see the wood for the trees'.

For this reason, it is up to the producer of the information – the report-writer or speaker – to show the crucial relationships between various bits of information, and to pick out from all the information available only that which is critical to the person who will use it.

In this chapter we shall look at

- the different methods of presenting statistical and other data, so that you can choose the method which is best suited for any particular purpose
- the ways in which it is possible to distort the message conveyed, by presenting it in a particular way, so that, as a communicator, you can avoid misleading your reader, and as a receiver, you will be alert to the possibility that other people might be misleading you.

Graphic aids

Graphic aids are the names we give to charts and other illustrations which are used for presenting data. Used effectively they can simplify and speed up the communication or instruction. Used to present statistical data they cannot usually totally replace words but they can considerably reduce the number of words necessary. Graphic aids, plus a brief commentary in words, can make an invaluable combination to help you communicate, even if, strictly speaking it is not true that 'a picture is worth a thousand words'.

Graphics aids are, therefore, excellent supplements to the written or spoken word. Your reader or listener may find it difficult, or at least hard work, to take in the relationships when reading or, worse, hearing that 'demand for Easter eggs grew by 2 per cent between April and August 2002, 4 per cent in the next 7 months (August 2002 to March 2203), but 9 per cent between March and April 2003'.

However, if that same data can be seen in a graph, a better and stronger mental image of the events is received than from words alone. Look at the simple graph in Figure 18.1.

Remember that meanings are in people and not in words.

By quantifying information and presenting it in graphic form, you can help to reinforce the meaning of the words in your reports. Charts, graphs and tables are tools that help you make this presentation of quantitative data more efficiently by enabling your reader to compare and contrast data. Diagrams and pictures help still further to produce concrete mental images out of abstract and often ambiguous concepts. Your readers or listeners will thank you for absolving them from the effort of understanding, and the consequences of misunderstanding.

Visual presentation

Advantages

- Gains attention if well done and pleasing to the eye
- Provides the maximum amount of information as quickly as possible
- Speeds comprehension if not unduly complex
- Relieves the monotony of solid text

- Conveys impression of overall trends and tendencies easily and quickly
- Helps the reader to pick out specific figures
- Helps the reader to see relationships
- Reinforces the verbal message
- Highlights differences.

Figure 18.1   **A simple graph.**

General principles

There are a few principles of visual presentation that you should bear in mind regardless of the type of aid you are using.

Is a visual aid needed?

While I have suggested that graphic aids can be invaluable supplements to your verbal message, and you should therefore never forget to consider using them, there are people who go to the opposite extreme and produce some sort of visual aid for practically everything they want to say on a subject which is not particularly technical, quantitative or complex.

A visual aid should be incorporated only when there is a clear purpose for it – a *need*. Aids should be included only when they will produce advantages like those listed above.

Visual aids should not be used simply to impress your receiver or make your presentation look more 'professional', or to 'make it look pretty'. What type should be used? Ask yourself:

Which visual aid will best tell my story?

It is easy to get into the habit of always using a certain table for one type of presentation, a certain chart for another, merely adapting them to suit every situation. This sort of habit runs the risk of not stretching your imagination enough to see if there might be another, better way of presenting the data or the idea.

The most appropriate method to use in a particular circumstance will vary according to the reader, the type of information (statistical or non-statistical) and the purpose (to contrast specific figures, to show trends, to explain a procedure, etc.).

Designing the content

You must not only choose the best type of visual aid, but also decide how complex or simple it should be in reference to the data and the receiver. One reader may be comfortable with five different graph lines on one chart (e.g. solid, broken, dotted, dashed and dot-dash). Another reader would require five different charts because they do not have sufficient ability, interest or motivation to analyse a single complex visual aid.

Prepare the reader

Always prepare your reader or listener for a visual aid. A visual aid forces your reader to pause in order to work out its purpose and this delay reduces the readability of the text. So introduce the visual aid. This does not have to be a lengthy business. Just mention it as you call attention to a particular piece of data. For example:

'In the table below (figure 6) you will see that wages increased by 10 per cent while sales only increased by 5 per cent.'

Explain the visual aid

Never assume that your readers will read and study a particular visual aid, and even if they do you can't assume that they will interpret it in the way you intended. It is therefore not enough to say: 'Table 6 is on p. 9' or 'Look at this graph' with no further comment. You must explain what you intend the graph or the table to convey.

Remember, visual aids are aids; that is, they should supplement the text not replace it.

18.2   Presentation of statistical data

Textual presentation

Most people cannot take in strings of facts and figures presented in the text and are therefore unable to recognise the significance of the information being presented or even pick out a specific figure which has particular importance or relevance.

However, you can *direct attention* or *emphasise certain figures* even in this type of presentation, and *can call attention to comparisons* which seem important. Consider this example:

Personnel managers are more likely to find jobs by replying to direct advertisements than by word-of-mouth or through agencies, according to a survey by executive recruitment consultancy MSL International. 26 per cent of personnel managers responded to direct advertisements while 16 per cent used agencies. Only 4 per cent got jobs by word-of-mouth while none admitted to being head-hunted. General managers are more likely to get jobs through the old-boy network or by being head-hunted. 42 per cent found jobs in this way. Head-hunting and the old boy network are also more common among managers earning more than £30 000 a year, the survey reports. For those earning less than £30 000 a year, replying to direct advertisements is the method used most often.

At least this has presumably extracted the important figures and comparison, but it is still fairly indigestible and would be difficult to take in aurally. However, as a commentary to a visual presentation of all the figures it would be very useful in helping to highlight significant figures and comparisons.

As an alternative to the textual presentation of information in this way, the most common types of graphic aid available to choose from are tables, graphs and charts. However, numerous variations and combinations of these basic types are possible.

Types of graphic aid

Tables

Strictly speaking tables are not graphic aids, but they are usually discussed in connection with visual aids because they do have a visually different effect compared with expressing the same information in the text, as we have just seen.

They are the simplest form of visual aid and consist of an orderly arrangement of figures in columns and horizontal lines, enabling the receiver to grasp the significance of the figures presented and at the same time to discard from consideration those figures which are irrelevant.

By arranging in tabular form (see Figure 18.2) the figures that were presented in the verbal statement above, it is now possible to include all the other figures and still see how much more readily comparisons can be made.

Check-Points: Table Presentation

- Convenient devices for displaying large amounts of data in a relatively small space.
- Useful for reference – comparisons and contrasts can be seen easily and specific figures picked out.
- Each vertical column should be headed clearly and concisely.
- Data to be compared should be placed in the same horizontal plane from left to right.
- Decimals rather than fractions should be used.
- Tables should be laid out very carefully with careful ruling and plenty of white space.

Graphs and charts

'Continuous' or 'discrete' information? When deciding whether to use charts or graphs, one important judgement has to be made.

HOW MANAGERS FIND THEIR JOBS					
Salary/ Source	to £20k (%)	£20-30k (%)	£30-£40k (%)	£40k + (%)	Total (%)
Internal	34	37	31	47	36
Head-hunted	2	3	13	8	5
Consultant advert	3	10	11	5	7
Company advert	34	24	13	13	24
Word-of-mouth	10	10	22	19	13

Figure 18.2 **Presentation of data in a table.**

- Is the information 'continuous' in that every point on the line of graph is valid, for example speed, acceleration, population growth, resource usage, sales, plotted against time; or conversion graphs like °C to °F, or £ to $?
- Or is the information 'discrete' in that it is not directly related to other items of information being plotted: it occurs in distinct steps, for example children per family, population in one country at a particular moment in time compared with population in other countries at the same moment. Compare Figures 18.3, 18.4 and 18.5 to see the difference.

Generally speaking 'continuous' information is best displayed on some sort of line graph whereas 'discrete' information is best shown on a chart. However, sometimes a line graph can be constructed by plotting vertical bars. This is called a histogram and must not be confused with a conventional bar chart.

18.3 Presenting continuous information

Graphs

Graphs are useful for showing trends in continuous information over periods of time. They are easy to make and most people are familiar with them from maths and science classes at school.

Simple graph

A graph is an aid in which points on a scale are connected with a line in order to show increases and decreases. The degree of slope to the line provides a better impression of the intensity of activity as well as a picture of the trend over a given period of time. See the graph shown in Figure 18.3 and the histogram in Figure 18.4.

Multiple graph

Sometimes it is useful to show trends of more than one thing as a basis for comparison. This is possible by the use of solid, dotted and broken lines where there would be any confusion as the lines cross (see Figure 18.6).

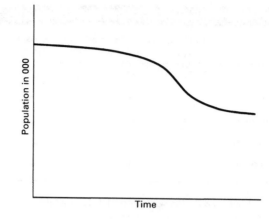

Figure 18.3 **Presenting continuous information as a simple graph.**

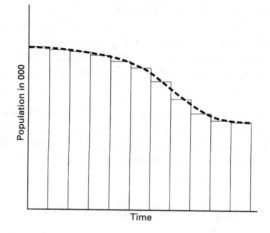

Figure 18.4 **Presenting continuous information as a histogram.**

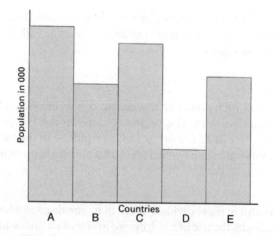

Figure 18.5 **Presenting discrete information as a bar chart.**

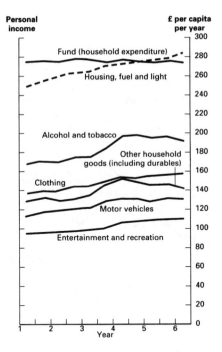

Figure 18.6   **A multiple graph.**

Divided compound graph

This shows the value of both the total and its parts by a series of lines on the graph. In order to distinguish it from a multiple graph, the area between each successive line should be coloured or shaded distinctly and shown in a key or labelled clearly (see Figure 18.7).

Scatter graph (scattergram)

A single dot to represent one value is plotted against scales drawn on two axes at right angles drawn in the normal way. Both may be independent variables. The points are not joined by a line. The graph consists of a scatter of dots and from this the basic message is read, for example, the scatter of dots (loosely enclosed) will indicate a possible discernible trend (see Figure 18.8). Scatter graphs are often used when considering statistical correlations.

Histograms

These are used to display the patterns behind a large volume of figures, for example, income of a large number of employees. The information is divided into 'intervals' and the vertical measurement represents 'frequency'. Columns need not have the same widths since this is a measure of the intervals used – they need not be uniform (see Figure 18.9).

However, where the intervals are uniform then a line may be used to join the tops of the columns and the profile of the graph becomes a curve. The area below the

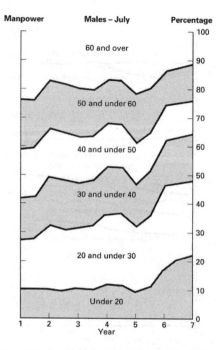

Figure 18.7 **A divided (compound) graph.**

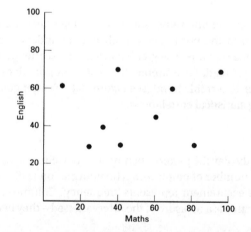

Figure 18.8 **Scatter graph (showing results of English and Maths examinations. Each dot indicates one student's score in both examinations).**

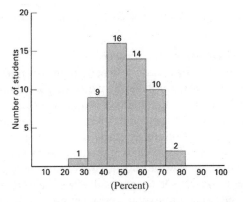

Figure 18.9 **Histogram (showing the frequency of distribution of examination marks of 52 students in 10% intervals).**

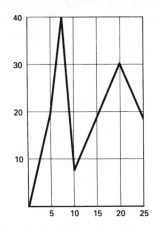

Figure 18.10 **Tall and narrow graph.**

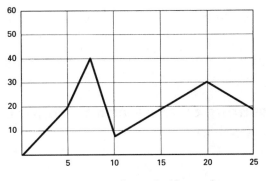

Figure 18.11 **Flat and wide graph.**

line can be shaded so that a section of the curve may now represent 'frequency' on the histogram.

Beware! A histogram looks like a vertical bar chart but the bars are not separated and their *width* as well as their *height* is significant.

18.4 Presenting discrete or non-continuous information

Bar charts

Bar charts are used to convey discrete or non-continuous information about different kinds of things (e.g. ownership of cars or washing machines, mortality rates in different places), sometimes at different moments in time.

They are particularly useful for conveying a quick comparison of quantities (e.g. barrels of oil in different areas) or sums of money (e.g. gross national product

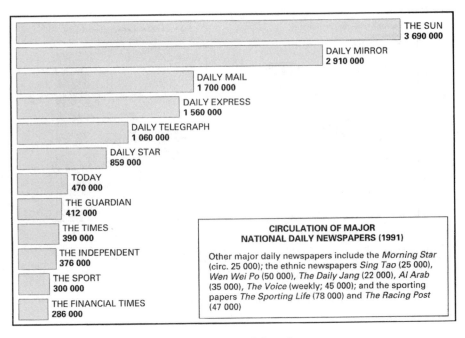

	THE SUN 3 690 000
DAILY MIRROR 2 910 000	
DAILY MAIL 1 700 000	
DAILY EXPRESS 1 560 000	
DAILY TELEGRAPH 1 060 000	
DAILY STAR 859 000	
TODAY 470 000	
THE GUARDIAN 412 000	
THE TIMES 390 000	
THE INDEPENDENT 376 000	
THE SPORT 300 000	
THE FINANCIAL TIMES 286 000	

**CIRCULATION OF MAJOR
NATIONAL DAILY NEWSPAPERS (1991)**

Other major daily newspapers include the *Morning Star* (circ. 25 000); the ethnic newspapers *Sing Tao* (25 000), *Wen Wei Po* (50 000), *The Daily Jang* (22 000), *Al Arab* (35 000), *The Voice* (weekly; 45 000); and the sporting papers *The Sporting Life* (78 000) and *The Racing Post* (47 000)

Figure 18.12 **Simple bar chart.**

Source: Guinness Publishing Ltd.

Assignment: Find out the circulation figures for the last complete year and show those figures and the 1991 figures in an appropriate chart.

in different countries) where exact figures are not so important. However, where items are plotted at various time intervals they can also depict trends.

They are drawn by showing a series of values plotted against two axes, but instead of being indicated by a line, the values are represented by vertical or horizontal bars or columns. Vertical charts are used when chronological data or other quantitative data is presented. Horizontal charts are generally used when making comparisons of data which is classified qualitatively or geographically (see simple bar chart in Figure 18.12).

Each bar is usually kept separate from its neighbour to emphasise that the information is discrete, not continuous as in a histogram. No attempt should be made to join the tops or ends of the bars to form a curve.

Divided (component) bar charts

Each bar may be divided into any number of parts to compare the constituents as well as the total value (e.g. population broken into different age groups or percentages). Each part is shaded differently and must be indicated by a key or labelled (see Figure 18.13).

Component bar charts can be confusing, since they can also be used to compare two sets of data, as in Figure 18.14.

When looking at component bar charts you should be sure that you know the difference between these two methods of using a component bar chart. The

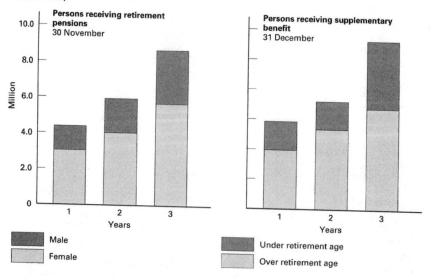

Figure 18.13 **Divided (component) bar chart.**

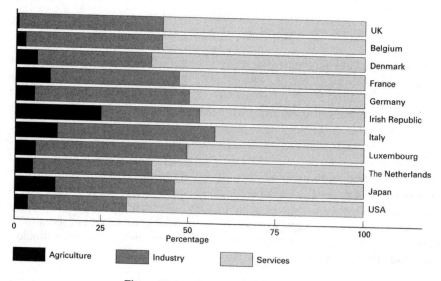

Figure 18.14 **Component bar chart.**

information in the chart in Figure 18.14 would be less ambiguously represented in a multiple bar chart.

Multiple bar charts

Bar charts can be used to compare any number of different items by producing a bar for each item and setting them in groups (see Figure 18.15).

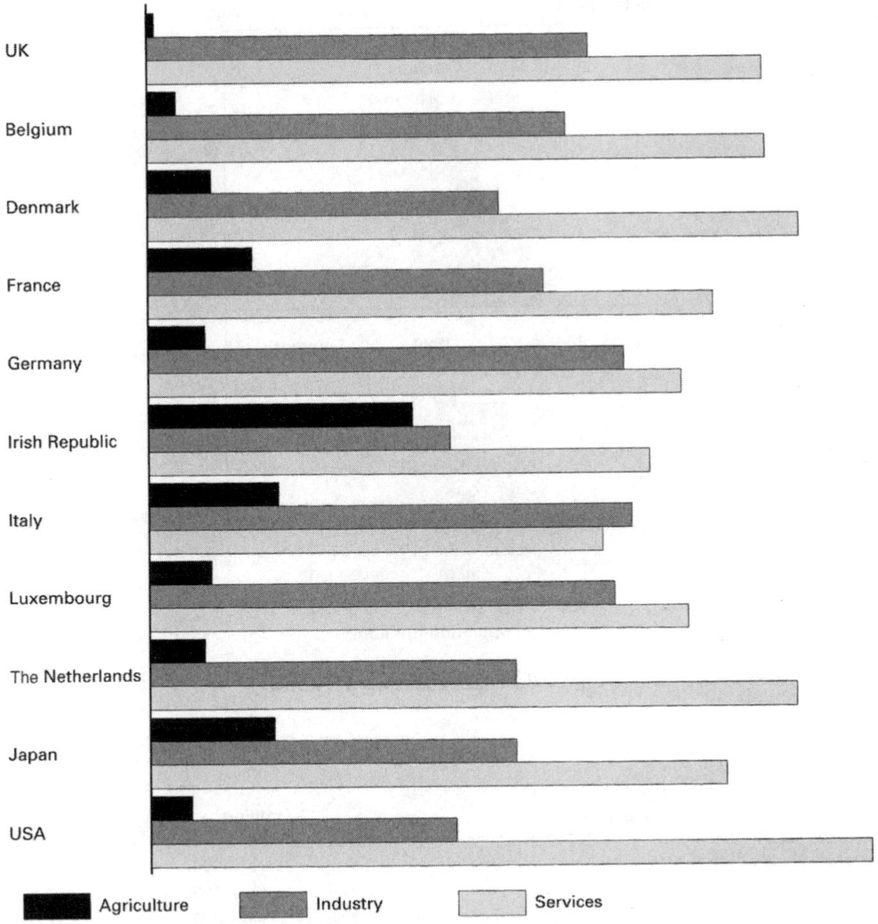

Figure 18.15 **Multiple bar chart (showing civilian employment by sector).**

The chart shows civilian employment by sector for: UK, Belgium, Denmark, France, Germany, Irish Republic, Italy, Luxembourg, The Netherlands, Japan, USA.

Legend: ■ Agriculture ▨ Industry ▢ Services

Population pyramid

This allows the representation of both the age and sex structure of population, by building up the age groups, male on one side and female on the other. The ages can be grouped every 1, 5 or 10 years and the information can be read, apart from the length of the bar, by comparing the shape of the pyramid with another (Figure 18.16).

Floating bar charts

The bar 'floats' either in the area of the graph or above and below a zero line from which a value runs down as well as up, for example, for plotting variations in a quantity (see Figure 18.17).

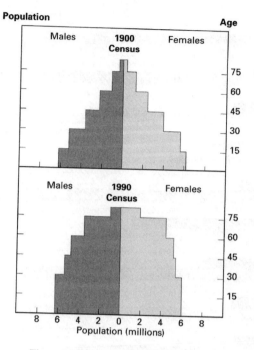

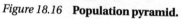

Figure 18.16 **Population pyramid.**

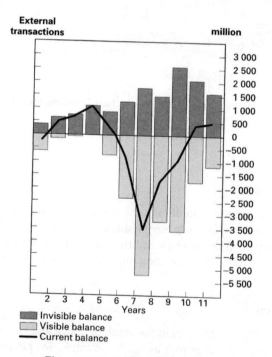

Figure 18.17 **Floating bar chart.**

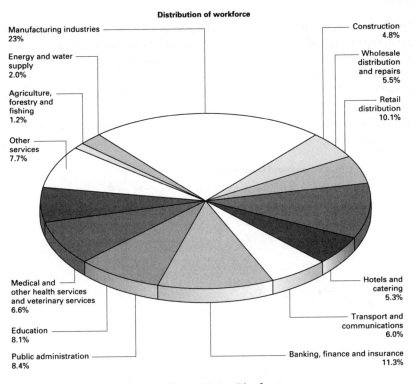

Figure 18.18 **Pie chart.**
Source: Guinness Publishing Ltd.

Pie or circle charts

The 'pie' or circle chart is one of the most common visual aids used. It is easy to interpret, can easily be produced on most computers and communicates its basic message with clarity and simplicity. Although each segment represents a different percentage, the total comes to 100 per cent. Each section is proportional to the value it represents, for example, distribution of the workforce between different sectors (see Figure 18.18).

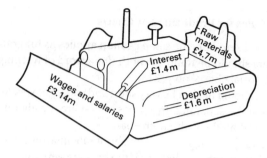

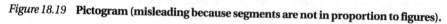

Figure 18.19 **Pictogram (misleading because segments are not in proportion to figures).**

Pictograms

The pie chart can be presented in a variety of ways. Some firms use a picture of their product to represent their 'pie' and divide it into appropriate segments to represent cost of materials, salaries, depreciations and so on. However, this can lead to distortion if the various segments are out of proportion (see Figure 18.19).

The reader should also be aware of the pie which has segments labelled only in words but with no percentage figures.

Each segment in a pie chart or pictogram should be identified and show the percentage it represents.

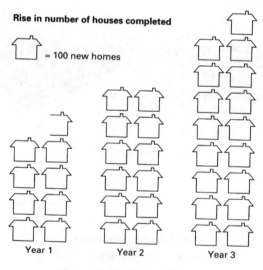

Figure 18.20 **Pictorial chart.**

Pictorial chart

The pictorial chart or pictograph is an adaption of the bar chart but it aims to overcome the lack of appeal of the bar chart by actually representing the subject. The pictorial chart is ideal for the reader who is in a hurry or disinclined to interpret a conventional bar chart. They can quickly see, for example, that the cost of living has gone up a little if shopping baskets are shown marching up a chart, or that more houses have been constructed this year than last year if five additional houses are shown (see Figure 18.20).

The symbols, such as people, homes, aeroplanes or £ signs should all be uniform in appearance and size. Each should represent the same quantity and dimension (which should be shown in a key). For this reason, they are rather more difficult for the amateur to produce accurately. The symbols should be simple and so easily recognisable that it would be almost impossible for two readers to interpret them differently.

Only a limited amount of information can be represented in a pictorial chart. For data which has several facts and requires thoughtful interpretation, other visual aids are preferable.

Check-Points: Rules and Warnings for Pictorial Charts

1 Symbols should be self-explanatory.
2 Pictorial charts should give an overall picture, not minute details.
3 Pictorial charts make comparisons between things, not flat statements about things.
4 Changes in numbers are shown by more or fewer symbols, not by larger or smaller ones.

Assignment: Look at Figure 18.21.
Does Mr B earn twice as much as Mr A?

Figure 18.21 is adapted from Darrell Huff's book, *How to Lie With Statistics* (Penguin, 1991), which is compulsive reading and which I strongly advise you to read in order to discover how other people may mislead you, and how you may unwittingly mislead others. The author goes on to explain how easily we can be tricked by a pictorial chart like this, which breaks rule 4:

> *The catch, of course, is this. Because the second bag is twice as high as the first, it is also twice as wide. It occupies not twice but four times as much area on the page. The numbers still say two to one, but the visual impression, which is the dominating one most of the time, says the ratio is four to one. Or worse, since these are pictures of objects having in reality three dimensions, the second must also be twice as thick as the first. As your geometry book puts it, the volumes of similar solids vary*

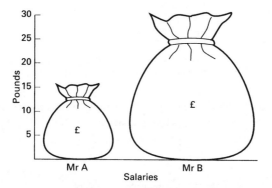

Figure 18.21 **A misleading chart.**

as the cube of any like dimension. Two times two times two is eight. If one money bag holds £15, the other, having eight times the volume, must hold not £30, but £120.

Statistical maps

Statistical maps are a particular kind of graphical device for showing quantitative information geographically (see Figure 18.22). They consist of representations of geographic areas shown either shaded, hatched or coloured.

Statistical maps sometimes also include dot or pin maps, the frequency of the dots indicating the relative density of the statistic being shown. Sometimes the size of the dots is varied as the magnitude of the data being presented varies.

Absence from work a year (days)

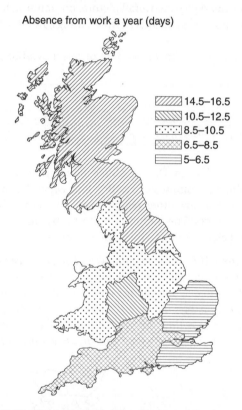

14.5–16.5
10.5–12.5
8.5–10.5
6.5–8.5
5–6.5

Figure 18.22 **Statistical map (showing annual average days of incapacity per person – males aged 16–44).**

Assignment: Now go back to the visual presentation which you made of the data concerning greetings cards and display stands in the first Assignment of this chapter. On the basis of what you now know about the advantages and disadvantages of different charts and graphs, would you present the data differently?

Now look at Examples 1–8 in Figure 18.23 – all ways of presenting the same information, but some more effectively than others.

Sales of greeting cards 15-20 March

Example 1

Shop	Total Sales
A	175
B	410
C	220
D	187
E	435
F	475
G	286
H	575
I	275
J	525

Shows specific data, but not very effectively

Example 2

Shop	Traditional Stand	Revolving Stand
A	175	
B		410
C	220	
D	187	
E		435
F		475
G	286	
H		575
I	275	
J		525

Example 3

Shop	Traditional Stand	Revolving Stand
A	175	
C	220	
D	187	
G	286	
I	275	
B		410
E		435
F		475
H		575
J		525

Example 4

Traditional Stands		Revolving Stands	
Shop	Traditional	Shop	Revolving
A	175	B	410
C	220	E	435
D	187	F	475
G	286	H	575
I	275	J	525

Shows specific data: well organised

(Continued on p. 316)

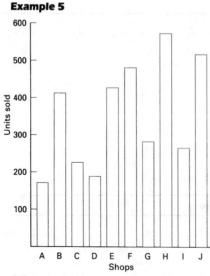

Example 5

Units sold

Reflects data but not very precisely and difficult to assimilate

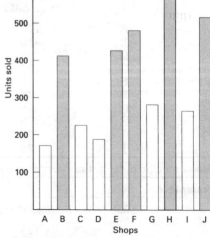

Example 6

Units sold

Reflects data; attempts to show comparison but effect is confusing

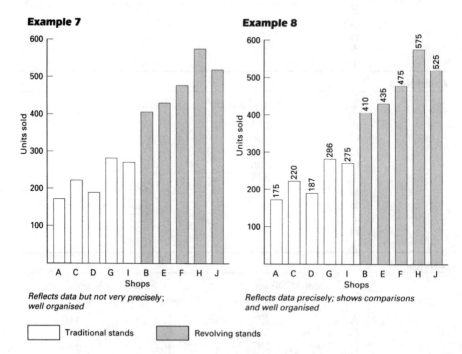

Example 7

Units sold

Reflects data but not very precisely; well organised

Example 8

Units sold

Reflects data precisely; shows comparisons and well organised

Traditional stands   Revolving stands

Figure 18.23 **Different ways of presenting the same information.**

Let's examine the choices we would have in presenting that data as effectively as possible. At first sight, we have to choose whether to present specific sales figures, or trends in sales, a combination of the two, or a picture of the information (pictogram).

The information to be represented is discrete: the sales figure in each newsagent shop is distinct and separate from the others and since we are given no information on time of sales, there is apparently no trend to present, so a graph is not appropriate, and little is to be gained from showing a lot of little pictures of display stands. We are also told that the importance of the data is in the *comparisons* of sales using the two different stands, not which shop or shops had the highest sales.

From this we can deduce that a table or bar chart is the best visual aid to use, as they will convey specific data and allow comparisons to be seen if we organise the data sensibly.

Look at the eight examples in Figure 18.23. Examples 2, 3, 4, 7 and 8 show specific data and the bar charts give a visual reinforcement of the message. However, 1, 5 and 6 are confusing as they do not emphasise the comparison between the two types of display stand, whereas when the data is grouped by display stand it is easier to see what is important straightaway.

Example 4 (table) and 8 (chart) show the data the most effectively. Which of the two would you prefer? Would it depend on your purpose and/or your audience?

Distortion by omission

'There are three kinds of lies: lies, damned lies and statistics', said Disraeli, and statistics in the hands of the ignorant, the inexperienced or the downright dishonest can be made to mislead the reader. A writer has to select facts for a chart, graph or table and omit others. The facts he does present may be accurate, but the impression

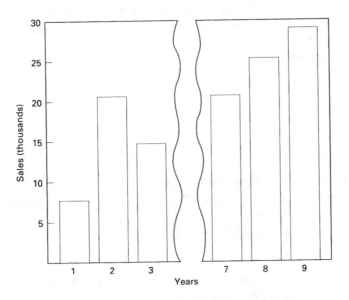

Figure 18.24 **Example of selective omission: 1.**

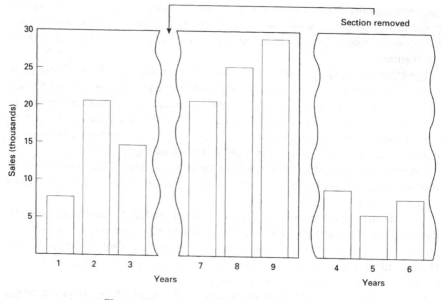

Figure 18.25 **Example of selective omission: 2.**

they create may be misleading. Look at the bar chart (Figure 18.24) for an example of selective omission. The casual reader might simply assume that sales rose steadily from year 1 to year 9. However, if we look at the section of the chart which has been removed (see Fig. 18.25), ostensibly to save space, the picture is rather different. Sales have not gone up consistently. The chart showing a broken line to indicate the missing years 4, 5 and 6 would be accurate, but misleading.

The moral, therefore, is that when we read charts, graphs and illustrations, or interpret statements which quote statistics, we must do so very *critically:* are the ideas accurate and complete? And when we transmit ideas through graphic aids or statistics we must continually ask ourselves whether we are being complete and honest in our intentions.

Exercise 18.1

1 List five advantages of visual presentation.
2 List the specific factors which should influence you in your choice of visual aid.
3 What specific advantages do tables have that make them particularly useful for presenting large quantities of statistical data?
4 If you wanted to present 'continuous' information would you use line graphs or bar charts?
5 List at least five ways in which someone presenting statistical data could intentionally mislead the reader.

Assignment: Get a copy of Darrell Huff's *How to Lie with Statistics* and start by reading as far as the end of the chapter called 'The Well-Chosen Average' (Chapter 2 in my copy). Find out how easy it is to be misled (and to mislead) by using the common expression 'on average'.

Using this knowledge, what particular cautions would you recommend to the reader if the following figures were presented as (a) mean, (b) modal and (c) median averages?

Salaries of directors	£
Mrs Simmonds	15 000
Mr Clough	70 000
Mr Langham	16 000
Mr Green	13 000
Mrs Shaw	14 000
Mr Beg	60 000

Incidentally, Darrell Huff's book will not only amuse and horrify you with its examples of how easy it is to lie with statistics, but it will also teach you quite a lot about the subject.

18.5 Presenting non-statistical information effectively

It is not just statistical information which can benefit from being presented visually. A chart showing the steps in the process, or a diagram showing the constituent parts of a piece of equipment, can save thousands of words, and reduce the likelihood of misunderstanding. Sometimes, reducing the number of words can be not only time-saving, but the only way to communicate where the message is aimed at a large audience of such different people from different backgrounds and with different abilities that a verbal message may be in the wrong language and incomprehensible to many, including those who are unable to read.

Public and directional information

Geographical maps are probably the most obvious form of visual aid in this category, but in offices, shops, public places and work places, signs, symbols and cartoons are increasingly used to direct and inform visitors, the public and the workforce. In our Western society, the use of symbols is now widespread and assumes a fairly sophisticated level of 'visual literacy' (the ability to 'read pictures') on the part of the whole population. The well-known ambiguity of road signs may cause much amusement but could have serious consequences in failing to communicate the intended message (see Figure 18.26).

Parachute
dropping area?

Danger: Someone
opening umbrella?

Figure 18.26 **Ambiguous visual communication?**

Do you know what these signs are really conveying? The first one signifies 'hazard' and the second 'roadworks'. Some road signs are considerably more difficult to understand immediately. However, the words would take up more space, take longer to read and would probably still be ambiguous, if not incomprehensible to some, for example, 'heavy plant crossing' may conjure up something from a horror movie. Where language barriers may cause problems in interpreting written or spoken words, for example, between different ethnic workers on the same workforce, the use of signs and symbols allied with a touch of humour may be a very effective method of presenting information.

Although visual communication can be very effective, and we are generally used to receiving messages visually, since we are said to gain 83 per cent of our information in this way, nevertheless some people are 'visually illiterate': they find interpreting visual communication more difficult than reading words. For this reason, messages should perhaps be communicated by both verbal and visual media, wherever possible.

Instructional or problem-solving information

Flow or process chart

Flow charts are very useful in representing in graphic form all the steps in a process. They begin at the very beginning and take the reader, or trainee perhaps, through a logical sequence of steps to the completion of the operation. In some cases this will involve assembling the materials or ingredients, processing them, and then channelling them in all directions to other user groups. In other cases, it may be a very simple operation. Represented visually, the flow chart needs no special symbols. A sequence of written statements, linked by arrows to indicate the line of reasoning, is enough. However, method study officers, systems analysts, training officers and others who analyse jobs and processes tend to use a series of simple symbols to represent the various kinds of activity involved, as in Figure 18.27.

> **Assignment:** Using these symbols, or a simpler system of your own, draw a flow chart showing the process of someone preparing a cup of instant coffee. Start with 'person seated on chair in lounge' and end with 'person seated on chair with coffee'. There are approximately 25 stages in the process. Assume the person is using an electric kettle. Then look at the suggested version in Figure 18.28.

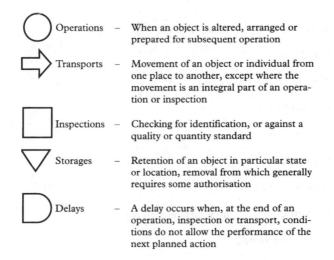

<table>
<tr><td>Operations</td><td>–</td><td>When an object is altered, arranged or prepared for subsequent operation</td></tr>
<tr><td>Transports</td><td>–</td><td>Movement of an object or individual from one place to another, except where the movement is an integral part of an operation or inspection</td></tr>
<tr><td>Inspections</td><td>–</td><td>Checking for identification, or against a quality or quantity standard</td></tr>
<tr><td>Storages</td><td>–</td><td>Retention of an object in particular state or location, removal from which generally requires some authorisation</td></tr>
<tr><td>Delays</td><td>–</td><td>A delay occurs when, at the end of an operation, inspection or transport, conditions do not allow the performance of the next planned action</td></tr>
</table>

Figure 18.27 **Flow/process chart symbols.**

It is useful to be able to break down a job or process into stages in this way. It is easier to explain it to someone learning the job and it enables processes and jobs to be made quicker, easier and generally more efficient by working out where there may be wastage of time or energy (unnecessary movement, for example) and where unnecessary or avoidable delays occur.

Algorithms

An algorithm is a set of instructions and decisions which will always give an answer, provided a procedure is followed correctly. Algorithms are very similar to flow charts in their function, but they also include a breakdown of the *decision-making element*. At any point in the system where a decision has to be made, the chart can show the alternative choices open to the operative and the subsequent route they must take depending on the particular decision made. For this reason, they are sometimes called 'decision-trees' and the chart resembles a tree with various branches showing all the possible routes and the re-entries back into the main route.

Again, although simple boxes and arrows are perfectly adequate the representation is helped by a set of standard symbols as in Figure 18.29.

The example of an algorithm given in Figure 18.30 is part of a fault-finding algorithm for a machine. More complex and extended algorithms may incorporate other symbols.

This kind of charting adapts well to computer-programming and is also very useful for diagnostic testing and fault-finding. It is also an extremely efficient way of getting forms completed properly and is therefore often used in public administration, for example, to discover quickly if people are eligible for social services, or to determine their legal position and so on.

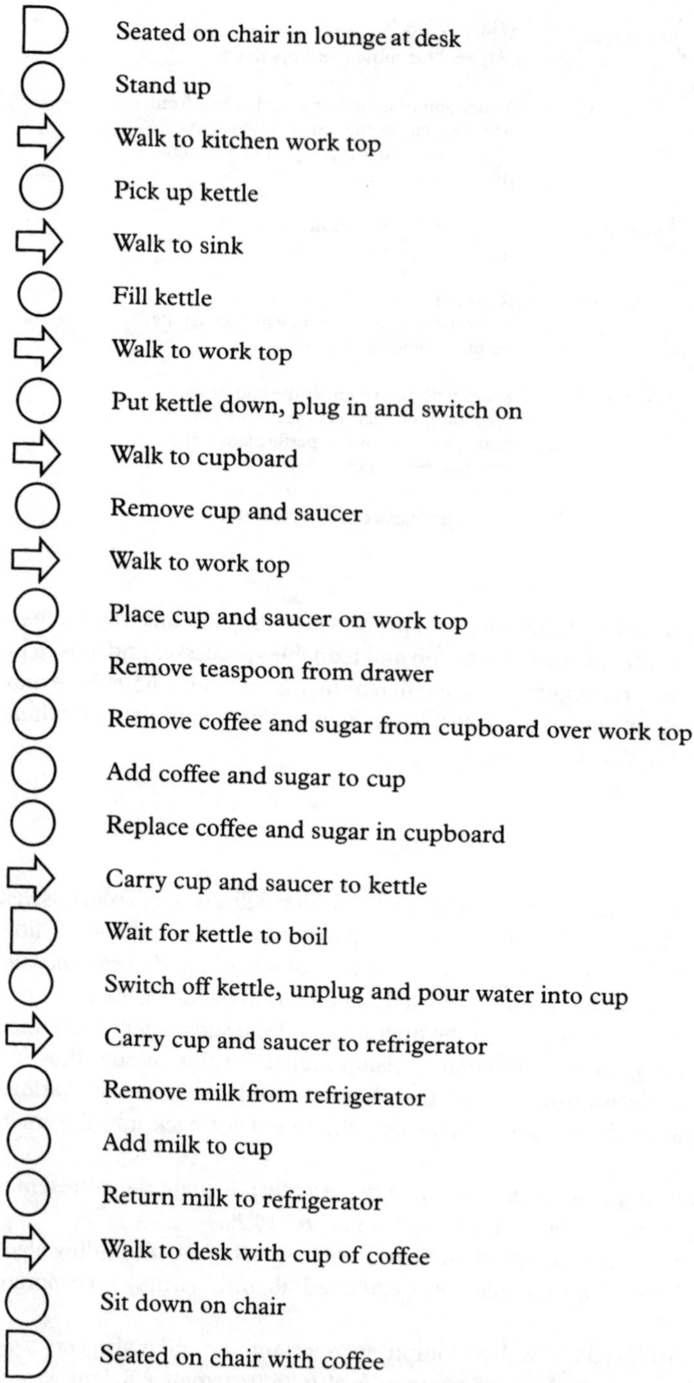

D	Seated on chair in lounge at desk
O	Stand up
⇨	Walk to kitchen work top
O	Pick up kettle
⇨	Walk to sink
O	Fill kettle
⇨	Walk to work top
O	Put kettle down, plug in and switch on
⇨	Walk to cupboard
O	Remove cup and saucer
⇨	Walk to work top
O	Place cup and saucer on work top
O	Remove teaspoon from drawer
O	Remove coffee and sugar from cupboard over work top
O	Add coffee and sugar to cup
O	Replace coffee and sugar in cupboard
⇨	Carry cup and saucer to kettle
D	Wait for kettle to boil
O	Switch off kettle, unplug and pour water into cup
⇨	Carry cup and saucer to refrigerator
O	Remove milk from refrigerator
O	Add milk to cup
O	Return milk to refrigerator
⇨	Walk to desk with cup of coffee
O	Sit down on chair
D	Seated on chair with coffee

Figure 18.28 **Flow or process chart for preparation of cup of instant coffee.**

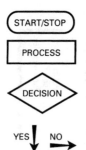

A START or STOP box to begin or end a sequence

A PROCESS box in which instructions may be placed to initiate action

A DECISION box where a question is asked, preferably a question with only two possible answers

ARROWS to lead the reader through the algorithm stage by stage.
Decisions 'made' are written on the arrows

Figure 18.29 **Algorithms: standard symbols.**

To show relationships

Where we are concerned with showing what a piece of equipment or an organisation consists of, and the relationships between the constituent parts, we can use diagrams and drawings and 'family tree' type charts.

Line drawings

These are probably the simplest type of visual aid of all. However, without perspective it is sometimes difficult to see the relationship between the parts.

Cutaway and exploded drawings

Cutaway and exploded sketches or photographs are excellent for showing the reader the component parts of a piece of equipment as well as sub-surface areas ('what goes on inside').

A cutaway can often convey a much clearer picture of the interior working parts of a complex mechanical device than could a 5000-word description (see Figure 18.31).

An exploded diagram (see Figure 18.32) presents the component parts of a device. Each piece is drawn to show how it fits into, or next to, a contiguous piece. If it is a pie chart, for example, each of its segments is exploded. Dotted lines are sometimes used to illustrate how the entire unit is attached to the larger mechanism.

Cutaway and exploded diagrams are most often used in technical reports or training manuals. They really require the services of an artist who can draw with care and precision, and can also use imagination, but if you have a little talent for drawing you could always be prepared to have a go. Computer-aided drawing packages can nowadays make artists of us all.

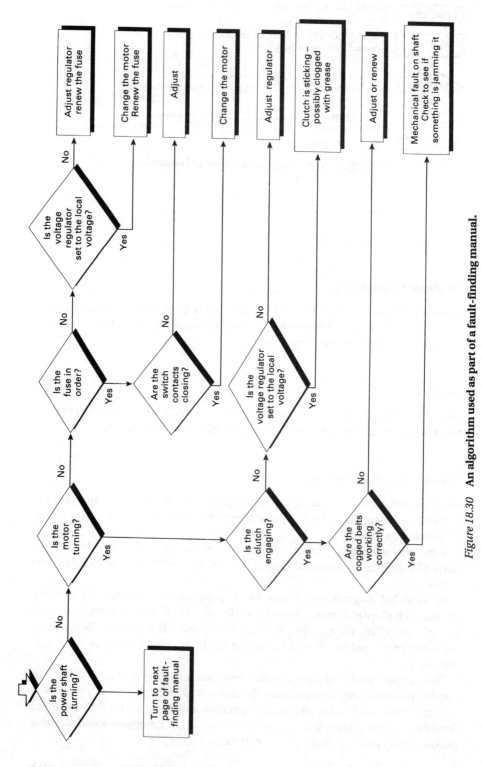

Figure 18.30 **An algorithm used as part of a fault-finding manual.**

Acoustically tuned chambers to give maximum
sound attenuation with minimum power loss

Baffles have lipped holes to
give greater rigidity

Case and endplates
lock-seamed to give
a secure gas-tight seal
and greater corrosion
resistance

CO_2 welded to give
consistent quality
and strength

Double skin acoustically
deadens silencer case

Tubes are 'press-fitted' into baffles for
greater strength and durability

Endplate damper prevents acoustical vibration
being transmitted through endplate

Figure 18.31 **Cutaway diagram showing the inside of a car
exhaust silencer.**

This drawing shows the crankshaft on
a conventional four cylinder in-line
engine with three main bearings.

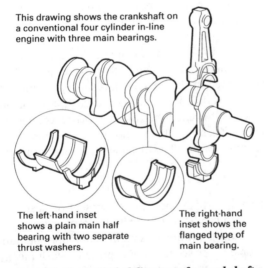

The left-hand inset
shows a plain main half
bearing with two separate
thrust washers.

The right-hand
inset shows the
flanged type of
main bearing.

Figure 18.32 **Exploded diagram of a crankshaft.**

Family tree charts

Organisation charts

Modern organisations are so complex that it is often difficult to have a clear
understanding of who reports to whom and how exactly you fit in. Every employee
usually feels more comfortable when they know exactly where they stand within a
company, who is their boss, who is their boss's boss and so on.

There are several kinds of organisation chart, but probably the most common is
the vertical chart like the one shown in Figure 18.33, which reads from top to bottom.

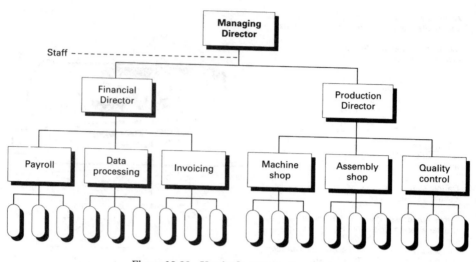

Figure 18.33 **Vertical organisation chart.**

There are also horizontal charts which read from left to right and circle charts that show authority emanating from the centre. In most organisation charts, solid lines indicate direct relationships and broken lines indirect, often consultative or advisory, relationships.

Although authority and the chain of command usually differ between the real situation and what is depicted on paper, the organisation chart does serve an important purpose. Something is needed to give an appreciation of the structure of the company and nothing does it so quickly and easily as an organisation chart. At the same time, it is well to remember that the *actual* centres of authority in an organisation usually differ from what is shown on the chart, and the *real* lines of communication do not always follow the lines on an organisation chart.

Information trees

If the set of information which you want to present or need to consider can be classified into subsets, it can be displayed in the form of 'trees' rather like a family tree. However, unlike the algorithm, this method of representation is not problem-solving or instructional in the sense of being prescriptive. It merely gives a historic view of the 'problem' showing all related facets and leaves the reader to interpret the relationships and draw conclusions.

It is incidentally, a useful method of taking notes (see Figure 18.34).

Information mapping and charting

A variation on the idea of information trees, this system allows you to show all the information on one subject on a single sheet of paper, chart or transparency. It does not necessarily rely on the existence of subsets or close relationships, but it does allow you to see at a glance all the items which make up your subject, and you may find that having written down your information in boxes placed almost at random on the paper, you will detect relationships between one 'box' and another. These

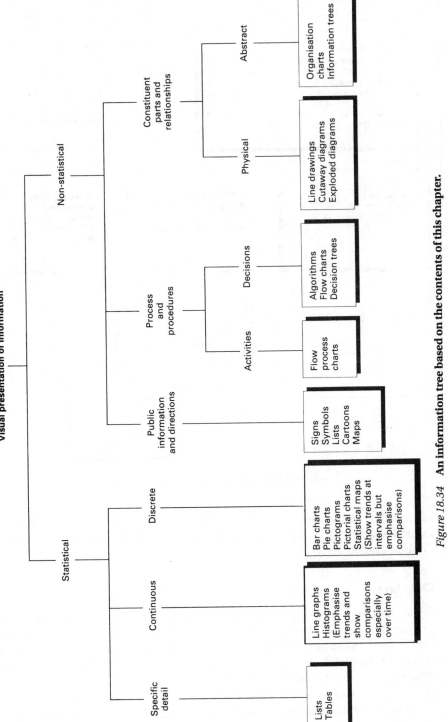

Figure 18.34   **An information tree based on the contents of this chapter.**

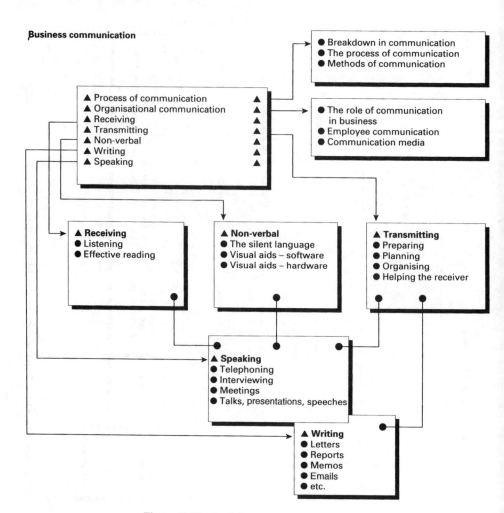

Figure 18.35 **An information map or chart.**

relationships can be shown by arrows, or by cross-links in the form of ●—●, as in Figure 18.35 which represents a quick information chart on the subject of 'Business Communication'.

Overlays

When the visual aid is to be part of an oral presentation, a useful method of presenting statistical information is the use of transparent overlays. All the graphic aids mentioned can be used in this way. A base chart gives the scale, grid, title and so on, and comparatively simple data is gradually superimposed through the use of different transparent overlays made with different coloured transparencies. This combination could be used as a line graph, a bar chart or even a statistical map.

Obviously, all the same rules apply but it is a very effective method of presentation in that a specific comparison can be made and then removed. In other words, whereas on a chart of a single dimension, once all the information is on the chart it is difficult for the reader to eliminate some of the information, when overlays are used, the reader can be shown only those overlays in which they are particularly interested. Another advantage is that overlays allow the presenter to show the cumulative effect of different numerical data.

The same advantages, of course, apply to building up complex diagrams and charts of non-statistical information.

Exercise 18.2

1 Suggest two reasons why visual communication may be more effective than verbal communication.
2 What is 'visual literacy'?
3 What kinds of visual aid might you consider using to convey a process or procedure?
4 If you were trying to devise an instruction manual or leaflet which would enable a mechanic to discover why a washing-machine has stopped working so that they can repair it, which method of presentation would be the most effective?
5 Which visual symbols would you use to indicate the following activities on a flow chart?

- Check typing of a letter
- A worker waiting for materials
- Papers filed in a filing cabinet
- Picking up a screwdriver
- An object moving on a conveyor belt
- Signing a document.

Assignment

1 Draw a cutaway diagram of any simple object, for example a felt-tip pen, a cigarette lighter
2 Try to draw a flow chart tracing the process of application for your course or your job

- You will probably need to interview people concerned with admissions, or recruitment and selection to find out what documents are involved and what happens to them
- From examining the steps in the procedure do you think that the process could be made any simpler? More efficient?

Further reading

Bradbury, Andrew, *Successful Presentation Skills*, Kogan Page, 2000
Huff, D., *How to Lie with Statistics*, Penguin, 1991

19 Getting to grips with grammar

You may not know what a verb is, or for that matter what a noun, or a preposition, or an adverbial clause, is. Furthermore, you may feel that it is not necessary to know. Perhaps you feel that these things are the stuff of English lessons, English teachers and dusty grammar books. Or perhaps you feel that these words are just another kind of jargon: useful for the specialists in the field of English but unnecessary double-dutch to everyone else. And you may be right!

19.1 Why does grammar matter?

Many people speak and write English quite correctly without knowing very much about the rules and conventions of the English language. They automatically apply them without thinking or realising that they are doing so. Most of us, because we have been brought up to speak English as our mother tongue, are able for the most part to put down words in the right order; that is, in a way that other people expect, and understand fairly easily. Most of us, for example, would recognise that to write: 'I haven't never been their' is wrong. It is wrong because 'their' is used when we are indicating possession of something – 'their coats', 'their children' – but it is not spelled like that when we are referring to a place. It is also wrong because two negatives cancel one another out – 'I haven't never' = 'I have not never' = 'I have', which is presumably the exact opposite of what the speaker meant to say.

The problem is that all of us, to a greater or lesser extent, make mistakes through either ignorance or carelessness and these mistakes can lead to misunderstandings, confusion and sometimes failure to communicate in the way we intended.

As we saw in the earlier chapters, we communicate by means of previously agreed symbols, but if we don't use the correct symbols, or if we don't use them in the way other people expect, they will have difficulty understanding what we mean. If we break the rules of the code they will at worst not be able to understand, and at best be irritated at being obliged to make what they consider to be an unnecessary effort to work out what we mean.

More and more business people are coming to accept that the key test is:

Does the text I have written mean the same to the reader as I meant it to say?

If it does, then successful communication has happened.

19.2 What is grammar?

Because our language is in daily use, it is constantly being modified by those who speak it. But there have to be some points of agreement about what is acceptable at any point in time (correct usage) and in any one geographical place (dialect) or we would not be able to communicate with one another – the code would not be understood. These points of agreement about how we put words together and what is acceptable (i.e. understood by the majority of people) are what make up grammar and usage.

However, since the language changes slowly, so usages that once were thought to be incorrect are now a part of everyday usage. For example, 'different to' has now become widely acceptable, particularly because American English uses it all the time; whereas in Britain until the 1970s 'different from' would have been insisted upon, and by many people still is.

The trouble is that some of the potential readers of our business writing may not accept that such modifications are happening. They may insist that certain usages are simply *wrong*. Since we need them to accept what we are writing, we would do well to work to their rules, however tedious this may be. Therefore, although the 'rules' of grammar are, in reality, not *instructions* but *observations* about how the language is structured, we need to treat them like rules for some of our more finicky readers.

Another reason for trying to use good English is that otherwise, rightly or wrongly, others may judge us ignorant, ill-educated, lazy or careless – all characteristics which are not very desirable in our society. As we have seen, it is unfortunately often the case that the unintended non-verbal communication – in this context, poor spelling or bad grammar or awkward sentence structure – will have a greater impact on the reader than the real *content* of what we are trying to say.

Self-Check

Check your knowledge of grammar. Can you

1 Identify each word in a sentence as being a particular part of speech (*verb, noun, adjective,* etc.)?

2 Recognise which words form the *subject* of a sentence and which words form the *verb* and the *object* (*predicate*)?

3 Find the *main verb* in a sentence and identify its *subject* and the *object* or *complement*?

4 Distinguish between a *phrase*, a *clause* and a *sentence*?

---

5 Recognise the three different kinds of sentence: *simple, compound* and *complex*?
6 Describe what a *paragraph* is, and what it is for?
  • Can you do all these things?
  • Did you understand all the grammatical terms (in italics) used in the questions?

If you answered 'No' to either question, you would do well to read this chapter through fairly carefully. But you will probably need to do some more work on grammar, usage, sentence construction and punctuation since these form the basis of effective written communication. Try *Mastering English Grammar* by S.H. Burton in the Palgrave Macmillan Masters Series which has lots of practical exercises. The more you know, the more you will be able to find out from other reference books, some of which are suggested in the Bibliography on p. 412.

But, you may say, while all this may be true, and acceptable justification for learning and obeying the generally accepted rules and conventions of the English language, why is it necessary to know the names of the various parts of a sentence or the functions of the parts of speech? The reason is simple if you think about it. It is almost impossible to explain to people where and why they are making mistakes, how they are breaking the rules of the code or even what those rules are, unless they know the names of the things you are talking about. Imagine trying to explain to other people how to do your job or some part of your hobby perhaps, without first describing what things are called and how they relate to one another. For example, it would be very difficult to teach people to drive a car unless they knew the names of the various pedals and switches and so on. It might be possible, if you and the learner were both sitting in the car, to get by with instructions like 'Unless you move this like this and that like that while moving your foot like this and gradually putting your other foot on that, the car won't move!' but it would make understanding what to do much more difficult and would depend on a practical visual demonstration in the car. Similarly, any explanation of accepted English language practice depends on knowing at least some of the terminology.

In this chapter and Chapter 20 we shall be looking briefly at the way we should try to use the English language in order to reduce the chances of our being misunderstood, or of causing unnecessary irritation in our receivers. Above all, these two chapters will concentrate on:

• the more common problems and errors in using the language
• the bare essentials of English grammar and usage necessary to solve the problems and avoid the more common errors.

If you find that you need more detailed explanation than is possible here, or that you become hooked on what can be a really fascinating study and want to go further, you will find some suggestions for further reading as you progress through the chapters.

19.3   How good is your English?

Self-Check

Let's start by finding out what you know already. Look at the following sentences and decide whether in your opinion they are correct or contain errors. Make any corrections you think necessary. There may be more than one error in a sentence and some sentences may have no errors. Unless you need to rewrite the whole sentence in order to correct it, you should rewrite only the word or words which are wrong.

1 Thanking you for your letter of 6 Febuary in which you complained about the control mechanism.
2 Furnished accomodation is required by young woman about to be married for one year.
3 Each of the new members are to be introduced seperately.
4 The office needs redecorating, but its carpet is in good condition.
5 The manager, together with his assistants, is working on the project now.
6 Toys, which are dangerous, should not be given to children.
7 She is one of the students who is taking the examination.
8 He found the job very different to what he had expected.
9 Please book the seats for my wife and I.
10 She is the woman who we expect to be the next vice-president.
11 Looking at it the next morning, the task seemed easier.
12 We complained about them having taken the notice off the board.
13 She cannot type as quickly as I.
14 Its the type of product that we need in order to be competitative.
15 She does not remember the incident as well as me.
16 He is the only one who you could ask.
17 Nothing succeeds like success.
18 I do not remember him having told me about the meeting.
19 Although they were dissapointed they had only theirselves to blame.
20 The power of her arguements, which were very persuasive, were not enough.
21 A cue of people stretched along the pavement, which was getting longer.
22 Our trading had not only increased beyond our expectations but also our hopes.
23 There was less paper than was needed to do the job.
24 Neither of the rooms were laid out like he had requested.
25 This is the section from the Deanfield report, which they wrote last week.
26 It looks like he will succeed.
27 In my opinion he never has, and never will be, a success.
28 He swims like a fish, but runs like an elephant.
29 They ordered an extra a hundred boxes for the new season.
30 Due to become the next president, he was hurt not to have been invited.
31 They finished there work before going home.
32 Due to the holidays, production was severely delayed.

33 The two company's were not only in competition but also at risk.
34 He asked me to carefully correct the errors before giving it back.
35 She is the tallest of the two girls.
36 There were less papers in this year's exams.
37 Surprisingly, he did not deny that he was not guilty.
38 Entering the office, she saw her colleague already typing the report.
39 She writes reports as well, if not better than, her boss.
40 They survived the scandal without hardly a dent in their reputation.
41 The report will take me some time to read.
42 These kind of problems are very difficult to solve.
43 Due to shortage of supplies, we are unable to dispatch the goods today.
44 Cycling along the lane, the bull suddenly charged out in front of me.
45 Less problems might have meant success instead of failure.
46 If I was you I would go to the meeting.
47 Going into the office, the secretary could be seen already typing the memo.
48 Having opened the meeting, there was no way of avoiding the issue.
49 Having stolen the cash, the manager had no option but to sack me.
50 There was fewer people and less questions than had been expected.

Answers

Altogether there were 50 mistakes in the sentences. How many did you recognise? Check your answers carefully with the correct sentences below. The number of mistakes in the original sentence is indicated by the number in brackets. You only get a point if you spot a mistake, not for recognising that a sentence was correct. Take off points if you invented mistakes that weren't there!

Refer to
Page

357   1 Thank you for your letter of 6 February in which you complained about the control mechanism. (2)

367   2 Furnished accommodation is required for one year by young woman about to be married. (2)

348   3 Each of the new members is to be introduced separately. (2)

372   4 The office needs redecorating, but its carpet is in good condition. (√)

348   5 The manager, together with his assistants, is working on the project now. (√)

376   6 Toys that are dangerous should not be given to children. (1)

348   7 She is one of the students who are taking the examination. (1)

382   8 He found the job very different from what he had expected. (1)

370   9 Please book the seats for my wife and me. (1)

371 10 She is the woman whom we expect to be the next vice-president. (1)

354 11 When we (he/she, etc.) looked at it the next morning, the task seemed easier. (1)

357 12 We complained about their having taken the notice off the board. (1)

370 13 She cannot type as quickly as I. (√)

372	14 It's the type of product that we need in order to be competitive. (2)
370/382	15 She does not remember the incident as well as I. (1)
371	16 He is the only one whom you could ask. (1)
382	17 Nothing succeeds like success. (√)
357	18 I do not remember his having told me about the meeting. (1)
368	19 Although they were disappointed, they had only themselves to blame. (2)
348	20 The power of her arguments, which were very persuasive, was not enough. (2)
367	21 A queue of people, which was getting longer, stretched along the pavement. (2)
383	22 Our trading had increased not only beyond our expectations but also beyond our hopes. (1)
365	23 There was less paper than was needed to do the job. (√)
348/383	24 Neither of the rooms was laid out as he had requested. (2)
368	25 This is the section, which they wrote last week, from the Deanfield report. (1)
383	26 It looks as if he will succeed. (1)
384	27 In my opinion he never has been, and never will be, a success. (1)
383	28 He swims like a fish, but runs like an elephant. (√)
364	29 They ordered an extra hundred boxes for the new season. (1)
364	30 Due to become the next president, he was hurt not to have been invited. (√)
372	31 They finished their work before going home. (1)
364	32 Owing to the holidays, production was severely delayed. (1)
372	33 The two companies were not only in competition but also at risk. (1)
352	34 He asked me to correct the errors carefully before giving it back. (1)
364	35 She is the taller of the two girls. (1)
365	36 There were fewer papers in this year's exams. (1)
385	37 Surprisingly, he did not deny that he was guilty. (1)
354	38 Entering the office, she saw her colleague already typing the report. (√)
384	39 She writes reports as well as, if not better than, her boss. (1)
385	40 They survived the scandal with hardly a dent to their reputation. (1)
367	41 The report will take me some time to read. (√)
348/364	42 This kind of problem is very difficult to solve. (1)
364	43 Owing to shortage of supplies, we are unable to dispatch the goods today. (1)
354	44 As I was cycling along the lane, the bull suddenly charged out in front of me. (1)
365	45 Fewer problems might have meant success instead of failure. (1)
359	46 If I were you I would go to the meeting. (1)
354	47 As I entered the office, the secretary could be seen already typing the memo. (1)

357	48 Having opened the meeting, I (we/they) had no way of avoiding the issue. (1)
354	49 Since I stole the cash, the manager had no option but to sack me. (1)
348/365	50 There were fewer people and fewer questions than had been expected. (2)

The numbers in the left-hand margin refer to the numbers of the pages in Chapter 20, where you will find an explanation of the errors in the test sentences.

How did you score?

If you spotted fewer than 30 mistakes out of 50, you would do well to read through the whole of this and the next chapter carefully. If you spotted 30–45 mistakes, look particularly at the relevant sections in the next chapter, but you obviously write fairly correct English (even if you are not always sure of the rules). 45+ Congratulations!

Self-Check

Before we discuss the reasons why some of those sentences were incorrect and why some of them which perhaps you thought were incorrect are strictly speaking correct, see what you can remember about the eight main parts of speech by describing what each of them does and providing some examples of each.

Part of speech	Function	Examples
Noun		
Pronoun		
Adjective		
Verb		
Adverb		
Preposition		
Conjunction		
Interjection		

19.4 The parts of speech in brief

Every word in an English sentence belongs to one or another of the eight parts of speech, according to the work it is doing in that sentence. Some words can belong to more than one part of speech but we will come to that later. These parts of speech are as follows:

Nouns are words which *name* persons, places or things
    e.g. 'man', 'Peter', 'Bristol', 'book', 'anger'

Pronouns are words which are used *instead of nouns* in order to save repeating the noun several times in the sentence

    e.g. 'The manager met *her* assistant and *they* went to the meeting'

Adjectives tell us more about nouns and pronouns; they *qualify* or describe persons, places and things

    e.g. 'This *beautiful* picture is the *finest* in *this* collection'

Verbs are the '*doing words*'; they are the words around which the whole sentence turns, for they show what is done or happens or is

    e.g. 'The factory *closes* for three weeks' (i.e. what is done)
       'She *gave* him the letter' (i.e. what is said to have happened)
       'He *is* the brother of my friend' (i.e. what is)

Adverbs are to verbs what adjectives are to nouns and pronouns: *they modify the verb* or, in other words, describe the circumstances (how, when, where, why etc.) in which the action represented by the verb is done

    e.g. 'He writes *slowly* but types *quickly*.'

Prepositions are words placed (usually) before a noun or pronoun to show its *connection* or relation with the other words in the sentence

    e.g. 'She came *into* the room'
The preposition '*into*' shows the connection between her coming and the room; if we change the preposition to '*from*' that connection is altered.

Conjunctions are used to *connect* words, phrases or clauses in the sentence

    e.g. 'Matthew *and* his partner have arrived'
       'The company has the same name, *but* is owned by his brother'

Interjections are used to show emotion or draw attention and do not strictly speaking form part of the sentence

    e.g. 'Hello!' 'Indeed!'
They are not normally used in business writing.

Self-Check

Now look back at your list and assess how well you did. You may still be uncertain about some of your answers because parts of speech are not always as simple to distinguish as this brief explanation may suggest, but it should provide you with a quick reference list.

Now try this exercise. Give the different parts of speech that each of the following represents:

arm
maroon
as
rough
base
second
best

---

set
desolate
where
error
why
fish
wrong

To check your answers, look up each word in the dictionary. As you will realise, often a word is used as more than one part of speech. The different ways a word can be used are indicated in the dictionary by the abbreviations n. (noun), adv. (adverb), v.t. (verb transitive) and so on. So, in this sentence: 'She bruised her arm', the word 'arm' is being used as a noun, and in this sentence: 'The soldiers picked up their arms and marched on', although the meaning of the word 'arm' is different from the first sentence, it is still being used as a noun. However, when we say: 'They were armed with shovels and pickaxes', we are using 'arm' as a verb – in this case, as part of the past tense of the verb 'to arm'.

In looking up these words you may have come across abbreviations which you did not understand. If so, you will probably find somewhere near the front of the dictionary a list of the abbreviations used in the dictionary together with their meanings. However, this may still pose problems. Perhaps you are none the wiser when you find that a word can be used as a 'verb transitive' and its 'past participle' is such and such. In this case, you could first try looking up the word itself in the dictionary. For example, you will find the word 'transitive' under 'transit n.'. Look it up now. Found it? You will probably find something like this: 'adj. transitive' (i.e. 'transitive' is the adjective formed from the noun, 'transit') 'passing over: having the power of passing: taking a direct object (gram.).'

From this we discover the meaning of the word and, in particular, that in *grammatical* terms it means 'taking an object', so a transitive verb is a verb which takes an object, or in other words, 'passes over' an idea from the subject to object, from the *doer* to the *receiver*.

Put another way, a transitive verb needs an object to complete its meaning, for example, 'She *hit* the tree.' Without 'the tree' we would be left asking: She hit *what*?

Assignment: What, then, do you think an 'intransitive' verb is? Now look it up to check that you have guessed correctly. Can you think of five examples of intransitive verbs? Look them up in the dictionary to see whether they are transitive (v.t.) or intransitive (v.i.)

Perhaps you found that some could be used as both, or that with one meaning the verb is transitive, but with another meaning it is intransitive. Let's look at an example of a verb which can be both transitive and intransitive.

'She manages.'

In this sentence the verb 'manage' must mean 'get by' or 'cope' because there is no object and yet the verb is complete – it makes sense. So 'manage' used like this is intransitive. Now look at this sentence:

'She manages the company.'

Here 'manage' means 'handle', 'conduct' or 'control' and needs the object 'the company' to complete it, so 'manage' used this way is transitive.

Most of the time you will probably not need to know the difference between transitive and intransitive verbs because you will naturally use them correctly without thinking twice. However, it is important to know the difference because some of the more unusual verbs are frequently used incorrectly:

e.g. 'require' when it means 'need' is a transitive verb which requires an object, and should not be used intransitively as in

'A special programme requires to be arranged for their visit.'

A correct version might be

'A special programme needs to be ...' or 'A special programme will have to be ...'

> **Assignment:** Can you see anything wrong with this sentence?
> 'The report which you wanted was laying on the table.'

If you cannot see anything wrong with it, look up the verbs 'to lay' and 'to lie' in the dictionary.

'To lay' is transitive and must therefore have an object: 'Hens lay eggs' (Present); 'I laid the report on the desk' (Past); 'They were laying the table' (Past continuous); 'To lie' is intransitive: 'I lie down to go to sleep' (Present); 'I lay on the bed' (Past); 'They were lying on the floor' (Past continuous).

Notice the difference between the past versions of the two verbs. These are frequently confused.

'The report was laying next to the typewriter' *wrong*

'Was laying' is the past tense of the verb 'to lay' which is transitive and must therefore have an object, but there is no object in the sentence. If we want to say what the report was doing we must make sure we use the correct verb in the correct form:

'The report ... was lying next to the typewriter' *right*

Without care the same confusion can occur in the present tense:

'They are laying the table' (transitive) but 'The books are lying on the desk' (intransitive), not 'The books are laying on the table?'

19.5 The framework of English

The parts of speech are used in *paragraphs, sentences, clauses* and *phrases*.

- The **paragraph** should contain a single thought unit and its development (explanation, examples, details). Two distinct points should not be dealt with in a single paragraph, but the development of a single point may fall into logical sections that can properly be expressed in separate paragraphs. The main idea of the paragraph should normally be expressed in a clear and concise sentence (topic sentence) usually placed near the beginning of the paragraph or occasionally towards or at the end of the paragraph (see Figure 13.1).

- The **sentence** is a complete statement:

  'The manager arranged the audioconference.'
  'You should not lie.'
  'Press the lever now.'

  Note that all three sentences have verbs; the first has a subject (manager) and an object (audioconference), the second has a subject only (you) and the third has an object (lever), but the subject (you) is understood but not stated.

  Sometimes single words, or phrases without verbs, can stand as sentences, usually in replies during conversation:

  'Not at all.'
  'Good heavens.'
  'Naturally.'

  Occasionally, we find constructions like:
  'The building was empty. No people. No furniture. Nothing.'

- The **clause** is an incomplete statement, used to expand another statement:

  'She called the meeting *when the news broke.*'
  '*Because results were better than last year,* morale was high.'
  'The fax machine, *which is now so common,* has changed our working lives.'

  The first is an adverbial clause of 'time' modifying *called* (saying when the 'calling' took place).

  The second is an adverbial clause of 'reason' modifying *was* (saying why morale 'was' high).

  The third is an adjectival clause describing *fax machine.*

- The **phrase** is a group of words without a verb, used to expand another part of the sentence:

  '*Last on the scene,* she acted very quickly' (adjectival phrase, describing *she,* the subject)

  'He spoke *in a very boring manner*' (adverbial phrase, describing how he *spoke*)

  You need to take great care in placing clauses and phrases, or your meaning can easily be ambiguous or even absurd. The moral is to keep clauses and phrases as close as possible to the other words they are related to.

  For sale, piano, by lady going abroad, in a walnut case (!)

19.6 The architecture of the sentence

Subject and predicate

Every sentence must have a 'subject' – the person or thing under discussion; and every sentence must have a 'predicate' – what is said about the subject. Example:

Subject		Predicate
The manager	+	has interviewed all the candidates

The subject is usually a noun or pronoun; the predicate must have a verb, since it is the verb that tells us what is done or said to be.

Where there is another person or thing directly affected by the verb, this is called the 'object'. Example:

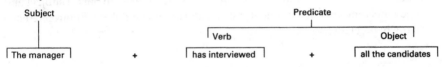

It is possible to go on dividing the parts of a sentence into twos in this way and this process of breaking down the structure of a sentence, called 'binary analysis' can be quite a useful way of making the structure of a sentence clearer, like this:

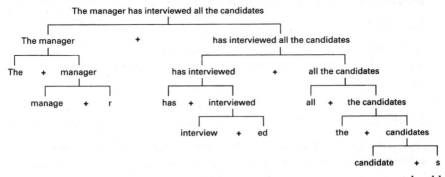

Now I am not suggesting that every time you write or utter a sentence you should go through this process. Fortunately most of the time we are able to speak and write quite fluently and work out, without thinking, how to structure our sentences. But, sometimes things go wrong: we get stuck in the middle of a sentence and are not sure how to finish it grammatically; or we re-read a sentence and it sounds wrong and we are not sure why. Sometimes in these circumstances it is helpful to be able to work out the *architecture* of the sentence in order to solve the problem. Try it out next time you need help in constructing a sentence. In the meantime, it may be worth bearing it in mind as we go on to look at more complicated sentences and the parts of speech in more detail.

More complicated sentences

We do not usually write in a series of short sentences like the ones we have analysed so far; we *link* two or three sentences together. This can be done by:

- *Joining them with conjunctions* (In this case we call the 'sentences' that combine to make the main sentence 'main clauses' – they each have a subject and a verb and without the conjunction could stand alone.)

  Example:

  sentence

  main (or independent) clause   *main (or independent) clause*

  The manager has interviewed   but   he has not made a decision.
  all the candidates,

  (The manager has interviewed all the candidates.) (He has not made a decision.)

Sentences consisting of two or more main clauses are called '*compound sentences*'.

- *Making one sentence the central one and having one or more others depending on it* (The 'sentences' which are depending on the main clause to make sense are called 'dependent' or 'subordinate clauses'; although they too have a subject and predicate, they are not completely and clearly understandable without reference to the main clause.)

Example 1

main clause	*subordinate clause*
He has seen all the candidates	who have applied for the job.

'Who have applied for the job' is a subordinate or dependent clause because it depends for its meaning on the main clause.

Example 2

subordinate clause	*main clause*
Although he has seen all the candidates,	he has not made a decision.

Or:

main clause	*subordinate clause*
He has seen all the candidates,	although he has not made a decision.

Note: 'although' is a conjunction but it cannot join main clauses because it is a subordinate conjunction, not a 'pure' conjunction. See 'Conjunctions', pp. 379–83.

Sentences consisting of a main clause and at least one subordinate clause are called '*complex sentences*'.

- *Turning the less important sentences into 'phrases' or even single words and adding these to the central sentence* (A 'phrase' is a group of related words, *without* a subject and a predicate, used as a part of speech, so a phrase could be called an adverbial phrase if it functions like an adverb in the sentence.)

In the following example, mark the main clause, the subordinate clause and the adverbial phrase.

> Although he has interviewed all the candidates with great care,
> he has not made a decision.

subordinate clause

Although he has interviewed all the candidates with great care

main clause	*phrase*
he has not made a decision	*(adverbial)*

'With great care' is a phrase because it does not have a subject and a predicate and it certainly cannot stand alone. It acts in this sentence as an adverb in that it describes how the interviewing was done.

It is useful to be able to recognise phrases, clauses and sentences because, as we shall see, you will be better equipped to avoid grammatical and punctuation errors.

In addition, you should be able to combine them in different ways to serve different purposes and create different effects.

See what you think of the following passage:

> Telecom Italia has been created from the merger of five companies. The need for a new, single entity has many causes. One is rapid technological development. Another is the growing liberalisation of the telecommunications sector. Finally, there is market globalisation. The new entity will benefit from the past experience and results of the five separate companies. It will be able and ready to assume a prominent and significant position in the international telecoms market.

As one writer said: 'The human mind welcomes variety and a change of pace. It craves the freshness of different kinds of sentences. It does not want them to come marching out all the same, like so many cartridge boxes off the end of an assembly line.' The sentences in the passage above are all *simple* sentences and the effect on the reader is likely to be very similar to that produced by watching identical boxes falling off the end of an assembly line.

Assignment: Try rewriting the passage using a variety of sentence structures – simple, compound and complex.

Without too much overhaul it would be possible to produce something like this:

> Telecom Italia has been created from the merger of five companies. Rapid technological development, the growing liberalisation of the telecommunications sector and market globalisation have generated the need for a new, single entity which will benefit from the past experience and results of the five separate companies. It will now be able and ready to assume a prominent and significant position in the international telecoms market.

The effect is still direct and clear. None of the sentences is too long for the reader to cope with and yet the passage flows more smoothly and provides a variety of pace which should keep the reader's interest.

However, in trying to avoid a series of simple, staccato-like sentences, there is always a danger of going to the other extreme. You might be amused (or bemused!) to read the original version of this passage, which was borrowed from an advertisement for Italy's telecoms operator, Telecom Italia. The paragraph consists of one sentence that is 66 words long!

Rapid technological development, the growing liberalisation of the telecommunications sector and market globalisation have generated the need for a new, single entity, Telecom Italia, which has been created from the merger of five companies and which, benefiting from the past experience and results of the five separate companies, will now be able and ready to assume a prominent and significant position in the international telecoms market.

There are not many readers who would be able to keep up with that sentence and still fewer who would be able to pick out the main idea of the sentence.

Further reading

Burton, S.H., *Mastering English Grammar*, Palgrave Macmillan, 1984

Hilton, Catherine, *Getting to Grips with Punctuation and Grammar*, Letts 1992

Peck, John and Coyle, Martin, *The Student's Guide to Writing*, Palgrave Macmillan, 1999

Rose, Jean, *The Mature Student's Guide to Writing*, Palgrave Macmillan, 2001

20 Common problems with English

You should now be aware of the basic framework of the English language and of some of the basic terms used to describe the various parts of speech and their functions. We now need to look at these in rather more detail in order to discover some of the typical problems which arise from not sticking to the accepted rules and conventions. It is not simply a case of obeying the rules for the sake of obeying rules. It is more a case of trying to obey the conventions in order to avoid being unclear and ambiguous when we are communicating.

20.1 Subject–verb agreement

A verb must agree in number with its subject, so we say: 'The man *catches* the ball', but 'the men *catch* the train'. We make the verb 'to catch' plural because its subject, 'the men', is plural. That is fairly straightforward and in most simple cases the majority of people don't have too much difficulty. The problems arise when the sentence becomes complicated and it is difficult to be sure exactly which word or words represent the subject of the sentence.

Multiple subjects

(i) 'and'. When two subjects are joined together by 'and', the verb must be plural rather than singular:

right   The man catches the train.
right   The man *and* his son catch the train.
wrong In the garden there *was* a fountain and a swimming pool.
right   In the garden there *were* a fountain and a swimming pool.

But when two singular nouns represent one subject they are followed by a singular verb: 'The chairman and the founder of the company *are* (both) to be invited', *but* 'The chairman and founder of the company *is* to be invited'. (In the latter case, the chairman is the founder of the company, that is, one person. Note also that in this case the definite article 'the' is used only once.)

Similarly, when the two words connected by 'and' represent one idea or are closely connected in thought, for example whisky and soda, fish and chips, they take a singular verb:

'The bread and butter *was* piled high on the plate.'

(ii) 'With', 'together with', 'as well as' are also prepositions which can join two subjects. However, they have the effect of making one subject subordinate to the other so that the verb in this case is singular not plural:

The man, with his son, *catches the train.*
The boy, as well as his sister, *goes* to that school.

Other prepositions which have this effect are 'in addition to' and 'including'.

Collective nouns

Some nouns are called collective nouns. It is important to recognise them because they affect the use of verbs. Traditionally, a collective noun, for example, 'army', 'committee', 'audience', 'class', is treated as singular and therefore takes a singular verb and a singular pronoun:

An army *fights* on *its* stomach.
The audience *was* most impressed by the speaker.

However, this rather inflexible rule has been relaxed in recent years so that the verb can now be either singular or plural according to whether our attention is directed to the group as a single unit or to the individuals composing the group:

The audience *was* too large for the room.
The audience *were* talking quietly among themselves.

Beware! Whether singular or plural is selected as the more appropriate, it is important to be consistent; you cannot change from singular to plural in the same sentence, as in this confusing example:

The committee was not unanimous because some of them felt that it had not had enough time to discuss all the issues.

Either 'the committee were' and 'they had' or 'some of the members felt' would make the sentence consistent and therefore acceptable.

But when a collective noun is followed by 'of' plus a plural noun as in: 'a committee of women', 'a team of engineers', 'a collection of stamps', a common mistake is to treat it as a plural subject:

wrong   A committee of women were formed.
right   A committee of women was formed.

As in the last example the problem of uncertainty often arises when the subject is separated from the verb by a number of other words: 'The reasons for the move to the new building *were* explained'. By the time you get to the verb it is easy to forget which of the nouns is the real subject. This is probably the main reason for the errors described in the next three sections.

Other singular nouns

But, kind, sort and type

These are all singular nouns:

> *wrong* These kinds of problems are the most difficult.
> *right*   This kind of problem is the most difficult.

It is true that *'these kind'* and *'those sort'* are often heard in conversations, but whereas this might be acceptable in informal spoken English, in business writing it is wiser to use the correct form. In practice the error is usually made even worse by non-agreement of the demonstrative adjective ('this', 'that', 'these' and 'those') as well!

> *very wrong*   These *kind of problems are* the most difficult.

In this example, neither does the verb agree with its subject ('kind') nor the demonstrative adjective agree with its noun, so we end up with this muddle:

> pl.   s.   pl.   pl.
> These kind of problems are ...

To conclude this very confusing area with some advice, it is probably wiser to make sure all the constituent parts of the subject and verb are kept in the singular whenever possible and then the rule is simpler to obey.

Each, every, everyone, everybody, anyone, anybody, no one, nobody, none

These, too, are all singulars. While it is easy to attribute the idea of a lot of people to words which include 'every' and 'any', perhaps it would be helpful to think always of the idea of 'one' which is either expressed or understood in these words, so:

> each = each (one)
> everybody = every*one*
> anybody = any*one*

> *wrong* All the students have a book (only one book among them all?).
> *right*   Each of the students has a book.
> *right*   None of the students has a book.
> *right*   None of the passengers was injured. (frequently heard in news broadcasts)

Either, neither

Both 'either' and 'neither' are also singular: 'Neither of the secretaries *knows* when the meeting starts.'

The use of 'either ... or' and 'neither ... nor' can present a few problems though. The rule is that the verb agrees with the nearer of the subjects. However, while 'Neither my husband nor I am able to drive' is correct it sounds rather odd. In cases like this it is better to try to find another way to express it: 'Neither my husband nor I can drive' replaces the verb with another which sounds the same in the singular and plural. Where this is not possible it may be necessary to recast the sentence completely: 'My husband and I are unable to drive.'

Work out carefully the exact subject in the sentence and check that the verb agrees. Don't be misled by elements that fall between the subject and the verb, or by the fact that the normal word order – subject, verb, object – is reversed.

Self-Check

Now re-check your answers to **3, 5, 7, 20, 24, 42** and **50** in the test in Chapter 19 (Section 19.3).

Answers

3 Wrong The subject is 'each' which takes the singular, so 'are' should be 'is'. There is also a spelling mistake in this sentence – 'separately' should be 'separately'. This is a very common spelling mistake. If you didn't spot the spelling error, learn the correct spelling now.

5 Right 'Together with' has the effect of making 'his assistants' subordinate to 'the manager' so, although they are both subjects, the verb must agree with 'the manager' which, is singular.

7 Wrong 'who is taking the examination' is a subordinate clause in which 'who' is the subject, but 'who' is a relative pronoun referring back to 'the students'. It is the students who are taking the examination, so the verb 'to be' must agree with the students and must therefore be plural – 'are taking'.

20 Wrong In this sentence 'the power' is the real subject of the verb 'to be', so the sentence should read: 'The power of her arguments, which were very persuasive, *was* not enough.'
Did you also notice that 'arguments' was spelled incorrectly in the original sentence? The verb 'argue' drops its 'e' when it is turned into the noun 'argument'.

24 Wrong 'Neither' is the real subject of the sentence, and as we have seen 'neither' is singular and must therefore take a singular verb, so the sentence should read: 'Neither of the rooms *was* laid out ... .' There is another mistake in this sentence, but we will come to that when we look at problems associated with the use of 'like' and 'as' (p. 382.)

42 Wrong There are several pitfalls in this sentence. Did you sort them out? The real subject is 'kind' which as we have seen is usually better left singular, so its verb should be singular – 'is' (very difficult). But if 'kind' is singular then its adjective (in this case a demonstrative adjective) should also be singular – '*This* kind' – and 'problems' should also be singular: 'This kind of problem is very difficult to solve.' If you at least managed to get everything to agree – '*These* kinds of problems *are* very difficult to solve – then you deserve half marks; but as we have seen, the whole phrase is better when it is all singular.

50 **Wrong**   Here the subject of the sentence is 'people and questions' so the verb must be plural – 'were' instead of 'was'.

There are also some problems in this sentence concerned with 'less' and 'fewer' but we will look more closely at these when we come to problems with the correct use of adjectives (see Section 20.3, p. 365).

20.2   Problems with verbs

Main and subordinate verbs

The verb, as we have seen, indicates what is said or done, and is the key word in the sentence, since without a main verb you cannot have a sentence. But what is a main verb?

Self-Check

Try to pick out the main verbs in the following sentences.

1 She answered the letter.
2 She read out the minutes of the meeting and then signed them.
3 While she was signing them someone began to speak.
4 While she was signing them, someone began to speak, although the discussion had not officially begun.

In **1**, 'answered' must of course be the main verb because it is a simple sentence and a simple sentence has only one main verb. **2** consists of two simple sentences joined by 'and' to make a compound sentence, so there are two main verbs – 'read out' and 'signed'. When we come to **3** things become more difficult because this is a complex sentence consisting of one main clause and one subordinate clause, so the main verb is the one in the main clause, that is, 'began'. **4** is again more difficult because this too is a complex sentence but this time with a main clause and *two* subordinate clauses. The main verb is therefore the verb in the main clause – 'began'.

It is important to be able to recognise the main verb because, as we shall see, several common errors arise from not being able to recognise which is the main verb, which is the subordinate verb, or which is just a part of a verb – like a participle – which sometimes behaves more like a noun than a verb.

Active and passive voice

When you want to show that the subject of the sentence is performing the action, you should use a verb in the *active* voice:

The auditor *approved* the accounts.

But when the subject of the sentence is being acted upon, having something done to it by something or someone else, you can use a verb in the *passive* voice:

The accounts *were approved* by the auditor.

It is important to be able to recognise the difference between the active and the passive voice because it is sometimes useful to draw attention away from the person who did the action and concentrate the reader's attention on the thing that was acted upon:

The management *shut* the factory for three weeks every year.
The factory *was shut* for three weeks every year.

If the person who does the action is not as important as the thing that is acted upon, then the passive voice is a useful mechanism for focusing on what is important.

However, traditionally there has been a tendency to use the passive voice too much in business writing, particularly in reports. This habit has probably been encouraged by the need for 'objectivity' and the consequent removal of 'people' with their subjective opinions from formal factual reporting. This had led to a style of writing which is therefore very cold and lacking in vitality.

Self-Check

Which of the following do you prefer?

The consent of H M The Queen to the merger of the Department of Employment with the Department of Education was given with effect from 15 July.

H M The Queen has consented to the merger of the Department of Employment with the Department of Education with effect from 15 July.

Neither of the sentences is particularly readable but in the first sentence we have to wait until almost the end of the sentence before we discover what happened to the 'consent'. In the second sentence at least the style is more direct and the main 'idea' of the sentence is brought nearer the beginning of the sentence.

'The consent ... was given' in the first sentence is an example of the *passive*, whereas in the second sentence I have changed it into the *active*: 'has consented'. If the Grammar-Checker on your computer says you have used the passive, find the verb and ask the question 'by whom' was this done. Then make that the subject. A passive verb always contains the verb 'to be' (*was, is, were, have been, etc.*) + the past participle, which with most verbs ends in '-ed' (*arranged, joined*) but with irregular verbs may end with -t or -en (*given*).

In order to encourage business writing to be more straightforward and lively there is now a trend towards using the active voice wherever possible and appropriate. In particular you should try to avoid the 'impersonal passive' such as 'It is felt that ... ' for 'We feel that ... ' or 'It is regretted that ... ' for 'We (or I) regret that ... '

In letters, too, the use of the impersonal passive gives the reader the impression that they are dealing with robots rather than human beings. Active verbs make for an active style which is easier to read and gives an impression of liveliness and action.

Infinitives

Infinitives are verb forms that indicate in a general way an action, or a state of being. They are identified by 'to', which is either expressed or just understood. Infinitives can be used as nouns, adverbs or adjectives:

noun (subject)	*To err* is human.
noun (predicate)	His intention is *to work*.
adjective	Here are the letters *to be signed*.
adverb	She has gone *to get* the report.

After some verbs – 'make', 'hear', 'watch', 'bid', 'let', 'help', 'dare', 'feel', 'see' – the sign of the infinitive 'to' is, or can be, omitted:

He heard him *shout out*.
They watched her *start* the conveyor belt.

Beware the split infinitive! If an adverb is placed between 'to' and the main stem of the verb – 'to carefully follow', 'to quickly discover' – we call it splitting the infinitive and it is still regarded by many people as incorrect. However, in colloquial English people do split infinitives all the time – 'You're not going to actually rewrite it all?' or 'We will have to completely reconsider the decision'. Probably the most famous split infinitive is 'to boldly go', and it is worth noting that Americans split their infinitives all the time without even being aware of it. Despite the objections of the purists, successful modern writers occasionally do use the split infinitive for the sake of clarity or emphasis. Indeed, there is a school of thought that claims that the real infinitive is a single word, that is, 'follow', 'discover', 'go' and the particle 'to' is not part of the infinitive or part of the verb at all. Consequently, it is perfectly ok to put another word, between the 'to' and the verb. As with other matters of style it is a question of judgement.

There are two things to consider: first your reader. If you know you are writing to someone who will react badly to a split infinitive, then make sure the adverb is placed before or after the infinitive.

split	We therefore ask you to carefully consider this proposal.
normal order	We therefore ask you to consider this proposal carefully.

Your second consideration should be one of style. In the majority of cases a split infinitive just sounds awkward and should therefore be avoided on those grounds alone. However, very occasionally, it may sound more awkward *not* to split the infinitive. In this case, if your reader would be offended both by a split infinitive and by the awkward style arising from avoiding it, it is probably wiser to recast the phrase or sentence completely. (Not, you notice, 'wiser to completely recast the phrase or sentence'.)

Yes; it contains a split infinitive and should read: '... to correct carefully...' not '... to carefully correct...' or better still put 'carefully' after 'the errors'.

Participles

The present participle is the form of the verb ending in 'ing' and denotes action in progress, for example 'I am starting the report now'. The past participle of a regular verb is formed by adding 'd' or 'ed' to the present tense of the verb, for example.

rain   rained   It has rained hard today.
walk   walked   I have walked five miles across the fields.

Some irregular verbs form their past participle differently, for example 'give, given; speak, spoken; write, written'.

Verbal adjectives

Both the present and past participles can function as adjectives.

present participle   The secretary *taking* notes is very efficient.
('taking' is an adjective qualifying the noun 'secretary'; it is also a verb taking the object 'notes')
past participle   The notes *taken* by the secretary were used after the meeting.
('taken' functions as an adjective qualifying 'notes')

Misrelated and unrelated participles

Participles which are acting as adjectives *must* be attached to nouns, and to the *right* noun.

Having read the report, she was prepared to make the decision.
(She has read the report and she is prepared to make a decision.)

Thanking you for your letter, *we* are enclosing your order.
(We are enclosing your order and we are thanking you.)

One way of checking whether you have attached the participle to a noun is to turn the sentence round so that you start with the subject followed by the participle and ask yourself whether it still makes sense:

Walking into the room, the secretary gasped.
The secretary, walking into the room, gasped.
(The secretary is the same person who walked into the room and gasped.)

Misrelated participles

Careless writing often leads people into the trap of relating the participles to the wrong subject.

Self-Check

Compare this sentence with the one above about the gasping secretary.
Walking into the room, the secretary was already typing the memo.

If 'walking' relates to 'secretary', which it should according to the rules of sentence construction, then we are left with an absurd picture of the secretary typing while on the move! So, if it wasn't the secretary who was walking into the room, who was it? Someone else? The sentence must be expressed:

Walking into the room, *I* saw the secretary already typing the memo.

Now, in the above example because the possibility of secretaries typing while walking is rather remote, we can work out roughly what is meant, having recognised that something is wrong. However, sometimes the same error is committed but because it appears still to make sense, we misunderstand the sentence without realising that we have done so. This is why it is so important to understand the rule and check your writing carefully. For example, let's go back to the gasping secretary:

Walking into the room, the secretary gasped.

Anyone who knows the rules about participles would be right in assuming that it was the secretary who walked into the room and then gasped. However, this is the kind of sentence that can easily and innocently be written by someone who does not know the rule and really meant: someone else walked into the room which caused the secretary to gasp – which is quite another thing altogether.

Self-Check

What about this one?
Unhappy about the decision, the meeting ended.

Who was unhappy about the decision? We would be right in assuming from the statement that the meeting (i.e. all the members present) were unhappy about the decision. However, the truth of the matter is that it was the speaker who was the only one unhappy about the decision. To say what they really meant, they should have said:

Unhappy about the decision, I realised that the meeting was ending.

Or:

Although I was unhappy about the decision, the meeting ended.

Self-Check

Now re-check **11, 38, 44, 47, 49** (Section 19.3). They all contain participles: some used correctly and some used incorrectly. Can you work out which are wrong?

Answers

11 Wrong Who is doing the looking? Not 'the task' which is the subject of the sentence at the moment. The sentence must be recast if it is to be correct.

either   Looking at it the next morning, we (or another pronoun) thought the task seemed easier.

or   When we looked at it the next morning, the task seemed easier.

38 Right   She saw and she entered.

44 Wrong   Surely the bull wasn't cycling? A correct version would be:

As I was cycling along the lane, the bull suddenly charged out in front of me.

47 Wrong   The secretary could not be going into the office at the same time as typing. It must be someone else.

As I entered the office, the secretary could be seen …

49 Wrong   The manager is the subject of the sentence but did not steal the cash – 'I' did, so once again the sentence must be recast:

Since I stole the cash, the manager had no option …

Unrelated participles

Another trap awaiting the careless writer is the unrelated participle. Instead of being related to the wrong noun or pronoun, which is bad enough, the participle is not related to anything at all.

Having thanked the speaker for his contribution, there was nothing more to do.

Not only do we not know who thanked the speaker, but also we do not know who had 'nothing more to do'. The person who thanked the speaker? The speaker? The audience? This error can also lead to absurd pictures:

Putting the letter on the desk, there was an enormous crash and the ceiling fell down.

The unrelated participle is often related to errors of punctuation. For instance, a mistake commonly found at the beginning of letters leaves the sentence unfinished and the subject of the participle, at best, in the next sentence:

Thanking you for your letter of 3 May, in which you ordered shelving.
Unfortunately we are unable to complete your order at the moment.

The first 'sentence' is not a sentence because it has no subject and no main verb. 'Thanking' is only a participle, that is, a part of a verb, and not a main verb. The reader is left in mid-air. Eventually their curiosity about who or what might be doing the thanking is more or less satisfied in the second sentence when the pronoun 'we' appears, but it is all very unsatisfactory and not guaranteed to create a very good impression of the writer or the writer's organisation.

Self-Check

How would you correct the example above?

Either the two sentences must be joined together to make one:

Thanking you for your letter of 3 May, in which you ordered shelving, we are unfortunately unable to complete your order at the moment.

Or, it would be even better expressed if two new sentences were produced:

(We) Thank you for your order for shelving of 3 May. Unfortunately, we are unable to complete your order at the moment.

Similarly, the ends of letters often present the same problem if the hackneyed expression 'Thanking you in anticipation. Yours faithfully' is used. This is a legacy from the days when it was normal and correct to end a letter:

Thanking you in anticipation of a favourable reply, we remain, dear sirs, your obedient and humble servants,

G. Pentwhistle & Sons.

Notice the punctuation. Though this expression is now outdated and should never be used, it is correctly expressed and punctuated as one whole sentence from 'Thanking' to 'Sons'.

Although most people now drop 'of a favourable reply, we remain, dear sirs, your obedient and humble servants' some people still treat what is left as a sentence, putting a full stop after 'anticipation' even though the clause no longer has a main verb, and leaving the reader in mid-air again. If in doubt therefore, it is probably better to avoid these expressions completely and use instead a straightforward sentence like:

We look forward to hearing from you.

Now let's turn to another problem.

Beware! The present participle looks the same as a verbal noun (gerund) which serves a different function.

Verbal nouns (or gerunds)

Verbal nouns, or gerunds as they are sometimes called, are verb forms which can function in a sentence, as their name suggests, as nouns. The words 'writing', 'dictating', 'selling', 'advertising' are examples of gerunds which can often occur in business messages!

Writing good reports requires skill.
She was congratulated on stepping in at short notice.

Self-Check

Which of the following are present participles (or verbal adjectives) and which are gerunds (or verbal nouns)?

1 The woman writing the letter is the managing director.
2 Writing the letter is the hardest job.

---

3 He does not like speaking in public.
4 Looking closely at the evidence, you will see that the conclusions are justified.

Answers

1 'Writing' is a participle acting as a verbal adjective which qualifies, or describes 'the woman'.
2 In this sentence 'writing' is a gerund. It is acting as a noun and the subject of the sentence and as a verb taking the object 'the letter'.
3 Similarly in this sentence, 'speaking' is a gerund but this time it is acting as the object of the verb 'does not like'.
4 This one is more difficult. Don't be misled by finding 'looking' at the beginning of the sentence where the gerund often is if it is acting as the subject of the sentence. In this case, 'looking' is a participle acting as an adjective to qualify 'you'. The sentence could equally well read:

You, looking closely at the evidence, will see that the conclusions are justified.

Perhaps you didn't get them all right, but you should try to learn the difference because a common error arises from ignoring the difference.

Self-Check

Is the following sentence correct?
He disliked me reading the memo.

Strictly speaking it is incorrect, because 'reading' functions as a noun and therefore, as with any other noun, the qualifying noun, or pronoun, in this case 'me', should be in the possessive form 'my'.

In other words, it wasn't that he disliked 'me' in the act of reading the memo; he disliked the act itself. The sentence should therefore read:

He disliked *my* reading the memo.

Similarly:

He regarded *my* leaving the company as a mistake.
The shop's opening was reported on the front page.

Of course, as with many other correct usages, too rigid adherence to the rule can lead to problems of style. In this case, the possessive form can lead to very awkward-sounding sentences:

The manager complained about the treasurer's and the secretary's being late for the meeting.

Owing to John's and David's falling ill, the completion of the project will be delayed.

Most careful writers, despite knowing the rule, would probably omit the possessives in sentences like these, or better still, find another less cumbersome way to express them:

> The manager complained that the treasurer and the secretary were both late for the meeting.
>
> Because John and David have fallen ill, the completion of the project will be delayed.

or even better, to avoid the passive *will be delayed*:

> Because John and David are both ill, we shall have to delay the project.

Self-Check

Now check **1**, **12**, **18** and **48** (Section 19.3). Can you see what is wrong?

Answers

1 Wrong   The 'sentence' is incomplete because there is no subject. A correct version would be:

'(We) Thank you for your letter of 6 February in which you complained about the control mechanism.'

(*Note:* it is acceptable to leave out the pronoun 'we' or 'I' as it is understood.) Did you also notice that February needs an 'r' in the middle?

12 Wrong   We did not complain about 'them', but about the act of having taken the notice off the board. 'Having taken' is a gerund or verbal noun in this sentence so 'them' should be 'their'.

18 Wrong   The same mistake again. It should be:

'I do not remember his having told me about the meeting.'

48 Wrong   This is an example of an unrelated participle. 'Having opened' is not related or attached to anything in particular. Who opened the meeting? The same person or people who could not avoid the issue?
A better version might be:

'Having opened the meeting, I had no way of avoiding the issue.'

Or:

'The meeting having opened (or having been opened) there was ... ' which avoids the problem of stating who exactly was concerned, but does not leave a participle unattached.

The Subjunctive

Self-Check

Is there anything wrong or strange about these two sentences?

If I were in his place, I should resign.
The committee recommended that the procedure be introduced.

The *subjunctive mood* of the verb used for hypotheses and commands has now almost disappeared from use but it is still retained to express a supposition, a wish or a doubt. In the two sentences above you may have thought that 'were' should have been 'was' and that 'be' sounded rather odd because we usually say 'I was' and 'the procedure is'. However, they are both perfectly correct uses of the subjunctive which have survived, and should be used if you wish to write correctly. The first is an example in common use of the subjunctive to express a hypothesis that is not a fact, and the second is an example of established idiomatic use of the subjunctive after any words of command or desire. The subjunctive is still therefore commonly used in the following examples:

1 *Wishing, hypothesis:*

You are a very good speaker; I wish I were. (I *wish*, but I'm not)

2 '*If ... were*' clauses
Note: where an ordinary condition is expressed 'is' and 'was' can be used as usual but note the difference:

If the speaker *is* here, we can begin. (I don't know whether she is or not)
If the speaker *were* here, we could begin. (But she is not here)

3 *Supposition*
Suppose she *were* to arrive late.

4 *Command and desire*
This use is particularly well established in modern business writing and formal English:

Public opinion demands that an inquiry *be* held.
I move that a chairman *be* appointed. (Always used in a formal motion at a meeting.)
It is suggested that traffic lights *be* installed to reduce the danger.
He has asked that the ban *be* temporarily lifted.
She is anxious that the truth *be* known.

Note: In these examples an acceptable alternative is to use 'should be', but whichever form you choose, take care to be consistent, using instructions which are 'grammatically parallel', for example, when listing recommendations.

Unfortunately, the following horrific example of inconsistency in recommendations, which appears all too frequently at the end of many reports, reveals not only the writer's unease with the use of the subjunctive, but also their inability to 'hear' the jarring effect of mixing structures:

It is recommended that:

1 a course be held to provide training for staff;
2 a training officer should be appointed;
3 two staff will be seconded to organise the training course.

If you cannot grasp the rules about the subjunctive you will certainly be in good company, since many well-respected writers believe that rather than misuse it we should avoid it, and Somerset Maugham went even further when he said: 'The subjunctive is in its death throes, and the best thing to do is to put it out of its misery as soon as possible.'

However, even if you prefer to join the band of scholars devoted to the abolition of the subjunctive, you should never be guilty of saying: 'If I *was* you.' All sorts of people who are not at all familiar with the rules of grammar and have probably never heard of the subjunctive will frown on this error.

Self-Check

Now re-check **46** (Section 19.3).

Answer

Yes; it should read: 'If I were you ... (because I'm not you)'

Tenses

The tense is that form of the verb or use of the verb which indicates the *time* of an action. The three main tenses are present, past and future:

'I walk' (present), 'I walked' (past), 'I shall walk' (future).

Unfortunately the tense of the verb can cause difficulty but the whole subject of tenses is sufficiently complicated as to be worthy of a book of its own. However, the accurate timing of verbs is an important communication skill and it is worth becoming familiar with the different tenses and their uses so that you can write precisely what you mean. The verb must indicate the exact time of the action.

Self-Check

Compare the different meanings indicated by:

They promised that they will pay.
They promised that they would pay.

In the first example, though they promised in the past, they have not paid yet, and are not expected to pay until some time in the future. In the second example, the act of paying was in the future at the time they promised, but may or may not have been done yet – a subtle difference which could have great significance!

Similarly:

I should like to have visited New York.
I should have liked to visit New York.

The first means that at the present moment, 'I wish I had visited New York', but the second means that at some time in the past I wanted to visit New York. Some people try to make it even more complicated (or simpler!) by writing instead of either sentence:

I should have liked to have visited New York.

Strictly speaking this has yet another meaning:

At some time in the past I wished that I had visited New York at a time even further back in the past.

However, this meaning is usually not the one intended and is more likely to be the result of mere clumsy use of the past infinitive ('to have visited'), which should certainly not be used unless absolutely necessary to convey a very particular meaning. Look back at **12** (Section 19.3). Many people might have written:

We complained about their taking the notice off the board

But presumably the act of taking the notice off the board must have taken place further back in the past than the act of complaining, so it is more correct to say:

We complained about their having taken the notice off the board

Similarly in **18** (Section 19.3) if the act of remembering is taking place in the present, then the act of telling must have taken place in the past, so it is more correct to say:

I do not remember his having told me about the meeting

This brief selection of the complex range of meanings which can be conveyed by the use of different tenses should be enough to persuade you that, at the very least, considerable care needs to be given to the choice of tense, if you are to say what you really mean. However, if you are already completely bemused you might be happier referring to a basic explanation of English verbs (see *The Oxford Guide to English Grammar*, Oxford University Press, 1994).

shall and will

A common error is to assume that 'shall' and 'will' are interchangeable without altering their meaning.

Future

I shall	We shall
You will	You will
He will	They will
She will	
It will	

So, in a simple statement using the future tense:

I shall sit the exams next month.
He will take his exams later.

Determination. However, if you wish to convey the meaning of determination in the future, 'shall' and 'will' are reversed:

I will pass my exams. (I am determined to)
He shall go. (I shall see that he goes)

Conditional. 'Should' and 'would' follow the same rules as 'shall' and 'will'. They are used in conditional sentences referring to the present time:

I shall go if you will come with me.
I should go if you would come with me. (There is doubt about going)

However, all tenses take 'should' when it means 'ought to':

He should go without me. (He ought to go without me.)

This distinction between the use of 'shall' and 'will' and 'should' and 'would' is now considered rather old-fashioned and, particularly in spoken and informal English the modern practice is to use 'will' and 'shall' in all persons, though 'will' is the more common of the two.

20.3   Problems with adjectives

Normally adjectives do not present too many problems but frequent confusion arises over the difference between the comparative and superlative forms.

Comparative

Used to compare *two* objects:

- normally formed by adding 'r' or 'er' to simple adjectives of one syllable and to a few of two syllables:

strong   stronger
wise   wiser
angry   angrier

- most adjectives of more than one syllable form the comparative by adding the word '*more*' (or '*less*') before the simple adjective:

careful   more careful
expensive   less expensive

He is the stronger of the two boys.
This car is more expensive than that one.

Superlative

Used to compare *three or more* objects:

- normally formed by adding *'est'* to adjectives of one syllable and to a few of two syllables:

  fast   fastest
  angry   angriest

- most adjectives of more than one syllable form the superlative by adding *'most'* (or *'least'*) before the simple adjective:

  effective   most effective
  variable   least variable

  This is the fastest car in the world.
  That would be the least expensive method (of several methods).

Self-Check

Choose the correct form of the adjective from those in brackets to complete these sentences:

She was the . . . . . . of the two sisters. (more beautiful, most beautiful)
This is the . . . . car in the range. (faster, fastest)

Don't be misled by the presence of 'the' in the first sentence. Always concentrate on the number of objects being compared. So, 'more beautiful' and 'fastest' are the correct answers.

Other adjectives that deserve attention

This, that, these, those

'This' and 'that' are the only adjectives that have a *plural* form. 'These' and 'those' must be used with plural nouns:

   wrong   *Those* kind ...
   right   *This/That* kind or *those* kinds ...

'Them' is not an adjective and should never be used to qualify a noun:

   very wrong   Can you pass me *them* books?

Either, neither

'Either' or 'neither' refers to *one of two*
'Either' should be used with 'or', 'neither' with 'nor'.

First, last

The words 'first' and 'last', when used with adjectives that express number, are placed before the adjectives:

The first three pages
The last ten issues

Each other, one another

'Each other' refers to *two* objects only; 'one another', to *more than two*:

The two women help each other.
The three women help one another.

Above, below:

'Above' is normally an adverb or a preposition; but modern dictionaries are beginning to recognise its usage as an adjective. 'Below' is an adverb or a preposition; it is not recognised as an adjective and should not be used as one:

right	*Below*, we could see the river in the valley. (adverb)
right	The road ran *above*. (adverb)
right	Put it *below (above)* the other. (preposition)
right	The *above* comments must be checked. (adjective)
wrong	The *below* comments must be checked.

The word 'above' is sometimes used in combinations as in 'above-mentioned', 'above-listed'. Although correct they are usually avoided by careful writers as they create foggy English and a style which is now rather old-fashioned.

Numbers as adjectives

See Appendix C, 'Using numbers'.

Using the articles a, an, the

'A' and 'an' are indefinite articles used to describe a noun as anything in a particular class:

a letter; *an* order

Note: use 'a' before nouns beginning with a consonant: 'a company'; 'a product'. Use 'an' before words beginning with a vowel sound: 'an employee', 'an angry man', 'an HND'.

'The' is the definite article, so named because it selects a specific or definite individual or object from a particular class.

The officer who issues the order (a specific officer; a specific order).

Note: when two nouns in a sentence need different articles, for example, 'a' and 'an', do not make one article do the duty of the other:

Entries to the competition should be sent in an envelope or box (or *a* box).

When two separate things are intended, the article 'the' should be repeated:

I was introduced to the chairman and the managing director (i.e. two people).
I was introduced to the chairman and managing director (i.e. one person).

Be careful not to repeat the indefinite article unnecessarily:

wrong They produced *a* further *a* hundred samples.
right   They produced a further hundred samples.

Self-Check

Now re-check **29** (Section 19.3). Did you spot it as an error the first time?

due

Strictly speaking, 'due' is an adjective but it is often used as a prepositional phrase – 'due to'. This may be frowned on by the purists and you should try not to use it where 'owing to' or 'because of' is what you really mean. You should note that this usage is in the process of changing. For the time being, the safe assumption to make is that the people who read your work may regard the older usage as correct. Unless you are *sure* that you are writing for people who are not pedantic, try to remember to use 'because of' when it fits instead of 'due to'.

right   Absenteeism due to illness is increasing.
wrong Due to illness he missed the meeting.
right   Because of illness, he missed the meeting.

In the first sentence 'due' is an adjective qualifying 'absenteeism' and the sentence could equally well read: 'Absenteeism, which is due to illness, is increasing.' However, in the second sentence 'due to' is being used as a prepositional phrase and should be replaced by 'owing to', 'because of' or 'as a result of' as in the third sentence. In fact, Gowers in The Complete Plain Words says: 'Many readers feel very strongly against the "incorrect use" of "due to", common though it is. Sensible writers should therefore try to form the habit of using it correctly, though they may well feel that there are many points more worth their attention.(!)'

Self-Check

Now re-check **30, 32, 35, 42** and **43** (Section 19.3).

Answers

30 Right 'Due' in this sentence is being correctly used as an adjective to describe 'he'. He was due to become the next president.

32 Wrong 'Due to' really means 'because of' in this sentence so you must either say 'owing to the holidays' or 'because of the holidays'.

35 Wrong There are only two sisters so the comparative should be used not the superlative:

She is the taller of the two girls.

42 Wrong As we have already seen in this sentence there are all kinds of agreement problem but 'these' is an adjective which goes with a plural noun – 'these kinds' – or better still, 'this kind of problem'.

43 Wrong Here again 'due to' should be 'because of' or 'owing to'.*

less and fewer

Frequently 'less' is confused with 'fewer'. 'Less' can only be used to describe a noun which is *uncountable* and is therefore used to describe the degree, the quantity or the extent of something; 'fewer', on the other hand, is used to describe the number of *countable* things:

less expenditure   fewer expenses
less paper   fewer papers
less money   fewer pounds

Note: 'less' is always followed by a *singular* noun; 'fewer' is always followed by a plural noun.

Self-Check

Now re-check **23, 36, 45, 50** (Section 19.3).

Answers

23 Right 'Paper' is singular, it cannot be counted and the sentence is concerned with the quantity or amount of paper, so 'less' is correct.

36 Wrong In this case, we are concerned with the number of papers, so 'fewer' would be correct.

45 Wrong Again we are concerned with a number of problems, so it should be 'fewer' problems.

50 Wrong 'Fewer people' is correct but 'less questions' is wrong; it should be 'fewer questions'. Of course, as we have seen, this sentence is also wrong because the verb 'was' should be plural 'were' to agree with its subject 'people and questions'.

20.4   Problems with adverbs

Common problems

as ... as, so ... as

If equality is stated, use 'as ... as'; if negative comparison is made, use 'so ... as'.

Profits are *as* good this year *as* they were last year.
Profits are not *so* good this year *as* they were last year.

farther, further

There is a great deal of controversy surrounding the correct use of these two words (which can both be used as adverb or adjective); 'farther' is usually preferred for reference to spatial distance, and 'further' for reference to time, quantity or degree:

He lives farther away than I do.
You will not succeed without further effort.

real, very

'Real' is an adjective of quality. 'Very' is an adverb of degree. 'Real' must be used with a noun; 'very' to modify an adjective or an adverb:

As a singer, she has *real* talent.
This report is *very* (not *real*) good.
He spoke *very* (or *really*, not *real*) slowly.

sometime, some time

'Sometime' (one word) is an adverb meaning at one time or other not definitely known. 'Some time' (two words) is a phrase consisting of a noun 'time' qualified by the adjective 'some', indicating length of time:

They visited us *sometime* during last year.
They visited us for *some time* last year.

Placing adverbs

Adverbs should be placed as close as possible to the words they modify. Frequently the wrong meaning is conveyed by careless positioning of the adverb. There is an important difference between:

He did not fly happily. (He did not like flying) *and*
Happily he did not fly. (... because the plane crashed)

Self-Check

How could you punctuate those sentences in order to avoid any doubt about the intended meaning?

'Happily, he did not fly' would remove any doubt.

Some adverbs ('merely', 'hardly', 'scarcely', 'too', 'also', 'almost', 'even' and, above all, 'only') need special care. 'I was only trying to help' is a common statement but what does it really mean? I was trying only to help, not hinder, or I was only trying, that is, not helping but only trying.

Assignment

'Only' can be placed in four different positions to give four different meanings to the following sentence.
She has given £2000 to that charity.
Try it.

Only she has given £2000 to that charity.
(She and nobody else has given that sum.)

She has *only* given £2000 to that charity.
(She has given money but not helped the charity in any other way.)

She has given *only* £2000 to that charity.
(She has given neither more nor less than the sum mentioned.)

She has given £2000 to that charity *only*.
Only to that charity has she given £2000.
(She has given money to no other charity.)

Self-Check

Now re-check **41** (Section 19.3).

Answer

You might have been tempted to join 'some' and 'time' together, but in this sentence 'some' is an adjective describing 'time' and the two should therefore be written as two separate words.

Not only should single-word adverbs be placed as closely as possible to the word they modify, but so also should groups of words acting as adverbs; these are called adverbial phrases or clauses.

Self-Check

Look back at **2, 21, 25** (Section 19.3).

Answers

2 Wrong This sentence is not so much wrong as ambiguous because we are left with the impression that the poor young woman is going to be married for only one year. This impression is caused by misplacing the adverbial phrase 'for one year'. In order to avoid any ambiguity it is necessary to move the phrase closer to the word it modifies – 'required':

Furnished accommodation is required for one year by young woman about to be married.

(Did you also notice that accommodation was spelled incorrectly in the original sentence?)

21 Wrong Similarly in this sentence it sounds as if the pavement is getting longer because the adverbial clause 'which was getting longer' is too far away from a 'queue of people' which it really modifies. (Note also the wrong spelling of 'queue' in the original sentence. 'Cue' is the spelling of the thing used to play billiards.) To avoid ambiguity the sentence must be reordered:

A queue of people, which was getting longer, stretched along the pavement.

25 Wrong This is the same problem but rather more difficult to put right. At the moment we are not sure whether 'which they wrote last week' refers to the report or the section. Slightly better might be:

This is the section, which they wrote last week, from the Deanfield report.

20.5 Problems with pronouns

Pronouns are useful since they act as substitutes for nouns and therefore reduce the need for repetition. However, their use is fraught with problems, if we are to ensure that we write correct English and above all English which is not ambiguous. We have already looked at some of the problems associated with pronouns while exploring the problems of other parts of speech, for example, collective nouns, subject–verb agreement. Now let's look at others.

The main types of pronoun are:

personal	I, me, you, he, him, she, her, one, it, we, us, they, them
relative	who (whom, whose), which, that
demonstrative	this, these, that, those, such, the other, the same
possessive	mine, yours, his, hers, its, our, theirs, whose
interrogative	who? which? what? whom? whose?
reflexive and emphatic	myself, yourself, himself, herself, itself, oneself, ourselves, yourselves, themselves

---

Self-Check

Now re-check **19** (Section 19.3).

Answer

19 Wrong 'Theirselves' does not exist as a pronoun, but is frequently invented as a pronoun to replace 'themselves'. This sentence also contains a spelling mistake. Did you spot it? 'Dissapointed' should be spelled 'disappointed'.

Subject–object confusion

In English, unlike some other languages, most words do not change their form when they are being used as the object of a verb rather than the subject, for example,

The child hit the ball.
The car hit the child.

In both these sentences 'the child' remains the same even though in the first sentence 'the child' is the subject of the verb and in the second sentence 'the child' is the object of the verb.

However, pronouns do change their form depending on their function in the sentence:

I walk (*I* is the subject)

He walks towards me (*me* is in the objective form because it follows a preposition *towards* and prepositions take the objective form)

Those books are mine (*mine* is a pronoun in the possessive form)

Self-Check

Which of the pronouns in the middle of p. 368 can be used only in the objective form, that is, as the object of the verb or preposition?

Answer

'Me', 'him', 'her', 'us', 'them', 'whom'

One of the commonest errors is to use the subject instead of the object form, or vice versa:

Matthew and me went to the cinema.

If you take away 'Matthew and', it becomes obvious that you would not say: 'me went to the cinema' so the sentence above should have read:

Matthew and *I* went to the cinema.

Similarly:

I booked seats at the theatre for my wife and I.

This sounds correct and in colloquial (i.e. everyday) English is frequently heard, but 'I' is governed by the preposition 'for' and you would never say 'for I', so the sentence, if written correctly, should read:

I booked seats at the theatre for my wife and *me.*

A similar confusion seems to arise when comparing persons or things using 'than' or 'as'. The rule is that they can both be subject or object but they must both be in the same case:

She is better than I at working alone: *right* (both subjective)

She is better than me at working alone: *wrong* (*she* is subjective, *me* is objective)

One way to check is to insert the missing but understood 'am'. It then becomes obvious that you cannot say 'me am'.

Self-Check

Which of the following is correct?

1 It helped him more than I.
2 It helped him more than me.
3 She is as tall as I.
4 She is as tall as me.

Answers

Remember, each of the two things compared must be in the same case. The first sentence is therefore wrong because 'him' is an object so 'I' should be 'me'. Similarly the fourth sentence is wrong because 'she' and 'me' are not in the same case. However, this last example demonstrates the 'I/me' controversy. Though it is incorrect, the last sentence sounds right and might be forgiven though noticed in spoken English. But although 'It is I' is correct because the verb 'to be' always takes the nominative or subjective case, you would probably be regarded as pedantic if you insisted on using it in spoken English. However, 'it is me', which is acceptable but incorrect in speech, would probably be regarded as improper in writing.

Self-Check

Now re-check **9**, **13** and **15** (Section 19.3).

Answers

9 Wrong   It should read:

Please book the seats for my wife and me.

13 Right   She cannot type as quickly as I (can).

In this sentence 'as quickly as' is an adverbial phrase describing how I type. 'Can' is understood, but if it had been written it would be clear that since we cannot say 'as quickly as me can' the pronoun in this sentence is correct.

15 Wrong   From the previous explanation it should be clear that the same rule applies in this sentence so it should read:

She does not remember the incident as well as I (do)

Although we may be forgiven for making these mistakes in everyday spoken communication, it is important to know the rules so that our written English is correct and we don't irritate our readers.

Relative pronouns

Who and whom

This subject–object confusion arises in the same way with 'who' and 'whom' which are relative pronouns.

'Who' is the subject and the equivalent of 'he', 'she' or 'they'.
'Whom' is the object and is the equivalent of 'him', 'her' or 'them'.

Apart from knowing the difference, the problem seems to be which one to use, because, as a relative pronoun, 'who/whom' refers back to its antecedent, or noun, but may function in its own clause in a different case from its noun:

She spoke to the man who/whom we hope will be the next chairman.

Although we would say 'She spoke to him' which seems to suggest 'whom' would be correct, or argued another way, in the subordinate clause 'we' might be thought to be the subject of the verb 'hope' making 'whom' the object; however, *the relative pronoun takes its case from its function in the part of the sentence to which it belongs.* Therefore to find out whether it must be 'who' or 'whom' we must isolate the clause in which the relative pronoun appears, make it a separate sentence and replace the relative pronoun with the right personal pronoun:

She spoke to the man. He (we hope) will be the next chairman.

In this way, it becomes clear that the equivalent relative pronoun must be 'who'.

Self-Check

Now re-check **10** and **16** (Section 19.3).

ANSWERS

10 Wrong As with the last example in the text, we must divide the sentence into two clauses:

She is the woman. Her (we expect) to be the next vice-president.
Or:
She is the woman. We expect her to be the next vice-president.

Notice that this time the verb is the infinitive – to be – unlike the last example in the text. In that example the pronoun would have been 'she' but in the test sentence the pronoun must be 'her' so the equivalent relative pronoun must be 'whom'.

She is the woman whom we expect to be the next vice-president.

16 Wrong 'Who' should be 'whom'. Again if we divide the sentence into two we get:

He is the only one. You could ask him.

So the sentence should read:

He is the only one whom you could ask.

Personal and possessive pronouns

Its and it's

A very common error is to use *it's* as a possessive pronoun:

The cat was licking it's coat.

Personal pronouns in the possessive form do *not* require the apostrophe ('). The sentence should read:

The cat was licking its coat.

Its is the correct possessive form of the personal pronoun *it*.
It's is the contraction for *it is*.

Note: the confusion probably arises because nouns *do* form their possessive with an apostrophe, for example, *the boy's book; the boys' books*. Some people seem to be obsessed with using an apostrophe where it is incorrect and even use it when only a simple plural is required. The plural of *company* is companies not *company's*, which is the singular possessive form.

Self-Check

Now re-check **4, 14,** and **33** (Section 19.3).

Answers

  4 Right   *Its* without the apostrophe is correct in this sentence because *its* is being used as the possessive form of *it*.

14 Wrong   In this sentence *its* means *it is* and should therefore be *it's*.
   Note: it is normally better to avoid this contraction in most business writing anyway, so when checking through anything you have written you might be suspicious if you come across *it's* at all. Did you also spot the spelling mistake? *Competitative* should be *competitive*.

33 Wrong   *Company's* should be *companies* because it is a simple plural not a possessive.

Master the difference between *its* and *it's* (and the correct form of plural nouns and plural possessives) *now!* They are basic mistakes which will cause you embarrassment otherwise. If you are still confused turn to the section on 'the apostrophe' in Appendix A.

Possessive pronouns and adjectives of place

Their, there and they're

Another common but very basic mistake is to confuse *their, there* and *they're*.
Their is the possessive form of *they*, for example, *their coats, their ideas*.
There is an adverb of place, eg Here, *there* and everywhere.
They're is a contraction of *they are* (and is not, therefore, often used in written business English).
Note: '*They're* hot so they have put *their* coats in *there*.'

Self-Check

Now check back to **31** (Section 19.3). Did you spot the wrong spelling of 'their'?

Agreement of pronouns

A pronoun must agree with the noun or pronoun which *precedes* it.

Each of the departments has submitted *its* budget.
One must always consider *one's* colleagues.
All the students passed *their* exams.
Anyone may come if he pays *his/her* way.
Each student must obtain *his/her* own grant.

However, this rule perhaps more than any other is causing problems nowadays. Increasingly, there is a tendency to write:

Anyone may come if *they* pay their way.
Each student must obtain *their* own grant.

This may be good anti-sexism, but it is strictly speaking bad grammar and will offend many people – probably as many as the sexism would offend! Even in this book I have found it necessary to write sentences like:

The speaker must always maintain good eye contact with their audience in order to avoid being guilty of sexism.

But in doing so, I have been guilty of breaking one of the strongest rules of grammar. However, the use of 'their' with a singular noun or pronoun preceding it is becoming increasingly accepted as the solution to the sexism dilemma. It is certainly better than having to write 's/he' and 'his/her' all the time and it is not always possible to turn the antecedent into a plural, which is a common solution to the problem:

Speakers must always maintain good eye contact with their audience (or audiences?).

In much of business writing, it is often possible to solve the problem by writing in the second person (you) and it has the advantage of making the writing more friendly and personal.

Compare:

Any member of staff who cannot show her/his pass will be refused entry.
All members of staff who cannot show their passes will be refused entry.
If you cannot show your pass, you will be refused entry.

One

The indefinite pronoun *one* also tends to get people into a tangle. It is inadvisable to substitute *you* for *one* in formal business writing. For instance, in a formal report the readers are made to feel under unjustified attack if they suddenly read:

It has to be said that you can never succeed completely.

when all that is being referred to is people in general. However, it is possible to err the other way:

One does not feel that one has the right to force one's opinion on others when one is not as directly involved as one would like to be.

Repetition of 'one' in this way sounds rather pompous and should be avoided by completely recasting the sentence in a different style.

However, in some cases 'one' is the right and proper pronoun to use, in which case care should be taken to maintain consistency in the pronouns used:

wrong   *One* is bound to agree that *you* can never completely eradicate the problem.

wrong   What could *one* do in the circumstances but consider *their* battle lost?

Which pronoun refers to which?

A very common ambiguity is caused by careless use of pronouns, when the reader is left to guess which of several antecedents is referred to by the pronoun:

She said her mother had moved when she got married.

Who got married? 'She' or 'her mother'?

As with other ambiguities, the error can often cause amusement but in doing so it enables us to work out what was really meant:

Please send me a form for cheap milk. I have a two-month old baby and did not know about it until a neighbour told me.

or, on a slightly more serious note:

Mr Frank Dyer, prosecuting, told the court that he was one of a number of people involved in certain incidents which took place at the school that evening. He said he had gone with a friend to the Youth Club earlier that evening, but they had decided to go to a local pub on their motorcycles.

Presumably Mr Dyer, the prosecuting lawyer, was not the same person who was involved in certain incidents, nor the person who went to the youth club and then to the local pub on a motorcycle! The confusion arises because we are not sure to whom the pronoun 'he' refers.

> *All pronouns must clearly refer to the appropriate antecedents*

In the passage above the antecedent of the first 'he' appears to be Mr Dyer, but obviously this cannot be the case. The correct antecedent should have been inserted to make it clear to whom the pronouns refer:

Mr Frank Dyer, prosecuting, told the court that *Jason Dale* was one of a number of people involved in certain incidents which took place at the school that evening. He said *Dale* had gone with a friend to the Youth Club earlier that evening, but they had decided to go to a local pub on their motorcycles.

Exactly the same problem can arise with careless use of relative pronouns:

This is the chapter from the book which he has just written.

Does 'which' refer to 'chapter' or 'book'? Has he just written the chapter, or just written the book? In order to avoid this kind of ambiguity, it may be necessary to recast the sentence completely:

This is the recently completed chapter from his book.

Moral: if you are to communicate exactly what you intend you must make sure that it is clear to which antecedents your pronouns refer.

Which and that

The correct use of these two pronouns is difficult and complicated, but choosing the wrong one can completely change the intended meaning.

wrong Sweets, which do not contain sugar, should be given to diabetic patients.
right Sweets that do not contain sugar should be given to diabetic patients.

In the first sentence the meaning seems to be that all sweets do not contain sugar, which is untrue. What is meant, and is better expressed by the alternative, is that only sweets containing no sugar should be given to diabetics.

Sir Ernest Gowers in *The Complete Plain Words*, which explains the complexities of these two words in much greater detail, suggests a very useful general rule:

On the whole it makes for smoothness of writing not to use the relative which *where that would do as well, and not to use either if a sentence makes sense and runs pleasantly without.*

Fortunately for us, he also says:

The truth is that for nearly all writers, whatever their level of excellence, the ear is a reliable guide.

So take his advice when in doubt and try speaking the sentence aloud. More than likely you will be able to hear which one is correct, and whether it is possible to drop either without changing the sense.
For instance, in this sentence:

He said that the report that he needed was that one.

it would be possible to remove the first two 'thats' without altering the sense and it would sound a lot easier on the ear:

He said the report he needed was that one.

Beware! Sometimes, particularly when writing in haste and using the words 'say' and 'think' which can generally do without 'that', it is easy to omit words which are essential to the sense of a particular sentence:

The doctor said the patient was ill.

In order to make it absolutely clear that it is the patient who is ill and not the doctor, 'that' must be inserted into the sentence:

The doctor said that the patient was ill.

Of course, if we really wanted to say that the doctor was ill, we would need to punctuate the sentence differently:

'The doctor', said the patient, 'was ill'.

Duplication of that

It is also easy to insert 'that' more than once:

> She said that, in order to keep costs down, that it would be necessary to reduce the workforce.

The sentence needs one 'that' but not two.

Where it is necessary to repeat 'that' in a sentence, special care should be taken to remember which words introduced the first 'that':

> The general spoke to the troops in order to dispel the idea that they might be losing the battle, and that they should be attacking the enemy.

Put like this the general is likely to have had the opposite effect from the one intended. If we remove the first 'that' clause, we are left with:

> The general spoke to the troops to dispel the idea that ... they should be attacking the enemy!

It is important always to check back to make sure that the constructions suit each part of the sentence, particularly with long complex sentences.

Self-Check

Now re-check **6** (Section 19.3).

Answer

6 Wrong   At the moment it sounds as if all the toys are dangerous.
'Toys that are dangerous should not be given to children' makes the meaning clearer, or
'Toys which are dangerous should not be given to children' without commas in both cases.

20.6   Problems with prepositions and conjunctions

Prepositions and conjunctions are both 'connectives' and as their name suggests they are words used to connect ideas which are closely related.

Self-Check

In the following passage all the prepositions and conjunctions have been omitted. Insert the words which have been left out:

> They presented their recommendation (   ) us (   ) the first meeting of the committee, (   ) that was not, (   ) my opinion, the best moment (   ) its discussion.

Self-Check

Which of those omitted words are prepositions and which are conjunctions?

Functions of prepositions

A preposition is a word used to connect a following noun or pronoun to some other word or elements in the sentence. In making the connection, the preposition always indicates the relationship:

… *to* us *at* the first meeting *of* the committee

The preposition is followed by its object, which is a noun, pronoun or the equivalent:

… to *us* at the first *meeting* of the *committee*

To identify the object of the preposition ask 'what?' or 'whom?' after the preposition:

To whom?	to us
At what?	at the meeting
Of whom?	of the committee

A preposition is always followed by an *object* so when the object is a pronoun it must be in the objective case:

So – to me	*right*
Not – to I	*wrong*

Most commonly used prepositions

aboard	around	by	of	toward
about	at	concerning	on	under
above	before	down	till	underneath
across	behind	during	over	until
after	below	except	past	up
against	beneath	for	round	upon
along	beside	from	through	with
amid	between	in	throughout	within
among	beyond	into	to	without

'But' when it means 'except' is also a preposition (see p. 379).
Some prepositions consist of two or more words:

instead of	contrary to
on account of	in reference to
in addition to	to the extent that
devoid of	from beyond

Prepositions and word order

The old rule maintained that sentences should never end with a preposition. However, if this rule is applied too strenuously, it can lead to very awkward-sounding sentences. Winston Churchill, in a successful effort to show how absurd the rule could be when taken too far, is renowned for having said:

This is the sort of English up with which I will not put.

Normally it is fairly easy to avoid putting the preposition at the end of the sentence. However, it is more difficult to avoid when the verb in the sentence is a compound verb (i.e. made from a verb and two prepositions) where the last preposition is essential to the meaning of the verb, as in Sir Winston Churchill's example – 'to put up with'.

So let your ear be the best judge. If the preposition sounds best at the end of the sentence, leave it there.

However, ending a sentence with several prepositions can sound rather odd:

'What', the small boy asked his mother, 'did you want to bring the book I didn't want to be read out of up for?'

But it probably sounded perfectly understandable with the small boy's emphasis on the appropriate words.

Self-Check

Which of these do you prefer?

Have you seen the house she lives in?
Have you seen the house in which she lives?
Have you seen the house she inhabits?

The first sounds acceptable, though perhaps the second would be better in written English, but the third just sounds pompous even though it is correct.

Prepositional idiom

It is also important to use the right preposition, that is, the preposition which is normally accepted as being the correct one:

She answered the teacher. (no preposition)
He had to answer *to* the committee *for* having failed to produce the report (we answer *to* someone *for* doing something).
She substituted the tin trophy *for* the silver one.
The silver trophy was replaced *by* the tin one.
She replaced the silver trophy *with* the tin one.
He communicated his answer *to* the staff.
He communicated *with* his staff regularly.

Other prepositional idioms

to be averse to	to be endowed with
to connive with	to gloat over
to culminate in	to be impervious to
to be deterred from	to be intent upon
to be devoid of	to be marred by
to dissent from	to be sensitive to

Note: to consist of BUT *to comprise* (no preposition) NOT *to comprise of, to be comprised of.* 'A consists of B and C' or 'A comprises B and C'.

An even more common cause of uncertainty arises with the verbs 'compare' and 'to be different':

right   Compared *with* her he is lazy.
wrong   Compared *to* her he is lazy.
right   This problem is different *from* that one.
wrong   This problem is different *to* that one. (But, in US English this is acceptable)
right   He was indifferent *to* her plea.

However, 'compare to' can be used when it means 'to liken or represent as similar'.

Margaret Thatcher compared herself to Winston Churchill.

Among/amongst/between

People often have difficulty determining which of these is correct. Most authorities on the subject seem to agree that 'amongst' is obsolete, as is 'whilst', and has now been replaced by 'among'. If in doubt, therefore use 'among'. However, do not confuse 'among' and 'between'. 'Among' is used where there are three or more items or people, whereas 'between' refers to two only.

Functions of conjunctions

Conjunctions are words which are used to connect words, phrases and clauses:

She will arrive at Heathrow *or* Gatwick (connects words)
He usually arrives in a long plastic mac *and* white tennis shorts (connects phrases)
Her performance is improving, *but* her progress is slow (connects clauses)

Note: in the example above 'but' is a conjunction. Compare its use in that sentence with its use in the following sentences.

But for him, we would have lost the match.
Everyone *but* the MD was there.

In these last two sentences 'but' means 'except' and is therefore used as a preposition (see p. 377).

There are two sorts of conjunctions: coordinate and subordinate.

Coordinate conjunctions

These join elements of equal rank or grammatical relation:

Men *and* women are treated equally here.
She will take a long time, *and* may not complete the work.

The 'and' in the first example connects two nouns, and in the second connects two independent clauses. The principal *coordinate conjunctions* are:

and	likewise
but	moreover
for	neither – nor
neither	nevertheless
nor	not only – but also
or	notwithstanding
accordingly	now
as well as	so
besides	so that
both – and	still
consequently	then
either – or	therefore
furthermore	thus
hence	whether – or
however	yet

pure conjunctions

Note on punctuation: It is important to know which are the 'pure' conjunctions because you should use a *comma* to separate independent *clauses* which are in pairs or in series joined by a 'pure' conjunction:

Men *and* women are treated equally here ('and' is not joining clauses)
First she planned the letter, *and* then she dictated it. (In this instance, 'and' is joining two independent clauses and so a comma is used)

Use a *semi-colon*, however, between independent clauses which are joined by a conjunction that indicates a greater change of thought than is indicated by a 'pure' conjunction. Typical of such conjunctions are:

accordingly
consequently
hence
however
moreover
nevertheless
notwithstanding
therefore

She did not work very hard; consequently she failed the exam.

Correlative conjunctions

These are coordinate conjunctions which are used in pairs:

both – and
either – or
neither – nor
not only – but also
whether – or

Make sure that correlatives are placed *just before* the words or phrases connected:

right   Let me have either the report or the draft.
wrong Let me either have the report or the draft.

Put another way, the words should always be balanced after each half of the correlative:

wrong He will not only make a good secretary but also a good treasurer.
right   He will make not only a good secretary but also a good treasurer.
wrong Either he will be promoted or sacked.
right   He will be either promoted or sacked.

The reason for this rule is that it helps to emphasise the two ideas clearly in the mind of the reader. It is of course also an example of grammatical parallelism. (A good check is to see that the correlatives are followed by the same parts of speech: a pair of nouns, a pair of verbs, etc. for example 'a good secretary/a good treasurer'; 'promoted/sacked'; 'the report/the draft'.)

Subordinate conjunctions

These are used to join a subordinate or independent clause to some word in the main clause:

She was away from work *because* she was ill.
He agreed to do it *on condition that* his family could accompany him.

The main subordinate conjunctions are:

after	so that
although	supposing (colloquial)
as	than
as soon as	that
because	though
before	till
if	unless
in the event that	until
in order that	when
inasmuch as	where
lest	whereas
on condition that	whether – or
provided	while
since	

Beware

No one doubted *that* (not *but that*) he was successful.
He will try *to* (not *and*) come to the meeting.

Like and as

'Like' is a preposition, but frequently it is used incorrectly as a conjunction instead of its corresponding conjunction 'as', which should be used to join clauses:

right   He looks like a kind man. (preposition)
wrong   It looks like they will come.
right   It looks as if they will come.
wrong   I wish I could write like she does.
right   I wish I could write as she does.

Providing and provided

Strictly speaking 'providing' is a present participle and should not be used as a conjunction to replace 'provided'. However, dictionaries are beginning to reflect the more widespread use of 'providing' as a rough alternative to the more accurate 'provided':

less desirable   Providing she chairs the meeting, I will present the report
more desirable   Provided she chairs ...

Self-Check

Now re-check **8, 15, 17, 22, 24, 26, 28** (Section 19.3).

Answers

8 Wrong   This is a very common mistake but will still upset some people so it is important to use the right preposition:

He found the job very different *from* what he had expected.

Some people would even go further and write:

He found the job very different from that which he had expected.

But this produces a rather pompous piece of English, even though it is correct.

15 Wrong   The sentence *really* means:

She does not remember the incident as well as I do 'As' is therefore a conjunction not a preposition, so 'me' should be 'I'.

17 Right   If the sentence read

'Nothing succeeds like success does' we would have to replace 'like' with the conjunction 'as'.

22 Wrong The two halves each side of the correlative conjunctions 'not only –
but also' do not balance. To correct the sentence we must write:

Our trading had increased not only beyond our expectations but also
beyond our hopes.

Or:

Our trading had increased beyond not only our expectations but also our
hopes. (This is correct but sounds rather more awkward than the first
correct version)

24 Wrong As well as the mistake of not making the verb agree with its subject
'neither' which is singular, this sentence is also wrong because again 'like'
is being used incorrectly as a conjunction and should be replaced by its
corresponding conjunction 'as'.

26 Wrong Again, 'like' is being used incorrectly as a conjunction and should
be replaced by 'as if'.

28 Right Here 'like' is being used correctly as a preposition introducing a
phrase.

20.7 Problems with ellipsis

Ellipsis is the process whereby we leave out some words because they are
'understood' in a sentence. In this way we can avoid using the same word twice in
a sentence and use one word to do the job of two, or sometimes more. So

The first examination was Economics, the second examination was Biology and
the third examination was English

can be shortened by ellipsis to

The first examination was Economics, the second Biology and the third English

Or:

They had worked hard for and saved hard for their summer holiday

becomes

They had worked and saved hard for their summer holiday

However, it is important that the words that are understood really are the same as
the words in the sentence which are doing double duty. When this is not the case it
is called *faulty ellipsis*, and without care this fault is easy to commit, as we have seen
with the use of 'a' and 'an' (see p. 363).
Here are some examples of faulty ellipsis:

wrong   The police were preventing people coming and going from the scene of
the accident.

right   The police were preventing people coming *from* and going *to* the scene
of the accident. ('coming' and 'going' take different prepositions)

wrong   She swims as well, if not better than, her brother.

right	She swims as well *as*, if not better *than*, her brother. (the conjunction 'than' cannot take the place of 'as')
wrong	The pet shop owner said that she had black and white rabbits for sale.
right	The pet shop owner said that she had black rabbits and white rabbits for sale.
	(If this is what is meant, the omission of 'rabbits' after 'black' gives the impression that each of the rabbits was black and white.)
wrong	His hair was dark but his eyes blue.
right	His hair *was* dark but his eyes *were* blue. (a singular verb cannot serve for an understood verb which is plural)

Self-Check

Now re-check **27** and **39** (Section 19.3).

Answers

27 Wrong The understood part of the verb must be the same as the part expressed in the sentence; so the sentence should read:

In my opinion he never has been, and never will be, a success.

39 Wrong Similarly in this sentence, since 'as well' takes 'as' not 'than', the sentence should read:

She writes reports as well as, if not better than her boss.

20.8 Problems with negatives

In English two negatives cancel one another out and produce a positive, just as in mathematics. In spoken English we often use double negatives: 'I shouldn't be surprised if he isn't coming' can mean 'I think he's coming'. Sometimes even in written English the use of two negatives creates an effect which would not be created by using the positive form:

This is not to imply that the job is impossible.

is not the same as

This is to imply that the job is possible.

However, using negatives requires a great deal of care and skill or we are liable to say the opposite of what we intended:

There is no reason to doubt that what he says in his statement ... is not true

when we meant to say:

'There is no reason to doubt that his statement *is* true.'

Even if you manage to work out the effect of multiple negatives and say what you mean, your receiver will be at best irritated at having to work out what you mean, and at worst completely and utterly confused. So, they are really best avoided.

Virtual negatives

Hardly and scarcely

These words are virtually negative in meaning and therefore can cause the same problems as the more conventional negative forms if they are used with other negatives:

> *wrong* He hadn't scarcely the energy to go on.
> *right* He had scarcely the energy to go on.

Or with words that have a negative effect:

> *wrong* Without hardly another thought, she agreed to take on the responsibility.
> *right* With hardly another thought, she agreed to take on the responsibility.

Self-Check

Now check **37** and **40** (Section 19.3).

Answers

37 Wrong It could be argued that this sentence is not so much wrong as ambiguous, but the word 'surprisingly' leads us to believe that he did something unusual. People usually deny that they are guilty so in this sentence we are surprised he did not deny he was guilty. If the other negative – 'wasn't guilty' – is left in, we are left with a negative to spare, which means that he said he was not guilty which would not fit the tone of the sentence conveyed by 'surprisingly'. The sentence should surely then read:

Surprisingly, he did not deny that he was guilty. (he admitted his guilt)

If you are completely confused, perhaps it proves the point about the confusion caused by multiple negatives – avoid them!

40 Wrong Similarly 'without hardly' means 'with'. Are we to understand that they did have a dent? No; 'with hardly' is the right construction.

20.9 Revision of grammar

If you have worked carefully through all the sections in this chapter, now try the test in Section 19.3 again.

Come back to the test in a few weeks' time and see if you can improve your score. Try to analyse where your particular weaknesses are. Verbs? Spelling? Agreement of verbs and subjects, or pronouns and their antecedents?

If you did well the first time, or feel that now you have been through the various problem areas, you are ready to move on to greater things, you might be interested in the following books which go into the subject of grammar and usage in much greater detail than is possible here.

Further reading

Burton, S.H., *Mastering English Grammar*, Palgrave Macmillan, 1984

Crystal, David, *The Cambridge Encyclopaedia of the English Language*, Cambridge University Press, 1997

Chambers Guide to Common Errors, Chambers, 1999

Chambers Guide to Punctuation, Chambers, 1999

Eastwood, John, *Oxford Guide to English Grammar*, OUP, 1994

Fowler, H.W., *Modern English Usage*, Oxford University Press, 2002

Gowers, Sir Ernest, *The Complete Plain Words*, Penguin, 2003

Manser, Martin H., *Bloomsbury Good Word Guide*, Bloomsbury, 2000

Oxford Manual of Style – The Essential Handbook for All Writers, Editors, and Publishers, Oxford University Press, 2002

Partridge, Eric, *Usage and Abusage*, Penguin, 2003

Peck, John, and Coyle, Martin, *The Student's Guide to Writing*, Palgrave Macmillan, 1999

Rose, Jean, *The Mature Student's Guide to Writing*, Palgrave Macmillan, 2001

Strunk, William Jr, and White, E.B., *The Elements of Style*, Allyn & Bacon, 2000

and particularly:

Hilton, Catherine, *Getting to Grips with: Punctuation and Grammar*, Letts, 1992
as it contains Exercises and Answers as well as clear explanations

☑ Appendix A **Punctuation made easy**

Full stop

▪ The strongest punctuation mark of all. Should be used:

1   At the end of a complete sentence (not a question or an exclamation).
2   At the end of an imperative sentence (Shut the door.)
3   After all initials and some abbreviations (N. R. Baines, etc., Feb., n.a., c.i.f.).
4   Between pounds and pence expressed in figures (£3.65).

Comma

▪ The weakest pause mark, but the most important, since its omission can sometimes change the meaning of the sentence.

- *Don't* pepper your sentences with commas – use the meaning of the sentence as a guide.
- *Never* separate subject from verb by a single comma.
- *Never* separate verb from object or predicate by a single comma.

Should be used:

1   To separate words or word groups in a series when there are at least three units:

   Sales are increasing, productivity is increasing, and profits are increasing.

2   To separate a subordinate clause which precedes a main clause:

   Although we are not yet sure of the position, work will continue.

3   To separate a relative clause whose removal would *not* change the basic sense of the sentence:

   This product, which is one of our traditional lines, is not expensive.

   Compare:

   The product that you have selected is not expensive.

4   To separate a phrase or word of explanation from the rest of the sentence:

   London, the swinging city, stands besides the Thames.

Note: the rule here is the same as for relative clauses, so:

He read the article, 'Management Training for Tomorrow's Managers', before tackling the report.

5 To separate coordinate *clauses* joined by one of the 'pure' conjunctions: *and, but, or, neither, nor, for:*

She opened the safe, and took out the files.

6 To separate an introductory phrase containing a verb from the main sentence:

To complete the contract on time, we will need extra men.

Note: an introductory phrase without a verb has no comma following it, unless it is parenthetical:

Following your request, here are the samples.

7 Before a short quotation.

8 To mark a dependent word or word group that breaks the continuity of the sentence:

The manager, her decision over-ruled, conceded defeat graciously.

Semi-colon

Marks a longer pause than a comma. A rather neglected punctuation mark, which is worth learning how to use. Should be used:

1 Between parts of a compound sentence when no conjunction is used:

The comma is over-used in punctuation; the semi-colon is under-used.

2 Between the clauses of a compound sentence before the so-called con-junctive adverbs: *also, consequently, for, hence, nevertheless, on the other hand, otherwise, thus, however, therefore* and so on, for these – unlike other conjunctions – do not join, but they do imply a close connection with the preceding clause:

The matter had been discussed at length; however, a decision had still not been made.

3 Before the following expressions: *as, namely, i.e., e.g., viz,* when they intro-duce an illustration that is a complete clause or an enumeration that con-sists of several items:

Business English should be concise; that is, as brief as is consistent with conveying a clear meaning.

4 To separate the parts of a compound sentence when one or both parts already contain commas:

The report will be finished today; the diagrams, tomorrow.

5 To separate serial phrases or clauses which have a common dependence on something that precedes or follows:

They recommended that the department should be expanded; that a new manager should be appointed; and that work should start immediately.

6 To emphasise parts of a series of clearly defined units:

The true entrepreneur recognises a great opportunity; moulds the resources necessary to take advantage of it; and creates a thriving business.

Colon

A stronger mark than the semi-colon, but used as an *introducer*. Should be used:

1 Between two independent groups not joined by a connecting word, when the first group points forward to the second:

Success lies ahead: better sales and higher productivity.

2 To introduce a long quotation:

In his inaugural address as President, John F. Kennedy said: 'Ask not what your country can do for you; ask what you can do for your country'.

3 To introduce a list of items:

She has good qualifications: a good business education, five years of work experience, and an excellent personal reputation.

4 To separate independent clauses when there is a sharp antithesis:

Man proposes: God disposes.

But a semi-colon would be sufficient.

Question mark

It is equivalent to a full stop and should therefore be followed by a capital letter. Should be used:

1 After a direct question:

Can you come to the meeting?
He asked, 'Where is the letter?'

Should *not* be used after an indirect question; that is, one that does not require an answer:

He asked where the letter was.

Need not be used after a courtesy question; that is, a sentence disguised as a question, but actually expressing a request or a command:

Will you please let me know as soon as possible.

2 After the individual parts of a speech, each of which might be expanded into a complete sentence:

Have you finished typing the report? The illustrations? The binding?

Exclamation mark

 After a word, phrase or sentence to indicate strong emotion or to express sharp emphasis:

No! That is not the point at all!

Quotation marks

Are placed immediately before and after the actual words spoken or quoted. Should be used:

1 To enclose a direct quotation:

He was reported as saying that 'time is running out'.

2 To enclose both parts of an interrupted quotation:

'Let us hope', she said, 'that next year will be a better one for us all'.

3 To enclose the titles of subdivisions of published works (parts, chapters, sections, etc.) and the titles of magazine articles, reports, lectures and the like. Titles of books, newspapers, magazines, plays and other whole publications should be italicised.

His lecture 'Communicate or Perish' was reproduced in *Management Today.*

4 To enclose unusual or peculiar terms, words that are used in a particular sense, or words to which attention is directed to make the meaning clear:

'Gobbledygook' is a term often used to describe foggy English in which a great deal of technical and business jargon is used.

Note: when quotation marks are used with other punctuation marks, the rule is that punctuation marks go inside the quotation marks if they apply to the quotation or direct speech only, and outside when they apply to the whole sentence:

He said, 'Are you going?'
Did he say, 'I am going'?

When both the whole sentence and the quoted words require a question mark, *one* question mark is made to serve both purposes, and is placed inside the quotation mark:

Did he ask, 'Are you going?'

Note: where a quotation is included within a quotation, double quotation marks should be used for one quotation and single quotation marks for the other:

The lecturer said, 'The importance of good written English was summed up by Winston Churchill's words, "Men will forgive anything except bad prose." '

Apostrophe

Beware of the apostrophe; it causes untold problems for people who do not seem to know the correct use of *it's* and *its*. *It's* stands for *it is*. *Its* stands for *belonging to it*.

Should be used:

1   To indicate possession (by a noun):

   (a) man – *man's* hat: singular noun not ending in *s* adds *'s* to show possession

   (b) Charles – *Charles's* hat: singular noun ending in *s* adds *'s* to show possession. (Some people do not like the effect of double *s* and therefore add only an ', but this can cause other mistakes, so it is safer to add *'s* to all singular nouns, whether they end in *s* or not.)

   (c) men – *men's*: plural noun not ending with *s* adds *'s* to show possession

   (d) *boys'* coats – plural noun ending with *s* merely adds ' to show possession

Note: Fortnum and Mason's store (joint possession), *Matthew's and Abigail's premium bonds* (individual possession), *my brother-in-law's house* (one brother-in-law), *my brothers-in-law's houses* is correct but better would be *the houses of my brothers-in-law*

2   To indicate missing letters: *haven't, can't, isn't.*
3   To indicate contracted dates: the swinging *'60s* (not *'60's*).
4   To indicate the plural of letters and numbers:

Your handwriting is not very clear: your *u's* are difficult to distinguish from your *n's*.
'How many *9's* in 36?'

But omit the apostrophe in abbreviations and in 'collective' dates: *MPs, 1960s.*

Dash

A much over-used punctuation mark. It should never be used merely as substitute for commas, semi-colons or full stops. It has its own useful functions. (Make it long enough to avoid confusion with the hyphen.)

Should be used:

1   As a separator, to indicate that a sentence has been broken off, or to indicate a new direction of thought:

We used a similar campaign for the Marsh account – but of course you'll be familiar with it, won't you?

The Prime Minister admitted the desperate need for housing, hospitals, schools – thereby, you may think, invalidating her policy of public spending cuts.

2 To mark a parenthesis or apposition:

One director attended the party – Mr Gideon.

He asked for only one document – the Walker contract.

3 To give strong emphasis:

Those who voted against him – and there were many – still spoke warmly of his courage.

4 To mark off a contrasting or summarising statement:

Accuracy, brevity and clarity – such are the qualities of good business writing.

Parentheses (round brackets)

 Distinguish between round and square brackets. Round brackets should be used:

1 To mark off explanatory or supplementary material:

Commas are the weakest marks for this purpose; dashes are stronger; round brackets (parentheses) are the strongest.

In future advertisements (watch out for them in the press) we will give dates and times of free trial sessions.

The trend this year is encouraging (see Figure 3a).

2 To enclose numbers or letters in enumerations in the text:

The report is written in three parts: (1) the introduction (2) the body, and (3) the conclusion or final section.

3 To express an amount in numbers previously expressed in words:

The annual salary will be fifteen thousand pounds (£15000).

Brackets (square)

☐ Square brackets should be used to enclose explanation, comment, or criticism inserted by someone other than the person quoted:

'The economy [of Britain] has never looked worse.'

Omission marks (or ellipses)

… Signify the omission or deletion of letters or words in quoted material:

'Man … is a being born to believe.' – Disraeli

Hyphen

- 1 To indicate the division of a word at the end of a line.
2 To join parts of certain compound words. There appear to be no definite rules; however, the following guides represent current practice:

(a) With prefixes *ex, self* and *vice:*
  ex-managing director, self-centred

(b) To join a prefix to a proper noun:
  pro-British

Note: it is not used with short prefixes like *co, de, pre, pro* or *re* except to prevent misinterpretation or mispronunciation:

  recover – to regain, but *re-cover* – to cover again

(c) Between two or more words serving as a single adjective before a noun:

  first-class mail; forty-hour week; up-and-coming company; well-presented report; long-term solution; up-to-date figures

Note: when an adverb ending in *ly* is used with an adjective or a participle, the compound is usually not hyphenated:

  highly regarded employee; the universally held view

(d) To join numbers, quantities and fractions:

  a one-third-share but *one third of the total sum; a ninety-nine-year lease*

(e) To express a series of hyphenated compounds dependent on a common element which is omitted in all but the last compound:

  short- and long-term objectives

(f) To join a single letter to another word:

  X-rays; H-bomb; Z-cars

(g) To separate repetitions of certain letters:

  semi-invalid; taxi-ing

(h) To avoid ambiguity:

  the sweet-shop girl; the black-bearded politician

When in doubt – consult a dictionary. The 'rules' of punctuation given above are frequently a subject of debate and, like much of English language usage, constantly undergoing a process of change. For a more comprehensive examination of the irregularities and exceptions, try *Chambers Guide to Punctuation* edited by Kay Cullen (Chambers) 1999.

◼ ✓ Appendix B **Using capitals**

Try to use capital letters as little as possible. However, use capital letters:

1 For proper names – a proper name is the name of an *individual* person, place, company, ship, product, and so on:

   Maximilian Forsythe-Rhodes; the British; Concorde; the Houses of Parliament.

2 To start a sentence or quotation.

3 For names of the week and months of the year but *not* for seasons:

   Wednesday; March; spring; autumn.

4 For the titles of books, magazines, films and so on:

   The Dogs of War; the *Daily Mirror* (but note: *The Times); Management Today.*

5 For the particular and not the general:

   the Chairman, Managing Director and senior directors; Oxfordshire County Council
   but when you refer to them a second time:

   The council deferred the decision.

6 For points of the compass which name a particular geographical area; but *not* when they express direction:

   You travel north-east to get to the North-East; the Far East; far eastern crafts; southern Britain; North America.

7 For divisions of knowledge when you use them as titles of specific courses; but *not* when they are used to refer to studies in general or common divisions of knowledge:

   I am taking Principles of Marketing and Personnel Management as well as some economics and politics.

▼ Appendix C **Using numbers**

General rule

Traditionally the rule has been to write the numbers from one to nine as words; from 10 upwards write them as figures. However, recently the modern style seems to be to write all numbers as figures. In either case the following exceptions seem sensible and worth considering.

Exceptions

1 *Beginning a sentence* – Numbers are often spelled out when they begin a sentence, although this rule is dying out. Try not to start sentences with complicated numbers; for example:

   Fifty-three million nine hundred and eighty-five thousand three hundred and sixty cars were produced last year. (!)

2 *Round numbers* – These should be spelled in full, except when they are used in the same sentence with other numbers that cannot be expressed in words conveniently:

   We cancelled the meeting about ten days ago.
   The report contained more than fifty pages.
   These machines range in price from £50 to £13 500.

3 *Adjoining numbers* – When one number immediately follows another, it is best to spell out the smaller number, or the first number:

   ten 40-seater coaches; four 25p notebooks; twelve 2p pieces

4 *Numbers in parallel constructions* – Write all the numbers in figures, unless all are small or are round numbers that can be written easily in words. If the first word is a number, it may be written out, even though the rest of the numbers are written in figures; but it may be possible to recast the sentence so that the first word is not a number:

   She ordered 65 diaries, 43 ring binders, and 125 felt-tip pens.
   One hundred and sixty-two men, 75 women and 53 children were in the plane when it was hijacked.
   When the plane was hijacked there were 162 men, 75 women and 53 children on board.

5 *Sums of money* – Write sums of money in figures except in legal documents:

   £53; £5.36; 36p

6 *Ordinal numbers* – Ordinal numbers in lists in figures – 1st prize, 2nd prize, 3rd prize; the date is in figures – 4th February 1992 (although the practice of writing 4 February, 2 March, etc. is increasing); but elsewhere in words – first, second, third.

7 *Quantities and measurement* – Quantities and measurements are usually written in figures.

◪ Appendix D **Business clichés or commercialese**

A number of words and phrases that were once commonly used in business English are now regarded by most people as bad business English. Many of these terms still survive but you should try to avoid them:

Commercialese	Better English
above-mentioned	this/these
in accordance with	under
acknowledge receipt of	have received
advices	letter, instructions
advise/inform	tell, say, let you know, mention
I would advise	DON'T USE
kindly advise us as to your wishes	please let us know your requirements
are in agreement	agree
in answer to same	in reply to your query
assistance	aid, help
as to	DON'T USE
at your (earliest) convenience	as soon as possible
attached hereto	attached
awaiting/thanking/trusting	TRY NOT TO USE
beg	DON'T USE (unless bankrupt!)
commence	start, begin
communication	letter/fax/phone call
comply with	keep to
in conclusion would state	we therefore conclude/finally
in connection with	… about
consequently	so
despatch	send
due to the fact that …	because of
enclosed please find/enclosed herewith	we are/I am enclosing/here is
in the event	if/when
in excess of	more than
forward	send
furnish	supply/give/send
furthermore	… also
to hand	DON'T USE
herewith/heretofore/hereinunder/ hereby	DON'T USE
please do not hesitate to	please

implemented	carried out/done
indicate	show
learn	hear, see, read
matter	BE SPECIFIC
in the near future	soon (or better, give the date)
we should be much obliged if you would	please …
obtain	have, get
only too pleased	glad to
per annum/per diem	a year/a day
peruse	read
prior to	before
proceed	go
provided that	if
purchase	buy
on receipt	when we/you get
with reference to	about/concerning
referring to your letter of…	your letter of… mentioned
we note your comments regarding	you mention that
request	ask
regret	am sorry, concerned about
in respect of/with respect to/ with regard to	about/concerning
same as in … your order. We have now received *same* (or *the same*)	… it
state	say, mention
terminate	end, complete
trust	hope (is usually better, but not always)
we wish to point out/we would remind you	DON'T USE
under separate cover	in a separate letter/in my letter dated …
utilise	use
viz	namely
and… please do not hesitate to contact me if I can be of further assistance	FIND SOMETHING ORIGINAL!

■ ⍗ Appendix E **Commonly misused and confused words**

American spelling is increasingly influencing spelling rules, particularly as more and more people rely on American computer spellcheckers. But this list gives the English spelling as many readers will still be indignant at anything else.

accept:	to receive, to give an affirmative answer
except:	to exclude, to omit, to leave out
advice:	counsel, recommendation (noun)
advise:	to suggest to, to recommend (verb)
affect:	to influence, to alter (verb)
effect:	to bring about (verb)
effect:	result or consequence (noun)
all ready:	prepared
already:	previously
all right	completely right
alright:	OK (coll.) – considered by some as incorrect usage of 'all right'
altogether:	completely or thoroughly
all together:	in unison, in a group
among:	refers to three or more
between:	refers to two only
amount:	quantity (of uncountable material)
number:	a total of countable units
anyone:	any person in general
any one:	a specific person or item (e.g. any one suggestion)
complement:	that which completes or supplements
compliment:	flattery or praise, expression of regard
confidant:	person in whom one confides (noun)
confident:	positive or sure (adjective)
continual:	taking place in close succession, frequently repeated
continuous:	without stopping, without a break
council:	an assembly of people (noun) – similarly, *councillor*
counsel:	to advise (verb), advice (noun), legal adviser – similarly *counsellor*

credible:	believable or acceptable
creditable:	praiseworthy
credulous:	gullible
currant:	fruit
current:	belonging to present time, motion of air or water
dependent:	depending, relying (adjective)
dependant:	one who depends on another for support (noun)
discreet:	prudent, circumspect
discrete:	separate entity, individual
disinterested:	neutral, not biased
uninterested:	not concerned with, lacking interest
disorganised:	disordered
unorganised:	not organised or planned
eminent:	outstanding, prominent
imminent:	very near, impending, threatening
farther:	refers to geographical or linear distance
further:	more, in addition to
forgo:	abstain from, go without – similarly *forgone*
forego:	precede, go before – similarly *foregone*
formally:	according to convention
formerly:	previously
imply:	to hint at, or to allude to in speaking or writing
infer:	to draw a conclusion from what has been said or written
its:	a possessive singular pronoun
it's:	a contraction for *it is*
less:	smaller quantity of uncountable material
fewer:	a smaller total of countable units
licence:	permission, authorisation (noun)
license:	to permit, to authorise (verb)
maybe:	perhaps (adverb)
may be:	indicates possibility (verb)
militate (against):	be a strong factor in preventing
mitigate:	make less severe, serious or painful, lessen the gravity (an offence or mistake)
moral:	a principle, maxim, or lesson (noun); ethical (adjective)
morale:	a state of mind or psychological outlook (noun)
oral:	by word of mouth
verbal:	in words whether oral or written

personal:	private, not public or general
personnel:	the staff of an organisation
practical:	not theoretical, useful, pragmatic
practicable:	can be put into practice (should not be used to refer to people)
practice:	action, performance, habitual action (noun)
practise:	to put into practice, to perform (verb)
proceed:	to begin, to move, to advance
precede:	to go before
principal:	of primary importance (adjective), head of a college, original sum, chief
principle:	a fundamental truth
stationery:	writing paper or writing materials
stationary:	not moving, fixed
their	belonging to them (possessive of *they*)
there	in that place (adverb)
they' re:	a contraction of the two words *they are*
weather:	climate or atmosphere
whether:	introduces the first of two alternatives
wether:	a castrated ram
who's	a contraction of *who is*
whose:	possessive of *who*
your	a pronoun (possessive)
you're	a contraction of *you are*

Appendix F **Ten (simple?) rules of spelling**

1 *i* before *e* except after *c*, when the sound is *ee*:

achieve, receive, piece, perceive

Except

seize, weird, weir, sheik

Note: the words *neighbour, height, weight, heir, their,* are not exceptions, since the sound is not *ee*.

2 Words ending in a silent *e* drop the *e* before a vowel when forming compound words but not before a consonant:

love – lovable – loving; move – moving

but: like – likely; safe – safely

Except: the *e* is retained

(a)   after *c* and *g* to soften the sound:

noticeable, knowledgeable, manageable

(b)   for reasons of distinction:

singing, singeing

dying, dyeing

Note: the *e is* dropped before consonants in words of one syllable:

due – duly; true – truly

and judgment and judgement
   acknowledgment and acknowledgement } *both acceptable*

3 Words ending in *l* take *ll* when *y* is added:

hopeful – hopefully
faithful – faithfully

4 Words ending in a single vowel and a single consonant double the final consonant before adding -*ed*, -*ing*, -*er*:

win – winning   commit – committed
run – running   refer – referring

but: feel – feeling

as long as the stress is on the final or only syllable.

If the accent is not on the last syllable, the consonant is not doubled:

differ – differing
alter – altering
Except:

worship – worshipping
travel – traveller

5   When the word begins with *s* the *s* is retained after *mis-* and *dis-*:
misspelling, dissolve, dissatisfy, dissuade

but: mislead, disappoint, disappear

6   When *all, full, till,* and *well* are used to form compound words they usually drop
one *l*:

full – fulfil   careful
skill – skilful   until
well – welfare

Except:

farewell, well-being

7   Words ending in *-ceed, -cede, -sede*

pro ⎫
ex ⎬ ceed   super-sede
suc ⎭

All others take *cede*:

concede, intercede, precede

Note: proceed but *procedure; proceedings*

8   Words ending in *-our* usually drop *u* before *-ation*, *-ate* and *-ous*:

humour – humorous
vigour – vigorous – invigorate

Note: 'humor', 'color' are American spellings

9   Words ending in *y* preceded by a consonant, change *y* to *i* when a syllable is
added:

merry – merrily
lady – ladies
rely – relied
likely – likelihood

10   *c* changes to *s* when the noun is used as a verb in English spelling:

pract*ice* (I am going to do some practice)
pract*ise* (I am going to practise)

licen*ce* (I have a driving licence)
licen*se* (I am licensed to drive)

adv*ice* (Can I give you some advice?)
adv*ise* (Can I advise you?)

☑ Appendix G **Commonly misspelled words**

absence
accessible
accommodate
achieve
acquainted
advertisement
agreeable
all right
among
appearance
arrangement

beautiful
beginning
behaviour
believed
benefited
business

certain
choice
circumstances
colleagues
coming
commitment
committee
comparative
competent
competitive
conceal
conscientious
conscious
correspondence
criticism

decision
definite
dependant (noun)
dependent (adj)

disappear
disappointed

eighth
embarrassed
emergency
environment
especially
essential
excellent
excitement
exercise
expenses
extremely

faithfully
familiar
February
forego (foregone)
forgo (forgone)
forty
friend

gauge
government
grateful
guarantee
guard

height
honour

immediately
independent
instalment
knowledge

library
losing
lying

maintenance
management
miniature
minutes
miscellaneous

noticeable
nuclear

occasionally
occurrence
omitted
opinion

parallel
parliament
personal
personnel
planning
possesses
preceding
principal
principle
privilege
procedure
proceed
professional
pronunciation
psychological

quantitative
quiet
quite

really
receipt
received
recommend
relieved

responsibility
restaurant

safely
safety
scarcely
secretary
separately
similar
sincerely

successfully
supersede
surprising

tendency
transferred

unconscious
undoubtedly
unnecessary

until
usually

valuable
view

Wednesday
withhold
twelfth

⬛ ⌄ Appendix H **Tips on modern business style**

Be...

    Clear

        Concise

            Courteous

                Constructive

                    Correct

                        Complete

Use active verbs wherever possible.
We know not *knowledge has been acquired; we regret* ... not *it is regretted* ...

Use concrete nouns rather than abstract nouns wherever possible.
Civilian deaths not *collateral damage.*

Prefer verbs to nouns.
We confused them rather than *we caused them confusion; we anxiously waited for him to arrive* not *we awaited his arrival with anxiety.*

Use adjectives and adverbs not adjectival and adverbial phrases – the single word not several.
Soon not *in the near future; rudely* not *in a way which could only be described as rude; if so* not *in the contemplated eventuality.*

Use adjectives and adverbs sparingly – only to make meanings more precise and rarely more emphatic.
An economic crisis not *a serious crisis.*

Prefer the short word to the long.
Use transport not *transportation; use* for *utilization; buy* not *purchase; start or begin* not *commence.*

Prefer the familiar word to the unusual.
Although it is always debatable how many different words there are in the English language and new words are always being introduced, it is probably wiser to use words that your recipient is sure to understand.

Avoid ambiguity – use pronouns with care – clearly referring back to the right noun.
Avoid: *If the baby does not thrive on cow's milk, boil it.* Turn the sentence round: *Boil the cow's milk if the baby does not thrive on it.*

Avoid the dangling participle.
Not *standing on the bank of the river, the fish could not be seen by the angler* but better *standing on the bank of the river, the angler could not see the fish* (which also cuts out the passive).

Avoid jargon.
A language of a few. It's dull, snobbish, vague, fence-building, an attempt to impress, and should only be used with the specialist group who created it – and never with customers or clients.

Avoid clichés and hackneyed expressions.
Out of the woods; the thin end of the wedge; at the end of the day; basically; the bottom line; going forward (for *in the future*) are all boring and mean different things to different people.

Avoid commercialese/businessese.
Please find enclosed; we acknowledge receipt of; thanking you in anticipation; please do not hesitate to contact me if I can be of further assistance.

Avoid foreign words.
Per se; per annum; a priori; de facto.

Avoid verbiage or gobbledygook – the abundance of words without necessity and without much meaning.
In view of the fact that = because; in relation to = for, of, with, about; during such time as = while; cause an investigation to be made with a view to ascertaining = find out. As to, so far as ... is concerned, from a ... point of view are usually quite unnecessary and *it may be stated with some confidence that ...* is completely unnecessary!

KEEP THINGS SIMPLE AND STRAIGHTFORWARD

COMMUNICATE TO EXPRESS NOT IMPRESS

■ M Appendix I **Differences between men and women communicating**

Since the early 1990s, research into men and women's behaviour and conversation both in and out of work have led to some interesting conclusions which prompt wry expressions in both sexes as they recognise the differences. Although not true of everyone of course, these tendencies should at least be borne in mind when we are communicating.

Generally, women tend to be more concerned with networking, empathising or fostering good relationships, whereas men tend to worry more about status and their position in the hierarchy and whether they are one-up or one-down in dialogues with others. So ...

Men tend to:	Women tend to:
use active channels of communication (face-to-face and phone)	use active channels too but make more time for e-mail and mail
worry about status and control	worry about other people and empathise
see their appearance as an expression of power	be more concerned by social pressure to be attractive
identify themselves by the jobs they hold	identify themselves in more complex ways than by their job
maintain their one-up relationship	maintain good relationships
choose a steady, continuous pace of action	choose a fast and steady pace with breaks
like to get to the point and keep to the point	like to consider the background, compare and consider options, debate, be sure before deciding or acting
prefer not to waste time on planning and reflection	prefer to reflect, imagine and allow for contingencies
in meetings speak more often and for longer, interrupt twice as often as women, control the topics and ignore topics raised by women	in meetings, listen and reflect, raise subtly associated points, get silently frustrated if ignored
use power in decision-making	avoid displaying rank or power in decision-making

be logical and rational	be concerned with feelings and emotions
prefer impersonal talk that avoids emotion	prefer personal talk that builds rapport
like to get evidence in the form of hard facts and statistics	like to hear case histories, consult, gather a variety of information and opinions, including people's feelings and reactions
want to have information	want to share information
control circumstances	adapt to and influence circumstances
talk about one thing at a time	want to see continuity between points and therefore to jump quickly between and on to subjects that they see as related
see success as being at the top	see success as being at the centre of things rather than at the top
view work as a means to an end and therefore focus on completion rather than the actual doing of tasks	take account of the larger context of work, and therefore focus on the process as well as the completion of tasks
focus on work without interruption	make time for activities not directly related to work
concentrate on the job in hand	spend time on relationships important to achieving objectives
use strong, direct language and express more hostility	use more qualifying and modifying language – adjectives and adverbs
express preferences directly and are often blunt	express preferences by asking a question
hear questions as direct requests for information	hear questions as a way of keeping the conversation going
think silence is a sign of approval or neutrality	use silence to express disapproval and respond to offensive comments
think nodding and smiling mean approval and agreement	nod and smile to encourage, not necessarily as an expression of opinion
think an impassive expression is attentive and businesslike	think an impassive expression is cold and disapproving
not to look at a woman when talking to her but focus on a man nearby	sometimes refuse eye contact with men in case it appears hostile or inviting
not to notice non-verbal messages or think women are 'imagining things'	be better at coding and decoding non-verbal messages, especially tone of voice and changes in tone

see aggressiveness as OK, a way to get things moving in a conversation	see aggressiveness as almost always inappropriate and negative
respond to hearing a problem by offering advice and solutions	respond to hearing a problem by offering comfort and reassurance, except when directly asked for advice
not to admit to needing help or advice when they have a problem	want comfort and reassurance when they have a problem unless they specifically ask for advice
… want to get on with it!	… want to talk about it!

◪ A final word

Throughout this book we have concentrated on the basic principles that lie behind effective communication in business, but you will have discovered that there is no magic lamp that you or I can rub to make you an effective communicator. It is a question of being aware of the nature of communication and the principles which govern the process, and then being prepared to make the effort to put those principles into practice.

If you are willing to think sensitively when you communicate and always keep the other person – the receiver – constantly in mind before you communicate and while you are communicating, you will automatically discover the answers to those familiar questions:

- What shall I say?
- How shall I say it?
- What do they mean?
- Why did they say that?

In other words, communication is a selfless process in which, to stand any chance of success, we have to fight constantly our natural instinct to be self-centred. We have to guard against the very natural inclination to concentrate on ourselves, on what *we* want to say, and try instead to consider the other person and focus on what we *need* to say and do, both to help them understand what *we* mean and to help them tell us what *they* mean.

Real communication, then, is a two-way process. We must be prepared to listen as much as speak and we must listen effectively to what is really being said – and to what is *not* being said. We must be conscious of what may be communicated between the lines when we listen and read, and when we speak and write – in other words we must be aware of the potential difficulties that beset communication, and alert to the ways in which we can strive to overcome them, or at least reduce their effect.

We will not always succeed. Communication is by nature a human and therefore imperfect process, but our efforts to improve will be rewarded in countless ways. In any case, just trying to understand how communication works and how we can try to perfect our ability to communicate effectively can in itself be a rewarding task.

Nicky Stanton

◪ Bibliography

Argyle, Michael, *The Psychology of Interpersonal Behaviour*, Penguin, 1994

Bandler, R. and Grinder, J. *Frogs into Princes, Neuro Linguistic Programming*, Real People Press, Utah 1979

Barker, Alan, *How to Manage Meetings*, Kogan Page, 2002

Berne, Eric, *Games People Play: The Psychology of Human Relationships*, Penguin Books, 1968

Bloomsbury Good Word Guide, Bloomsbury, 2000

Bradbury, Andrew, *Develop Your NLP Skills*, Kogan Page, 2000

Bradbury, Andrew, *Successful Presentation Skills*, Kogan Page, 2000

Buzan, Tony, *Use Your Head*, Harper Collins, 2000

Buzan, Tony, *Speed Reading*, BBC Consumer Publishing, 2000

Buzan, Tony, *Mind Map Book*, BBC Consumer Publishing, 2001

Buzan, Tony, *How to Mind Map: The Ultimate Thinking Tool That Will Change Your Life*, Harper Collins, 2002

Burton, S.H., *Mastering English Grammar*, Palgrave Macmillan, 1984

Cartwight, Roger, *Mastering Marketing Management*, Palgrave Macmillan, 2002

Chambers Guide to Common Errors, Chambers, 1999

Chambers Guide to Punctuation, Chambers, 1999

Choices: Jobs Through the Internet, Omnia Books, 2002

Cottrell, Stella, *The Study Skills Handbook*, 2nd edn Palgrave Macmillan 2003

Crystal, David, *The Cambridge Encyclopaedia of the English Language*, Cambridge University Press, 1997

Crystal, David, *Language and the Internet*, Cambridge University Press, 2001

Citrine, Lord, *The ABC of Chairmanship*, Fabian Society, 4th edn, 1995

Eastwood, John, *Oxford Guide to English Grammar*, OUP, 1994

Fairbairn, G.J. and Winch, C., *Reading, Writing and Reasoning*, Open University, 1998

Flynn, Nancy and Flynn, Tom, *Writing Effective E-mail*, Kogan Page, 2000

Forsyth, Patrick, *Powerful Reports and Proposals*, Kogan Page, 2003

Fowler, H.W., *Modern English Usage*, Oxford University Press, 2002

Goleman, Daniel, *Emotional Intelligence: Why It Can Matter More Than IQ*, Bloomsbury, 1995

Goleman, Daniel, *Working with Emotional Intelligence*, Bloomsbury, 1998

Goleman, Daniel, Boyatzis, Richard, McKee, Annie, *The New Leaders*, Time Warner Books UK, 2002 (originally published in US by Harvard Business School Press, 2002)

Gowers, Sir Ernest, *The Complete Plain Words*, Penguin, 2003

Handy, Charles, *Understanding Organisations*, Penguin, 1993

Harris, Thomas A., *I'm OK, You're OK*, Arrow, 1995

Harris, Amy and Harris, Thomas A., *Staying OK*, Arrow, 1995

Havard, Bob, *Performance Appraisals*, Kogan Page, 2000

Hayes, Marion E., *Make Every Minute Count*, Kogan Page, 2000

Hilton, Catherine, *Getting to Grips with: Punctuation and Grammar*, Letts, 1992

Hudson, Diane, *Designing for Desktop Publishing*, How To Books, 1998

Huff, D., *How to Lie With Statistics*, Penguin, 1991

Inglis, John and Lewis, Roger, *Clear Thinking*, Harper Collins, 1993

Keats, Daphne, *Interviewing: A Practical Guide for Students and Professionals*, Open University Press, 2000

Knight, Sue, *Introducing NLP*, Chartered Institute of Personnel and Development, 1999

Knight, Sue, *NLP at Work*, Nicholas Brealey Publishing, 2002

Kump, Peter, *Breakthrough Rapid Reading*, Prentice Hall, 1998

Maitland, Iain, *Make That Call!*, Kogan Page, 2000

Maitland, Iain, *Write That Letter!*, Kogan Page, 2000

Morris, Desmond, *Peoplewatching*, Vintage, 2000

O'Connor, Joseph and Seymour, John, *Introducing NLP Neuro-Linguistic Programming*, Aquarian/Thorson, 1993

Oxford Manual of Style – The Essential Handbook for all Writers, Editors, and Publishers, Oxford University Press, 2002

Partridge, Eric, *Usage and Abusage*, Penguin, 2003

Pease, Allan, *Body Language: How to Read Others' Thoughts by their Gestures*, Sheldon Press, 1997

Peck, John and Coyle, Martin, *The Student's Guide to Writing*, Palgrave Macmillan, 1999

Rinaldi, Arlene H., *The Net: User Guidelines and Netiquette*, www.fau.edu/netiquette/net/netiquette.html

Rose, Jean, *The Mature Student's Guide to Writing*, Palgrave, 2001

Tannen, Deborah, *You Just Don't Understand*, Virago, 1991

Tannen, Deborah, *That's Not What I Meant*, Virago, 1992

Strunk, William Jr and White, E.B., *The Elements of Style*, Allyn & Bacon, 2000

Studner, P. and McDonald, M. (Eds) *Super Job Search: The Complete Manual for Job-Seekers and Career-Changers*, Mercury Books, 1996

Wainwright, Gordon, *Read Faster, Recall More*, How To Books, 2001

Yate, Martin, *The Ultimate, CV Book*, Kogan Page, 2002

Zinsser, William, *On Writing Well*, Harper Collins, 1998

■ ⌄ Answers to exercises

1 The process of communication

Exercise 1.1

1 Look back to pp. 4 and 5.

3 Listening

Exercise 3.1

1 45 per cent listening (9 per cent writing; 16 per cent reading; and 30 per cent speaking).
2 One-tenth of the original message is remembered after 3 days.
3 See p. 27 – 'Listener responses'.
4 See p. 27 – 'Resist distractions'.
5 People who tend to concentrate on their own thoughts and interrupt might do well 'holding back' and 'reflecting back' the ideas of others before making their own contribution. They would probably find 'reflecting back' extremely difficult but very instructive.

Managers who try to appear good listeners but end up talking about their own problems might also benefit from 'reflecting back' and 'holding back' but could also try 'helping the speaker' by more use of listener responses.

The student needs to be alert for messages which affect them, constantly asking themselves: 'how can I make use of this?' 'Being interested' is not something that just happens: it requires hard work, preparation and a readiness to listen and show you're interested. They might also make a real effort to 'resist distractions' and increase their concentration in the middle of a lecture. 'Listening for the main ideas' would help their concentration.

And finally, the person who is quick to judge a person's ideas on the basis of superficial things, like the appearance and dress of the speaker, needs above all to 'keep an open mind' and 'resist distractions'.

4 Human interaction and non-verbal communication

Exercise 4.1

1 'Metacommunication' literally means 'in addition to communication', so the term is used to refer to all those things which we take into account in interpreting what someone is saying, over and above the actual words.

2 By remaining silent at strategic moments we may encourage someone to carry on talking, and in doing so we are providing them with the opportunity to communicate feelings and attitudes which they might not otherwise have done. It can therefore encourage feedback and real two-way communication.

3 They may think:
   (a) You are not a very punctual person.
   (b) You are not very interested in getting the job.
   (c) You are not very concerned about other people, since it apparently doesn't bother you that you may have caused someone inconvenience.
   (d) You are rude and discourteous because you did not apologise.

4 'Kinesics' is the study of body movements which convey information in the absence of, or in addition to, speech.

5 The four types of distance are: intimate, personal, social and public.

6 You are likely to be perceived as more confident, more believable and more interested in your audience than the content of your speech.

7 Shifts of gaze and head nods, as well as grunts, gestures and changes of body orientation, help to synchronise speech in conversations.

8 We are more likely to believe the non-verbal message.

5 Talking on the telephone

Exercise 5.1

1 (a) What does 'today' mean? Since the message has no date, Matt will not necessarily know to which day 'today' refers. If Matt is out all day on the day the message is received, when he comes in the next day he would be justified in assuming 'today' refers to that day. It is therefore possible that he will miss the appointment and turn up on the wrong day to find no one is there.

   Furthermore, what does 'lunch time' mean? This will depend on whether the lunch hour is taken at the same time every day for both Mr Strange and Matt. Finally Matt has no means of finding out the answers to any of these queries because the message is not signed, so he has no idea who took it.

   Telephone messages should always include the date and time the message was taken and the name of the person who took the message.

(b)   Same deficiencies as 1(a). It also does not include the name of the person to whom it is addressed. The message is very vague suggesting that the message-taker has not heard the words very clearly and has not read it back to the caller. If the message-recipient has no idea what the message is about he may even wonder if it really is for him. He cannot check with the message-taker (no name), he cannot check with the caller (caller's name not given) and he is probably left, either to ignore it and hope he will eventually find out what it is all about, or to start a detective hunt perhaps starting with appointments in his diary on Mondays (he doesn't know *which* Monday).

Make sure the message contains all the necessary details.

(c)   *Who* rang? *What's* all fixed? Now, the message-recipient has just been talking to a chap at Dawson's asking him to arrange a special delivery, so perhaps the message refers to that and he can rest assured that his requirements will be met. On the other hand, he spoke to someone else at Dawson's the day before about another matter in which a special price was being negotiated. That chap also said he would ring back and let him know if the price had been accepted. Perhaps the message refers to that matter. Perplexed, the recipient has no alternative but to make another, otherwise unnecessary, call to clear up the confusion.

Perhaps a worse consequence of this kind of incomplete message is that the message-recipient could have assumed that the message referred to the most recent matter.

Never assume that the message-recipient will know what the message is all about.

2   This illustration shows a message pad with all the headings necessary to remind the message-taker what they should make a note of. But no message pad can ensure that the details of the actual message are taken down clearly and completely – *that is up to you:*

Date: ....Time:	
Message for:	
Message from: (Name)	
(Address)	
....	
(Tel. no.)	
(email)	
Message:	
....	
....	
....	
Message taken by:	

3   The conversation could have been like this:

'Paul Jeffries. Mr Sloane's secretary. Can I help you?'
'Good afternoon. This is Trent of Partridge's. Is it possible to speak to Mr Sloane? I'm meeting him in London tonight.'
'I'm afraid he's at a meeting at the moment, Mr Trent. Can I give him a message?'
'Yes please.' (Trent thinks quickly.) 'He said he might be able to meet me at the airport. Tell him: Trent (Partridge's, Manchester) is arriving at Heathrow at 6.27 p.m. on Flight No. ML-367. That's Terminal One. I will wait until 7 p.m. If he has not arrived by then I will make my own way to Tudor's where we've booked dinner for 8 p.m. If he wants to ring me I shall be at Manchester 675071, until 4 o'clock this afternoon.'
'Can I just check that, Mr Trent?' (He reads back the message.) 'Is that correct?'
'Fine. Thanks very much.'
'I'll see he gets it as soon as possible, but in any case before he leaves the office this afternoon.'
'Thank you. Goodbye.'
'Goodbye, Mr Trent.'

Where possible, the conversation has been shortened by giving the essential details early on in the conversation. However, it cannot be greatly reduced because Mr Trent must give the necessary information and the secretary must read the message back to check he has heard it correctly and written down what Mr Trent wants written down.

The major difference, however, between this and the original conversation is that Trent knows exactly what is going to happen and has built in a contingency plan which will operate if Sloane cannot meet him. Provided the secretary passes on the message (and he sounds efficient) everyone will know what is happening. If by any chance he fails to contact his boss, Trent's contingency plan will work and they will meet for dinner at 8 p.m. All this has been completed in one phone call instead of possibly two in the original situation.

This was achieved because Trent thought in advance about the call; worked out at least two possibilities – he might speak to Sloane himself or he might have to leave a message; thought of a contingency plan in case Sloane could not meet him so that an additional call was not necessary; and had all the details at his fingertips.

Despite making the call as brief as possible, consistent with being clearly understood, both parties were polite and helpful, and the purpose of the call was achieved. Efficient telephoning!

6   Interviewing

Exercise 6.1

1   An interview has a purpose and is planned and controlled.
2   (a)   problem-solving but mainly decision-making;
     (b)   research and discovery of new information;

(c) research and discovery of new information;

(d) problem-solving and decision-making; seeking behaviour (and perhaps belief) change;

(e) seeking belief and/or behaviour change.

3 (a) Probably all of them: a good selection interview should not focus on any one type of information.

(b) A market research interview could focus on any one or all of the possible types of information.

(c) An interview with a witness will usually focus on description and factual knowledge. It might include statements of the interviewee's behaviour before and during the accident, but it should avoid subjective statements of attitudes, beliefs, feelings and values.

(d) The performance appraisal interview will concentrate on statements of behaviour. Although the interviewee may be encouraged to express attitudes, feelings and values, the interviewer should avoid making these statements and should concentrate on an objective discussion of facts, that is, what the interviewee has done, is doing and could do.

(e) The sales interviewer will be particularly concerned with eliciting attitudes, beliefs, feelings and values as a basis for his persuasive skills.

Exercise 6.2

Obviously there are no right answers. It would depend entirely on the particular context of the interview and your specific purpose. However, here are my suggestions:

employment	moderately structured
appraisal	moderately structured
counselling	unstructured
discipline	moderately structured
termination	moderately/highly structured
induction	moderately structured
consulting	highly structured
sales	moderately/highly structured
data-gathering	highly structured/standardised
order-giving	moderately structured

Exercise 6.3

1 A direct question allowing only a 'yes' or 'no' answer, so not very useful. Good for opening the interview and putting interviewee at ease but might be better worded: 'How was your journey?'

2 Pulling rank and begging for pity are both inexcusable and it is a leading, if not even a loaded, question. A good alternative would depend on the purpose of the interview, but something along these lines would be an improvement: 'How can I help you to cope better with your job?'

3 This is a leading question revealing the interviewer's own views on 'job-hopping' and not giving the interviewee a really fair chance to explain what may be perfectly acceptable reasons for changing jobs. Better: 'Why did you move from … to …?'

4 Such a mixture of questions is far too complicated and long-winded for us to analyse, let alone for anyone to answer. Ask one question at a time: 'Why did you take a mixture of O levels and CSEs?'

7 Being interviewed for a job

Before the Interview

1 Be informed about the organisation: its history, geographical location, general methods of doing business, reputation, and so on.

2 Anticipate questions that might be asked: factual questions as well as 'trap' questions.

3 Make a note of questions you want to ask.

During the interview

4 State why you are applying for the job and show you know something about it.

5 Present your qualifications in terms of having something of value to offer the company. Deal as much as possible in specific details and examples – job experiences, interests, travel, activities, offices held, organisations and school.

6 Don't depend merely on a 'smooth front' (appearance and smile) to sell yourself. Provide full information to the prospective employer.

7 Don't hesitate to admit potential weaknesses. Under no circumstances attempt to bluff or fake on these, but wherever possible make a transition from a weakness to a strength; or, at least, when the facts justify it, show some extenuating circumstances for the weakness. (This doesn't mean supplying alibis or excuses!)

8 Generally attempt to expand your responses beyond a simple 'yes' or 'no'.

9 Treat the interviewer as a human being, not an ogre!

10 Remember the normal rules of etiquette.

11 Get as much information as possible about the job requirements and organisation, and on 'sensitive' matters such as salary (usually in terms of range, or the 'going average').

12 Try never to have an interview concluded without some sort of understanding about where you stand, what happens next, who is to contact whom and so on.

13 Try to enjoy it.

14 Be sincere – be yourself.

8 Communicating in groups

Exercise 8.1

1 Large and more complex business organisations have made it impossible for any one person or area to make decisions without consulting other areas in the organisation. People want to be involved, to be given a chance to express themselves and be heard, to be 'given a voice' in matters that concern them. They are then more likely to be committed to the resulting decisions which may affect them.

2 Groups are likely to make better decisions than an individual because (a) more information is available in the form of several people's knowledge and experience, and (b) by dividing responsibilities for research among a number of people, more information can be brought into the discussion.

Taken together these two advantages explain the statement 'two heads are better than one'. A group consisting of five or more people can conduct more interviews, read more reports, or conduct more surveys than one member acting alone.

Exercise 8.2

	Democratic	Autocratic	Laissez-faire
(a)	2	1	3
(b)	4	6	5
(c)	9	7	8
(d)	10	11	12
(d)	15	13	14
(e)	16	17	18

Exercise 8.3

1 Look back at Figure 8.1.
2 The optimum size of group is 5 (certainly no more than 7), as this size allows complete interaction among the members and yet provides sufficient variety of talent and personality to tackle problems imaginatively.
3 No. A group needs to be compatible, and this means that personalities should be complementary. A group consisting of members who all have dominant personalities and want to lead would probably not be effective.
4 The 'hidden agenda' refers to the personal objectives of individuals in a group. These personal objectives may conflict with the group's objectives and to be effective a group must, by some means or another, encourage individuals to see the group's objectives as more important than their own.
5 Who am I in this group? What is the pattern of influence? What are my personal needs and objectives?
6 Physical proximity increases interaction. The location of the meeting communicates a message. Shared facilities, even poor facilities, can encourage cohesiveness in a group.

Exercise 8.4

1 Seeking opinion and/or gatekeeping.
2 Summarising.
3 Expressing group feeling.
4 Probably an example of 'blocking', but if it is followed up with reasons it could be an example of 'evaluating'.
5 Standard-setting.
6 Competing.
7 Giving information.
8 Seeking sympathy.
9 'Diagnosing' but also 'initiating activity' and 'seeking opinion'.
10 'Giving opinion' but worded the way it is, it is likely to serve an 'encouraging' function as well.

9 Running and taking part in meetings

Exercise 9.1

Brainstorming is a good way to encourage ideas but the *question technique* encourages quieter members and controls the more talkative members.

Exercise 9.2

1 *False.* This is a definition of democratic leadership. A definition of autocratic leadership might be: where the leader plays a strong directive role in setting group goals and in planning and directing the activities of the group, delegating few of the functions of leadership to the group.
2 *True.* Effective participation means that you at least are aware of the responsibilities and functions of the leader and are willing to carry out some of those functions, particularly those concerned with group maintenance, if the leadership style invites it. As an effective participant you will also not sit silently through a meeting depriving the group of the chance to consider your ideas and benefit from your knowledge and experience, but will be alert to the moments when your contribution will be most usefully received.
3 *False.* Routine items and items requiring little discussion should be placed high on the agenda, but the amount of time allowed for their discussion should be carefully controlled by the chairperson to allow sufficient time for discussion of more lengthy items.
4 *False.* Solutions should only be invited after the problem has been carefully identified and diagnosed; otherwise there is a danger of solving the wrong problem.
5 *True.* All the basic principles of good communication concerning purpose, audience, timing, two-way communication, listening, and so on apply to participants in meetings.

Exercise 9.3

1 A meeting should be held at a time and in a place convenient to as many members as possible.

2 Payne started off well by explaining 'the object of the meeting', but in trying to stimulate discussion he was guilty of talking too much rather than asking questions, and being too ready to express his own very detailed opinions and experiences.

3 'Just for the sake of getting on with the business', Crass makes a proposal. This is as good a reason as any, and might have prompted a proposal earlier if Payne had realised he should invite proposals.

4 A '*proposition*' is a suggestion, a call for action or an opinion, put forward by a member of the meeting. As soon as it is seconded and submitted for discussion and vote it is called a '*motion*'. If and when the motion is agreed upon by a majority of those present, it becomes a '*resolution*'.

In practice, the term 'proposition' is not used very often since most propositions have been seconded, and therefore become motions before the meeting discusses the matter. However, if a proposition is put forward but fails to gain a seconder it is dropped.

A motion should be very clearly and positively worded and many committees insist that a motion is submitted in writing, preferably before the meeting starts. In any event, it should be clearly recorded by the secretary and should be repeated by the chair from time to time so that everyone is quite clear what they are discussing. Positive wording is advised because when the voting takes place, it may be confusing for members who are in favour of something, for example, the reintroduction of capital punishment, to find that in order to vote in favour of that idea, they must actually vote against the negatively worded motion: 'That capital punishment should not be reintroduced.'

5 Rules for speaking are indicated in the standing orders of a committee or organisation but will usually include:
- Members of the meeting may only speak by permission of the chair, one at a time. 'Catching the chairperson's eye' is therefore a skill worth developing.
- Anyone who speaks must be standing. The speaker then 'has the floor'.
- A speaker must address their remarks to the chair and not to any individual member of the meeting; hence the frequent use of 'Mr Chairman/Madam Chair'.

6 Other terms which relate to the standing orders are:
(a) and (d) A *point of order* must deal with the *conduct* or *procedure* of the debate, for example, an objection raised by another member of the meeting that the speaker is departing from the subject, that the standing orders concerning the rules of debate are not being operated, or that offensive language is being used. Harlow 'rose to a point of order' justifiably, I think, since the meeting needed to be reminded that they should not decide where the Beano was to take place without first deciding *if* the Beano should take place. However, it is up to the chair to rule an objection 'in' or 'out of order' and they therefore need to know the standing orders.
(b) *call the chairman to order* – strictly speaking, there are only two ways you can object to the chairman's chairmanship: (i) challenge the chair's ruling, and

(ii) propose a motion of *no confidence in the chair*. However, in practice the chair's ruling is normally regarded as final, other than in exceptional circumstances.

(c) and (d) A *point of information* is made by a member of the meeting rising either to ask the chair's permission to correct a misrepresentation or to give or ask for information. Again, since this is often used as a device for taking the floor out of turn, the chair is empowered to *rule it out of order*.

(e) An *amendment* is a proposition to change the wording of a motion either by deleting or adding words. The amendment must also be seconded before it can be discussed, and it must be voted on before discussion of the main motion is resumed.

7 The chairperson should repeat the motion clearly to make sure that everyone understands the motion they are voting on. They should also be aware of the different methods of voting – ballot, show of hands and so on – and the advantages and disadvantages of each method.

11 Using visual aids

Exercise 11.1

1 Probably some kind of magnetic board. This would allow you to move pieces representing furniture, people and department names around the board as you put forward your alternative office layouts. It would also provide the facility for building up pictures of alternative suggestions from the meeting, so that everyone could see what is being suggested.

However, the problem with using build-up boards for presenting distinct alternatives is that you also need a permanent record of each alternative for reference purposes when you get to the point of comparing them. You might therefore consider supporting your initial presentation with separate charts for each alternative which can be distributed to everyone present for reference purposes both during and after the meeting. Large charts at the front of the room may possibly be difficult to see in a group as large as 30, so individual handouts would be better, but this is where judgement of the particular circumstances comes in. It would depend on the actual room, the seating arrangements and the degree of detail which you want everyone present to see.

An alternative, expensive and rarely available, would be a whiteboard that produces photocopies. The ideas could be drawn and a photocopy produced at each important stage and as a final record.

Handouts. The idea of reproducing your visual aids as individual handouts is always worth considering. The timing of the issue of these handouts is crucial: produced early in a presentation they can provide your audience with individual copies of detailed material to refer to, but they draw attention away from you, the speaker, and can be distracting; produced late in the presentation or at the end they can cause frustration because people often take notes from visuals which they then discover they do not need. The solution is to tell your audience, as you speak, which visuals they will receive at the end as handouts.

2   If you are right-handed you should stand on the left of a board or flip chart when facing the board; if you are left-handed you should stand on the right. This will obviously affect where you position a free-standing board, so that you can reach your notes and move around easily.

3   To provide an example of something the audience may not have actually seen before; to provide an everyday example as an analogy of some more complex process you are talking about; to provide interest, vitality and reality.

4   If you will be able to gain access to the room where you will give your talk well before the session begins, you would probably be advised to draw the diagram carefully on the board very faintly. In this way you will be able to draw in each part of the piece of equipment as you explain it and following the faint guidelines which only you can see. This method will prevent you frightening your audience to death by revealing a large complex visual aid right at the start.

    To be successful you will have to make sure that you can get into the room sufficiently early to be able to draw the diagram very carefully. You should also make sure that you will be able to draw it sufficiently large for the back row of the audience to see it.

    If you will be unable to get into the room beforehand, then a large wall chart might serve as well. In this case you might consider sticking lift-up flaps over sections of the drawing, so that you can reveal the diagram fairly gradually as you go along.

5   The most appropriate form of visual aid for recording a discussion is probably a flip-chart board with lots of paper. The audience's contributions can be written up and the torn-off sheets can be fixed to the wall as they are completed. These can then serve as the basis of the report for the newspaper. You would also be able to produce your own prepared visual aids on flip charts as and when they seemed appropriate in the context of the discussion. An alternative to flip charts might be overhead projector transparencies or a roll of OHP film which could be used in the same way as flip charts, but cannot be hung up on the walls.

Exercise 11.2

1   You should ask for a 35 mm slide projector, unless your transparencies (photos) are in your computer, in which case you need a data projector.

2   You might try to avoid using more than one aid which requires a screen, since you would have to move the overhead projector to prevent it getting in the way of the film or slides, and you might have to use the whiteboard in order to show OHP slides. The overall principle is to be able to arrange as much as possible beforehand, and cut any movement of equipment or general fiddling-about down to a minimum once the presentation has started. However, a coffee break in the middle of the proceedings might allow you to rearrange things if you want to.

3   Any process which depends on movement is obviously best shown on video. If you can't get hold of a commercially produced video of the operation you want, you should seriously think about the possibility of making your own, especially if it is likely to be of use again in the future.

4   Know how to replace it with the one you've brought along in case. Failing that, give a prearranged signal to someone in the audience who will seek out the technician while you carry on talking. Failing that, abandon the slides because you thought about this eventuality beforehand and have arranged your presentation so that you can do without them – at a push. As an absolutely last resort, if the visual aids are vital and if the audience is quite small and fairly close to you, and if the walls are plain, you might just get away with holding them up against the wall!

12   Faster reading

Exercise 12.1

1   NEFARIOUS (c); evil; vicious, villainous; for example, a nefarious plot (Latin: – 'wrong, crime').
2   CENSURE (c) to blame; criticise; reprimand officially; for example, to censure a member of Parliament (Latin: *censere* – 'to assess').
3   NEBULOUS (b) vague or unclear; hazy; cloud-like; for example, a nebulous statement (Latin: *nebula* – 'mist').
4   SALUTARY (a) beneficial; promoting health; wholesome; for example, a salutary experience (Latin: *salus* – 'health').
5   TORTUOUS (d) winding; full of twists and turns; for example, a tortuous path; also, devious; e.g. a tortuous argument (Latin: *torquere* – 'to twist').
6   PREMISE (a) basic assumption; proposition from which a conclusion may be drawn: 'He started with the premise that "All men are mortal" ' (Latin: *praemittere* – 'to place ahead').
7   CREDIBLE (d) believable; apparently worthy of belief or confidence; for example, a credible story (Latin: *credere* – 'to believe').
8   INVALIDATE (b) cancel; render of no force or effect; for example, to invalidate a will (Latin: *invalidus* – 'weak').
9   BIZARRE (a) odd; eccentric; fantastic; strikingly out of the ordinary, or at variance with accepted standards; for example, bizarre behaviour (Italian: *bizzarro* – 'gallant, brave').
10 DEFUNCT (a) extinct; dead; for example, a defunct system (Latin: *defunctus* from *defungi* – 'to finish, discharge').

13   Better reading

Exercise 13.1

1   The value of reading material can be assessed against these three categories: *essential, useful* and *irrelevant*.
2   Skimming helps you with the final reading task because at each level of depth of detail it familiarises you with the structure of the material you are about to read, before you read it.

3 In discursive or factual writing the main idea is usually contained in a 'topic sentence' which is normally the first sentence of the paragraph, but is sometimes the last.

4 For examples of 'verbal signals or signposts' see pp. 186–8.

5 The five stages of reading are: *survey, question, read, recall* and *review*. This method of reading is usually referred to as the SQ3R method.

6 You should not start taking or making notes until you start the *recall* stage. Having to make notes at this stage helps you to recall what you have read.

14   Writing business letters

Exercise 14.1

1 The cost of a letter includes internal handling costs, filing time, filing equipment and space, cost of writer's and WP operator's time as well as stationery and postage – estimated by some companies at a total of £25 per letter on average – and no cheaper even if the letter is sent electronically.

2 An *adjustment letter* seeks to satisfy a complaint, make reparation for a fault or deficiency; a *credit reference enquiry* is written at periodic intervals in the process of trying to obtain payment of a debt. Different letters are written at different stages in the process.

3 Letters fall into four main categories: favourable; neutral; unfavourable; persuasive.

4 When a letter introduces the negative elements too early the reader may switch off and not be prepared to be convinced by any reasons or justification which follow.

   Negative elements can be made to seem less important if they are subordinated through positive word choice, careful sentence structure and positioning in the letter. Since the first and last sentences in a letter should be reserved for views you want to emphasise, negative elements should not be put in the first or last sentences.

   By using inductive word order, which presents the reasons and details first and then introduces the negative idea, the reader may be persuaded to accept it.

5 Questions (or exclamations) are very acceptable beginnings for letters of a sales or persuasive nature. They may be used to start any letter in which your objective is to gain the reader's attention quickly. A question involves the reader quickly and provides a bit of mystery and suspense to keep them reading until you can explain where they fit into the picture. A question can also be flattering to the reader by asking for their opinion.

6 Favourable elements: it is always desirable to end a letter with a favourable element, a positive tone, to leave the reader in a good frame of mind.

   - *Goodwill* – Without overdoing it, you should take every opportunity to build goodwill in a letter. Pleasant-sounding words throughout the letter are always welcome but endings which include 'Thank you' 'Good luck', 'Best wishes', are especially useful for ending letters which have contained disappointing news.

- *Resale* – Sometimes it is appropriate to end a letter by reassuring the reader that the purchased product is right for the customer, or that the company the customer is dealing with is the one that can do the best job for him, but this should not be done too blatantly.
- *Action* – This is perhaps the most useful way to end any letter in which some action is required by the reader or writer. Specify near the end of the letter exactly what is going to happen next:

  'I will let you know as soon as I have the information you need', 'Please ring me on ext. 252 to let me know whether you will be able to attend', 'Please reply on the enclosed reply-paid card.'

  Don't end a letter with: 'Please do not hesitate to contact me if I can be of further assistance.' This is now a really hackneyed expression. Try to think of something more sincere and original.

15 Applying for a job

Exercise 15.1

1 *False.* The first stage in applying for a job is deciding what sort of a person you are and what sort of a job would suit you. The second stage involves finding the vacancies and discovering exactly what the advertisers are looking for. Only then should you think about actually replying to advertisements.

2 *True.* More people will see Internet and newspaper advertisements (especially those in national newspapers) than those publicised anywhere else, so there are likely to be more applicants. The first letters received may get more careful attention. Furthermore, the quality of promptness is a personal virtue that employers may consider a business virtue.

3 *False.* Careful consideration of the style of the advertisement, the tone of the wording, what is omitted and what is included can often tell you more about what the company wants, than the obvious statements of qualifications and experience required.

4 *True.* Any contact you have with the prospective employer, however informal, can help or hinder your application, and therefore deserves thought and preparation.

5 *False.* You *must* think of something to say. Most employers will give you a black mark if you cannot write a short coherent statement in this section, and seem to be content to limit your application to the straightforward factual questions in the rest of the form.

6 *False.* Two sheets are preferred – one that gives the facts in easy-to-locate summary form (the curriculum vitae – CV) and another that states clearly which job is being applied for, interprets the CV information, and gives reasons for applying (the covering letter). This method is actually easier for you. It avoids problems of style and, if you are applying for lots of similar jobs, it allows you to reproduce copies of the facts for use as you need them.

7 *False.* The duties and attributes required for certain manual jobs may be required also for the office-type jobs you are seeking. For example, if you have

worked in a shop-floor manual job this may provide evidence of such qualities as initiative, reliability, cooperativeness and punctuality, as well as a willingness to dirty your hands, mix well with all sorts of people, or try anything once. Even a temporary or holiday job may display evidence of wanting to gain experience, earn your own living or provide the means of achieving some other goal, all qualities which would count in your favour.

8 *True.* If two headings 'General education' and 'Business education', or 'Technical qualifications' and 'Other qualifications', allow you to link some of your qualifications and experience more closely to the job you are seeking, then you should use whichever headings you feel are appropriate.

9 *False.* While the covering letter does serve the invaluable purpose of showing how well you can express yourself, it should never merely repeat the facts in the CV. It represents a chance to expand on some of the bare facts, draw out and pull together those that are significant, emphasise what responsibilities and opportunities certain jobs have given you, explain why you want the job. Above all, in doing all this you should be able to *imply* those qualities which you possess and recognise as significant for the job.

10 *True.* Copying someone else's letter will at best cause you to commit inadvertent inaccuracies (between the CV and the letter, for example) and at worst will cause you to be caught out if you do get an interview. As for using your present employer's stationery or making negative comments about them – both would reveal a disloyalty, a lack of good manners and an underhandedness – undesirable qualities in themselves but hardly likely to recommend you as a prospective employee. Other common errors made by applicants which should be avoided are:

writing as if the letter were an autobiography
overworking 'I', 'me', and 'my'
sounding unduly humble
begging or pleading
asking for sympathy
sounding too flippant or casual
seeming to lecture the reader
seeming to brag about accomplishments
making assertions about your qualities and qualifications without giving evidence to support the statement
writing about educational qualifications as if they were the only things needed
using vague, general terms
repeating instead of interpreting CV information
using colloquial or hackneyed expressions

16 Writing reports

Exercise 16.1

1 The 'terms of reference' define your task and should state exactly what is needed. Your instructions must be precise, not vague; they should explain why the report

is needed; and what kind of report is required. Without clear terms of reference your task is impossible.

2 The main elements of any report are: terms of reference (including the objective or statement of the subject, and the authorisation, if appropriate); procedure; findings; conclusions, and recommendations (if asked for).

3 Any report should contain **three** main sections: introduction; body of the report; and final section.

4 A summary is a miniaturised version of the whole report, usually placed very near the beginning of the report, and providing the busy reader with a quick idea of the scope and objective together with a brief version of the conclusions and recommendations of the report.

5 A 'functional' paragraph does not add information, but is used to introduce, conclude or link sections of the report.

6 The main stages of writing a report are setting the objectives; researching and assembling the material; organising the material and planning the report; writing the first draft; editing the report; and producing the report.

17 Memos, messages, forms and questionnaires

Exercise 17.1

This question is unsatisfactory because it:

- is not personalised ('you' form) to make it clear who is being asked
- isn't clear whose pay the question is asking about
- provides no yardstick against which to judge how good pay is
- demands a black-or-white answer.

The question should have been put as follows:

How do you think your pay rate compares with what you could get from other employers in your industry?

Better   About the same   A bit worse   Much worse

18 Visual communication

Exercise 18.1

1 Turn back to pp. 297–8, 'Advantages of visual presentation', to check your answers. But here is a quick checklist:
- gains attention
- provides information quickly
- speeds comprehension
- relieves monotony
- conveys trends and tendencies
- highlights specific figures
- shows relationships

- reinforces the words
- highlights differences.

2 In choosing a visual aid, your first consideration will be, is a visual aid needed? Will it produce some of the advantages above? Then you should consider:
- what exactly you are trying to 'say'
- the complexity of the information
- the ability and motivation of the reader
- whether you want to highlight specific figures, show trends, or compare and contrast differences.

3 Tables are particularly useful for:
- displaying large amounts of data in a relatively small space
- providing an easy reference device from which specific figures can be picked out
- making comparisons between and among statistics
- conveying quantitative data in a more comprehensive form than submerged in the body of the text.

4 Generally speaking line graphs are used to present 'continuous' information and bar charts to present 'discrete' information. However, histograms, which look like bar charts but should not be confused with them, can be used to present 'continuous' information.

5 Graphic presentation can mislead by:
- omitting a zero line
- starting a graph just below the lowest point on the graph line
- condensing or extending the scale on the two axes in relation to one another
- omitting percentages and producing disproportionate wedges on a pie chart
- showing increase in number by showing wider bars or bigger symbols on bar charts or pictorial charts
- choosing to shade particular areas rather than others on a statistical map
- selective omission; omitting certain facts which if they were included would tell a rather different story!

Exercise 18.2

1 Visual communication can be more effective than verbal communication for the following reasons:
- Visual aids can often communicate more quickly and in less space than the equivalent verbal message would require.
- Visual presentation is often the only way to communicate where language and literacy barriers would make a verbal message incomprehensible.

2 'Visual literacy' is the ability to 'read' pictures, signs, symbols, charts and so on.

3 Flow charts, algorithms and decision trees are all variations of plotting visually the steps in a process or procedure.

4 An algorithm. Algorithms are particularly useful for diagnosing faults and problem-solving, since they should provide an answer to every possible question, provided that the procedure is followed correctly *and* the algorithm has been designed logically.

5 Checking typing of a letter – *inspection*: □

A worker waiting for materials – *delay*: D

Papers filed in a filing cabinet – *storage*: ▽

Picking up a screwdriver – *operation*: ○

An object moving on a conveyor belt – *transport*: ⇨

Signing a document – *operation*: ○

☑ Index